Human Rights Education

HUMAN RIGHTS EDUCATION

Theory, Research, Praxis

Edited by

Monisha Bajaj

Afterword by

Nancy Flowers

PENN

UNIVERSITY OF PENNSYLVANIA PRESS

PHILADELPHIA

Published by
University of Pennsylvania Press
Philadelphia, Pennsylvania 19104-4112
www.upenn.edu/pennpress

Printed in the United States of America
on acid-free paper

10 9 8 7 6 5 4 3 2 1

Library of Congress Cataloging-in-Publication Data

Names: Bajaj, Monisha, editor. | Flowers, Nancy, 1940– writer of afterword.
Title: Human rights education : theory, research, praxis / edited by
    Monisha Bajaj ; afterword by Nancy Flowers.
Other titles: Human rights education (University of Pennsylvania)
Description: 1st edition. | Philadelphia : University of Pennsylvania Press,
    [2017] | Includes bibliographical references and index.
Identifiers: LCCN 2016053346 | ISBN 9780812249026 (hardcover : alk.
    paper)
Subjects: LCSH: Human rights—Study and teaching.
Classification: LCC JC571 .H8668 2017 | DDC 323.071—dc23
LC record available at https://lccn.loc.gov/2016053346

CONTENTS

ABBREVIATIONS

ACAS	Advisory, Conciliation and Arbitration Service
AIM	American Indian Movement
ASPnet	Associated Schools Project Network
ATL	Association of Teachers and Lecturers
BBC	British Broadcasting Corporation
BSV	Buckingham Student Voice
CAT	Convention Against Torture and Other Cruel, Inhumane or Degrading Treatment or Punishment
CEDAW	Convention on the Elimination of All Forms of Discrimination Against Women
CEP	Community Empowerment Program
CPC	Community Peace Committees
CRC	Convention on the Rights of the Child
EFA	Education for All
ELL	English Language Learners
ESL	English as a Second Language
GCE	Global Citizenship Education
GLSEN	Gay, Lesbian, and Straight Education Network
HRA	United Kingdom Human Rights Act
HRC	Human Rights Commission
HRE	Human Rights Education
HREA	Human Rights Education Associates
HRE USA	Human Rights Educators USA
HRFS	Human Rights Friendly Schools
HRINGO	Human Rights International Nongovernmental Organization
HRW	Human Rights Watch
HURITER	Center for Promotion of Human Rights Teaching and Research
ICCPR	International Covenant on Civil and Political Rights

ICERD	International Convention on the Elimination of All Forms of Racial Discrimination
ICESCR	International Covenant on Economic, Social and Cultural Rights
ICT	Information and Communication Technology
IDP	Internally Displaced Person
IGNOU	Indira Gandhi National Open University
IGO	Intergovernmental Organization
IHRE	Institute of Human Rights Education
ILO	International Labor Organization
INGO	International Nongovernmental Organization
IOM	International Organization for Migration
KDP	Kurdistan Democratic Party
KRG	Kurdistan Regional Government
LGBTIQ	Lesbian, Gay, Bisexual, Transgender, Intersex, Queer
MDFC	Movement of Democratic Forces of Casamance
MDG	Millennium Development Goals
NCERT	National Council of Education and Training
NCTE	National Council for Teacher Education
NGO	Nongovernmental Organization
NHRC	National Human Rights Commission
NHRI	National Human Rights Institution
NIHR	National Institute of Human Rights
NOW	National Organization for Women
NUT	National Union of Students
Ofsted	Office for Standards in Education
OHCHR	Office of the High Commissioner for Human Rights (United Nations)
ORAM	Organization for Refuge, Asylum, and Migration
PD	Professional Development
PUK	Patriotic Union of Kurdistan
RRSA	Rights Respecting Schools Award
RSC	Resettlement Service Centers
RTE	Right to Education
SLT	Senior Leadership Team
SOGI	Sexual Orientation and Gender Identity
UDHR	Universal Declaration of Human Rights
UFW	United Farm Workers

UGC	University Grants Commission
UIC	Unique Identifier Code
UNDHRET	United Nations Declaration on Human Rights Education and Training
UNESCO	United Nations Educational, Scientific and Cultural Organization
UNGEI	United Nations Girls' Education Initiative
UNICEF	United Nations Children's Fund
UPR	Universal Periodic Review
WHO	World Health Organization

Introduction

Monisha Bajaj

Human rights education (HRE) as a field utilizes teaching and learning processes to educate *about* basic rights and *for* the broadening of respect for the dignity and freedom of all people(s). Since the founding of the United Nations and the adoption of the Universal Declaration of Human Rights (1948) after World War II, HRE has been held out as an ideal to ensure that schools become sites of promise and equity rather than breeding grounds for hate and violence.

Human Rights Education: Theory, Research, Praxis provides a thorough introduction to the past, present, and future of human rights education as a scholarly field. This book has four overarching goals: (1) to formulate working definitions of HRE; (2) to foreground the field's relevance for scholarship, policy, curricular reform, pedagogy, and practice; (3) to analyze tensions in, and discontinuities among, the contested realizations of human rights education in diverse contexts; and (4) to offer new critical insights and directions on theory, research, and praxis for students, scholars, and practitioners of this growing and expanding field.

The collection of chapters in this book offers the voices of thought leaders and researchers deeply engaged in understanding the politics and possibilities of human rights education as a field of inquiry. Many of the authors in this volume teach undergraduate and graduate courses on human rights education in diverse institutions and contexts internationally. The various chapters, some overlapping boundaries notwithstanding, are broadly grouped here into three larger categories: (1) Theoretical and Conceptual Foundations of Human Rights Education, (2) Global Research in Human Rights Education, and (3) Transformative Human Rights Education Praxis. Similar to the folktale of a group of blind men who seek to describe an elephant by touching its various parts and who disagree about its nature based on their positioning (e.g., touching the tusk, trunk, feet, tail, etc.), human rights education may look different depending on the angle and perspective one takes. Some scholars in this volume examine the rise of HRE and the reasons for the field's increasing popularity as an educational project in the decades after the end of the Cold War; others posit models for conceptualizing and practicing HRE and how different forms of HRE may operate in different "vernaculars" (Merry 2006); yet others zoom in on specific programs and particular questions of implementation, including lessons learned and insights for those seeking to put HRE into practice in classrooms and communities across the globe. In the afterword, Nancy Flowers, a pioneer and leading voice in human rights education, reflects on questions of HRE praxis. Following the work of Paulo Freire (1970), "praxis," largely synonymous with "practice," involves an active and reflexive engagement with the tensions inherent in applying and localizing concepts that exist in idealized forms—here, those of human rights laws, norms, and values.

Taken together, the chapters in this book chart the rise, emergence, and nature of human rights education as a field of scholarly and engaged practice in global, national, and local settings. The book offers a comprehensive introductory text on human rights education that is both global in scope and attentive to the diverse forms of HRE, whether implemented through governmental policies and textbook reforms; through the work of intergovernmental organizations (i.e., UN agencies like UNESCO and UNICEF); through colleges and universities; through nongovernmental organizations (NGOs) engaging in professional development, curriculum design, or direct instruction; or through the work of individual educators, schools, and community activists. The idea for this book project emerged in 2014 when I assumed leadership of the first master's program in human rights education in the United States at the University of San Francisco. I found a pressing need for a textbook on human rights education that historicizes HRE while offering concrete grounding for students, educators, researchers, advocates, and activists who seek entry into this dynamic field of scholarship and practice.

Collectively, the chapters that follow offer a primer on the international field of human rights education. In 1997, during the United Nations Decade for Human Rights Education (1995–2004), a seminal book was published, entitled *Human Rights Education for the Twenty-First Century* (Andreopoulos and Claude 1997). Almost two decades into the twenty-first century, this book builds upon that work to take stock of the contemporary scholarly field of human rights education as it has been institutionalized through UN, national, and community-level programs and initiatives; significant conferences and reforms; numerous publications and reports; and ever-increasing programs of study in human rights and human rights education at universities across the globe (Suárez and Bromley 2012). While cataloguing every effort under way across the globe is beyond the scope of this book, we do seek here to offer key insights, perspectives, and common threads woven through the numerous programs that exist under the banner of HRE.

History, Definitions, and Models of Human Rights Education

Despite its initial mention in the 1948 Universal Declaration of Human Rights (UDHR), human rights education as a global movement gained considerable momentum only after the end of the Cold War in the early 1990s. Article 26 of the UDHR identifies, first, the right to education, and second, the right to an education directed toward "the full development of the human personality and to the strengthening of respect for human rights and fundamental freedoms" (UDHR 1948). There have been many antecedents to HRE in individual initiatives and community-based efforts over centuries past. Yet the 1993 UN World Conference on Human Rights in Vienna was a watershed moment for HRE. The Vienna Declaration stated that "human rights education, training and public information is essential for the promotion and achievement of stable and harmonious relations among communities and for fostering mutual understanding, tolerance and peace." The Vienna Declaration and Program of Action resulting from the conference had an extensive subsection on human rights education and called for a UN Decade for Human Rights Education, which subsequently lasted from 1995 to 2004 and which brought policymakers, government officials, activists, and educators into more sustained conversation.

While there are many approaches to human rights education, there is broad agreement about certain core components.[1] First, most scholars and practitioners agree that HRE must include both *content* and *processes* related to teaching human rights (Flowers 2003; Meintjes 1997; Tibbitts 2002). Second, most literature in the field discusses the need for HRE to include goals related to cognitive (content), attitudinal or emotive (values/skills), and action-oriented components (Tibbitts 2005). Amnesty International's

Human Rights Friendly Schools framework weaves together the intended outcomes of HRE by highlighting three prepositions linking education and human rights in a comprehensive manner: education *about* human rights (cognitive), education *through* human rights (participatory methods that create skills for active citizenship), and education *for* human rights (fostering learners' ability to speak out and act in the face of injustices).[2]

As the UN Decade for Human Rights Education came to a close, the UN World Programme for Human Rights Education was established in 2005, housed within the UN Office of the High Commissioner for Human Rights (OHCHR). In 2011, the UN General Assembly adopted the Declaration on Human Rights Education and Training (UNDHRET), further highlighting the importance of HRE at the level of national policy and reform. As defined by the United Nations:

> Human rights education can be defined as education, training and information aiming at building a universal culture of human rights through the sharing of knowledge, imparting of skills and molding of attitudes directed to
> (a) the strengthening of respect for human rights and fundamental freedoms;
> (b) the full development of the human personality and the sense of its dignity;
> (c) the promotion of understanding, tolerance, gender equality and friendship among all nations, indigenous peoples and racial, national, ethnic, religious and linguistic groups;
> (d) the enabling of all persons to participate effectively in a free and democratic society governed by the rule of law;
> (e) the building and maintenance of peace;
> (f) the promotion of people-centered sustainable development and social justice.

Emphasized in the United Nations' definition of HRE is knowledge about human rights and tolerance/acceptance of others based on such knowledge. UN initiatives are largely directed toward member states, and they attempt to foster adoption of national plans of action for integrating HRE into their educational systems.

Nongovernmental organizations (NGOs) and community-based organizations have also long been active in human rights education, utilizing human rights discourse as a strategy to frame the demands of diverse social movements—a more bottom-up approach to HRE. At the grassroots level, HRE has often taken the form of popular education or community education to mobilize constituencies for expanding social movements (Kapoor 2004). In Latin America, for example, many efforts aimed at HRE blossomed immediately after the end of dictatorships, when NGOs that had fought for human rights turned their attention to education as a tool for reconciliation and the prevention of a return to authoritarian rule (Magendzo 1997). As such, human rights education efforts are seen as both a political and a pedagogical strategy to facilitate democratization and active citizenship.

For purposes of definition, human rights education can take a variety of forms. In formal schooling, human rights can be integrated into textbooks or other subjects such as civics or social studies. In some places, direct instruction in a "human rights" class is mandated or offered as an elective in public or private schools at the secondary level. In universities, undergraduate and graduate programs in human rights, and increasingly in human rights education, are emerging and becoming institutionalized. More commonly, optional programs—either during the school day, after school through clubs or co-curricular programs, or through summer camps and other programs—offer students exposure to human rights. In professional settings across the globe, human rights training—either optional or required, ad hoc, or sustained—has been offered for judges, police officers, military personnel, health workers, and teachers, among others. Additionally, nonformal HRE is flourishing in community-based settings worldwide. Further, the types of rights brought into focus (civil, political, social, economic, cultural, or a cross-section of equality rights for a specific group) depends on the context and the approach. Thus, human rights education varies in content, approach, scope, intensity, depth, and availability.

Drawing on the promise of grassroots-level efforts to impact awareness about human rights, Amnesty International defines human rights education as follows:

> Human rights education is a deliberate, participatory practice aimed at empowering individuals, groups, and communities through fostering knowledge, skills, and attitudes consistent with internationally recognized principles. . . . Its goal is to build a culture of respect for and action in the defense and promotion of human rights for all. (Amnesty International 2015)

The Amnesty International definition places greater responsibility on human rights learners becoming activists for human rights through the process of HRE by sharing information with others and actively working to defend human rights. Both social change as an outcome, and learners becoming agents of this process of claiming their own rights and defending others' rights, are central to this definition. Differences in the way individuals or organizations approach HRE account for the ways it is conceptualized as an education reform or strategy.

Existing Models

As is generally the case with fields in development and in motion, many articulations of models and approaches emerge to understand phenomena and chart the boundaries of a field; HRE is no exception. Within the broad parameters of convergence discussed above, some differences in approaches and definitions have been put forth to further explore human rights education depending on what side of the "elephant" one is looking at, to follow up on the metaphor introduced before. More recent articulations have elaborated the definition of what HRE must include in different contexts—beyond the teaching of international human rights norms and standards—and have cited a variety of goals and learners.

HRE models provide productive schemas for theorizing its emergence, conceptualization, and implementation across the globe. One vital forum is the online list-serve and "epistemic community" coordinated by the U.S.-based Human Rights Education Associates (HREA). As noted by scholar David Suárez (2007), this organization allows its more than 16,000 members from over 170 countries to—"through discourse and active reflection"—"practice, negotiate, refine, and mold HRE" (66). Populated by many government officials and staff of UN agencies as well as educators and human rights activists globally, the discursive engagement on various issues of HRE through the online community has played a significant role in facilitating international discussions (e.g., creating opportunities for feedback as the UN Declaration on Human Rights Education and Training was being drafted). Since many posts are from practitioners seeking advice, materials, or input, the online community can also influence practices as well.

With the global diffusion of ideas related to the teaching and learning of human rights, various scholars in this volume and elsewhere have proposed different models for human rights education. Felisa Tibbitts in Chapter 3 builds upon her seminal 2002 work in creating a three-tiered model for human rights education that explores differing levels of implementation by distinct actors. Tibbitts differentiates among the socialization approach of values and awareness of human rights that can be utilized in formal and nonformal settings to socialize learners into basic knowledge about human rights; the accountability or professional development approach for those working directly with victims of rights abuses (e.g., by police, health workers); and the more activist transformation approach which offers a holistic understanding of human rights knowledge, attitudes, and actions. This model suggests productive areas for researchers and practitioners to examine, and frameworks for analyzing such action.

I have argued elsewhere (Bajaj 2011) for the importance of following the varying ideologies of human rights education initiatives as they have proliferated across the globe. Depending on relationships to power and conditions of marginalization, the perceived and actual outcomes of human rights education may differ based on social location (Bajaj 2012). Some programs, particularly those adopted at national and international levels or in situations of relative privilege, may discuss global citizenship as an outcome. In conflict settings, coexistence and respect for difference may be prioritized. In disenfranchised communities, HRE may be a strategy for transformative action and empowerment (Bajaj 2011; Tibbitts 2002 and in this volume). Recent critiques (Keet 2007) have noted that the overly "declarationist" approach of HRE, which anchors itself in normative standards, limits its emancipatory potential since it fails to consider broader debates in the field of human rights. Several chapters in this volume heed Keet's call for a more critical human rights education approach to move the field forward, closer to its emancipatory promise.

Initiatives working toward human rights education tend to fuse Freirean notions of consciousness-raising with the philosophical tradition of cosmopolitanism, as others and I have noted elsewhere (Bajaj 2014; Bajaj, Cislaghi, and Mackie 2016; Meintjes 1997; Osler and Starkey 2010; Tibbitts 2002). Paulo Freire's (1970) notion of *conscientization* results from individuals—often those from marginalized groups—collectively analyzing conditions of inequality and then acting and reflecting to inspire new action in an iterative fashion in order to overcome situations of oppression and subordination. Cosmopolitanism is a philosophical position that posits a shared human community and a global notion of citizenship and belonging (Appiah 2007).

Pairing these philosophical orientations together results in local action and critical analysis (à la Freire) informed by global solidarity and connection (as is posited in some versions of cosmopolitanism). Some scholars have termed this type of HRE "transformative human rights education" (THRED) and have documented its principles and components across formal and nonformal settings (Bajaj et al. 2016).

For such transformative HRE approaches, a basic theory of change—drawing on Freire's notions and cosmopolitan ideas of global citizenship—that unites the purpose of human rights education for empowerment efforts (in its ideal form, though in practice it may look different) is posited as follows:

1. Learners (in formal or nonformal settings) learn about a larger imagined moral community where human rights offers a shared language.
2. Learners question a social or cultural practice that does not fit within the global framework.
3. Learners identify allies (teachers, peers, community activists, NGOs) to amplify their voice, along with other strategies for influencing positive social change.

While the theory of change posited above can account for the way in which transformative human rights education is conceptualized, there are often many tensions and contradictions in actual practice. What has yet to be elaborated fully, as suggested in some of the chapters that follow, is the need for strategies to deal with the unintended consequences of human rights education (see Chapter 5 by Audrey Osler and Chalank Yahya as well as Chapter 7 by Sam Mejias) and corresponding action as well as the co-optation of rights language for entirely different ends (see also Bajaj 2012 and Wahl 2013). Additionally, nation-states and policymakers have diverse reasons to support human rights education—that may or may not include a transformative vision—as several chapters in this book discuss. These are areas that the field of human rights education must continue to engage and contend with.

In the field as well as in this volume, HRE scholars use various methodological approaches to look at different levels of implementation and operation. The worldwide increase in the use of human rights language and subsequent textbook reforms is one angle into the field (see Chapter 1). Putting different fields of work and scholarship (e.g., human rights or peacebuilding) in conversation with human rights education is another (see the discussions in Chapters 4 and 11 on the right to HRE and on peacebuilding and HRE, respectively). Examining the impact and "micropolitics" of programs and initiatives at secondary and tertiary levels of education that espouse rights language is another (as in Chapters 6 and 7). Providing research-based insights for practice is yet another way that scholars approach studies of human rights education (see Chapters 8, 10, and 12).

Whether offering prescriptive insights, models for engagement, research findings, or analyses of global trends, scholars of human rights education have much to offer vis-à-vis ongoing discussions of globalization, citizenship, and education.

About the Book

This book is divided into three sections: Part I covers theoretical and conceptual foundations of human rights education, Part II examines dimensions of research across the globe, and Part III offers insights from endeavors engaging in transformative HRE praxis. The chapters in Part I draw from research and literature to offer conceptual perspectives and theoretical underpinnings to the field of human rights education. The research and praxis sections explore quantitative and qualitative case studies that reveal the strengths, possibilities, and contested processes of localization of human rights education as practiced in diverse contexts across the globe. The chapters that follow historicize human rights education, explore tensions and contradictions in conceptualizing education for human rights, review assorted local struggles to implement and realize HRE, and highlight the dynamics and contestations among the various actors involved, from academics to UN organizations to NGOs at the community level. Taken together, the chapters of this book offer grounded insights and new directions for the field.

In the first part, on the theoretical and conceptual foundations of human rights education, the authors set the stage for our understanding of why and how HRE has become a global phenomenon, the role of emotions in HRE, what approaches and models it entails for diverse audiences, and HRE's legal standing.

In Chapter 1, Susan Garnett Russell and David Suárez discuss how human rights education has become central to the global human rights movement, complementing the immediate goals of protecting victims and promoting international treaties with education about human rights for the prevention of abuses. Drawing on world polity theory, the authors argue that HRE gains international traction because of widely held cultural scripts about progress, justice, and the individual. Suárez and Russell review world polity theory and then chart HRE over the past several decades through policy documents, curricula, and textbooks as they have become infused with human rights language. The authors conclude with recommendations for new research on HRE that can address important gaps in the field.

Chapter 2, by Michalinos Zembylas, explores the entanglement of emotion, pedagogy, and human rights education on a theoretical level. Specifically, it suggests that a theory of HRE that acknowledges the significance of emotion and sentimentality in critical ways can provide productive pedagogical orientations to human rights. The chapter begins by reviewing human rights critiques, focusing in particular on how the rhetoric of human rights often remains at a metaphysical level or ends up being an empty and abstract moral ideology. To provide a different view, the chapter discusses the relation between emotions and human rights, and offers an overview of the different ways in which emotions may be implicated in the experiences of those who perceive, mobilize, or claim human rights; the argument here is that there is a need to engage in a political analysis of emotions in human rights theory. Then the chapter turns to philosopher Richard Rorty's proposal of "sentimental education" and acknowledges his contributions to theorizations about the role of emotions and sentimentality in HRE, as well as the limitations of his views. Building on this analysis, the chapter suggests three elements that may contribute to a critical pedagogy of emotions in HRE, namely: "(1) the significance of pedagogic discomfort, (2) the pedagogical principle of mutual vulnerability, and (3) the value of compassion and strategic empathy."

In Chapter 3, on the evolution of human rights education, Felisa Tibbitts builds upon her 2002 work positing three models for HRE in formal, professional, and nonformal education sectors: Values and Awareness, Accountability, and Transformation. The author proposes amendments to the models to reflect developments in HRE over the past fifteen years. Some revisions include a stronger association of the Values and Awareness Model with socialization, the linking of the Accountability Model with professional development, and the alignment of the Transformation Model with activism. Additionally, the institutional context as well as the background of the learners is analyzed vis-à-vis each of the typologies of HRE discussed. Tibbitts argues for ongoing reflexive praxis that can result in an increased presence of HRE in formal settings, along with adult learners in communities and the workplace espousing critical pedagogy to engender human rights activism and social transformation.

Chapter 4, by Peter Kirchschlaeger, explores the right to human rights education as defined in international law. Exploring moral and legal justifications for this right, and how nation-states may seek to either hide poor human rights records behind their efforts in HRE or co-opt the language of rights, the author delineates the justification in various realms for the human rights education enterprise. The UN Declaration on Human Rights Education and Training is discussed in terms of its potential as well as the ways in which nation-states may subvert its expansive call for HRE to permeate all state organs and institutions.

Rooted in conceptual underpinnings, Part II explores research from various parts of the globe on human rights education. From India to the United Kingdom to Senegal to Iraqi Kurdistan, the chapters in this part discuss how intentions sometimes vary from outcomes in HRE programs and how different actors utilize rights language in diverse ways. The findings from some of the chapters also suggest promising outcomes related to the broadening expanse of rights for marginalized groups such as refugees who identify as lesbian, gay, bisexual, transgender, intersex, or queer (LBGTIQ; see Chapter 8), but also some limitations vis-à-vis how schools that adopt a human rights–friendly framework fail to live up to the promise and ideals they purport to espouse (see Chapter 7). Research in HRE includes a variety of methods, as evidenced by the approaches throughout this section.

In Chapter 5, Audrey Osler and Chalank Yahya examine tensions in the implementation of HRE in schools in Kurdistan, Iraq. Drawing on documents and fieldwork (observations and interviews) in two governorates, the authors discuss how educators and policymakers make sense of HRE amid international and aspirational calls for children's rights, gender equity, and nation-building. Osler and Yahya find that, in practice, rights operate in tension and may be denied in societal contexts where conservative, patriarchal values prevail. They discuss teachers' attempts to reconcile tensions with limited resources and to become advocates in contexts where many violations of basic rights occur.

In Chapter 6, Monisha Bajaj and Rachel Wahl chart the convergence of Indian educational policy toward human rights language and discourses beginning in the 1980s and 1990s alongside India's adoption of neoliberal economic policies. Diverse nongovernmental organizations and educational institutions have sought to operate in the space opened up by the policy focus on human rights education, although what HRE means in practice differs greatly across the country and in different institutions. Examining distinct levels—postprimary, secondary, tertiary, professional education and training, and community-based popular education—Bajaj and Wahl offer a complex case study of how, in one nation-state, diverse actors give multiple meanings and differentially "vernacularize" a particular education project: human rights education.

In Chapter 7, Sam Mejias draws on his extensive ethnographic research in a London secondary school to discuss gaps between the vision, implementation, and outcomes of Amnesty International's global whole-school human rights education initiative, Human Rights Friendly Schools (HRFS). Mejias discusses how, rather than aligning school practices with HRE, the school used the program and affiliation with it as a political tool to showcase during national inspections. Later, disgruntled teachers and students utilized HRE to destabilize the school's leadership team and, ultimately, the school itself. The promise of HRE was held out in the face of a wide gap between rights and actual realities in a contested school setting. Through an examination of the "micropolitical" activity in the school, Mejias explores some of the limits of human rights education discourse when co-opted by various actors for divergent purposes.

In Chapter 8, Oren Pizmony-Levy and Megan Jensen examine how international organizations over the past decade have advocated for the protection of LGBTIQ (lesbian, gay, bisexual, transgender, intersex, and/or queer) individuals who face persecution in their home countries. The authors note that the UN High Commissioner for Refugees (UNHCR) published a guidance note on refugee claims relating to sexual orientation and gender identity in 2008. This chapter engages with the participants in training programs aimed at helping UNHCR personnel and NGO workers engage with LGBTIQ individuals. Utilizing data from an exit survey collected in seven different locations (India, Israel, Jordan, Kenya, Malaysia, Senegal, and Turkey), Pizmony-Levy and Jensen find that participants respond in various ways to the content of the training as well as to exposure to trainers who identify as LGBTIQ. The authors point to various ways ahead for expanding and deepening HRE to include the rights of sexual minorities across the globe.

Through community engaged projects, the chapters in Part III focus on transformative human rights education praxis. In this part, through collaborative approaches as well as through the historicizing of human rights with concepts of social justice and peacebuilding, the authors offer rich insights into HRE praxis. From West Africa to refugee and other marginalized communities in the United States, Colombia, and Mexico, the global reach and resonance of HRE as a form of critical and transformative education is highlighted by the four chapters in this part.

In Chapter 9, Melissa Gibson and Carl Grant argue for the rooting of liberatory pedagogies in the language and history of universal human rights to provide a concrete means of resisting social injustices. The authors offer a detailed history of the relevance of human rights for the United States context through the nation's engagement with debates around the drafting of the Universal Declaration of Human Rights. Gibson and Grant then explore international human rights vis-à-vis American movements for racial, economic, and gender justice, often understood as the genesis of social justice education in the United States. The authors bring this historicization into U.S. discussions of social justice teaching as a way of expanding the frame to reflect global visions of solidarity. In the face of U.S. arguments about its exceptionalism regarding international human rights, the role of declarations and their critical history offers key insights for those involved in education for social justice in the United States and elsewhere.

In Chapter 10, Beniamino Cislaghi, Diane Gillespie, and Gerry Mackie discuss the nonformal human rights education program of Tostan, an NGO operating throughout West Africa. Through a multiyear study of Tostan's Community Empowerment Program (CEP), which lasts 2.5 years in each village where it operates, the authors discuss how participants experienced the first module of the CEP. That module includes, among other content, sessions on visioning and human rights and responsibilities. Cislaghi, Gillespie, and Mackie found that participants came to advance human rights in their larger communities in ways that aligned with local practices to further their vision of community well-being. By reviewing the curriculum, pedagogy, and participants' experiences, the authors offer insightful perspectives on how HRE is localized by Tostan.

In Chapter 11, Tracey Holland and Paul Martin examine three human rights education programs that combine legal reforms with the educational work of human rights organizations on the ground in various regions and nations of Latin America and sub-Saharan Africa. While each example of HRE is unique, they argue that all have resulted in significant shifts in thinking about deeply embedded social and cultural practices, and in the actual life conditions of the people who have experienced HRE. Chapter 11 seeks to demonstrate how HRE programs compensate for the absence of effective government support and services by building up resources such as skills in community-building, self-help, and self-reliance, and leading people to see human rights as an essential and motivating source of laws and norms. The authors posit that human rights education is one peacebuilding activity that helps communities rebuild, and therefore should not be ignored by policy-makers.

In Chapter 12, Carol Anne Spreen and Chrissie Monaghan discuss a unique collaborative action-research project involving diverse high school students, university students, and professors (in law and education) in Virginia. For the participants, some of whom are refugee and migrant children in local high schools, the authors find that notions such as democratic values, rights, and citizenship are mostly discussed rhetorically and never address these students' on-the-ground realities or day-to-day experiences in American society. Spreen and Monaghan explore the limitations of traditional ap-proaches to history and civic education and demonstrate the strengths and possibilities for rights-based approaches in enabling high school–age learners to explore their communities. The chapter profiles a high school course called "Becoming a Global Citizen," in which refugee and migrant students (from Africa, the Middle East, Europe, Asia, and Latin America) partnered with a diverse group of American students (who were from various racial, ethnic, and socioeconomic backgrounds) to learn about human rights and civic engagement.

In the Afterword, entitled "Theory, Research, and Praxis: The Way Ahead for Human Rights Education," human rights education pioneer Nancy Flowers reflects on more than three decades of active involvement in the field through work with organizations like Amnesty International, various agencies of the United Nations and the Council of Europe, as well as through the development of groundbreaking scholarship on human rights education. She considers the contributions of the chapters in this volume vis-à-vis the past, the present, and the future of the field of human rights education. Flowers offers insights and perspectives, and points the way ahead for edu-cators, students, activists, and scholars of human rights education.

Overall, this edited collection of voices from scholars deeply engaged with human rights education globally offers a rich compilation of theoreti-cal insights, engaged research, and lessons from grounded praxis. While the intention of the book is to draw some working maps of and directions for the field, it is our sincere hope that the book will raise more questions than it provides answers. Through exploration, new generations of scholars should develop ways to make HRE their own through research and practice. In the words of UN High Commissioner for Human Rights Zeid Ra'ad Al Hussein, speaking at the Holocaust Memorial Museum in Washington, DC, in 2015, "We do not have to accept the world as it is; indeed, we must not. We do not have to give in to the dark allure of hatred and violence: indeed, it is vital that we find the energy to resist it." It is imperative that we consider how educational spaces have become sites of such transformational resistance utilizing global understandings of human rights and seek to expand such spaces in the pursuit of hope, possibility, and visions for a more just future.

Notes

1. Some sections of this introduction draw from a previously published article entitled "Human Rights Education: Ideology, Location, and Approaches" (Bajaj 2011).

2. See Amnesty International, Human Rights Friendly Schools Project, http://www.amnesty.org/en/human-rights-education/projects.

References

Amnesty International. 2015. "Human Rights Education." http://www.amnesty.org/en/human-rights-education.

Andreopoulos, George J., and Richard Pierre Claude. 1997. *Human Rights Education for the Twenty-First Century*. Philadelphia: University of Pennsylvania Press.

Appiah, Kwame Anthony. 2007. *Cosmopolitanism: Ethics in a World of Strangers*. New York: W. W. Norton.

Bajaj, Monisha. 2011. "Human Rights Education: Ideology, Location, and Approaches." *Human Rights Quarterly* 33:481–508.

Bajaj, Monisha. 2012. *Schooling for Social Change: The Rise and Impact of Human Rights Education in India*. New York: Bloomsbury.

Bajaj, Monisha. 2014. "Human Rights Education: A Path Towards Peace and Justice." Proceedings of the Peace and Justice Studies Association Conference, San Diego, CA, October 16–19, 2014.

Bajaj, Monisha, Beniamino Cislaghi, and Gerry Mackie. 2016. "Advancing Transformative Human Rights Education" (Appendix D to the Global Citizenship Commission Report). New York: New York University. https://www.openbookpublishers.com/shopimages/The-UDHR-21st-C-AppendixD.pdf

Flowers, Nancy. 2003. *What Is Human Rights Education?* Hamburg: Bertelsmann Verlag. http://www.hrea.org/erc/Library/curriculum_methodology/flowers03.pdf.

Freire, P. 1970. *Pedagogy of the Oppressed.* New York: Continuum.

Kapoor, Dip. 2004. "Popular Education and Social Movements in India: State Responses to Constructive Resistance for Social Justice." *Convergence* 37(2):55–63.

Keet, André. 2007. "Human Rights Education or Human Rights in Education: A Conceptual Analysis." Ph.D. dissertation, University of Pretoria.

Magendzo, Abraham. 1997. "Problems in Planning Human Rights Education for Re-emerging Latin American Democracies." In G. Andreopoulos and R. P Claude, eds., *Human Rights Education for the Twenty-First Century* (pp. 469–483). Philadelphia: University of Pennsylvania Press.

Meintjes, G. 1997. "Human Rights Education as Empowerment: Reflections on Pedagogy." In G. Andreopoulos and R. P Claude, eds., *Human Rights Education for the Twenty-First Century* (pp. 64–79). Philadelphia: University of Pennsylvania Press.

Merry, Sally. 2006. *Human Rights and Gender Violence: Translating International Law into Local Justice.* Chicago: University of Chicago Press.

Osler, Audrey, and Hugh Starkey. 2010. *Teachers and Human Rights Education.* London: Trentham Books, 2010.

Suárez, David. 2007. "Education Professionals and the Construction of Human Rights Education." *Comparative Education Review* 51(1):48–70.

Suárez, David, and Patricia Bromley. 2012. "Professionalizing a Global Social Movement: Universities and Human Rights." *American Journal of Education* 118(3):253–280.

Tibbitts, Felisa. 2005. "Transformative Learning and Human Rights Education: Taking a Closer Look." *Intercultural Education* 16(2):107–113.

Wahl, Rachel. 2013. "Policing, Values, and Violence: Human Rights Education with Law Enforcers in India." *Oxford Journal of Human Rights Practice* 5(2):220–242.

PART I

Theoretical and Conceptual Foundations of Human Rights Education

CHAPTER 1

Symbol and Substance: Human Rights Education as an Emergent Global Institution

Susan Garnett Russell and David F. Suárez

Introduction

In early 2014, Human Rights Education Associates (HREA), an international nongovernmental organization (INGO), hosted an online forum to discuss the progress of the World Programme for Human Rights Education. The Programme is an ongoing, multiphase initiative of the United Nations Office of the High Commissioner for Human Rights (OHCHR) that "seeks to promote a common understanding of basic principles and methodologies of human rights education, to provide a concrete framework for action and to strengthen partnerships and cooperation from the international level down to the grass roots" (OHCHR 2014b). Building on the UN Decade for Human Rights Education, which took place from 1995 to 2004, the first phase of the Programme (2005–2009) emphasized human rights education (HRE) in primary and secondary school systems. The second phase (2010–2014) expanded to tertiary education and to training for professionals in fields as diverse as education, law enforcement, and the military. The third phase (2015–2019) reinforces developments from the first two phases and expands training to journalists and others in the media. In accordance with the goal of strengthening partnerships, the OHCHR solicited input from civil society organizations regarding the draft plan of action for the third phase, relying on an NGO with a long history of facilitating discussions about human rights programming in formal and informal educational settings (Suárez 2007a).

The forum consequently presents an opportunity to reflect on many striking and important developments in HRE over the last few decades. Human rights education is an emerging global institution that has made many inroads and continues to garner support from diverse actors. NGOs, nation-states, and intergovernmental organizations (IGOs) all have played salient roles in the promotion and elaboration of human rights education (Ramirez, Suárez, and Meyer 2006; Suárez, Ramirez, and Koo 2009). As the World Programme suggests, human rights education applies to both formal and informal settings, and HRE is relevant for primary, secondary, and tertiary school systems. With the growing institutionalization of human rights education at the global level, theoretical accounts of how and why human rights education emerged and expanded merit further elaboration. Building on world polity theory, we argue that HRE gained traction at the global level because the broader social movement reflects widely held cultural scripts about progress, justice, and the individual. Furthermore, we suggest that the world educational revolution interacted with the human rights movement, bridging the social movement with informal and formal schooling (Ramirez et al. 2006; Suárez et al. 2009).

In order to expand and refine this argument, we provide an overview of world polity theory, and we clarify its relevance for explaining the diffusion of human rights discourse and practice. We then contextualize the role of education within the broader human rights movement and document the progression of HRE over the last few decades, highlighting the extent to which policy documents on education, curricula, and textbooks have become infused with human rights language. Finally, we offer an agenda for new research on HRE that addresses important gaps remaining in the literature on the impact of the reform and on sources of diversity. We discuss political and civil versus social and economic rights, regional variation, organizational strategies, and human rights within contexts of extreme violence.

Human Rights in World Society

World polity theory focuses on the role of the global environment in shaping the behaviors of actors such as nation-states and organizations. Blueprints about progress, justice, and the individual—often described as scripts or models—mold organizations in ways that are difficult to explain based solely on strategy, the technical task demands of work, or internal political dynamics (Ramirez 2012). Though many of the models are Western in origin, their diffusion intensified and globalized after the Second World War, greatly accelerated by processes of economic, social, and cultural exchange (Thomas et al. 1987). Empirical research has illustrated that these global models produce identifiable outcomes or consequences; one approach has been to show that countries frequently adopt similar policies and structures despite vast differences in national conditions and economies. For instance, much of the initial research in this tradition emphasized the emergence and growth of mass education, which occurred very rapidly and with a strikingly similar pattern across the globe (Ramirez and Boli 1987; Meyer et al. 1992). Subsequent studies have expanded to the school curriculum, secondary education, and tertiary education (Benavot et al. 1991; Kamens, Meyer, and Benavot 1996; Baker and LeTendre 2005; Schofer and Meyer 2005).

In addition to research on education, recent studies have demonstrated the role of global models in a wide array of fields and issues such as the environment, suffrage policies, and the growth of civic associations (Ramirez, Soysal, and Shanahan 1997; Frank, Hironaka, and Schofer 2000; Longhofer and Schofer 2010; Schofer and Longhofer 2011). To clarify the implications and effects of global models, a canonical paper elaborates an imaginary case or parable in which the modern world suddenly finds an undiscovered island with undiscovered peoples (Meyer et al. 1997). International consultants with diverse disciplinary backgrounds such as anthropology, economics, sociology, and political science descend upon the island and help the locals create a nation-state. Soon the island joins the United Nations, it develops a constitution, perhaps it gets a loan from the World Bank, and it establishes ministries or national-level offices (e.g., education, health, finance). International NGOs (INGOs) with professional staffs arrive and begin to implement social service programs and deliver humanitarian aid. These organizations also identify additional needs of the new citizens, they collect data on the race and gender of the citizens, and they even assist in developing a local civil society sector. Beyond showing how global scripts for justice and progress matter to nation-states, then, the parable draws attention to salient mechanisms and "carriers" of those scripts.

The island in the parable exists in a world of nation-states, a global field with dense patterns of interaction. DiMaggio and Powell (1983) identify three core mechanisms that produce isomorphism, or similarity across organizations in a field: coercive, normative, and mimetic. In a coercive form of isomorphism, countries or organizations follow global models because they are obligated to do so by more powerful actors. A donor country might tie foreign aid to a requirement that the recipient country provide education for minority communities, contributing to the coercive spread of education. Mimetic isomorphism refers to a more diffuse mechanism, the imitation of global models that occurs when actors scan the environment for "best practices" that will produce or maintain organizational legitimacy. When solutions to problems are unclear, nation-states frequently copy what successful or well-respected countries are doing, leading to the diffusion of global models. Finally, normative isomorphism refers to the spread of models via professional standards and networks of consultants—for instance, through international conferences and development experts—who offer templates for solutions based on their training and "unbiased" analysis (Chabbott 2003; Meyer et al. 1997).

These mechanisms also reveal some of the sources of variation and offer viable hypotheses. A country that is relatively closed or buffered from the global environment likely will be slower to adopt global models. As a formal argument, countries with stronger links to the world polity, as measured by ties to INGOs, should be more likely to adopt global norms and scripts. Similarly, countries should adopt global scripts at a faster rate as the world becomes more saturated with international organizations. Roughly paralleling the mimetic isomorphism mechanism, countries should be more likely to adopt global scripts as other countries in the world or in the same region adopt these models. Finally, aligning with normative isomorphism, countries should be more likely to adopt global models following major conferences that promote those ideas and practices. In many respects, all of these arguments are related to variability in the timing of adoption, with some countries never embracing a global model and others doing so very quickly. A different source of variability has to do with the enactment of the model itself. Not all countries will adopt a policy or reform in the same way, meaning that there is plenty of variation in terms of what a reform looks like in practice. World polity theory describes this as loose coupling, or a weak link between a reform and its implementation (Meyer and Rowan 1977; Bromley and Powell 2012).

Loose coupling, which occurs for a variety of reasons, is expected when countries adopt progressive global models or practices (Ramirez 2012). Some countries adopt a reform with every intention of implementing it faithfully, almost like an unmodified blueprint, but they might not have the technical expertise or the financial resources to do so. In other instances, there will be a temporal component in which policy and practice initially are loosely coupled, but over time the reform gradually becomes more aligned. A third possibility is that countries will take the reform and edit it to fit the cultural context, a process of "glocalization" or "externalization" (Schriewer 1990; Robertson 1992). Yet another possibility is that the implementation of policies at the local level will be uneven and not always aligned with the original intent of the policy, especially when countries are adopting global policies due to coercive pressures (Cole and Ramírez 2013). Finally, from a strategic perspective, countries may adopt a reform as an attempt to shield themselves from scrutiny through avoidance or concealment, creating a façade of compliance (Oliver 1991). In such circumstances there never is any intention whatsoever of implementation, creating extreme decoupling. Organizations may practice a form of hypocrisy in the superficial adoption of structures and ideologies to attain legitimacy (Brunsson 2002). In the following section we review the literature on human rights policy and practice, building on the core insights of world polity theory; we then focus specifically on human rights education.

Human Rights at the Global and National Level

The origins of a global rights consciousness can be traced back at least to discussions of human rights and racial equality during the drafting of the Covenant of the League of Nations (Lauren 2011). While ultimately the covenant (1924) did not explicitly reference "human rights" due to political constraints, the core ideas discussed laid the foundation for the international human rights regime codified in the post–World War II period.[1] The gross violations of human rights perpetrated by the Nazi regime during the Holocaust spurred the international community to articulate inviolable rights and freedoms in the drafting of the UN Charter and the Universal Declaration of Human Rights (Donnelly 2013; Stacy 2009). The UN Charter (1945) mentioned "human rights" and "human dignity" for the first time. The Universal Declaration of Human Rights (UDHR; 1948) and the subsequent elaboration of the International Covenant on Economic, Social and Cultural Rights (ICESCR) and the International Covenant on Civil and Political Rights (ICCPR) in 1966 formed the legal basis for the so-called International Bill of Human Rights and the foundation for human rights as a global institution.

The international human rights regime developed along with the United Nations, and thus human rights are infused within the mandates of post–World War II intergovernmental organizations. For instance, UNESCO was established in 1945 with the aim of "building peace in the minds of men and women" and was tasked with the promotion of human rights. The Office for the High Commissioner for Human Rights evolved out of an office in the UN Secretariat and was mandated by a 1993 resolution to monitor and implement global human rights treaties. The same year, the World Conference on Human Rights was held in Vienna. The tenets of the broader human rights movement have been diffused in part through the expansion and influence of intergovernmental organizations (IGOs) that promote global human rights norms. For instance, UNESCO and other IGOs serve as carriers of ideas and norms about human rights, influencing policies at the nation-state level (Finnemore and Sikkink 1998; Finnemore 1993). Table 1.1 documents the role of IGOs in promoting human rights awareness through the creation of human rights treaties and institutions, at both global and regional levels. IGOs that promote human rights have been established and elaborated since 1945 at the global level but also in Europe, Latin America, Africa, and Asia.

Complementing the expanding role of intergovernmental organizations in constructing human rights awareness, international nongovernmental organizations have also grown in number and influence during the past half century. Boli and Thomas (1997) document a quantitative increase in the number of nongovernmental organizations globally since 1945. Furthermore, there has also been a dramatic rise in the number of INGOs devoted specifically to human rights issues, from 96 in 1978, to 170 in 1988, to 499 in 1998 (Tsutsui and Wotipka 2004). Tsutsui and Wotipka (2004) analyze the growth in human rights international nongovernmental organizations (HRINGOs), finding that membership in HRINGOs is predicted by linkages to global civil society and international flows of human resources. Aligning with perspectives that stress the importance of the external environment, international factors grow more important over time, while domestic factors become less predictive of membership in HRINGOs.

International nongovernmental organizations and civil society networks and actors also serve an important role in disseminating information, ideas, discourse, and norms about human rights (Keck and Sikkink 1998; Sikkink 1993). For example, in several Latin American countries, including Argentina and Mexico, international and domestic advocacy networks have played a critical part in advocating for human rights protection and justice during periods of internal conflict (Brysk 1993; Sikkink 1993); however, in other cases, such as in Haiti and Guatemala, advocacy networks have not had the

Table 1.1. Creating Human Rights Awareness through IGOs

Global—United Nations

1945	United Nations established
1948	Universal Declaration of Human Rights
1967	International Covenant on Civil and Political Rights
1967	International Covenant on Economic, Social and Cultural Rights
1989	International Covenant on the Rights of the Child
1993	World Conference on Human Rights

Council of Europe

1949	Council of Europe established
1950	European Convention on Human Rights
1959	European Court of Human Rights
1961	European Social Charter

Latin America

1948	Organization of American States established
1948	American Declaration on the Rights and Duties of Man
1960	Inter-American Commission on Human Rights
1978	American Convention on Human Rights
1979	Inter-American Court of Human Rights
1988	Additional Protocol to the American Convention on Human Rights (San Salvador)

Organization of African Unity (now African Union)

1963	Organization of African Unity established
1981	African (Banjul) Charter on Human and Peoples' Rights
1998	African Court on Human and Peoples' Rights established
2002	African Union established

Association of Southeast Asian Nations (ASEAN)

2009	ASEAN Intergovernmental Commission on Human Rights (AICHR)
2012	ASEAN Human Rights Declaration (AHRD)

Note: This is not an exhaustive list, and emphasizes initial activities for each IGO.

same level of influence on domestic human rights practices (Sikkink 1993). Taken together, research on the human rights movement at the global level, from world polity theory and from other traditions in political science, demonstrates an unambiguous growth of organizations and institutions dedicated to promoting and protecting human rights.

While IGOs and INGOs have played an important role in promoting human rights norms globally, human rights discourse has also filtered to the national level. Several empirical studies demonstrate the diffusion of the global human rights discourse to national-level policies and institutions including treaties, national constitutions, and national human rights instruments. The number of international human rights instruments increased dramatically after World War II, particularly in the post–Cold War period (Elliott 2007). Additionally, the number of countries signing human rights treaties has also risen over time. The majority of countries in the world have signed on to the two main human rights covenants: 162 countries have acceded to the ICESCR and 168 countries have acceded to the ICCPR (treaties.un.org).

Many countries sign and even ratify international human rights covenants, but in practice they do not always enforce them, a clear example of loose coupling. For instance, some countries sign on to human rights treaties to deflect international criticism of human rights abuses but fail to implement them in practice (Clark 2010; Cole 2005; Hafner-Burton and Tsutsui 2005, 2007). In particular, repressive countries may sign on to human rights treaties to gain international legitimacy but do not implement them (Hafner-Burton and Tsutsui 2005, 2007). Hafner-Burton, Tsutsui, and Meyer (2008) find evidence that countries often fail to implement human rights treaties due to the lack of monitoring and enforcement mechanisms. Since the human rights regime is linked to a broader social movement via the "boomerang effect" (Risse, Ropp, and Sikkink 1999) or networks of national NGOs, social movements, and international NGOs advocating for rights, one would expect to find loose coupling between intention and practice.

Human rights discourse has also entered into realms of the nation-state, particularly in more recent years, providing an example of increasing human rights discourse as a result of the broader global context. In an analysis of national constitutions from 189 countries through 2005, Beck, Drori, and Meyer (2012) find that 60 percent mention the term "human rights" at least once, with an average of six mentions per constitution. Furthermore, they find that human rights language is prominent in newer constitutions and that it is influenced by the global environment. Nevertheless, constitutional rights are portrayed more regularly than human rights (Beck et al. 2012:488). Hence, human rights function symbolically rather than as a core component of national constitutions.

The establishment of national human rights institutions (NHRIs) also provides a good indication regarding the extent to which international human rights standards have been incorporated into national laws and practices. NHRIs function as "receptor sites" (Frank et al. 2000) for the diffusion of global human rights norms within a local context. Koo and Ramirez (2009) examine the adoption rates of NHRIs, finding that more democratic countries, countries with better human rights records, and countries with more international linkages are more likely to establish such institutions. According to their work, by 2004, 133 countries had established 178 NHRIs, including eighty-three classical ombudsman offices, seventy human rights commissions, and twenty-five human rights ombudsman offices. Despite their widespread adoption, NHRIs have a differential impact on human rights outcomes. Cole and Ramirez (2013) contend that while the existence of NHRIs has a positive effect on reducing violations of physical integrity such as torture and arbitrary imprisonment, this does not extend to abuses of civil and political rights (e.g., the right to vote and freedom of speech, assembly, and religion).

The proliferation of a global human rights discourse to national-level bodies, constitutions, and treaties, particularly for countries more linked to the world polity via INGOs, provides evidence for the way in which global norms are incorporated and diffused into local structures. The studies reviewed above indicate the extent to which the human rights movement has influenced national-level legal documents and institutions in countries linked to a "world culture" through international organizations, but also in countries seeking legitimacy through invoking an international human rights discourse. Having provided an overview of the broad human rights movement, in the next section we discuss the incorporation of the human rights movement into the educational sector.

The Emergence and Evolution of Human Rights Education

While numerous empirical studies have illustrated the extent to which a global human rights discourse has influenced national-level laws, policies, and institutions, the global human rights discourse also has influenced the educational realm. During the past three decades, human rights education (HRE) has emerged as an important component of the broader human rights movement, propelled by the work of international and local NGOs, the United Nations, and broader social movements emphasizing human rights. While the main aim of the human rights movement is the protection of the political, civil, social, cultural, and economic rights of individuals and marginalized groups, the prevention of human rights abuses and the promotion of an understanding of human rights through education have progressively become a central aspect of the broader human rights agenda.

Building on prior work, we suggest that the emergence and institutionalization of the field of human rights education is linked to three interrelated factors (see Figure 1.1): globalization, the expansion of mass education, and the consolidation of the global human rights movement (Ramirez et al. 2006). First, the advent of economic, social, and cultural processes of globalization has allowed for the diffusion of all kinds of models. In particular, human rights norms and models are spread via linkages to international nongovernmental organizations and networks of human rights professionals (Suárez 2007a). Second, the rise of mass education as part of the nation-building project has over time emphasized a postnational citizenship linked to a global model of human rights (Buckner and Russell 2013; Soysal 1994). The expansion of mass education, as evidenced by the Education for All (EFA) movement, is premised on a rights-based approach to education (Chabbott and Ramirez 2000). Third, the consolidation of the global human rights movement in the post–World War II era underscores the right to education generally, but also education about human rights. Importantly, human rights education has shifted from education about international human rights law to education about, through, and for human rights (Bajaj 2011; Tibbitts 2002).

In one of the more recent developments at the global level, the UN General Assembly adopted the UN Declaration on Human Rights Education and Training in December 2011 (UN A/RES/66/137), which states: "Human rights education and training concerns all parts of society, at all levels, including preschool, primary, secondary and higher education, taking into account academic freedom where applicable, and all forms of education, training and learning, whether in a public or private, formal, informal or non-formal setting. It includes, inter alia, vocational training, particularly the training of trainers, teachers and State officials, continuing education,

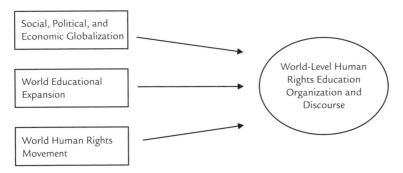

Figure 1.1. World polity explanation for the global expansion of human rights education. Based on Ramirez, Suárez, and Meyer (2006).

popular education, and public information and awareness activities" (Article 3.2). While a UN declaration is not as powerful as a treaty, it demonstrates an ongoing effort that complements the World Programme for Human Rights Education discussed earlier. The Declaration and the Programme are not the only ongoing initiatives for HRE at the global level. The UN Office of the High Commissioner for Human Rights also provides financial and technical assistance for the development of human rights education and training materials, and for the development of resources such as the Database on Human Rights Education and Training (www.ohchr.org).

Evidence of the institutionalization of human rights education abounds at the global level in other areas as well, as illustrated by the increase in human rights education publications and organizations promoting human rights (Ramirez et al. 2006). In their collection of data on publications, Ramirez et al. (2006) coded several databases in their entirety, but many of the publications did not mention human rights education explicitly. The database has continued to grow, and rather than presenting the same databases with more publications, we coded the database for publications since 2000 with the words "human rights education" in the title. As depicted in Figure 1.2, the number of publications with the term "HRE" in the title has risen from fifty-one in 2000 to 474 in 2013. This updated analysis reveals a cumulative increase over the past decade, evidence of the institutionalization of human rights education as a distinctive field.

Although many of the initial developments in human rights education, such as the publication of HRE documents, involved traditional human rights

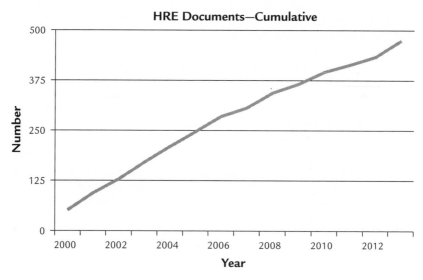

Figure 1.2. Mentions of "human rights education" in documents from the OHCRC and HREA databases.

organizations like Amnesty International, the role of tertiary institutions reveals the ongoing interaction between the human rights movement and education at all levels (Suárez 2006; Suárez and Ramirez 2007; Suárez and Bromley 2012). Several recent studies highlight the growing interest in human rights education at the tertiary level (Suárez and Bromley 2012, 2015). For instance, in Kenya, human rights is now a core course for undergraduates at several universities (OHCHR 2014a). Besides being a topic of interest for faculty members dispersed across a campus, some universities have created research centers to establish a central hub for human rights research. Moreover, in many countries, students can pursue a degree in human rights (MA degrees, LL.M. [law] degrees, and even undergraduate degrees exist).

Here we draw on data from various sources including curricula, textbooks from the past three decades, and research on pedagogy to update prior work and to document other aspects of the rise and institutionalization of human rights education. Overall, strong evidence demonstrates that the human rights education movement has evolved from a global discourse linked to the international human rights framework to a broader education movement incorporating concrete policy changes and actions in national and local contexts across diverse nations.

Curricula and Textbooks

In the area of curricula, Moon (2009) documents more than eighty-three countries across different regions of the world that have adopted human rights education in legislation, policy documents, and curricula since the late 1980s. Additionally, the International Association for the Evaluation of Educational Achievement (IEA) has carried out three studies on civic and citizenship education (1971, 1999, 2009) that offer a starting point for assessing the degree to which human rights is incorporated into curricula. In the most recent (2009) study of civic education in twenty-eight countries, the authors find that twenty-five of the countries emphasize human rights in the national curricula (Schulz et al. 2010:48).

In addition to the strong presence of human rights in educational curricula in recent years, the movement has also extended to student textbooks. In a cross-national study of secondary textbooks from around the world, Meyer, Bromley, and Ramirez (2010) document a rise in the discussion of human rights since 1995, especially in more developed and Western countries. Using an expanded and updated textbook data set, following Meyer et al.'s (2010) study of human rights in textbooks, we find that human rights terminology expands significantly after the 1980s, at both the textbook and country level (see Figures 1.3 and 1.4). Figure 1.3 shows an increase in the proportion of countries whose textbooks mention human rights over time; Figure 1.4 shows an increase in the proportion of textbooks in the sample that mention human rights across countries from 1945 to 2010.

Furthermore, we examine different discussions of human rights terms in textbooks and find a statistically significant increase in the post-1990 period in mentions of human rights across several dimensions (see Table 1.2). We also find that inclusion of human rights discourse increases in both Western and non-Western countries across all regions to varying degrees (see Table 1.3). Despite an increase in human rights discourse in textbooks globally, not all types of countries discuss human rights in their textbooks to the same degree: less democratic and non-Western countries are less likely to mention human rights (Meyer et al. 2010). Russell and Tiplic (2014) also find

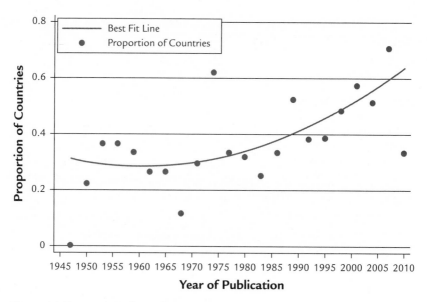

Figure 1.3. Proportion of countries mentioning human rights.

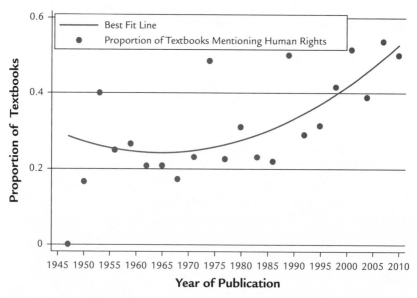

Figure 1.4. Proportion of textbooks mentioning human rights.

Table 1.2. Discussion of Human Rights in Textbooks (1945–2011)

	Pre-1990 (n = 349)	Post-1990 (n = 347)	
Percent with:			
Mentions of human rights	26.65	42.65	d
Discussion of political/civil rights as human rights	21.49	33.71	c
Discussion of economic, social, and cultural rights as HR	18.34	33.62	d
Reference to UDHR	10.03	17.58	c
Reference to national human rights bodies	0.57	5.19	c
Discussion of conflict as a human rights violation	13.75	21.84	c

[a] $p < .1$, [b] $p < .05$, [c] $p < .01$, [d] $p < .001$, one-tailed tests. Significance indicates t-test comparing difference between means of pre-1990 and post-1990.

Table 1.3. Discussion of Human Rights in Textbooks (1945–2011) by World Region

	West (n = 197)	Asia (n = 106)	E. Europe (n = 133)	Latin America (n = 79)	Middle East (n = 84)	Africa (n = 98)	
Percent with:							
Mentions of human rights	37.25	42.45	27.82	35.44	26.19	36.73	
Discussion of political/ civil rights as human rights	30.61	34.91	18.8	32.91	22.62	25.51	b
Discussion of economic, social, and cultural rights as HR	29.95	24.53	23.31	22.78	22.62	28.57	
Reference to UDHR	17.35	11.32	12.03	27.85	1.19	11.22	d
Reference to national human rights bodies	0.51	1.89	3.01	3.79	2.38	8.16	b
Discussion of conflict as a human rights violation	18.27	14.15	17.29	20.25	16.67	20.41	

[a] $p < .1$, [b] $p < .05$, [c] $p < .01$, [d] $p < .001$, one-tailed tests. Significance indicates F-test comparing difference across world regions.

that conflict-affected states are less likely to emphasize a rights discourse, although there is no difference in discussion of rights in post-conflict countries (Russell 2013).

Several studies illustrate the extent to which human rights discourse in educational texts is linked to other phenomena. For example, Buckner and Russell (2013) find that discussions of globalization and global citizenship are predicted by whether or not a textbook discusses human rights content. In an analysis of the presentation of the Holocaust in textbooks, Bromley and Russell (2010) show that discussions of the Holocaust are linked to human rights in texts. Similarly, mentions of transitional justice and conflict resolution mechanisms are linked to human rights mentions (Russell and Tiplic 2014), and discussion of gender-based violence in textbooks is also predicted by mentions of women's rights. In these instances, discussions of genocide, gender-based violence, and addressing past violence through transitional justice mechanisms are all framed explicitly within a human rights discourse.

Pedagogy and Practice

In addition to the presence of human rights language in educational curricula and textbooks globally (Ramírez et al. 2006), human rights education is also being implemented in schools to varying degrees across national and local contexts. In a quantitative, cross-national study using data from the 1999 IEA study (of 88,000 fourteen-year-old students), the authors consider student-level and country-level predictors of rights-related knowledge (Torney-Purta, Wilkenfeld, and Barber 2008). They find that student experiences with democratic practices and international issues and country-level participation in intergovernmental discourse contribute to human rights knowledge. Additionally, results from the 2009 study of civic education in thirty-eight countries demonstrate that human rights are discussed in classrooms and that students have some understanding of human rights issues. For instance, when students were asked about the fundamental purpose of the Universal Declaration of Human Rights, 68 percent of students answered the question correctly, with a range of 38 to 92 percent across the thirty-eight participating countries (Schulz et al. 2010:65). Thus, these studies point to the institutionalization of human rights as a topic at the classroom level across distinct national contexts.

Additional studies have sought to go beyond the presence of human rights as a topic in the classroom to investigate the influence of human rights education on knowledge and attitudes within the classroom context. Among the few studies of classroom learning, Bajaj (2004) finds that human rights education does change some behaviors among students in the Dominican Republic. In her more recent work on human rights programs in India, Bajaj (2011, 2012) shows that human rights education influences the way in which students conceive of their own rights and actions, and that human rights education has an impact on transforming students' sense of empowerment and agency at the community and school levels. Stellmacher and Sommer (2008) report an increase in knowledge and attitudes about human rights among German university students enrolled in a human rights seminar. In a study on global education, Gaudelli and Fernekes (2012) argue that teaching about human rights as a topic in a comparative world studies course leads to an increase in awareness about human rights among students.

Several studies examine the implementation of human rights education in various countries, including India, the United States, Argentina, and Costa Rica, providing evidence of loose coupling between policy and practice. In Bajaj's case study of human rights education in India, she finds decoupling between the intended national policy for HRE and the way in which some HRE is implemented as moral education or political ideology (2012). A study on HRE in the United States concludes that despite the global increase in HRE discourse, few programs are implemented in primary and secondary schools in the United States, and most programs are implemented by NGOs (Stone 2002). Suárez (2008) examines the inclusion of global citizenship and human rights in the civics education curricula and textbooks from two Latin American cases: Argentina and Costa Rica. Costa Rica incorporates citizenship and human rights in a conventional manner, while Argentina emphasizes global human rights due to its historical legacy of human rights violations. While HRE is present across different contexts, these studies show that implementation on the ground is variable.

In other contexts, such as in countries affected by violent conflict, human rights education is often controversial and difficult to fully implement in schools. In the South African case, human rights language is prominent across educational policy and school materials (Russell 2015; Thapliyal, Vally, and Spreen 2013). However, in practice, human rights education is rarely implemented in the classroom due to a lack of political will and teacher training (Carrim and Keet 2005). Similarly, in Rwanda, national policy and texts draw on a global human rights discourse to frame national and global citizenship in the post-genocide context. However, while human rights terms are present in school curricula and textbooks, human rights is also a contested and politically sensitive topic and is not often taught in practice (Russell 2013). Thus, human rights education may be most difficult to implement in countries that have experienced recent violations of human rights due to political sensitivities and resource constraints.

Future Directions: Impact and Variability in HRE

In prior sections we provided an overview of global developments in human rights and human rights education, building on world polity theory to offer an explanation for the diffusion of discourse and practices. We demonstrated that human rights education has gained traction, yet this argument does not imply that all countries throughout the world embrace the reform in the same way or with the same enthusiasm. We clarified that countries with more extensive ties to INGOs are more likely to adopt human rights policies and discourse than isolated countries. We also indicated that countries seeking external legitimacy are much more likely than others to utilize human rights discourse strategically; loose coupling can serve as a tactic for appeasing the international community without producing dramatic changes in national practices. Variability in implementation and practices undoubtedly increases as research perspectives become "narrower" too (i.e., comparative country case studies, within-country comparisons of policy implementation, and research on pedagogical practices across schools or teachers). Here we draw attention to new directions on the impact of human rights education and on underexplored sources of diversity.

While the International Bill of Human Rights[2] enshrines the protection of civil, political, economic, social, and cultural rights, some countries prioritize social and cultural rights (or vice versa), a pattern that extends to human rights education. In a recent study of Rwanda, for instance, Russell (2013) finds that women's rights and economic and social rights are less controversial and are thus emphasized over civil and political rights in national educational texts and policies (Russell 2013). A common explanation for differences involves the Cold War and ideological divisions between the United States and the Soviet Union, but recent work indicates that there is much greater complexity than tends to be presented in stylized depictions of a polarized world (Whelan and Donnelly 2007). A second explanation incorporates historical legacies and notions of positive versus natural law. Rather than reflecting ideological differences with respect to capitalism and communism, differences could have as much to do with legal traditions as with governance. Besides these two sets of explanations, variability could be related to political dynamics within countries, especially in terms of democracy and dictatorship. Finally, more economically developed countries could be in a better position to guarantee economic, social, and cultural rights through taxation and an expansive social safety net (welfare state).

Besides these lines of inquiry, another intriguing avenue for future research involves regional differences in the adoption of human rights education. For instance, in the aforementioned textbook analysis, 18 percent of textbooks from Eastern European countries mention political and civil rights as human rights compared to 33 percent in Latin America and 35 percent in Asia, respectively. A stark difference is found in reference to the UDHR, with only 1 percent of texts from the Middle East region mentioning the UDHR, compared to 28 percent in Latin America; additionally, only 0.5 percent of texts from the West discuss national human rights bodies, compared to 8 percent in African countries. Rates of incorporation of human rights discussion also vary by region: discussion of human rights in textbooks increased dramatically in textbooks from countries in sub-Saharan African in the post-1990 period, from 17 percent of textbooks to 65 percent, pointing to the strong emphasis on human rights in recent decades relative to other regions (see Table 1.4). New research, either incorporating indicators for world regions or focusing on specific world regions, could help to surface some of the mechanisms that produce these differences.

In addition to the need for research on regional variation and on which rights become institutionalized in discourse and practice, new studies are needed on how countries with histories of extreme violence and human rights abuses deal with these issues through education. Some countries, such as South Africa, place great emphasis on "historical memory"—educating future generations about the past so that history does not repeat itself—whereas other countries with extensive past violations, such as Spain, deemphasize their history of human rights abuses (Jelin and Lorenz 2004; Cardenas 2005; Bromley and Russell 2010). What explains differences in how countries recognize violations, and are such differences reflected in the reduction or prevention of future violations? Questions such as these push

Table 1.4. Discussion of Human Rights in Textbooks (1945–2011):
Sub-Saharan Africa

	Pre-1990 (n = 58)	Post-1990 (n = 40)	
Percent with:			
Mentions of human rights	17.24	65	d
A paragraph or more on human rights	17.24	65	d
Discussion of political/civil rights as human rights	13.79	42.5	d
Discussion of social rights as human rights	10.34	50	d
Discussion of cultural rights as human rights	6.9	15	a
Discussion of economic rights as human rights	10.34	27.5	b
Reference to international human rights documents	12.07	32.5	c
Reference to UDHR	8.62	15	
Reference to national human rights documents	6.9	20	b
Reference to national human rights bodies	0	20	d
Reference to national human rights documents and bodies	0	2.5	
Discussion of conflict as a human rights violation	12.07	32.5	c

[a] $p < .1$, [b] $p < .05$, [c] $p < .01$, [d] $p < .001$, one-tailed tests. Significance indicates t-test comparing difference between means of pre-1990 and post-1990.

research on human rights education in new directions, moving beyond general rights to specific discussions of national histories. More research is needed to determine the factors that influence countries to invoke a rights discourse within a conflict or post-conflict context; research is also needed on the differential application of the global human rights discourse across regions.

Thus far, all of the research directions we have suggested focus, at some level, on nation-states and educational systems. However, as mentioned earlier, plenty of research demonstrates that NGOs act as carriers and receptor sites for education reforms like human rights education (Frank et al. 2000; Mundy and Murphy 2001; Chabbott 2003; Suárez 2007a). Organizations thus are relevant to ongoing developments in human rights education, yet most extant research stresses the aggregate effects of NGOs. Put differently, just because civil society ties to NGOs increase the likelihood that countries will adopt reforms such as human rights education does not mean that all NGOs embrace those reforms or engage with them in the same way. There is plenty of diversity within organizations, and new research that explores variability in the structures and strategies of human rights organizations would be a welcome addition to the literature. Recent studies in political science, for instance, demonstrate that organizational configurations (particularly centralization) influence the activities of human rights organizations and humanitarian agencies (Wong 2012; Stroup and Wong 2013). Similarly, interorganizational networks help to explain tactical choices and other strategic behaviors among NGOs (Murdie 2014; Haddon 2014). Additional work on human rights NGOs would help to explain how professionalization and other factors influence engagement with education.

How do behaviors change after exposure to material on human rights education? To what extent are changes permanent, if indeed there are changes? How important is the curriculum for learning human rights? How does pedagogy matter for learning and retention of human rights material? Many of the studies mentioned earlier on textbooks and curricula demonstrate increasing amounts of human rights content, yet most cannot link the curriculum to student learning or to changes in attitudes and behavior over time. Similarly, while several studies reveal that students are exposed to human rights education across different contexts (Bajaj 2012; Torney-Purta, Wilkenfeld, and Barber 2008), further research is needed on the mechanisms through which human rights curricula and policies are implemented, on how students engage and learn about human rights, and on the extent to which human rights education leads to attitudinal or behavior changes. Important next steps include longitudinal studies of students and research on the direct impact of pedagogy.

In conclusion, human rights education has expanded dramatically over the last few decades, and ongoing scholarship has documented many of the changes in intergovernmental agencies, national-level discourse, curricular policies, and textbooks. World polity theory offers a powerful theoretical frame for understanding why and how the reform has gained traction, and the research tradition also offers many avenues for additional scholarship on the topic. We began with a broad discussion of human rights, situating the education component within the broader human rights movement. Much of the initial work on human rights emphasized the promotion of international treaties and the protection of victims of abuse. While those efforts have not diminished, the prevention of abuses through education has become a new pillar of the movement. The interaction between the human rights movement and formal education shapes both, meaning that it is not just human rights organizations that take on an education focus—formal education becomes infused with human rights discourse in primary, secondary, and tertiary education. Future research can clarify the linkages between discourse and practice through studies of pedagogy and student learning, and new work on organizations and differences in national-level practices would further contextualize many of the ongoing developments in human rights education.

Notes

1. Transnational advocacy networks to end slavery, female circumcision, and footbinding (often viewed as human rights issues) emerged well before the end of World War II (Keck and Sikkink 1998). The International Labor Organization (ILO) also predates the modern human rights movement.

2. The International Bill of Human Rights refers to the collective legal force of the Universal Declaration of Human Rights (1948), the International Covenant on Civil and Political Rights (1966), and the International Covenant on Economic, Social and Cultural Rights (1966).

References

Anderson, Benedict. 1983. *Imagined Communities: Reflections on the Origin and Spread of Nationalism.* New York: Verso.

Bajaj, Monisha. 2004. "Human Rights Education and Student Self-Conception in the Dominican Republic." *Journal of Peace Education* 1(1):21–36.

Bajaj, Monisha. 2011. "Human Rights Education: Ideology, Location, and Approaches." *Human Rights Quarterly* 33(2):481–508.

Bajaj, Monisha. 2012. *Schooling for Social Change: The Rise and Impact of Human Rights Education in India.* London: Continuum International Publishing.

Baker, David P., and Gerald K. LeTendre. 2005. *National Differences, Global Similarities: World Culture and the Future of Schooling.* Stanford, CA: Stanford University Press.

Beck, Colin J., Gili S. Drori, and John W. Meyer. 2012. "World Influences on Human Rights Language in Constitutions: A Cross-National Study." *International Sociology* 27(4):483–501.

Benavot, Aaron, Yun-Kyung Cha, David Kamens, John W. Meyer, and Suk-Ying Wong. 1991. "Knowledge for the Masses: World Models and National Curricula, 1920–1986." *American Sociological Review* 56(1):85–100.

Boli, John, and George Thomas. 1997. "World Culture and the World Polity: A Century of International Non-Governmental Organization." *American Sociological Review* 62(2):171–190.

Borgwardt, Elizabeth. 2005. *A New Deal for the World: America's Vision for Human Rights*. Cambridge, MA: Belknap Press.

Bromley, Patricia. 2014. "Legitimacy and the Contingent Diffusion of World Culture: Diversity and Human Rights in Social Science Textbooks, Divergent Cross-National Patterns (1970–2008). *Canadian Journal of Sociology* 39(1):1–44.

Bromley, Patricia, and Walter W. Powell. 2012. "From Smoke and Mirrors to Walking the Talk: Decoupling in the Contemporary World." *Academy of Management Annals* 6:483–530.

Bromley, Patricia, and Susan Garnett Russell. 2010. "Holocaust as History and Human Rights: Holocaust Education in Social Science Textbooks, 1970–2008." *Prospects: UNESCO's Quarterly Review of Comparative Education* 40(1):153–173.

Brunsson, Nils. 2002. *The Organization of Hypocrisy*. Copenhagen: Copenhagen Business School Press.

Brysk, Alison. 1993. "From Above and Below: Social Movements, the International System, and Human Rights in Argentina." *Comparative Political Studies* 26(3):259–285.

Buckner, Elizabeth, and Susan Garnett Russell. 2013. "Portraying the Global: Cross-National Trends in Textbooks' Portrayal of Globalization and Global Citizenship." *International Studies Quarterly* 57:738–750.

Buergenthal, Thomas, and Judith Torney. 1976. *International Human Rights and International Education*. Washington, DC: U.S. National UNESCO Commission.

Cardenas, Sonia. 2005. "Constructing Rights? Human Rights Education and the State." *International Political Science Review* 26(4):363–379.

Carrim, Nazir, and Andre Keet. 2005. "Infusing Human Rights into the Curriculum: The Case of the South African Revised National Curriculum Statement." *Perspectives in Education* 23(2): 99–110.

Chabbott, Colette. 2003. *Constructing Education for Development: International Organizations and Education for All*. New York: RoutledgeFalmer.

Chabbott, Colette, and Francisco O. Ramirez. 2000. "Development and Education." In Maureen T. Hallinan, ed., *Handbook of the Sociology of Education* (pp. 163–187). New York: Kluwer Academic.

Clark, Ann Marie. 2010. *Diplomacy of Conscience: Amnesty International and Changing Human Rights Norms*. Princeton, NJ: Princeton University Press.

Cole, Wade M. 2005. "Sovereignty Relinquished? Explaining Commitment to the International Human Rights Covenants, 1966–1999." *American Sociological Review* 70(3):472–495.

Cole, Wade M., and Francisco O. Ramirez. 2013. "Conditional Decoupling: Assessing the Impact of National Human Rights Institutions, 1981 to 2004. *American Sociological Review* 79(4):1–24.

DiMaggio, Paul J., and Walter W. Powell. 1983. "The Iron Cage Revisited: Institutional Isomorphism and Collective Rationality in Organizational Fields." *American Sociological Review* 48 (2):147–160.

Donnelly, Jack. 1983. "Human Rights and Human Dignity: An Analytic Critique of Non-Western Conceptions of Human Rights." *American Political Science Review* 76(2):303–316.

Donnelly, Jack. 1998. *International Human Rights*, 2nd ed. New York: Westview Press.

Donnelly, Jack. 2013. *Universal Human Rights in Theory and Practice*, 3rd ed. Ithaca, NY: Cornell University Press.

Dreeben, Robert. 1968. *On What Is Learned in School*. Reading, MA: Addison-Wesley.

Elliott, Michael. 2007. "Human Rights and the Triumph of the Individual in World Culture." *Cultural Sociology* 1:343–363.

Finnemore, Martha. 1993. "International Organizations as Teachers of Norms: The United Nations Educational, Scientific, and Cultural Organization and Science Policy." *International Organization* 47(4): 565–597.

Finnemore, Martha, and Kathryn Sikkink. 1998. "International Norm Dynamics and Political Change." *International Organization* 52(4): 887–917.

Frank, David John, Bayliss Camp, and Steven Boutcher. 2010. "Worldwide Trends in the Criminal Regulation of Sex, 1945 to 2005." *American Sociological Review* 75:867–893.

Frank, David John, Ann Hironaka, and Evan Schofer. 2000. "The Nation-State and the Natural Environment over the Twentieth Century." *American Sociological Review* 65:96–116.

Gaudelli, William, and William Fernekes. 2004. "Teaching about Global Human Rights for Global Citizenship." *The Social Studies* 95(1):16–26.

Graves, Norman, O. James Dunlop, and Judith Torney-Purta. 1984. *Teaching for International Understanding, Peace and Human Rights*. Paris: UNESCO.

Haddon, Jennifer. 2014. "Explaining Variation in Transnational Climate Change Activism." *Global Environmental Politics* 14(2):7–25.

Hafner-Burton, Emilie. 2008. "Sticks and Stones: Naming and Shaming the Human Rights Enforcement Problem." *International Organization* 62:689–716.

Hafner-Burton, Emilie, and Kiyoteru Tsutsui. 2005. "Human Rights in a Globalizing World: The Paradox of Empty Promises." *American Journal of Sociology* 110(5):1373–1411.

Hafner-Burton, Emilie, and Kiyoteru Tsutsui. 2007. "Justice Lost: The Failure of International Human Rights Law to Matter Where Needed Most." *Journal of Peace Research* 44(4): 407–425.

Hafner-Burton, Emilie, Kiyoteru Tsutsui, and John W. Meyer. 2008. "International Human Rights Law and the Politics of Legitimation: Repressive States and Human Rights Treaties." *International Sociology* 23:115–141.

Hathaway, Oona. 2002. "Do Human Rights Treaties Make a Difference?" *Yale Law Journal* 111:1935–2042.

Jelin, Elizabeth, and Federico Guillermo Lorenz, eds. 2004. *Educación y Memoria: La Escuela Elabora el Pasado*. Buenos Aires: Siglo Veinteuno de España.

Kamens, David, John Meyer, and Aaron Benavot. 1996. "Worldwide Patterns in Academic Secondary Education Curricula." *Comparative Education Review* 40(2):116–138.

Keck, Margaret, and Kathryn Sikkink. 1998. *Activists Beyond Borders: Transnational Advocacy Networks in International Politics.* Ithaca, NY: Cornell University Press.

Koo, Jeong-Woo, and Francisco O. Ramirez. 2009. "National Incorporation of Global Human Rights: Worldwide Expansion of National Human Rights Institutions, 1966–2004." *Social Forces* 87(3):1321–1353.

Landman, Todd. 2005. *Protecting Human Rights: A Comparative Study.* Washington, DC: Georgetown University Press.

Lauren, Paul Gordon. 2003. *The Evolution of International Human Rights*, 2nd ed. Philadelphia: University of Pennsylvania Press.

Longhofer, Wesley, and Evan Schofer. 2010. "National and Global Origins of Environmental Association." *American Sociological Review* 75(4):505–533.

Lutz, Ellen, and Kathryn Sikkink. 2000. "International Human Rights Law and Practice in Latin America." *International Organization* 54:633–659.

Meyer, John, W., John Boli, George Thomas, and Francisco Ramirez. 1997. "World Society and the Nation-State." *American Journal of Sociology* 103(1):144–181.

Meyer, John, W., Patricia Bromley, and Francisco O. Ramirez. 2010. "Human Rights in Social Science Textbooks: Cross-National Analysis, 1970–2008." *Sociology of Education* 83(2):111–134.

Meyer, John W., Francisco O. Ramirez, and Yasemin Nuhoglu Soysal. 1992. "World Expansion of Mass Education, 1870–1980." *Sociology of Education* 65(2):128–149.

Meyer, John W., and Brian Rowan. 1977. "Institutionalized Organizations: Formal Structure as Myth and Ceremony." *American Journal of Sociology* 83(2):340–363.

Moon, Rennie. 2009. Teaching World Citizenship: The Cross-National Adoption of Human Rights Education in Formal Schooling. Doctoral Dissertation, Stanford University, Stanford, CA.

Moon, Rennie, and Jeong-Woo Koo. 2011. "Global Citizenship and Human Rights: A Longitudinal Analysis of Social Studies and Ethics Textbooks in the Republic of Korea." *Comparative Education Review* 55(4):574–599.

Mundy, Karen, and Lynn Murphy. 2001. "Transnational Advocacy, Global Civil Society? Emerging Evidence from the Field of Education." *Comparative Education Review* 45(1):85–126.

Murdie, Amanda. 2014. "The Ties That Bind: A Network Analysis of Human Rights International Nongovernmental Organizations." *British Journal of Political Science* 44(1):1–27.

Neumayer, Eric. 2005. "Do International Human Rights Treaties Improve Respect for Human Rights?" *Journal of Conflict Resolution* 49:925–953.

Office of the High Commissioner for Human Rights (OHCHR). 2014a. "The Study of Human Rights Becomes a Core Subject in Kenyan Universities." http://www.ohchr.org/EN/NewsEvents/Pages/GradStudents.aspx.

Office of the High Commissioner for Human Rights (OHCHR). 2014b. "World Programme for Human Rights." http://www.ohchr.org/EN/Issues/Education/Training/Pages/Programme.aspx.

Oliver, Christine. 1991. "Strategic Responses to Institutional Processes." *Academy of Management Review* 16(1):145–179.

Ramirez, Francisco O. 2012. "The World Society Perspective: Concepts, Assumptions, and Strategies." *Comparative Education* 48(4):423–439.

Ramirez, Francisco O., and John Boli. 1987. "The Political Construction of Mass Schooling: European Origins and Worldwide Institutionalization." *Sociology of Education* 60:2–17.

Ramirez, Francisco O., Yasemin Soysal, and Susanne Shanahan. 1997. "The Changing Logic of Political Citizenship: Cross-National Acquisition of Women's Suffrage Rights, 1890 to 1990." *American Sociological Review* 62:735–745.

Ramirez, Francisco O., David F Suárez, and John W. Meyer. 2006. "The Worldwide Rise of Human Rights Education, 1950–2005." In Aaron Benavot and Cecilia Braslavsky, eds., *The Changing Contents of Primary and Secondary Education: Comparative Studies of the School Curriculum* (pp. 35–25). Hong Kong: CERC.

Risse, Thomas, Stephen Ropp, and Kathryn Sikkink. 1999. *The Power of Human Rights: International Norms and Domestic Change.* Cambridge: Cambridge University Press.

Robertson, Roland. 1992. *Globalization: Social Theory and Global Culture.* Newbury Park, CA: Sage.

Ron, James, Howard Ramos, and Kathleen Rodgers. 2005. "Transnational Information Politics: NGO Human Rights Reporting, 1986–2000." *International Studies Quarterly* 49:557–588.

Russell, Susan Garnett. 2013. The Role of Education in Promoting Reconciliation and Civic Identity in Rwanda: Global, National, and School Contexts. Doctoral Dissertation, Stanford University, Stanford, CA.

Russell, Susan Garnett. 2015. "Global Civil Society and Education Policy in Post-Genocide Rwanda." *International Sociology* 30(6): 599–618.

Russell, Susan Garnett, and Dijana Tiplic. 2014. "Rights-Based Education and Conflict: A Cross-National Study of Rights Discourse in Textbooks." *Compare* 44(3):314–334.

Schofer, Evan, and Wesley Longhofer. 2011. "The Structural Sources of Association." *American Journal of Sociology* 117(2):539–585.

Schofer, Evan, and John Meyer. 2005. "The Worldwide Expansion of Higher Education in the Twentieth Century." *American Sociological Review* 70(6):898–920.

Schriewer, Jurgen. 1990. "The Method of Comparison and the Need for Externalization: Methodological Criteria and Sociological Concepts." In J. Schriewer and B. Holmes, eds., *Theories and Methods in Comparative Education* (pp. 25–83). Frankfurt: Lang.

Schulz, Wolfram, John Ainley, Julian Fraillon, David Kerr, and Bruno Losito. 2010. *ICCS 2009 International Report: Civic Knowledge, Attitudes, and Engagement*

Among Lower-Secondary School Students in 38 Countries. Amsterdam: International Association for the Evaluation of Educational Achievement.

Sikkink, Kathryn. 1993. "Human Rights, Principled Issue-Networks, and Sovereignty in Latin America." *International Organization* 47(3):411–441.

Simmons, Beth. 2009. *Mobilizing for Human Rights: International Law in Domestic Politics.* New York: Cambridge University Press.

Soysal, Yasemin. 1994. *Limits of Citizenship: Migrants and Postnational Membership in Europe.* Chicago: University of Chicago Press.

Stacy, Helen M. 2009. *Human Rights for the 21st Century.* Stanford: Stanford University Press.

Stellmacher, Jost, and Gert Sommer. 2008. "Human Rights Education: An Evaluation of University Seminars." *Social Psychology* 39:70–80.

Stone, Adam. 2002. "Human Rights Education and Public Policy in the United States: Mapping the Road Ahead." *Human Rights Quarterly* 24(2):537–557.

Stroup, Sarah, and Wendy H. Wong. 2013. "Come Together? Different Pathways to International NGO Centralization." *International Studies Quarterly* 15:163–184.

Suárez, David. 2006. "The Institutionalization of Human Rights Education." In David Baker and Alex Wiseman, eds., *The Impact of Comparative Education Research on Neoinstitutional Theory* (pp. 95–120). Oxford: Elsevier Science.

Suárez, David. 2007a. "Education Professionals and the Construction of Human Rights Education." *Comparative Education Review* 51(1):48–70.

Suárez, David. 2007b. "Human Rights and Curricular Policy in Latin America and the Caribbean." *Comparative Education Review* 51(3):329–352.

Suárez, David. 2008. "Rewriting Citizenship? Civic Education in Costa Rica and Argentina." *Comparative Education* 44(4): 485–503.

Suárez, David, and Patricia Bromley. 2012. "Professionalizing a Global Social Movement: Universities and Human Rights." *American Journal of Education* 118(3):253–280.

Suárez, David, and Patricia Bromley. 2015. "Institutional Theories and Levels of Analysis: Diffusion, History, and Translation." In Jurgen Schriewer, ed., *World Culture Recontextualized* (pp. 139–159). Washington, DC: Taylor and Francis.

Suárez, David, and Francisco O. Ramirez. 2007. "Human Rights and Citizenship: The Emergence of Human Rights Education." In Carlos A. Torres, ed., *Critique and Utopia: New Developments in the Sociology of Education* (pp. 43–64). Lanham, MD: Rowman and Littlefield.

Suárez, David, Francisco O. Ramirez, and Jeong-Woo Koo. 2009. "UNESCO and the Associated Schools Project: Symbolic Affirmation of World Community, International Understanding, and Human Rights." *Sociology of Education* 82(3):197–216.

Thapliyal, Nisha, Salim Vally, and Carol Anne Spreen. 2013. "'Until We Get Up Again to Fight': Education Rights and Participation in South Africa." *Comparative Education Review* 57(2): 212–231.

Thomas, George, John Meyer, Francisco Ramirez, and John Boli. 1987. *Institutional Structure: Constituting State, Society, and the Individual*. Newbury Park, CA: Sage.

Tibbitts, Felisa. (2002). "Understanding What We Do: Emerging Models for Human Rights Education." *International Review of Education*, 48(3–4):159–171.

Torney-Purta, Judith, Britt Wilkenfeld, and Carolyn Barber. 2008. "How Adolescents in 27 Countries Understand, Support, and Practice Human Rights." *Journal of Social Issues* 64(4):857–880.

Tsutsui, Kiyoteru, and Christine Min Wotipka. 2004. "Global Civil Society and the International Human Rights Movement: Citizen Participation in Human Rights International Nongovernmental Organizations." *Social Forces* 83(2):587–620.

Whelan, Daniel, and Jack Donnelly. 2007. "The West, Economic and Social Rights, and the Global Human Rights Regime: Setting the Record Straight." *Human Rights Quarterly* 29(4):908–949.

Wong, Wendy. 2012. *Internal Affairs: How the Structure of NGOs Transforms Human Rights*. Ithaca, NY: Cornell University Press.

Wotipka, Christine Min, and Kiyoteru Tsutsui. 2008. "Global Human Rights and State Sovereignty: Nation-States' Ratifications of International Human Rights Treaties, 1965–1999." *Sociological Forum* 23(4):724–754.

CHAPTER 2

Emotions, Critical Pedagogy, and Human Rights Education

Michalinos Zembylas

Introduction

What role do emotions play in human rights education (HRE), especially in light of the proliferation of rational understanding of human rights (Barreto 2011) and HRE's reliance on a theory of human rights as universal principles (Sliwinski 2005)? In particular, how does the mobilization of emotion in HRE help cultivate in students the kind of emotional experiences that are valuable in creating sympathy for and solidarity with others, without leading up to "empty sentimentality" (Zembylas 2008, 2013a). These questions present some of the most important challenges that HRE currently faces (see Al-Daraweesh and Snauwaert 2013; Keet 2009, 2010, 2012). This chapter addresses these questions by looking at the entanglement of emotion, pedagogy, and HRE, exploring in particular the ambiguities and tensions that emerge from seriously taking into consideration the role of emotions and sentimentality in human rights teaching and learning. Specifically, it is suggested that a theory of HRE that acknowledges the significance of emotion in critical ways can provide productive pedagogical orientations to the teaching of human rights.

The chapter begins by reviewing human rights critiques, focusing in particular on how the rhetoric of human rights often remains at a metaphysical or rationalist level or ends up being an empty and abstract moral ideology. To provide a different perspective, the chapter shows the relation between emotions and human rights and offers an overview of the different ways in which emotions may be implicated in the experiences of those who perceive, mobilize, or claim human rights; the argument here is that the recognition of the role of emotion creates important openings for a different engagement with human rights. To demonstrate this, the chapter turns to Rorty's (1998) proposal of "sentimental education" as a point of departure that acknowledges the role of emotions and sentimentality in HRE; Rorty's contribution as well as the weaknesses of his proposal are discussed. The weaknesses point to the need for a more critical engagement with sentimentality so that the dangers of empty sentimentality are addressed. The chapter ends by suggesting a set of pedagogical practices that may contribute to a critical pedagogy of emotions in HRE.

Human Rights Critiques

Contemporary critiques of human rights are often grounded in the following arguments: Human rights, over the years, have become essentialized and universal norms often expressed in juridical terms, whereas their history indicates that human rights are a Western concept grounded in liberal views, serving the interests of Western powers (e.g., Mutua 2002) acting in neocolonial terms (Baxi 2007; Spivak 2004); human rights are vague, abstract, and more symbolic than substantive (Ignatieff 2001; Rorty 1998); and human rights are used to impose and legitimate political hegemony, even when they do not always intend to address the causes of social grievance and suffering (Brown 2004). Each of these critiques is briefly revisited below, not to provide a comprehensive review but to highlight their consequences in terms of how human rights are understood; these understandings have clear implications for how human rights may be taught, especially in relation to the role of emotion.

Some interpretations of human rights as a philosophical system have essentialized human rights and often reached the point of codifying them only in juridical terms (Donnelly 2003) or in terms grounded in problematic assumptions about a universal human nature and the sovereign subject (Douzinas 2000). As scholars from various philosophical perspectives have noted, the emergence and application of human rights ideas are embedded in power structures, whether national or international (Bhabha 1999; Evans 1998; Ignatieff 2001). This idea alerts us to the need to constantly reexamine whether current interpretations of human rights are really what we want them to be in order to prevent and correct—rather than simply recognize—human suffering, misery, and wrongs.

In particular, there are concerns about whether legalistic approaches to human rights—that is, approaches that treat human rights as legal norms—can adequately respond to the multiple complexities that are raised on human rights issues in conflict societies (Donnelly 2003). As Donnelly explains, the codification of human rights in legalistic terms cannot address the multiple social and political issues that arise when a human rights–based approach is followed in complicated situations—such as a conflict zone in which there are several groups involved and multiple violations of human rights by all sides.

In addition, there are concerns whether Eurocentric approaches to human rights eventually correct dominant power structures that are responsible for human suffering in the first place. Using a rather polemic tone, Mutua (2002) argues that interpretations of human rights are not neutral but very much embedded in cultural and political assumptions, contending that "The grand narrative of human rights contains a subtext which depicts an epochal contest pitting savages, on the one hand, against victims and saviors, on the other" (Mutua 2002:10). Human rights discourses, then, function as a subtle form of neocolonialist crusade, in which "civilized" nations must teach "primitive savages" the proper way of living and behaving. Mutua's main assertion is that, "Constructed primarily as the moral guardian of global capitalism and liberal internationalism, the human rights corpus is simply unable to confront structurally and in a meaningful way the deep-seated imbalances of power and privilege which bedevil our world" (157). Similar arguments are made by postcolonial theorists like Bhabha (1999), Chakrabarty (2000), Spivak (2004), and Baxi (2007), who further highlight the influence of colonial thinking and practices on human rights and argue that Eurocentric thinking entails the danger of perpetuating colonial power relations.

Another critique is that human rights are vague, abstract, and more symbolic than substantive (Ignatieff 2001; Rorty 1998). Liberal thinkers like Rorty and Ignatieff argue that the idea of universal human rights should not be based on a metaphysical or transcendental truth about humanity, but rather on the pragmatic consequences of suffering and the need for sensitivity to cruelty. Rorty (1998) argues that human rights are worthy ideas but are instrumentally fruitless; therefore, the best, and probably the only, argument for human rights, says Rorty, is sentimentalism grounded on a pragmatic basis (I come back to this). People may help others in the name of human rights, but they are really motivated by sentimental stories of cruelty and suffering. Similarly, Ignatieff (2001) emphasizes that human rights ideas are valuable because they are effective in limiting violence and reducing cruelty. As he writes: "That I take to be the elemental priority of all human rights activism: to stop torture, beatings, killings, rape, and assault and to improve, as best as we can, the security of ordinary people. My minimalism is not strategic at all. It is the most we can hope for" (173).

In her critique of human rights, Brown (1995, 2004) argues that liberal views on rights in general (and human rights in particular) are not intended to address the causes of social grievance and suffering. Brown's critique suggests that the ideology of liberalism that is embedded in human rights makes it difficult to see that they are grounded in particular forms of power—which do not only come in sovereign or juridical form, and which construct individuals in particular ways. Therefore, a faith in the capacity of human rights—as moral and legal rights—to alleviate social cruelty and suffering is pernicious because it distracts us from the work of changing the structures of exploitation and oppression. In addition, although human rights offer recognition and emancipation, they create a dependence upon the regime of the state, thus reinforcing existing power structures, as social inequalities are not really redressed through political and collective struggles for comprehensive justice. Brown argues that not only do human rights discourses fail to address these forms of power structures, they also construct political subjects that are dependable and vulnerable, and who must rely on the state to provide for their well-being (Hoover 2013). Therefore, the political possibilities that are produced do not always lead toward substantive justice or political empowerment.

Regarding the implications of these critiques for HRE, Keet (2012) argues that HRE has often been constructed "as a declarationalist, conservative, and uncritical framework that disallows the integration of human rights critiques into the overall HRE endeavor" (7). For example, the emphasis on teaching the articles of human rights from the UDHR—hence a "declarationalist" approach—limits the pedagogical value of HRE and most importantly its transformative possibilities. In fact, according to Keet, the "institutionalization" of HRE over the years—namely, the inclusion of human rights in structured and often highly formalized curricula, textbooks, and materials—has contributed to the spread of the declarationalist approach. The declarationalist approach refrains from reflections on how human rights and their critiques are integrated into HRE efforts (see Keet 2012; Sliwinski 2005). In addition, Sliwinski explains that the preferred curriculum strategy often follows a standard formula, beginning from the basic article of the UDHR, followed by specific case studies of oppression—usually about distant places and different peoples. The problem with this approach is that it fails to pay attention to local concerns and "offers a largely normative approach in which the steady re-articulation of this curricular strategy is combined with a justification of human rights education as a universal method for interpreting specific cultural violence" (221–222). It is not hard to see, then, how such a conceptual framing of HRE might lead to a perception of human rights as a sacred metanarrative discourse (Hopgood 2013)—namely, a view of human rights as a revered set of universal norms.

In summary, the review of human rights critiques discussed here highlights the importance of turning our attention to human rights culture and how it can be established in each society. At the same time, epistemic and ontological foundationalism often translates into pedagogical principles and practices in HRE that fail to address the structures of suffering and the role that emotions play in perceiving, mobilizing, or claiming human rights. In light of the fact that Western human rights theory has historically failed to seriously consider the role of emotions and sentimentality (Barreto 2006, 2011), the idea that sympathy is morally relevant to others' suffering is an important idea that deserves further attention. The next part of the chapter focuses on how emotions in general, and sympathy to others' suffering in particular, are relevant to human rights and have important implications for HRE.

Emotion, Suffering, and Human Rights

Emotions are intertwined with human rights in many different ways—not only because the rationalist approach in human rights discourses is "outdated," as Rorty (1998:170) argues, but also in that emotions (*together* with reason) constitute key players in the experiences of those who perceive, mobilize, or claim human rights (Abrams 2011). Rorty's resort to an ethics of emotions as ethics of human rights is a reaction to Kantian morality, "which is seen as hampered by a solipsist rationalism that lacks an account of the participation of sentiments in moral life" (Barreto 2006:74). In her discussion of the role of emotions in Rorty's work and its relevance to democracy,

Mouffe writes that the primary task of democratic politics is not the elimi-nation of passion and sentiment; on the contrary, the creation of a demo-cratic ethos "has to do with the mobilization of passions and sentiments, the multiplication of practices, institutions and languages games that provide the conditions of possibility for . . . democratic forms of willing" (1996:5).

Rorty has been one of the first scholars raising the issue of the signifi-cance of emotion and sentimentality in human rights discourse. In his essay "Human Rights, Rationality, and Sentimentality," which was prepared for the 1993 Oxford Amnesty International Lecture, Rorty (1998) argues that the idea of universal human rights should not be based on a metaphysical or transcen-dental truth about humanity, but rather on the pragmatic consequences of suffering and the need for sensitivity to cruelty. Rorty's attempt "to re-establish the central role that emotions had played in the early Enlightenment" (Bar-reto 2011:13) aims to assert that emotions are not under the control of reason but have a central role in morality. This is where the role of sympathy becomes important, because the key to morality is sympathizing with those who are oppressed by humiliation, cruelty, and pain; for Rorty, then, emotions form the basis or the content of the ethos of human rights (Barreto 2006). But what is the relation between emotions and human rights in general?

Abrams (2011) tries to bridge the abstract language of rights with the emotional experiences of those who assert and recognize their or others' rights. Stepping back from the theoretical analysis of rights, the relations between emotions and rights begin to emerge in the different ways in which emotions are implicated in the perception and mobilization of rights. For this purpose, Abrams formulates a typology in which she identifies five different processes that show how emotions are involved in the processes of rights assertion and recognition. The first process is responding to a moral shock; rights assertion often begins with the recognition of an injury. Understanding that one has sustained an injury is entwined with a range of emotions from grief or shock to fear, anger, and shame. The second process is coalescing with others; the recognition that one has sustained an injury may transform one's life circum-stances and may cause people to reach out to others. This outreach helps people regain their affective balance or strategize about possible ways of re-sponding. The third process is ascribing responsibility, which, for a particular injury, is often strongly mediated by emotions. These emotions may influence the assignment of responsibility as well as the mobilization to claim one's rights in response to the injury. The fourth process is mobilizing rights; the ability to mobilize a claim framed in the language of rights requires certain emotions. For example, the mobilization of rights through protest and social movement activity demands an appeal to particular affective tendencies or emotional cultures among the participants, or the creation of new emotional cultures that support particular forms of response. Finally, the fifth process refers to the emotional effects of mobilization; that is, the mobilization of rights is informed and infused by varied forms of affect, and it produces certain emotional consequences.

The multiple ways in which emotions and rights are related introduce the language of the emotional injury and transform both the content and the quality of the human rights discourse. Speaking about human rights from the perspective of the victim and the emotional consequences of human rights violations creates a discourse on human rights expressed in terms of *suffering*. As Barreto explains:

> One is obliged to face nakedly the fact of suffering. For the victims, the violation of their rights does not mean first of all the breaching of constitutions or international treaties, nor the negation of political ideas or ethical principles. For the victims, violence has material consequences in the body and mind, and is cause of immediate distress and physical or psychological pain. (2013:110)

Human rights theory, then, is inevitably entwined with suffering and the implicated emotions, because it is the language of emotions that would enable the injured to express his or her suffering. As Barreto further asserts, it is possible to speak about the victims of mass killings in the language of statistics or in terms of a political discourse of injustice, but the introduction of the language of suffering "is the immediate and sometimes the only speech or meaningful utterance available to those tormented by the torturers, to the mother facing the disappearance of her son, to the child who knows his father has been killed" (2013:111).

Although the language of emotions and suffering has not yet been admitted in the main body of the theory of human rights, there is no reason why this should continue (Barreto 2006, 2013). In fact, one could argue that a theory of human rights that fails to recognize the emotional consequences of suffering is unable to better explain many tensions and failures in human rights discourses (Cvetkovich 2012). The assumption behind this claim is that affective investments such as experiences of suffering can be a starting point for new insights into human rights struggles.

In fact, a critical issue that is highlighted by recent studies in the social sciences and humanities regarding the role of affect and emotions is how psychic elements of relationality as responses to suffering, violence, and trauma are entangled with historical, cultural, social, and political norms and conventions (Zembylas 2014). Affect and emotions shape and are shaped by "the political contours of our social imaginaries" (Rice 2008:206). This means that we are enabled to theorize affect and emotions—and thus "suffering" as a key concept in human rights theory—as intersections of language, desire, power, bodies, social structures, subjectivity, materiality, and trauma. The turn to emotions, then, points to a dynamism that recognizes bodily matters and their interrelations with political economies; this idea has profound implications in our attempts to theorize human rights without neglecting the concept of suffering and its implications, especially in relation to sentimentality.

A theory of human rights that acknowledges the role of emotions and suffering within the context of historical and political structures of power can give a powerful voice to human suffering. For example, in his postcolonial theory of human rights, Baxi characterizes the Third World as "the suffering humanity" and suggests that a major task of human rights narratology is to give language to histories of human pain and suffering (Baxi 2002:113–114). Thus, his notion of human rights is defined in terms of the emotional pain that the Third World has endured as a consequence of colonialism; analyzing suffering, then, becomes a crucial aspect of human rights theory. But the concept of "suffering humanity" is not limited to the incorporation of the unbearable pain endured by people in the Third World; rather, it acknowledges the emotional politics entangled with human rights violations. It does so by "bringing into awareness the role of vicissitudes the excluded community has had to endure since the beginning of modernity" (Barreto 2013:112). Awareness is established "in the sphere of sensibility as emotions form the basis or the content of the ethos of human rights" (Barreto 2011:13). This point brings up the issue of the role of emotions and sentimentality in Rorty's notion of sentimental education for and about human rights.

Rorty and Sentimentality

Rorty's (1998) main argument is that human rights violations can be contested through what he calls "sentimental education"—that is, the cultivation of a sympathetic and affective identification with others and the replacement of rationality by sentiment. As he writes: "This progress [the spread of the culture of human rights] consists in an increasing ability to see the similarities between ourselves and people very unlike us as outweighing the differences. It is the result of what I have been calling 'sentimental education'" (Rorty 1998:181). He rejects the Enlightenment's rationality, suggesting sentimentality in its place: "to rely on the suggestions of sentiment rather than on the commands of reason is to think of powerful people gradually ceasing to oppress others, or ceasing to countenance the oppression of others" (1998:181). In general, Rorty claims that sentimentality and sentimental education are the most important elements needed to strengthen human rights. For Rorty, then, sentimental education becomes a cultural, historical, and political project aimed at modifying the way individuals feel by cultivating moral feelings (Barreto 2011).

Rorty's proposal for sentimental education has two important implications for human rights (Barreto 2006, 2011). First, it expands the number of those whom we refer to as "people like us" (Rorty 1998:176) by making us more familiar with them and emphasizing the likeness between them and us; Rorty seems to believe that by perceiving similarities between ourselves and others, we will become "less tempted to think of those different" from ourselves "as only quasi-human" (176). Second, it offers opportunities for what he calls "sympathy," that is, putting ourselves in the place of those who suffer, who are the objects of cruelty, and who have been the victims of human rights violations. The first coaches us to think of our identity in a nonexclusionary fashion, while the second invites us to act in solidarity (Barreto 2006). In the first place, then, an education aimed at ensuring the acquisition of moral feelings, and particularly sympathy, could contribute to preventing the formation of victimizers; in the second phase, sympathy could also contribute to creating a sense of solidarity or a desire to eliminate the suffering of others (Barreto 2011). For Rorty, Barreto explains, both sympathy and solidarity are the effect of a process of sensibilization developed in specific historical circumstances, rather than characteristics of human nature.

Rorty suggests that sentimental education develops the capacity for sympathy and solidarity by manipulating our feelings through sad and sentimental stories. Reading stories about people who have been the object of oppression and cruelty can lead us to realize that they also suffer like we do and therefore they are entitled to the same dignity as we are. Such stories, he claims, "repeated and varied over the centuries, have induced us, the rich, safe, powerful people, to tolerate and even to cherish powerless people" (Rorty 1998:185). For Rorty, then, storytelling becomes the prime tool of the sensibilization of individuals and culture to the suffering of others. His strategy is to suggest a widening of our shared moral identity so that it is more inclusive of others who may be "strangers" (different from us) but who are our fellow sufferers; his aim is to create and strengthen an ethos of cooperation, respect, and democracy (Barreto 2011). Rorty traces the consequences of his reflection in the human rights arena by suggesting that this political culture cannot be other than one in which individuals and social groups are conscious of the contingency of the ways in which they are constituted, as well as the relative validity of their beliefs and opinions. A society immersed in this ethos is more likely to be open to learning from others, to widening its moral identity, to accommodating strangers, and to profoundly rejecting all forms of cruelty. This sort of sentimental education provides us an allegedly non-foundational, nonrationalistic version of moral obligation (Hayden 1999).

Although Rorty's basic intention is laudable and his notion of sentimental education could help strengthen respect for human rights by paying attention to emotions and suffering and by cultivating sympathy and solidarity, his proposal falls short of considering both the political and the pedagogical consequences, and especially the dangers of non-affective or empty sentimentality. To echo Berlant's (2000) acute critique of sentimental narrative or sentimental liberalism, reaction to injustice and human rights violations cannot be reduced to feeling bad about others' pain. Suffering, which is in part an effect of socioeconomic relations of violence and poverty, is problematically assumed to be alleviated by empathetic identification with others; there is no assurance that the feelings evoked will not be those of pity, a feeling which does not lead to any action (Zembylas 2013a). Woodward (2004:71) also argues that:

> the experience of being moved by these sentimental scenes of suffering, whose ostensible purpose is to awaken us to redress injustice, works instead to return us to a private world far removed from the public sphere. Hence, in a crippling contradiction . . . the result of such empathetic identification is not the impulse to action but rather a "passive" posture. . . . The genre of the sentimental narrative itself is morally bankrupt.

It is difficult to see how Rorty's appeal to a "shared ability to feel pain"—which is curiously grounded in a universal claim when he has made great efforts to reject universalism—prevents the danger of empty sentimentality. Rorty's proposal does not anticipate these implications and goes only as far as claiming that cultivating a greater awareness of and sensitivity to others' suffering will produce respect. As Hayden (1999:63) rightly observes:

> Surely a sympathetic familialization is valuable in helping to foster respect for human rights; however, would it necessarily produce that respect, and if it does not, then what? . . . What about would-be violators of human rights who do not care to read stories about those they would dominate and oppress, or who are unaffected by the stories they do read? Do we simply shake our heads in disappointment at the actions of torturers, rapists, and genocidal murderers and then encourage them to try reading some more sad stories about their victims?

Rorty does not describe how the ability to recognize others' suffering will necessarily lead to some kind of action to eliminate the causes of their suffering. He claims that solidarity will be created based solely on feelings of sympathy; however, he does not tell us how it is that individual empathizers would experience the "right" kind of feelings, such that they would be motivated to experience solidarity and thus strive to alleviate others' suffering (Hayden 1999). Rorty fails systematically to acknowledge the structures of injustice and oppression, and he restricts the efficacy of his sentimental education to our ability to read about and draw the "correct" sympathetic conclusions about others' suffering. He seems to underestimate the possibility that feelings of sympathy, when confined to the individual or when they are depoliticized from actual economic and political circumstances, may in fact reinforce the very patterns of economic and political subordination responsible for such suffering (Spelman 1997).

Finally, Rorty fails to consider that the overvaluation of suffering entails another danger: that of fixing others as the *sufferers/victims*, as those who can overcome their suffering only when the rest of the world feels moved enough to empathize with their suffering (Zembylas, 2013a). This is precisely the difference between Rorty's proposal and postcolonial theorizations of human rights (such as Baxi's); empathizing with the other's suffering does not automatically mean that the trap of turning the other into a passive and submissive victim is dismissed. Failing to address the political conditions of those who are marginalized and oppressed, and omitting any acknowledgment of the political necessity of improving their living conditions, limits the theory and practice of human rights within the realm of what Eagleton (2009) refers to as the "banality of goodness": a banal moral ethos grounded in the self-centered altruism of the everyday, while the asymmetry of power that must become the principle of solidarity upon which we act toward vulnerable others remains unrecognized (Chouliaraki 2011).

A Critical Pedagogy of Emotions in HRE

Rorty's proposal opens some possibilities for alleviating suffering by fostering feelings of sympathy and solidarity with others who suffer; however, the failure to acknowledge the asymmetry between the spectator and the sufferer is simultaneously a failure to realize that no matter how "sentimental" HRE is, it does not necessarily lead to action that aims to alleviate the structural conditions and effects of suffering (Chouliaraki 2008). Thus, human right educators need to trace the process of sentimentalization of narratives of suffering and how this process is related to the tendency of being fixed into self-centered accounts of others' suffering in our globalized world. The emerging testimonial culture of personalized stories of suffering makes the pedagogical challenges of human rights educators even greater, because, as Brown (1995) has shown, the fetishization and sentimentalization of narratives of suffering tend to turn all political claims into claims of injury, thus depoliticizing the histories that have produced suffering and rendering impossible any action to alleviate the structural conditions and effects of suffering. What is needed, therefore, is a pedagogical approach that goes beyond the weaknesses of Rorty's proposal. In the last part of this chapter I discuss some ideas and examples that offer the possibility of cultivating this approach in human rights teaching.

In particular, I will discuss three aspects of human rights teaching based on my longtime research in conflict-troubled and divided societies, in which I show how these aspects may inform a critical pedagogical approach by embracing the role of emotion (see Zembylas 2013b, 2015). These aspects are: (1) the significance of pedagogic discomfort, (2) the pedagogical principle of mutual vulnerability, and (3) the value of compassion and strategic empathy. Each of these aspects—along with their strengths and limitations—is briefly discussed below in terms of how they help navigate human rights teaching in more sensitive and critical, yet not therapeutic or naïvely sentimental, ways.

The Significance of Pedagogic Discomfort

Recent years have increasingly witnessed research that acknowledges how challenging students and teachers beyond their comfort zones and pushing them to deconstruct the ways in which they have learned to see, feel, and act constitutes a valuable pedagogic approach in social justice, citizenship, and antiracist education (e.g., Boler 1999, 2004; Boler and Zembylas 2003; Zembylas and McGlynn 2012; Zembylas, Charalambous, and Charalambous 2012). In fact, it has been argued that if a major purpose of teaching is to unsettle taken-for-granted views and emotions, then a "pedagogy of discomfort" is not only unavoidable but may also be necessary (Berlak 2004). "A pedagogy of discomfort begins," Boler explains, "by inviting educators and students to engage in critical inquiry regarding values and cherished beliefs, and to examine constructed self-images in relation to how one has learned to perceive others" (1999:176–177). For example, individuals who belong to a hegemonic culture experience discomfort when having to confront their privileges in relation to educational and social inequities (e.g., Leibowitz et al. 2010). Leibowitz and her colleagues, writing in the context of postapartheid South Africa, demonstrate how a pedagogy of discomfort is valuable in uncovering and questioning the deeply embedded emotional dimensions that shape some individual and group privileges (e.g., those of white students) through daily habits and routines. By closely problematizing these emotional habits and routines and their attachments to whiteness and structural injustices, it is shown that teachers and students in a context in which there have been and still are serious human rights violations can begin to identify the invisible ways in which they comply with dominant ideologies.

Additionally, Zembylas and McGlynn (2012) discuss the emotional tensions, ethical dilemmas, and transformative possibilities of using pedagogy of discomfort in a post-conflict society in which there are human rights violations from all sides (Belfast, Northern Ireland). These authors emphasize that discomforting pedagogies require considerable vulnerability, and thus the ethical responsibility of the teacher becomes a complex issue. Similarly, Bauer (2001) considers the institutional restrictions of using critical pedagogies in the classroom and suggests that there is less and less room to negotiate the ethics or politics proposed by critical pedagogies. These observations about ethical, political, and institutional restrictions reiterate the complexity of handling difficult emotional knowledge and why it is not always ethical or productive to address difficult knowledge on the basis of a predetermined collectivity that reiterates "we" and "they" distinctions.

When examined through the lens of a theory that attempts to instill a critical sentimental approach toward human rights, then, it becomes clearer how and why certain features of pedagogic discomfort can be helpful in identifying the complexity of human rights violations and their consequences in contextual terms. Students and teachers come into the classroom carrying their troubled knowledge about "conquest and humiliation, struggle and survival, suffering and resilience, poverty and recovery, black and white" (Jansen 2009:361). Unsettling this troubled knowledge demands emotional effort, careful listening to each other's traumatic experiences, and explicit discussion of the potential and the harm that troubled knowledge stimulates. The value of pedagogic discomfort cannot be overstated. This process should not be assumed to be always transformative in itself, or beyond question. In other words, there are no guarantees of change in the social and political status quo; a pedagogy of discomfort, especially in light of the tensions identified in this chapter, demands time and realistic decisions about what can and cannot be achieved. Also, concerns about the ethical implications of pedagogic discomfort must be foremost on the agenda. That is, is pedagogic discomfort concerning troubled knowledge always appropriate and effective? How far can critical pedagogy engage students' discomfort without violating some ethical sensibilities? Needless to say, not all students will respond in the same way or benefit from pedagogic discomfort in the same manner; some may adopt some sort of change, others may resist, and still others may experience distress (Kumashiro 2002). Thus, the concern here is not simply about overcoming resistance or motivating students who express apathy or hostility; "it is, rather, a pedagogical commitment to locate, interrogate, and engage troubled knowledge ... in ways that permit disruption of received authority" (Jansen 2009:267).

The Pedagogical Principle of Mutual Vulnerability

The second aspect that enriches the critical pedagogical role of emotion in HRE concerns the pedagogical principle of "mutual vulnerability" (see

Keet, Zinn, and Porteus 2009; Zembylas 2013a). The notion of mutual vulnerability is grounded in the idea that there is interdependence between human beings and that the recognition of all people as vulnerable has important pedagogical consequences concerning the possibility of assuming critical responsibility toward one's own life and the lives of others in a community. The argument that is developed here is grounded theoretically in the work of Butler (2004), particularly her essay "Violence, Mourning, Politics."

Butler (2004) presents a number of examples to show that "each of us is constituted politically in part by virtue of the social vulnerability of our bodies. . . . Loss and vulnerability seem to follow from our being socially constituted bodies, attached to others, at risk of losing those attachments, exposed to others, at risk of violence by virtue of that exposure" (20). This is evident, for instance, in the experience of losing someone to whom one is attached; thus each of us is mutually obligated to others because of this common vulnerability. The denial of such vulnerability unleashes violence against others, whereas its acknowledgment creates openings for an ethical encounter with others. Consequently, "we might critically evaluate and oppose," Butler emphasizes, "the conditions under which certain human lives are more vulnerable than others, and thus certain human lives are more grievable than others" (30). Once we consider how hegemonic power relations determine "who will be a grievable human" and what "acts" are "permissible" for "public grieving" (37), then we may begin to realize how a prohibition of grieving for others' lives extends the aims of violence and conflict.

The notion of vulnerability has important pedagogical consequences for the role of emotion in HRE because the mutual experience of loss and mourning reveals the possibility of an alternative moral responsibility and sense of community (Vlieghe 2010). Butler's theorization of common vulnerability constitutes the point of departure for a renewed pedagogical politics of recognition in contexts in which there are human rights violations—a politics that is not founded in a rationalist or metaphysical morality, but in the experience of vulnerability as such (Zembylas 2009). The notion of mutual vulnerability, then, enriches critical pedagogy because it disrupts normative frames of community on the basis of rationality and self-advancement and puts forward the notion of community on the basis of loss. This idea does not, however, imply an equalization of vulnerability, but the recognition that there are different forms of vulnerabilities.

Furthermore, mutual vulnerability provides "a new grammar" for critical pedagogy in HRE because the experiences of "the traumatized and the distressed and the micro-politics of peoples' struggles for survival become its central pre-occupation" (Keet et al. 2009:116). As Keet and his colleagues point out, writing in the context of postapartheid South Africa, the notion of mutual vulnerability enhances the emancipatory interests of education "because the frames of its interlocutor are made vulnerable and therefore hospitable to moderation" (116). In this sense, there is more exchange of troubled knowledge between different sets of meaning-making frames; thus, in pedagogic terms, the notion of mutual vulnerability can be the starting point for acknowledging the burden of troubled knowledge carried more or less by all participants in a given society.

The Value of Compassion and Strategic Empathy

Finally, the third aspect I want to share in this chapter concerns the value of compassion and strategic empathy in critical pedagogy for HRE (e.g., Zembylas 2012, 2013a). In light of the discussion so far, it is evident that troubled knowledge provokes strong emotional reactions in the classroom—reactions that can be quite discomforting for teachers and students alike. Teachers must find ways to constructively handle these reactions as well as the discourses that focus too closely on one's own traumatic experiences and ignore the other's sufferings. A constructive relationship with difficult knowledge, suggest Bonnell and Simon (2007), is based on the process of confronting and dismantling any taken-for-granted assumptions upon encountering such unfamiliar knowledge. Importantly, then, teachers need to establish trust in the classroom, develop strong relationships, and enact compassionate understanding in every possible manner. Critical pedagogy in the context of human rights teaching requires the strategic use of these pedagogical resources to enable the formation of new affective alliances among members of traumatized communities.

As noted earlier, attentiveness to mutual vulnerability is an important component of critical pedagogy for HRE. Students are enabled to establish and maintain this attentiveness when they begin to question and challenge arguments based on binaries such as us/them, perpetrators/victims, friends/enemies, and good/evil, a stereotyping of groups considered to be *more* or *less* grievable (Butler 2004). Jansen (2009) highlights two pedagogical tactics that I find particularly useful in teaching students how to learn compassion by challenging these binaries: first, the acknowledgment of brokenness by all sides—that is, the idea that humans are prone to failure and incompleteness, and that as such we constantly seek a higher order of living which cannot be accomplished without being in communion with others. Second, a pedagogical reciprocity is also required; all persons carrying the burden of troubled knowledge must move toward each other. As Jansen puts it in the context of postapartheid South Africa: "the white person has to move across the allegorical bridge toward the black person; the black person has to move in the direction of the white person. Critical theory demands the former; a post-conflict pedagogy requires both" (2009:268).

To promote the prospects of compassion in the classroom, I also argue that one of the pedagogical resources that will be needed is strategic empathy. Strategic empathy is essentially the use of empathetic emotions in both critical and strategic ways (Lindquist 2004); that is, it refers to the willingness of the critical pedagogue to make herself strategically skeptical (working sometimes against her own emotions) in order to empathize with the troubled knowledge students carry with them, even when this troubled knowledge is disturbing to other students or to the teacher. The use of strategic empathy can function as a valuable pedagogical tool that opens up affective spaces that might eventually disrupt the emotional roots of troubled knowledge—an admittedly long and difficult task (Zembylas 2012). Undermining the emotional roots of troubled knowledge through strategic empathy ultimately aims at helping students integrate their troubled views into compassionate and socially just perspectives.

Critical compassion is further cultivated if students begin to understand the conditions (structural inequalities, poverty, globalization, etc.) that give rise to human rights violations and therefore to troubled knowledge and suffering, and acknowledge some sort of human connection (e.g., mutual vulnerability) between themselves and others. But mere understanding is clearly not enough; students will become more susceptible to affective transformation when they enact compassionate action early on in their lives, starting with simple things such as learning to be more patient and tolerant with peers who do not grasp a difficult concept in language or mathematics. As they grow up, children are offered opportunities to enact more complex manifestations of compassion, including action to alleviate the suffering of people who experience difficult times, no matter which community they come from. What must follow the acknowledgment of mutual vulnerability is taking action that dismisses essentialized categories of "victims" and "oppressors" and highlights instead the impact of solidarity on reducing everyday inequalities.

Conclusion

This chapter began by reviewing human rights critiques to highlight how interpretations of human rights are often grounded in problematic assumptions. These assumptions have consequences in terms of how human rights may be taught, especially in relation to the role of emotion. My argument, then, has been to show that the recognition of the role of emotion creates important openings for a different engagement with human rights and therefore with HRE. After the presentation and discussion of Rorty's (1998) proposal for sentimental education, I made an attempt to construct a more "critical" engagement with sentimentality so that the dangers of empty sentimentality are addressed. What this means for the practice of critical pedagogy is that pedagogies of emotions are inevitably implicated in the way that HRE operates. Without a fundamental revision of our thinking about the role of emotion and sentimentality in human rights and its consequences for HRE, the radical potential of HRE to reconstitute the emotional connections of traumatized students and teachers may be compromised, in spite of our best intentions. This task requires a constant reconsideration of new pedagogical resources to enhance the potential of critical pedagogy such as those discussed here; undoubtedly, there are many more ideas that can contribute toward this effort.

At the same time, the limits and restrictions of using critical pedagogy in HRE need to be kept in mind. There are important unanswered questions in the effort to make the emotional complexities of human rights and HRE explicit and constructive: How can human rights educators avoid becoming some sort of therapists for their students when there is pressure in current times to provide therapeutic education? What are the limits of discomfort, mutual vulnerability, and compassion in settings that experience different human rights violations so that critical pedagogy retains its radical, but realistic, possibility? How far can human rights educators push their students to problematize their emotional responses toward human rights violations and to critique self and otherness in light of open wounds within a traumatized community? These and other important questions offer the potential to broaden the methods that incorporate the emotional implications of human rights into our understandings and practice of HRE.

References

Abrams, Kathryn. 2011. "Emotions in the Mobilization of Rights." *Harvard Civil Rights-Civil Liberties Law Review* 46:551–589.

Al-Daraweesh, Fouad, and Dale Snauwaert. 2013. "Toward a Hermeneutical Theory of International Human Rights Education." *Educational Theory* 63(4):389–411.

Barreto, José Manuel. 2006. "Ethics of Emotions as Ethics of Human Rights: A Jurisprudence of Sympathy in Adorno, Horkheimer and Rorty." *Law and Critique* 17:73–106.

Barreto, José-Manuel. 2011. "Rorty and Human Rights: Contingency, Emotions and How to Defend Human Rights Telling Stories." *Utrecht Law Review* 7(2):1–20.

Barreto, José-Manuel. 2013. "Human Rights and Emotions from the Perspective of the Colonized: Anthropofagi, Legal Surrealism and Subaltern Studies." *Revista de Estudos Constitucionais, Hermeneutica e Teoria do Direito* 5(2):106–115.

Bauer, Dale. 2001. "Classroom Spaces and the Corporate University." *Pedagogy* 1(3): 554–559.

Baxi, Upendra. 1997. "The Promise of the Third Millennium." In George Andreopoulos and Richard Pierre Claude, eds., *Human Rights Education for the Twenty-First Century* (pp. 142–154). Philadelphia: University of Pennsylvania Press.

Baxi, Upendra. 2002. *The Future of Human Rights.* Oxford: Oxford University Press.

Baxi, Upendra. 2007. *Human Rights in a Posthuman World.* New Delhi: Oxford University Press.

Berlak, Ann. 2004. "Confrontation and Pedagogy: Cultural Secrets and Emotion in Antioppressive Pedagogies." In Megan Boler, ed., *Democratic Dialogue in Education: Troubling Speech, Disturbing Silence* (pp. 123–144). New York: Peter Lang.

Berlant, Lauren. 1998. "Poor Eliza." *American Literature* 70:635–668.

Berlant, Lauren. 2000. "The Subject of True Feeling: Pain, Privacy, and Politics." In Sarah Ahmed, Jane Kilby, Celia Lury, Maureen McNeil, and Beverley Skeggs, eds., *Transformations: Thinking Through Feminism* (pp. 33–47). London: Routledge.

Bhabha, Homi. 1999. "The Postcolonial and the Postmodern: The Question of Agency." In Simon During, eds., *The Cultural Studies Reader* (pp. 189–208). London: Routledge.

Boler, Megan. 1999. *Feeling Power: Emotions and Education.* New York: Routledge.

Boler, Megan. 2004. "Teaching for Hope: The Ethics of Shattering World Views." In Daniel Liston and Jim Garrison, eds., *Teaching, Learning and Loving: Reclaiming Passion in Educational Practice* (pp. 117–131). New York: RoutledgeFalmer.

Boler, Megan, and Michalinos Zembylas. 2003. "Discomforting Truths: The Emotional Terrain of Understanding Differences." In Peter Trifonas, ed., *Pedagogies of Difference: Rethinking Education for Social Justice* (pp. 110–136). New York: Routledge.

Bonnell, Jennifer, and Roger Simon. 2007. "'Difficult' Exhibitions and Intimate Encounters." *Museum and Society* 5(2):65–85.

Brown, Wendy. 1995. *States of Injury: Power and Freedom in Late Modernity.* Princeton, NJ: Princeton University Press.

Brown, Wendy. 2004. "'The Most We Can Hope For': Human Rights and the Politics of Fatalism." *South Atlantic Quarterly* 103(2/3):451–463.

Butler, Judith. 2004. *Precarious Life: The Powers of Mourning and Violence.* London: Verso.

Chakrabarty, Dipesh. 2000. *Provincializing Europe: Postcolonial Thought and Historical Difference.* Princeton, NJ: Princeton University Press.

Chouliaraki, Lilie. 2008. "Mediation as Moral Education." *Media, Culture & Society* 30:831–847.

Chouliaraki, Lilie. 2011. "Improper Distance: Towards a Critical Account of Solidarity as Irony." *International Journal of Cultural Studies* 14(4):363–381.

Cvetkovich, Ann. 2012. *Depression: A Public Feeling.* Durham, NC: Duke University Press.

Donnelly, Jack. 2003. *Universal Human Rights in Theory and Practice*, 2nd ed. Ithaca, NY: Cornell University Press.

Douzinas, Costas. 2000. *The End of Human Rights: Critical Legal Thought at the Turn of the Century.* Oxford: Hart Publishing.

Eagleton, Terry. 2009. *Trouble with Strangers: A Study of Ethics.* Oxford: Wiley-Blackwell.

Evans, Tony, ed. 1998. *Human Rights Fifty Years On: A Reappraisal.* New York: Manchester University Press.

Hayden, Patrick. 1999. "Sentimentality and Human Rights: Critical Remarks on Rorty." *Philosophy in the Contemporary World* 6(3–4):59–66.

Hoover, Joseph. 2013. "Towards a Politics of Human Rights: Ambiguous Humanity and Democratizing Rights." *Philosophy & Social Criticism* 39(9):935–961.

Hopgood, Stephen. 2013. *Endtimes of Human Rights.* Ithaca, NY: Cornell Unievrsity Press.

Ignatieff, Micheal. 2001. *Human Rights as Politics and Idolatry.* Princeton, NJ: Princeton University Press.

Jansen, Jonathan. 2009. *Knowledge in the Blood: Confronting Race and the Apartheid Past.* Stanford, CA: Stanford University Press.

Kumashiro, Kevin. 2002. "Against Repetition: Addressing Resistance to Anti-Oppressive Change in the Practices of Learning, Teaching, Supervising, and Researching." *Harvard Educational Review* 72(1):67–92.

Keet, Andre. 2009. "Reflections on the Colloquium Within a Human Rights Discourse." In Mokubung Nkomo and Saloshna Vandeyar, eds., *Thinking Diversity, Building*

Cohesion: A Transnational Dialogue on Education (pp. 211–220). Amsterdam: Rozenberg Publishers.

Keet, Andre. 2010. *Human Rights Education: A Conceptual Analysis.* Saarbrucken, Germany: Lambert.

Keet, Andre. 2012. "Discourse, Betrayal, Critique: The Renewal of Human Rights Education." In Cornelia Roux, ed., *Safe Spaces: Human Rights Education in Diverse Contexts* (pp. 7–27). Rotterdam: SensePublishers.

Keet, Andre, Denise Zinn, and Kimberley Porteus. 2009. "Mutual Vulnerability: A Key Principle in a Humanising Pedagogy in Post-Conflict Societies." *Perspectives in Education* 27(2):109–119.

Leibowitz, Brenda, Vivienne Bozalek, Paul Rohleder, Ronelle Carolissen, and Leslie Swartz. 2010. "'Ah, but the Whiteys Love to Talk About Themselves': Discomfort as a Pedagogy for Change." *Race Ethnicity and Education* 13(1):83–100.

Lindquist, Julie. 2004. "Class Affects, Classroom Affectations: Working Through the Paradoxes of Strategic Empathy." *College English* 67(2):187–209.

Mouffe, Chantal. 1996. "Deconstruction, Pragmatism and the Politics of Democracy." In Chantal Mouffe, ed., *Deconstruction and Pragmatism: Simon Critchley, Jacques Derrida, Ernesto Laclau and Richard Rorty* (pp. 1–12). London: Routledge.

Mutua, Makau. 2002. *Human Rights: A Political and Cultural Critique.* Philadelphia: University of Pennsylvania Press.

Rice, Jenny. 2008. "The New 'New': Making a Case for Critical Affect Studies." *Quarterly Journal of Speech* 94(2):200–212.

Rorty, Richard. 1998. "Human Rights, Rationality and Sentimentality." In *Truth and Progress: Philosophical Papers*, vol. 3 (pp. 167–185). Cambridge: Cambridge University Press.

Sliwinski, Sharon. 2005. "Thinking Without Banisters: Toward a Compassionate Inquiry into Human Rights Education." *Educational Theory* 55(2):219–230.

Spelman, Elizabeth. 1997. *Fruits of Sorrow: Framing Our Attention to Suffering.* Boston: Beacon Press.

Spivak, Gayatri. 2004. "Righting Wrongs." *South Atlantic Quarterly* 103(2/3):523–581.

Vlieghe, John. 2010. "Judith Butler and the Public Dimension of the Body: Education, Critique and Corporeal Vulnerability." *Journal of Philosophy of Education* 44(1):153–170.

Woodward, Kathleen. 2004. "Calculating Compassion." In Lauren Berlant, ed., *Compassion: The Culture and Politics of an Emotion* (pp. 59–86). New York: Routledge.

Zembylas, M. 2008. "Trauma, Justice and the Politics of Emotion: The Violence of Sentimentality in Education." *Discourse: Studies in the Cultural Politics of Education* 29(1):1–17.

Zembylas, M. 2012. "Pedagogies of Strategic Empathy: Navigating Through the Emotional Complexities of Antiracism in Higher Education." *Teaching in Higher Education* 17(2):113–125.

Zembylas, M. 2013a. "The 'Crisis of Pity' and the Radicalization of Solidarity: Towards Critical Pedagogies of Compassion." *Educational Studies: A Journal of the American Educational Studies Association* 49:504–521.

Zembylas, M. 2013b. "Critical Pedagogy and Emotion: Working Through Troubled Knowledge in Posttraumatic Societies." *Critical Studies in Education* 54(2):176–189.

Zembylas, M. 2014. "Theorizing 'Difficult Knowledge' in the Aftermath of the 'Affective Turn': Implications for Curriculum and Pedagogy in Handling Traumatic Representations." *Curriculum Inquiry* 44(3):390–412.

Zembylas, M. 2015. *Emotion and Traumatic Conflict: Reclaiming Healing in Education.* Oxford: Oxford University Press.

Zembylas, Michalinos. 2009. "Making Sense of Traumatic Events: Toward a Politics of Aporetic Mourning in Educational Theroy and Pedagogy." *Educational Theory* 59(1):85–104.

Zembylas, Michalinos, Panayiota Charalambous, and Constadina Charalambous. 2012. "Manifestations of Greek-Cypriot Teachers' Discomfort Toward a Peace Education Initiative: Engaging with Discomfort Pedagogically." *Teaching & Teacher Education* 28:1071–1082.

Zembylas, Michalinos, and Claire McGlynn. 2012. "Discomforting Pedagogies: Emotional Tensions, Ethical Dilemmas and Transformative Possibilities." *British Educational Research Journal* 38(1):41–60.

CHAPTER 3

Evolution of Human Rights Education Models

Felisa L. Tibbitts

Introduction

Human rights education (HRE) is a newly established field of educational theory and practice that is garnering increased attention and significance across the globe. This effort, which has gained momentum since the early 1990s, has spawned a growing body of educational theory, practice, and research that often intersects with activities in other fields of educational study in schools, such as citizenship education, peace education, antiracism education, Holocaust/genocide education, education for sustainable development, and education for intercultural understanding. However, HRE is not only aimed at the formal education sector but has deep roots in the nonformal education sector; it also takes place in the training of professionals such as journalists, teachers, and law enforcement officials.

HRE is a deeply practical expression of the high-minded ideals of the Universal Declaration of Human Rights (UDHR)—a deliberate attempt to foster a worldwide human rights culture.

In 2002, I published three models for categorizing human rights education practice in the formal and nonformal education sectors: Values and Awareness, Accountability, and Transformation (Tibbitts 2002).[1] Infused within these models of HRE was an understanding of educational programming, learning theory, and social change. The original models were organized applying grounded theory from a practitioner's point of view about learner goals, target groups, and other practical elements of educational pro-gramming, such as content and methodologies. The emerging models of HRE practice were linked with praxis and strategies for social change.

In this chapter, I suggest revisions to these models, based on the interven-ing fifteen years of scholarship, documentation, and observation of practice across a range of teaching and learning settings globally, including my own.[2] This writing has been a reflexive praxis that has allowed me to distill my own understanding of how the field of human rights education has evolved. This process is consistent with grounded theory, which calls for researchers to continuously refine their definition of concepts and to check their models.

In the first half of the chapter, I present the goals of HRE as preventing human rights violations, and human rights activism as a subset of activities within a broader social change effort. I then consider the theories of change for the HRE models and learner outcomes in relation to both human rights activism and social change, recognizing the value of learners taking action in both the private and public domains in relation to social change. I identify new dimensions of the HRE models that add descriptive complexity and strengthen their analytical power. One new addition is teaching and learning practices, for which I present and critically review a range of methodologies used in HRE: didactic, participatory, empowerment, and transformational. Two other elements added to the models are the learning context/sponsoring organization and the learner.

In the second part of the chapter, I revisit the original HRE models, crit-ically applying these new dimensions. I argue that the original HRE models remain useful typologies for describing HRE practices and for critically an-alyzing their design in promoting agency in learners to take action to reduce human rights violations. However, I propose amendments to the models, in-cluding a stronger association of the Values and Awareness Model with so-cialization, the Accountability Model with professional development, and the Transformation Model with activism.

Key Concepts

Goals of Human Rights Education

The most widely accepted definition of human rights education (HRE) is that offered by the United Nations, whose General Assembly passed in December

2011 a Declaration on Human Rights Education and Training with the following language (Article 2):[3]

1. Human rights education and training comprises all educational, training, information, awareness-raising and learning activities aimed at promoting universal respect for and observance of all human rights and fundamental freedoms and thus contributing, inter alia, to the prevention of human rights violations and abuses by providing persons with knowledge, skills and understanding and developing their attitudes and behaviors, to empower them to contribute to the building and promotion of a universal culture of human rights.
2. Human rights education and training encompasses
    (a) education about human rights, which includes providing knowledge and understanding of human rights norms and principles, the values that underpin them and the mechanisms for their protection;
    (b) education through human rights, which includes learning and teaching in a way that respects the rights of both educators and learners;
    (c) education for human rights, which includes empowering persons to enjoy and exercise their rights and to respect and uphold the rights of others. (UN General Assembly 2011)

The first paragraph reaffirms the UN's long-standing definition of HRE as having a place in all forms of education and training, including the formal, nonformal, and informal sectors. These were represented across the original HRE models.

The second paragraph reflects the evolution of HRE practice, sharing more details than the original UN definition, as HRE *about*, *through*, and *for* human rights affirms the full spectrum of learner goals in accordance with knowledge/understanding, values, capacities, and actions, with a framework of personal empowerment. This new, extended definition also draws attention to teaching and learning processes and reaffirms the outcomes of HRE as being oriented toward taking action "for" human rights.

The goal of preventing human rights violations is central to HRE. Human rights norms are codified in international law in an ongoing manner and are intended to be protected in national law, policies, and practices. Human rights violations can result from direct action or inaction of governments or individuals. Combating human rights violations and the conditions of inequality and injustice that foster them requires a critical reflection and recognition of symptoms and sources, and taking action so such violations no longer occur. Human rights (legal) standards are oriented toward the changed behavior of governments, as they are the entities that sign human rights treaties and voluntarily commit themselves to uphold them. Human rights activism therefore is oriented toward changing the behavior of governments, although the obligations of certain nonstate actors such as multinational corporations and armed groups are increasingly addressed in human rights policy and scholarship.

Governments are not only lawmakers and foreign policy advisors but also flesh-and-blood people who are employees of the state, including the military, law enforcement officials, civil servants, social workers, health workers, and teachers. Human rights activism therefore, by definition, is first oriented toward the changed behavior of governments and their representatives at all levels—national, subnational, and local—in relation to their behavior, and the elimination of human rights violations. The original HRE Accountability Model was oriented toward the infusion of HRE within the training of government personnel so as to help ensure that they respect human rights in carrying out their responsibilities.

However, human rights activism takes place within a wider social change framework, one that involves the changed behavior of nonstate actors, that is, everyday people in their daily lives, regardless of whether or not they work for the government. The norms for such changed behavior can be fed through the human rights framework. The cross-cutting (human rights) values of nondiscrimination, equality, inclusion, and participation, as well as the norms associated with the human rights of specific groups, such as members of marginalized groups, women, children, migrants, and persons with disabilities, are eligible to contribute to social change processes more generally, inspiring behavioral changes in anyone. The original HRE Transformation Model highlighted the empowerment of disadvantaged groups for organizing collectively, not only to carry out human rights activism but also to carry forward social change more generally.

Social change and human rights activism are related, but they are not synonymous. Human rights activism can be defined as collective action undertaken to influence the behavior of governments so that laws, policies, and practices are consistent with human rights standards. An example of this would be mobilization for the release of prisoners of conscience or prisoners at Guantánamo who have not been provided with the opportunity of a trial. This is the approach of traditional human rights groups.

Social change is a long-term process involving changes in beliefs and behaviors of both state and nonstate actors. Human rights activism around changing government laws might be involved, but it would not represent the complete agenda. An example of this might be a lobbying effort to revise the criminal code to better protect victims of domestic violence, which might be part of a wider social movement to promote the equality of women.

The human rights movement as a whole has perhaps been overly defined by its association with legal standards and social action goals to influence political and legal environments. The women's movement has always recognized that gender equality would be brought about by a social movement that encompasses such legal and policy reforms, but also through the empowerment of individual women. The aims of women's human rights organizations toward influencing both national protection systems and grassroots social change has required any human rights education programming that is organized to potentially contribute toward both.

Thus, consistent with the higher aim of HRE to reduce human rights violations, HRE can be oriented toward changes in the public domain (the behavior of governments) but also changes in the private domain (the behavior of individuals). The former calls for activism and collective action, whereas the latter can occur through individual (nonlegal) actions taken in the privacy of one's home, school, or community.

In summary, the goals of HRE are oriented around the elimination of human rights violations. Through the lens of the legal standards, it is governments (signatories to treaties) that are ultimately responsible for preventing such abuses, both through their own behavior and through their ability to influence the actions of citizens whose conduct may be negatively affecting the rights of others. Through the lens of social change, the goals of HRE can also be oriented toward the hearts, heads, and hands of everyday people. This suggests that the original HRE Transformation Model would be more accurately described as promoting a goal of social change, incorporating both "activism" including *collective action* and *community development* as well as undertaking *individual actions to reduce violations in one's personal life* and immediate environment.

HRE Theory of Change and Models

The original HRE models generally associated program typologies with strategies for social change and human rights activism. The theory of change in these original models was linked with the learning process within formal and nonformal HRE programming. Thus, the first "link" in the logic chain leading from HRE to taking action to reduce human rights violations is the individual (learner) and his or her experience in the HRE program.

In the Values and Awareness Model, there is no specific theory of change in place in relation to social change. The goals of socialization may affirm the existing human rights discourse and provide learners with knowledge of human rights. However, the agency of the learner is not encouraged nor empowered to take action to reduce human rights violations.

In the Accountability Model, the theory of change was linked with the individual and his or her professional role. A successful HRE experience was intended to influence learners' knowledge, attitudes, and actions so that they would respect and promote human rights standards in their professional roles. The theory of change here is linked in part with the quality of the HRE learning experience and the disposition of the learner to apply the goals of HRE within the very specific roles and responsibilities they carry out in their work lives (see also Chapter 8 in this book, by Pizmony-Levy and Jensen, on the training of professionals who work with asylum seekers). The related theory of change is that learners who successfully absorb the goals of the HRE program and find them relevant for their work life may have changed behaviors, resulting in the reduction of human rights violations. Law enforcement officials may be less inclined to single out minority group members, and they may restrain themselves against use of excessive use of violence. Journalists may be more likely to report on human rights violations and to characterize them as such. Each of these behaviors, to the degree that they are associated with participation in an HRE program, can be seen as part of a logic chain between HRE and improved realization of human rights. In this approach, HRE methodologies that incorporate critical reflection on one's own work, and capacity development in relation to the application of human rights norms to work responsibilities, are key.

In the original Transformation Model, the HRE theory of change is quite prominent. In this approach, the HRE methodologies are associated with transformative and emancipatory learning (Bajaj 2011; Keet 2010).[4] HRE methodologies incorporate critical pedagogy and involve a critical reflection on society and conditions that result in injustice. This internal process can be a transformative one for those who have internalized oppression and have a "deficit" resulting from experiences of human rights violations. Thus, transformative learning and emancipatory learning—related critical pedagogies—can bring about profound change in the individual learner. The theory of change involves HRE leading to personal transformation, resulting in taking action to eliminate human rights violations.

The result is not only the cultivation of agency but specifically its application to reforming relationships and structures so that they are more equal, nondiscriminating, participatory, and consistent with human rights norms. As mentioned earlier, such changes might take place in the private domain (among family and friends) as well as in the public domain (in one's community and also including human rights activism).[5] Thus, within the Transformation Model, we locate a theory of change that is explicitly oriented to both personal and social change.

HRE Teaching and Learning Practices

The original HRE models did not address pedagogy or teaching methodologies in any depth, with the exception of the mention of transformative learning in relation to the Transformation Model. I propose a categorization of four kinds of methodologies used to deliver HRE. These methodologies intersect with other aspects of the HRE typologies, in particular the goals for HRE and the learning environment/sponsoring institution. These methodologies are not mutually exclusive, as will be explained, but they do tend to be associated with specific HRE models.

Didactic methodologies. This teaching and learning process is oriented toward the delivery of content to learners. It can intersect with schools and other environments influenced by a "traditional" culture of education in which there is distance between the educator and the learners, where memorization and rote learning are routine, and where learners are not given opportunities to influence their own learning, for example, through open discussion. Critical reflection, even in relation to the learning process, is not encouraged. An example is introducing the UDHR and asking learners to memorize its content, without any preceding or ensuing activities that involve critique or application to social realities. The teaching of human rights standards in a didactic, hegemonic manner has been associated with critiques of the human rights system itself as hegemonic and neocolonial (Baxi 2007).

Such methodologies reflect the "banking" approach and are associated with the Values and Awareness approach. Due to the lack of participation and critical reflection, this approach can be seen as one of (attempted) socialization. Given the definition of HRE being "about," "for," and "through" human rights, the focus on content and the application of didactic teaching methods reflects an incomplete, and potentially counterproductive, approach to HRE that is only "about" human rights.[6]

Participatory/interactive methodologies are now almost invariably used in HRE. These are seen as a means of motivating and engaging learners in the learning process. Such methodologies are applied instrumentally with the purpose of learners reaching a better understanding of human rights content and applying these values to issues at hand. An example is the popular "New Planet" exercise, which introduces learners to the UDHR through an activity in which small groups have to develop a "rights-based constitution" for a fictitious new planet and then compare their constitution with the content of the UDHR.

Participatory methodologies used for HRE result in engagement in the actual teaching and learning practices, but they are not actually intended to foster agency in the learner. Critical reflection on human rights values and standards and social problems may be addressed, but more as an analytical exercise, perhaps one aimed toward values clarification. Participatory learning takes place as part of the methodological recipe for both the Accountability and Transformation Models.

Empowerment methodologies are oriented toward the cultivation of agency in learners through specific capacities such as leadership development and the integration of practices of nondiscrimination in one's work roles. These various roads to empowerment are in relation to topics and issues of personal interest to the learner. What distinguishes empowerment methodologies from solely participatory ones is that empowerment methodologies explicitly see the learning process as instrumental for individuals having increased capacities to influence their environment.

The literature on HRE has gravitated toward empowerment as a key feature of successful programming and is associated most closely with the

Accountability Model and the Transformation Model. At the same time, empowerment is a multifaceted and nuanced concept that is difficult to define in concrete and observable terms. Empowerment methodologies can be easily linked with the skill development required in the Accountability Model. Having the opportunity to develop concrete skills, such as organizational or leadership skills, can also be considered a form of "instrumental empowerment" (Ross, Shah, and Wang 2011).

Knowledge itself can be a form of empowerment—for example, learning about the law and how to use it to protect one's rights. Reflecting and recognizing that one's personal values are consistent with those contained in international human rights standards, or that one's personal experiences of discrimination are shared by others, can also be empowering.

Transformative methodologies encompass and extend methodologies of instrumental empowerment. Both sets of methodologies are intended to cultivate agency in the learner. However, transformative methodologies are different in two respects. The first is that the agency of the learner is cultivated with the explicit aim of social transformation through human rights activism. HRE that prepares learners to organize human rights awareness-raising or campaigning can be associated with transformative methodologies, though this can still be considered a form of instrumental empowerment.

The second way in which transformative methodologies are different from empowerment methodologies is that they can explicitly foster personal transformation aligned with the concept of "intrinsic empowerment" (Ross et al. 2011). Transformative and emancipatory learning approaches, drawing from critical pedagogy, invite a critical reflection on power and oppression in one's local environment, usually as part of a close community of learners. Any subsequent reshaping of one's understanding of the world can result in taking actions to combat one's own oppression within one's family and immediate environment, consistent with wider processes of (privately experienced) social change in a society. When organized on a widespread basis with and for persons belonging to oppressed groups, such personal transformations are the basis of human rights activism.

The specific methodologies of transformative and emancipatory learning are associated with critical pedagogy and Paulo Freire (1968, 1973). The HRE literature is strongly associated with critical pedagogy, which encourages learners to think critically about their situation, to recognize connections between their individual problems and the social contexts in which they live, and to take action against oppression. Critical pedagogy was and continues to be associated with the Transformation Model, as this model is explicitly oriented toward a form of empowerment related to overcoming internalized oppression.

HRE Learning Context/Sponsor

The original HRE models included examples of representative programming but did not comment on the specific institution or agency carrying out the training. The motivation for the sponsors in carrying out HRE will be reflected in the goals (wither explicit or implicit) as understood by the sponsors (including the trainers and teachers) and as interpreted by the learners. *Status in the curriculum* in formal education environments is key. HRE taking place in the classroom will be validated if it is part of the official curriculum and carried out by regular staff. However, there are degrees of validation in formal education. HRE will be viewed by learners as a more serious enterprise of the sponsoring school or professional training institution (such as a police academy) if it is required (rather than optional), is taught by a regular member of the faculty (rather than a guest), and has a significant amount of time devoted to it (i.e., not just one lesson).

There are other features of the sponsoring institution that will have a bearing on the gravitas of HRE. One is the *consistency of HRE with the values of the institution sponsoring the HRE program*. In relation to the schools, training academies, and higher education, to what degree do these institutions as a whole reflect the values of human rights? What might the learner grasp in terms of the "intentionality" of HRE within the sponsoring institution and in the teachers or trainers themselves? HRE may be marginalized in formal education institutions that have not aligned themselves with human rights–related values in a formal way and are not attentive to the application of such values in the learning environment. On the other hand, HRE carried out by human rights NGOs and other civil society organizations associated with social change will have considerable legitimacy with learners.

This leads to another important consideration in relation to the HRE sponsor, namely the prospect of *follow-up and longer-term engagement*.[7] HRE that is carried out by human rights groups (usually in line with the Transformation Model) may provide the opportunity for learners to engage in ongoing HRE and activism. HRE carried out in a school or university setting might offer the opportunity for learners to self-organize in clubs or carry out activities in the local environment. Adult training institutions associated with the Accountability Model may also have a high commitment to HRE and follow up with internal accountability measures to ensure that staff members carry out their responsibilities in ways consistent with human rights principles. HRE carried out with a high level of commitment by the police can be followed up with strict oversight of staff behavior. In summary, it seems important to consider the institutional sponsors of HRE as a feature of the HRE models.

The HRE Learner

Another element of HRE not originally addressed in the models is the learner herself. It is understood that each learner comes with her or his unique set of experiences, values, and perspectives. HRE teaching and learning processes provide opportunities for these to be examined and potentially influenced. The identities of the learners in the original models were somewhat restricted: Values and Awareness—children, youth, and the general public; Accountability—adults who were members of professional groups; Transformation—members of marginalized groups. These are insufficient for understanding the potential of HRE to achieve its goals with learners.

A cross-cutting dimension of learner background is their preexisting values and attitudes, which are presumably related to previous experiences as well as personal dispositions. Learners who are attentive and empathetic to human rights violations and who have a deep sense of justice are more likely to resonate with the value system of human rights (Müller 2009). This key background feature is intrinsic to members of marginalized groups (whom we anticipate have personally suffered discrimination) and is recognized in the Transformation Model. However, such personal features can, in principle, can apply to anyone.

The self-selection of learners into HRE programming allows for an alignment of preexisting personal values with the message of HRE and increases the possibility that participation will lead to taking action of some kind. We would thus expect that the voluntary feature of nonformal HRE—found in the Transformation Model and in some adult trainings associated with the Accountability Model—would strengthen its potential to encourage human rights activism and social change behavior. In these environments, teaching and learning processes will still be essential for cultivating specific capacities in learners. However, motivation and mobilization for activism and social transformation can emerge quickly.

We might expect the opposite in environments where conditions for HRE are "required," such as in schools or adult training in institutions (Values and Awareness and Accountability Models). HRE that is incorporated within the curriculum of formal education systems will need to be designed in anticipation of potential resistance or apathy among learners. Under such circumstances, we may find that the teaching and learning processes and the environment, discussed earlier in this section, will be particularly critical in moving learners from minimal engagement in the learning process to outcomes associated with the cultivation of agency and taking action for social transformation.

Summary

In this section, on the basis of scholarship, documented practices, and my own experiences and field observations since 2002, I further defined and explored five conceptual categories relevant to HRE models. These five categories will be used in the next section of this chapter to systematically reflect upon the original HRE models and, in conjunction with additional information about HRE practices, suggest modification to these models that refine their underlying concepts and expand their descriptions and utility as analytic tools.

In terms of the goals of HRE and the reduction of human rights violations, I distinguished between the goals of changed behavior of *state actors* (the aim of human rights activism, in relation to human rights [legal] standards) and the goal of changed behavior of *individuals* (an aim of social change, influenced by the norms of human rights, including general values and standards). The HRE models collectively address HRE carried out for both human rights activism and social change (with human rights activism as a specific strategy related to broader social change). In making this distinction, it is possible for HRE to be analyzed in relation to its direct role in supporting activism as well as its role in supporting the behavior of individuals in the private domain.

In terms of the HRE theory of change, we first acknowledge that we are working with the individual learner, though this learner may be part of a community engaging in HRE. The theory of change for learners within the Accountability and Transformation Models is oriented toward professional development and changes in the personal and public domains that result in the reduction of human rights violations. We see that there is no direct link between the original Values and Awareness Model and social change, as taking action is not explicitly encouraged.

In terms of HRE teaching and learning practices, I proposed four clusters of methodologies. The first is the didactic methodologies, which I argue are antithetical to the substance and goals of human rights education if they are the only methodology used. The Values and Awareness Model is the only model that relies on didactic methodologies.[8] The remaining three methodologies are distinct, though linked—moving from participatory (oriented toward the learning process), to empowerment (oriented toward general capacities), to transformative methodologies (orienting action toward social transformation).

In regard to the learning environment/HRE sponsor, I have focused on the profile of the organization sponsoring HRE and its commitment to the values of human rights in its overall mission. In the formal education sector, such a commitment would be demonstrated in the placement of HRE within the curriculum of formal education, preparation of regular staff to carry out HRE (not just contracting out to NGOs), evidence of commitment to human rights values within the overall operation of the organization, and follow-up supports. These features can be discerned by learners and signal the level of seriousness with which HRE is taking place. Such commitments are generally found within NGOs carrying out HRE associated with the Transformation Model, but can also be found within the formal education sector for individual schools and training institutions.

Finally, in relation to learners, I have recognized that background features of the learners are a key ingredient in their "readiness" to engage in HRE teaching and learning processes and to respond by taking action. The Transformation Model had recognized this potential for a category of learners—those coming from marginalized groups and who have suffered human rights violations. However, many learners may come predisposed to the "message" of human rights and social justice, and with a desire to promote change. HRE that is provided on a voluntary basis is better positioned to bring about HRE learner outcomes than programs that are compulsory.

Revised Models of HRE

Models represent an idealized framework for understanding human rights education practice. The original HRE models were developed on the basis of grounded theory to distinguish among the primary practices at that time—efforts within the formal curriculum of schools, adult professional development, and nonformal HRE carried out by NGOs. The emerging models recognized target audiences, common approaches and topics, key program features, and the plausible link between each model and social change strategies.

In the first half of this chapter, I identified new dimensions of the HRE models that add descriptive complexity and strengthen their analytical power. In this part of the chapter, I revisit the original HRE models, critically applying these new dimensions.

For each of the models, I offer an overview of their key features, drawing on the first part of this chapter. New components of the HRE models include:

- the nature of the sponsoring organizations,
- whether learner participation is voluntary or involuntary,
- integration of critical stance,
- application of human rights norms,
- learner outcomes in relation to agency and transformation, and
- teaching and learning strategies.

For individual models I have revised my treatment of target audiences, content, and strategies for reducing human rights violations. In my narrative description of each model, I highlight those features that have been modified from the 2002 version (see Table 3.1).

Model 1. Values and Awareness/Socialization Model

Overview:

- Typically sponsored by government agencies or authorities.
- Learner participation usually involuntary.
- Usually found in the formal education sector, including schools through higher education, and in some public awareness campaigns.
- Common target audiences: students, sometimes the general public.
- Noncritical stance toward features of one's own society, the nature of power/authority, and the human rights system, though analytical

Table 3.1. Key Features of Revised Human Rights Education Models

Model Features	Values and Awareness/ Socialization	Accountability/Professional Development	Activism/Transformation
Sponsors	Typically government agencies or authorities	Both government agencies and civil society organizations, sometimes in partnership	Typically sponsored by civil society organizations
Kind of learner participation	Usually involuntary	Both voluntary and involuntary	Usually voluntary
Education sector	Usually in the formal education sector	Both formal (preservice) and nonformal (in-service) sectors	Usually in the nonformal education sector, including youth and community development
Common target audiences	Students, sometimes the general public	Law enforcement officials, lawyers and judges, civil servants, health and social workers, educators, journalists, religious leaders	Marginalized populations, youth
Incorporation of critical stance	Noncritical stance	Critical view of one's professional role in relation to prevention of HR violations	Critical stance toward one's society or local environment, the nature of power, the human rights system itself
Orientation	Transmission of information	Development of capacities related to work roles and responsibilities	Personal transformation, human rights activism, social change
Key content	General human rights theory, history, and content, with some attention to learner's rights	HR content relevant for group, with links to national protection systems and professional codes of conduct	HR content relevant for learner, with strong focus on learner's rights and contemporary local human rights violations
Treatment of human rights norms and standards	General treatment, with reference of norms to promote positive social behavior	Selected as relevant for professional group; may include appeal to personal value systems	Selected as relevant for the learners, with strong appeal to personal value systems

(continued)

Table 3.1. Key Features of Revised Human Rights Education Models (Continued)

Model Features	Values and Awareness/ Socialization	Accountability/Professional Development	Activism/Transformation
Teaching and learning strategies	Didactic to participatory	Participatory to instrumentally empowering	Instrumentally to intrinsically empowering/transformational
Strategy for reducing human rights violations	Passive: socialization and legitimization of human rights discourse	Active/agency: application of human rights values and standards within one's professional role	Active/transformational: integration within one's analytical framework, taking action to reduce violations in both private and public domains, participation in collective action and creation of social change agents

skills may be applied in relation to the learning of human rights content.

- Content oriented, with common topics such as the theory of human rights, human rights standards, the establishment of the United Nations, human rights institutions and NGOs, human rights violations in past history or "in other countries."
- Human rights norms and standards applied are general (e.g., "equality") and knowledge of one's rights is intended to promote positive social behavior.
- Teaching and learning strategies range from didactic to participatory.
- Strategy for reducing human rights violations (passive): socialization, legitimizes human rights discourse.

In this approach, we find a fragmented and incomplete approach to HRE, as analyzed through the UN definition including "about," "through," and "for." There is no infusion of a critical stance or an explicit aim to promote agency in the learner or social transformation. Human rights content and values are presented to be "learned." This model takes the risk of offering a superficial exposure to the human rights field that, in the worst case, can be experienced as primarily ideological. For this reason, I have extended the title of this model to include the term socialization.

The Values and Awareness/Socialization Model is common in the formal education sector and specifically in schools, though it can be found in HRE carried out with other target groups as well. In schools, topics such as the theory of human rights and the establishment of the United Nations may be included in the curriculum and incorporated within "official" learning resources. HRE topics are integrated in a descriptive manner within carrier subjects, such as world history, social studies, or citizenship education.

Human rights is not presented as an analytical framework or linked with social change, and lessons do not incorporate a critical perspective on one's own society, the nature of power/authority, or the human rights system itself. A key challenge for this model is how human rights educators working in schools and other settings can avoid the "banking" model of education warned of by Freire (1968).[9]

In this model, teaching and learning processes will likely reflect those that are already in use in the classroom. In schooling systems with traditional, didactic approaches, similar methodologies may be used for HRE. When these are applied to the learning of human rights standards, such as the Universal Declaration of Human Rights, such methodologies can be seen as focusing on compliance or political literacy (Keet 2012). Participatory exercises, to the degree that these are used in relation to human rights topics, will be carried out with the intention of promoting the learning of human rights concepts, rather than their application in the daily lives of learners. Learners' awareness of their own rights can be a by-product of this approach, but content is typically presented in a way that does not invite challenges to the political system or other power structures.

Individual teachers may on their own initiative carry out supplemental teaching and learning activities in order to further student engagement with human rights learning. These might involve resources provided by human rights NGOs. When teachers carry out such HRE in order to promote agency and activism with their students, this effort does not fall under the Values and Awareness/Socialization Model, but rather under the Activism/Transformation Model.

In some educational settings, the HRE programming may place a strong emphasis on values such as equality and respect for others. In this case, HRE in the Values and Awareness/Socialization Model is associated with socialization toward prosocial behavior. This highlights one of the many problematic areas of human rights in schools—that values can be separated out from the fuller body of critical reflection, individual rights, international norms and legal standards, and taking action. Moreover, core human rights values, such as nondiscrimination and participation, can be claimed by other value systems as well. What is unique to HRE is that such values are linked with the question of justice, the problematizing of state–citizen relations, and government accountability.

Public awareness campaigns involving public art and advertising, media coverage, and community events may also fall under the Values and Awareness/Socialization Model. In order to be eligible to be included, such awareness campaigns would not be directly linked with mobilization.

In the Values and Awareness/Socialization Model, the strategy for reducing human rights violations is a passive one. HRE programming is not directly linked with the goal of learners engaging in human rights activism or social change. The most optimistic view we could have is that the validation of the human rights discourse, concern for those suffering from human rights violations, and foundational knowledge about the international human rights system might be seen as a "primer" for other HRE efforts.

Model 2. Accountability/Professional Development Model

Overview:

- Sponsored by both government agencies and civil society organizations, sometimes in partnership.
- Learner participation can be voluntary or involuntary.
- Carried out in the formal (preservice training) and the nonformal (in-service training, further training) education sectors.
- Common target audiences: law enforcement officials, lawyers and judges, civil servants, health and social workers, educators, journalists, religious leaders.
- Critical review of one's professional role in relation to the prevention of human rights violations, implying a critical stance toward one's own society.
- Oriented toward agency: capacity and skill development as related to one's professional roles and responsibilities.
- Content will depend on the audience, but will include some content background on human rights, links with national protection systems and existing codes of ethics or potential human rights violations relevant for the professional group being trained.
- Human rights norms and standards applied are those relevant for the professional group, though appeals to personal value systems may be incorporated.
- Teaching and learning strategies range from participatory to instrumentally empowering.[10]
- Strategy for reducing human rights violations (active/agency): application of human rights values and standards within one's professional role in order to eliminate human rights violations carried out by self and others.

In this model, HRE is carried out with the explicit aim of developing the motivation and capacities of members of professional groups to fulfill their responsibilities in ways that are consistent with human rights values (i.e., they do not violate human rights) and/or that actively promote the application of human rights norms in codes of conduct, professional standards, and local laws. For this reason, the model is named the Accountability Model, though I have extended this title to include Professional Development, in order to make this approach clearer.

As this approach is skills-oriented, there is acute attention to teaching and learning processes that are successful with adult learners, moving beyond participatory engagement strategies to those that foster capacity development in areas relevant to the professional roles and responsibilities of the learner. This approach can, therefore, be directly associated with the principle of intrinsic empowerment, viewed from the perspective of increased capacities.

Under the Accountability Model, learners are already expected to be directly or indirectly associated with the guarantee of human rights through their professional roles. In this group, human rights education focuses on the ways in which professional responsibilities involve either (1) directly monitoring human rights violations and advocating with the necessary authorities, or (2) taking special care to protect the rights of people (especially vulnerable populations) for whom they have some responsibility. Because the nature of capacity development will be specific to the target audience, it is helpful to distinguish further among types of professional groups. I propose the following categories:

1. Professional groups, such as law enforcement officials, members of the armed service, civil servants and health and social workers, and business/private sector management, who need to understand and comply with human rights norms and related standards of professional conduct. Some key human rights principles that would apply would include nonviolation of human rights and nondiscrimination.
2. Lawyers, who need to know how to bring claims based on human rights norms, and judges, who need to be able to recognize such claims. The underlying strategy is advocacy for human rights using national legal norms.
3. Secular and religious community leaders and journalists, who can be trained to identify and report human rights violations and promote public knowledge about such violations.[11]
4. Educators, who can integrate human rights themes and pedagogy within their existing teaching in ways that promote agency and activism among learners.

Within this model, the assumption of all educational programming is that the learners will be directly involved in the protection of individual and group rights. The threat of violation of rights, therefore, is seen as inherent to their work, and the strategy for reducing human rights violations is to influence how people carry out their professional responsibilities. The specific content, skills, and applications of HRE are customized for each category, in accordance with the professional culture and violations that have been taking place in the local environment.

HRE carried out with professional groups can be organized through preservice courses within training academies or higher education institutes, and trainings carried out once these professionals are on the job. As with other kinds of trainings, when they are carried out by persons with the same professional background, this can assist in understanding the conditions under which people are working, and aim the HRE in a practical, applied, and sympathetic manner.

The overall educational context is highly relevant. HRE may take place as a "normal" part of induction training. HRE in-service trainings might also be organized as a high-level political response to educate members of the professional group to more carefully abide by human rights values. This can be the case when groups, such as police or health workers, are accused of systematic and widespread discriminatory behavior toward a certain group in society.

An important feature of the context for this model is where the HRE lies in relation to other standards or measures of accountability in relation to the application of HRE to the behavior of these professional groups. Is the HRE aligned with any revisions in professional standards or codes of conduct? Is there accountability in relation to how "human rights–abiding" members of these groups will be—for example, through the ability of members of the public to file complaints, internal monitoring and disciplinary procedures, or the presence of an active national human rights institution?

One of the findings of the past decade is the importance of incorporating within any HRE—including that for professionals who might technically be viewed as perpetrators—a core focus on the learner as a human being. This means understanding in a manner that is cross-cutting across all HRE programming that each learner brings his or her own mix of experiences and values, vulnerabilities and aspirations to HRE. Working with professionals as individuals first, and then as social workers, teachers, lawyers, or law enforcement officers, is essential for enabling contact with HRE to be one that is honest and critical. For this reason, HRE programming in the

Accountability/Professional Development Model can appeal to the personal value systems of learners. It is possible that this can lead to intrinsic empowerment and activism extending beyond the prescribed roles of the professional, though this is not the aim of this model.

Model 3. Activism/Transformation Model

Overview:

- Typically sponsored by civil society organizations (including human rights and development NGOs, community-service organizations, and faith-based groups).
- Learner participation is usually voluntary.
- Generally carried out in the nonformal education sector, including trainings, popular education, youth and community development.
- Common target audiences: marginalized populations, youth.
- Critical stance toward features of one's own society or local environment, the nature of power/authority, and the human rights system itself.
- Oriented toward transformation: increased self-confidence, capacity development for taking action, and participation in human rights activism/long-term social change.
- Content will depend on the audience and local context, but may include some content background on human rights, a focus on the learner's own rights, contemporary human rights violations, and the work of groups combating such abuses.
- Human rights norms and standards applied are relevant for the learners, with strong appeals to personal value systems so that human rights norms are internalized and solidarity is promoted.
- Teaching and learning strategies range from instrumentally empowering to intrinsically empowering/transformational.
- Strategy for reducing human rights violations (active/transformation): integration of human rights values and standards within one's analytical framework, taking action to reduce human rights violations within one's private and public domains, participation in collective action, and the creation of social change agents.

HRE programming falling under the Activism/Transformation Model is explicitly aimed at bringing about human rights activism and social change. I have added Activism to the title of this model to reflect this explicit aim. This kind of programming is usually nonformal and voluntary. It is often carried out by a range of civil society organizations oriented toward marginalized groups, youth, community development, and the training of human rights workers.[12]

Within this approach, HRE concentrates on the internationalization of human rights values and critical perspectives. Thus, in applying the human rights lens meaningfully in their own lives, learners may demonstrate new behaviors in their personal domain (e.g., addressing unequal relations in the family) as well as in the public domain (e.g., participating in campaigns or affiliating with a human rights NGO). The strategy for reducing human rights violations is thus immediate and personal as well as long-term, public, and collective.

Teaching and learning processes will involve methodologies of participation, empowerment, but also transformation by incorporating critical pedagogy within the HRE program goals. These kinds of HRE programming incorporate a critical stance toward features of one's own society, the nature of power/authority, and even the human rights system itself.

Different kinds of HRE programs fall under the Activism/Transformation Model. First, there are those that are solely focused on activism, such as the training of human rights workers. This link is self-evident and represents a form of instrumental empowerment.

Another type of HRE program falling within the category of Activism/Transformation is aimed specifically toward marginalized and excluded groups, such as women, migrants and refugees, minority groups that have experienced systematic discrimination, persons with disabilities, and the extreme poor. Learners coming from groups identified as marginalized may have personally experienced human rights violations and internalized oppression. An immediate aim of HRE is healing, intrinsic empowerment, and personal transformation as demonstrated through increased self-confidence and capacity for taking action to reduce human rights violations that are being experienced personally. These learners with enhanced critical consciousness may take action in their personal sphere and also engage in human rights activism and long-term social change efforts.

The Activism/Transformation Model also applies to HRE that is carried out as part of youth development and community development, of which

HRE may be one component of a wider strategy of leadership and capacity development. These programs share a common goal of encouraging learners to take action to reduce human rights violations. Some programs have used the critical HRE framework to review local conditions and to self-organize for change, as in the case of Tostan in West Africa, which has encouraged women to organize effectively around abandoning the practice of female genital cutting (see also Chapter 10 of this book, and Gillespie and Melching 2010). Human rights clubs in schools can serve this purpose by fostering an analysis of human rights issues, encouraging youth to take leadership in organizing awareness raising and mobilization actions. There are examples of Human Rights Cities (Marks and Modrowski 2008), where community members come together to review their community through a human rights lens, identifying ways in which human rights violations can be reduced and then organizing solutions.

Nonformal HRE is almost invariably carried out by civil society organizations. Such organizations are explicitly oriented toward the critical framework of human rights. This, combined with the voluntary nature of participation, creates ideal circumstances for fostering activism—in particular, activism driven by the goals and interests of the learners.

The self-selection of persons into HRE opportunities suggests a preexisting alignment of personal values with the human rights message. Students who decide to participate in Amnesty International school groups or women who participate in women's human rights training programs are likely to be predisposed to benefit from and act on the experiences they gain. The voluntary nature of their involvement suggests the potential for internalization of human rights norms and their application in ways that are personally meaningful.

Concluding Thoughts

In the second part of this chapter, I revisited the original HRE models. I argued that the original HRE models remain useful typologies for describing HRE practices and for critically analyzing their design in promoting agency in learners to take action to reduce human rights violations. I proposed amendments to the models including: a stronger association of the Values and Awareness Model with socialization, the Accountability Model with professional development, and the Transformation Model with activism.

The Activism/Transformation Model now includes any kind of HRE programming that cultivates activism (regardless of whether the learner is a member of a marginalized group). Within the Accountability/Professional Development Model, subgroups of adult learners are broken out, with implications for HRE program goals, content, and approaches. The Values and Awareness/Socialization model—if implemented in isolation and not as a first step toward more comprehensive HRE—continues to be problematic within HRE practice, as it is not designed to cultivate either learner agency or social transformation.

A considerable amount of HRE scholarship and programming remains focused on the formal schooling sector despite the challenges for carrying out critical HRE. In the years to come, I hope that ongoing reflexive praxis will result in the reorienting of HRE programming currently falling within the Values and Awareness/Socialization category. We should see a general movement of HRE methodology away from didactic approaches and toward those that foster empowerment and transformation.

Through revisiting and revising the 2002 HRE models, I have tried to offer a more complex and accurate description of the programming falling within each of them. These revised models should provide a clearer analytical framework for reviewing and designing HRE in keeping with its central mission to contribute to the reduction of human rights violations. Because of the international standards associated with HRE, I am convinced that this field will have staying power. However, these origins, the claims of universality, and the hierarchical nature of the government institutions sponsoring HRE means that there will be an inevitable and ongoing struggle to keep HRE close to critical pedagogy, its original mother. I am optimistic about this enterprise as long as we human rights educators continue to reflect upon, critique, and improve our efforts.

Notes

1. This article has been widely cited in the HRE literature and has been the basis for subsequent HRE models and critiques, some of which are identified in this chapter. I am using the term "transformation" rather than "transformational" in this article, a slight change from the original article, based solely on linguistic considerations.

2. Since 2002, I have continued to engage in HRE as an instructor of hundreds of teachers and adult learners in the human rights, humanitarian, and development

sectors through my position at Human Rights Education Associates (HREA) and as an adjunct faculty member at various universities. I have developed HRE-related curriculum guides for the formal and nonformal sectors and carried out impact assessments for national and cross-national programs. I have also engaged with intergovernmental human rights groups in developing policies, strategies, and technical resources for implementing HRE-related norms and practices. These experiences have continuously provided me with opportunities to dialogue with colleagues from all parts of the world about HRE concepts and practices, including ongoing challenges and opportunities.

3. I am using the UN policies as a key validator of HRE definitions, particularly as these have been influenced by practitioners, including NGOs such as Amnesty International, over the past decades. Thus, although the language of the documents remains general, they nevertheless offer normative guidance that is based in part on input from the grassroots level.

4. M. Bajaj has identified a similar approach as "HRE for Transformative Action" and A. Keet has referred to "resistance" and "empowerment" approaches to HRE.

5. Impact assessments the author has carried out for nonformal HRE has shown that learners have taken steps to reduce human rights violations in many parts of their lives, including relationships with family members, with friends, and with authority figures at school. (See Tibbitts 2010, 2012.)

6. Many textbook reforms, as discussed in Chapter 1, limit themselves to the "about." Training programs that facilitate educators applying participatory methods can help to overcome a purely didactic approach to HRE.

7. Teleki (2007) confirmed the importance of follow-up with adults participating in HRE in her review of twenty-seven HRE programs carried out for professional groups.

8. Although the Values and Awareness Model was linked with the schooling sector in the emerging models article, this approach is not restricted to the schooling sector and can be found in trainings of a range of groups.

9. According to Freire, "In the banking concept of education, knowledge is a gift bestowed by those who consider themselves knowledgeable upon those whom they consider to know nothing . . . a characteristic of the ideology of oppression [that] negates education and knowledge as a process of inquiry."

10. If didactic methods are used, then the HRE program belongs under the Values and Awareness/Socialization Model, even if adult professional learners are involved.

11. Although awareness-raising workshops carried out with these groups in a couple of the REAP sections were categorized within the Values and Awareness Model because of their sensitization goal, it is possible that these trainings might fall under the Accountability Model, depending on how relevant the training content was for the contexts these groups work in, and the emphasis placed on application in the workplace. Without further information on these specific trainings, this cannot be determined.

12. Teachers in schools who sponsor human rights or children's rights clubs normally do so in affiliation with such a group, and their efforts would thus fall under this model.

References

Bajaj, M. 2011. "Human Rights Education: Ideology, Location, and Approaches." *Human Rights Quarterly* 33:481–508.

Baxi, U. 2007. *Human Rights in a Posthuman World*. New Delhi: Oxford University Press.

Freire, P. 1968. *Pedagogy of the Oppressed*. New York: Seabury Press.

Freire, P. 1973. *Education for Critical Consciousness*. New York: Seabury Press.

Gillespie, D., and M. Melching. 2010. "The Transformative Power of Democracy and Human Rights in Nonformal Education: The Case of Tostan." *Adult Education Quarterly* 60(5):477–498.

Keet, A. 2010. "A Conceptual Typology of Human Rights Education and Associated Pedagogical Forms." *Journal of Human Rights Education* 2(1):30–41.

Keet, A. 2012. "Discourse, Betrayal, Critique: The Renewal of Human Rights Education." In C. Roux, ed., *Safe Spaces: Human Rights Education in Diverse Contexts* (pp. 7–27). Rotterdam: Sense Publishers.

Marks, S. P., and K. A. Modrowski (with W. Lichem). 2008. *Human Rights Cities: Civic Engagement for Societal Development*. Nairobi: UN Habitat, 2008.

Müller, L. 2009. *Human Rights Education in German Schools and Post-Secondary Institutions*. Research in Human Rights Education, Series, No. 2. Cambridge: Human Rights Education Associates.

Ross, H. A., P. P. Shah, and L. Wang. 2011. "Situating Empowerment for Millennial Schoolgirls in Gujarat, India and Shaanxi, China." *Feminist Formations* 23(3):23–47.

Teleki, K. 2007. *Human Rights Training for Adults: What Twenty-Six Evaluation Studies Say About Design, Implementation and Follow-Up*. Research in Human Rights Education, Series, No. 1. Cambridge: Human Rights Education Associates.

Tibbitts, F. 2002. "Understanding What We Do: Emerging Models for Human Rights Education." *International Review of Education* 48(3–4):531–549.

Tibbitts, F. (with D. Foong, T. Kasprzak, A. Keet, and M. Melouk). 2010. *Impact Assessment of Rights-Education-Action Program (REAP)*. Prepared for Amnesty International–Norway and Amnesty International–IS.

Tibbitts, F. (with E. Batik). 2012. *Impact Assessment of the Human Rights Education Program for Women (HREP)*. Prepared for Women for Women's Human Rights–New Ways, Istanbul.

United Nations General Assembly. 2011. *United Nations Declaration on Human Rights Education and Training*. GA 66/127, Art. 2, paras. 1–2. Geneva: United Nations.

CHAPTER 4

The Right to Human Rights Education: Conceptual Perspectives

Peter G. Kirchschlaeger

Introduction

The right to human rights education is defined in international law. This means that human rights education belongs to the essential elements and spheres of human existence needed for survival and for a life as a human being, which are protected by human rights. The right to human rights education, however, provokes doubts. On the one hand, the necessity for protection of human rights education is questioned by human rights theorists because there are doubts as to whether such education really belongs to the essential elements and spheres of human existence; questions are raised as to whether survival and life as a human is dependent on human rights education, as a challenge to the centrality of such rights.

On the other hand, the claim to universality of human rights in general faces critical concerns regarding their legitimacy. As a result, questions as to how human rights generally and how specific human rights—in particular, the right to human rights education—can be justified need to be addressed.

This question becomes even more pertinent when attempts are made to exclude a specific group of humans from human rights in general or from some specific rights, when human rights in general are neglected, or when some rights are denied. Facing the reality of countless human rights violations on a massive scale, as happens every day, and assuming that a convincing argument can make a difference, it is necessary to justify the reasoning.

This chapter will start by offering an overview of the right to human rights education on a legal level, on the universality of human rights, and on the multidimensionality of human rights. This will lead to a discussion of the different arguments that have been utilized to justify specific human rights, showing the necessity of a moral justification for the right to human rights education. Based on this, the necessary characteristics of a justification of human rights will be analyzed. This approach to justifying human rights will then be applied to the case of the right to human rights education.

The Right to Human Rights Education

The UN Declaration on Human Rights Education and Training[1] (UN-DHRET), adopted in 2011, emphasizes a right to human rights education that already existed in international law: "Everyone has the right to know, seek and receive information about all human rights and fundamental freedoms and should have access to human rights education and training" (Article 1). This declaration is not the first legal text claiming the centrality and need for human rights education. It builds upon numerous documents of international law that have embodied the right to human rights education (UN 1999, 2014; Alfredsson 2001:273–288). Since the Universal Declaration of Human Rights (UDHR) of 1948, a growing consensus and commitment by the international community to education on human rights for all can be noted.

The UNDHRET has been integrated in existing human rights law and must be read in this context. At the same time, the UNDHRET substantially surpasses the other documents due to its focus, its comprehensive character, and its conceptual contribution. The explicit description of the right to human rights education included in Article 1 forms a new element and therefore an added value to the already existing international law on human rights education and training. At the same time, a shortcoming of this descriptive formulation consists in its less appealing character as compared to a concise formula that "everyone has a right to human rights education."

A first group of human rights instruments embraces human rights education within the understanding of the right to education. Article 26 of the UDHR defines the right to education. Human rights education forms a goal of the education to which everyone has a right. In view of this, human rights education implicitly forms part of the content of the education to which everyone has a right. However, human rights education, understood as part of the right to education, has a limited group of addressees. Like the right to education, the legal claim of human rights education is restricted to the formal context, especially strictly speaking to the compulsory school years.

Besides this limitation, the character of the UDHR must be taken into consideration as well: it does not constitute a legal obligation, but is rather a common program adopted by nation-states which was to then be transposed step by step into international law treaties. Indeed, such guarantees under the UDHR were included regionally in the European Convention on Human Rights of 1950 (First Additional Protocol, Article 2); the International Covenant on Economic, Social and Cultural Rights (Article 13); and the UN Convention on the Rights of the Child of 1989 (Articles 28 and 29). Inclusion in these conventions created legal obligations that are enforceable. The right to education also contains a right to human rights education, as recorded at the regional level in the African Charter on Human and Peoples' Rights of 1981 (Article 25).

A second group of human rights instruments tends to open up the understanding of education, including the entire education system and all learning contexts. As a consequence, human rights education benefits from this development being part of the broader concept of education. Some examples of this second group are the International Convention on the Elimination of All Forms of Racial Discrimination of 1965 (Article 5), and the Convention on the Elimination of All Forms of Discrimination Against Women of 1979 (Article 14). The latter explicitly implies nonformal education as well. At the regional level, the Charter of Fundamental Rights of the European Union of 2000 (Article 14), for example, belongs to this group as it underlines that the right to education also implies vocational training and further training.

There is also a third group of human rights instruments recognizing the right to human rights education, embodying it no longer merely in the right to education but formulating it independently in human rights treaties, UN documents, and so on. The Convention Against Torture and Other Cruel, Inhuman or Degrading Treatment or Punishment (Article 10) belongs to this group with regard to the right to human rights education, with a specific focus on the educational process in the prohibition against torture. As in the case of the second group mentioned above, the understanding of education reaches further than the field of compulsory school education—for example, the Convention Against Torture and Other Cruel, Inhuman or Degrading Treatment or Punishment considers the education and further training of civil servants.

Obviously, the documents mentioned above have different legal statuses. While provisions of international treaties are strictly legally binding for those states that ratify or accede to them, other instruments such as declarations lack any strictly binding legal effect on states, but still formulate obligations that states have agreed to and therefore have an undeniable moral force. In addition, they provide, as a point of reference, conceptual and practical guidance to states with regard to their conduct. The recognition and acceptance of such documents by a large number of states should not be underestimated in terms of its value, as the documents may be seen as declaratory of broadly accepted principles within the international community.

The primary responsibility for implementation of the right to human rights education lies in the hands of nation-states. At the same time, while acknowledging the essential role played by civil society in the human rights tradition in general and specifically in the field of human rights education, it must be stated that civil society actors need to support, monitor, and be consulted in the implementation of the right to human rights education by national governments. Both nation-states and civil society may use the UNDHRET as an effective instrument in different ways to make progress in human rights education practice, advancing the full enjoyment of human rights by all human beings.

First, the UNDHRET includes the obligation to monitor and report on the implementation of the declaration by nation-states vis-à-vis their performance on human rights education and training in existing and well-established international and regional human rights mechanisms (Article 13). Here again, the principle has an effect: nation-states must explain themselves if they remain silent about their engagement in human rights education and training, or if they haven't undertaken any measures in the field of human rights education and training. A great deal can be expected from this, as it has been already happening in particular states, even without the declaration (see, for example, concluding observations of the Committee on the Elimination of Racial Discrimination: United Nations Human Rights 2002, 2003, 2003a, 2007, 2008, 2009, 2010) during country examining processes such as Universal Periodic Reviews by the UN Human Rights Council (e.g., 2008 in the case of Switzerland), which can create a corresponding demand for the member states to act.

Second, the declaration builds a strong argument to claim human rights education and training at local, national, regional, and international levels and for the opinion-forming and decision-making processes of policy-making and curriculum development. The member states can be reminded constantly that they have unanimously agreed to the declaration on the international stage.

Third, the declaration can serve as a tool for sensitizing and building awareness in society with regard to human rights education and training, as the declaration explains well the contribution of human rights education to the realization of all other human rights (e.g., the Preamble and Articles 1 and 4). This third point can interact with and enhance the previously mentioned second point.

Fourth, the understanding and definition of human rights education presented in the UNDHRET (see Articles 1–6) can provide conceptual guidance on the development of measures of implementation by nation-states. Additionally, governments can consult with various civil society actors in this process, especially those engaged in human rights education practice.

Fifth, the declaration serves as a frame of reference for monitoring and reporting the implementation of the declaration.

Sixth, the human rights education community can use the declaration (e.g., Articles 1–6) for theoretical clarification on issues relating to the ideas, aims, definitions, and the place of human rights education in the ensemble of human rights.

Seventh, the declaration can also be applied as a benchmark for quality management and for the further development and improvement of human rights education and training. (The seventh point is of high relevance as it furthers the credibility of human rights education practice.)

Eighth, the declaration enhances the significance of human rights education and training for the respect, implementation, and realization of human rights, which could be of help for human rights education practice (see the Preamble and Articles 1 and 4).

Justification for the Right to Human Rights Education

This section will examine whether the right to human rights education can be morally justified as a human right. A response to the question as to why every human is a holder of human rights is given by the principle of vulnerability. This explicative justification model consists of several elements that are grouped into first, second, and third steps of filtering.

First Step of Filtering

First, the principle of vulnerability begins with a human's self-awareness of his/her own vulnerability (see Kirchschlaeger 2013b:231–267). For example, a healthy human knows that he/she could fall ill in the future. This can be a frightening process for humans because it forces them to accept their vulnerability and their finite nature (see Hoffmaster 2006:42). Every human is exposed to the possibility of being attacked or hurt physically or mentally, including the inability to liberate oneself from vulnerability (see Schroeder and Gefenas 2009:113–121; Kottow 2004: 281–287). A human perceives all other humans, his/her context, and the world as possible sources of vulnerability. Humans therefore depend on themselves, other humans, the context, and the world, as all of them can activate their vulnerability or protect them from it (see Butler 1977). Vulnerability means, for example, that something can be done to a human without his/her agreement. This can make him/her feel powerless and out of control.[2] A human cannot free him/herself from this vulnerability, and it can limit their autonomy (see Lovell 2002:62–76). Furthermore, vulnerability highlights the transitory nature of human life (see Davis 1987:287–310).

Vulnerability therefore includes an external (possibility of attack or injury from outside) and internal (incapacity and lack of corresponding protection) dimension (see Schroeder and Gefenas 2009:116). Some aspects of a human's vulnerability can be reduced by power, intelligence, education, and resources. Linked to this observation is the conclusion that the distribution of power can lead to an increase in the vulnerability of the powerless.

In addition, the principle of vulnerability means that every human can lose something. Humans can be limited in their actions, and they cannot be without limits to what they want to be (see Fultner 1998:99). Humans are therefore integrated in power structures which can be a source of protection but also of violation. This vulnerability may even jeopardize the dignity of a human life.

Obviously, a distinction must be drawn between vulnerability that is not dependent on humans, or decisions or actions taken by humans,[3] and vulnerability that humans can prevent or influence in grade, volume, and reach (see Schroeder and Gefenas 2009:115–117). Vulnerability that is produced or initiated by a society or by societies must be ended or balanced or—in order to avoid paternalistic tendencies—be combated by empowering vulnerable individuals by strengthening their autonomy as a way to mitigate their vulnerability. In this context, it is helpful that all humans share vulnerability and cannot rid themselves of their common vulnerability. Humans must therefore, on the one hand, accept their fundamental vulnerability and plan their lives accordingly. On the other, humans must fight their vulnerabilities if they are depending on a society or societies. Between the two, in the case of modifiable vulnerabilities, humans need to find a balance between fighting against and accepting conditions of uncertainty. Awareness of one's own vulnerability—which is based on self-awareness and is independent of the empirical correctness of this self-perception—leads to uncertainty as it can also mean "a loss of opportunities to live better, loss of abilities to live well, and, at its extreme, loss of living" (Hoffmaster 2006:42).

Vulnerability embraces the past, the present, and the future, and does not know any spatial limitations. In humans this provokes an awareness that their vulnerability could transform into concrete violations and experiences of injustice. In addition, humans have a shared vulnerability with all humans of the present but also of the future, which leads to a global and intergenerational responsibility, and a universal interdependence.

Second, the "first-person perspective" (see Runggaldier 2003:143–221) is an essential part of the principle of vulnerability. The building of awareness of one's own vulnerability is a self-recognition process, the empirical correctness of which is not relevant. It is crucial that humans are willing to do something about this awareness, namely to protect themselves from vulnerability or to find a reasonable way to deal with it.

During this awareness-building process, a human recognizes *ex negativo* the first-person perspective. Humans understand that they make and interpret this basic anthropological situation of vulnerability as a subject (meaning as the first person singular) who is acting, deciding, and suffering, and who is living as a human.

> By acting and suffering, humans experience themselves as living beings, which are not just living like all other beings but which live by living their own lives. To relate to themselves, to act neither compulsively nor arbitrarily but to be guided by reasons and to pursue freely

chosen purposes constitutes the life form which connects them with all humans as their own kind. This life form makes them vulnerable as the self-relation which is inherent in this life form depends on fundamental conditions for realization." (Honnefelder 2012:171–172)

These fundamental conditions for realization (see Hoeffe 1991:15–36; Nussbaum 1993:324–363) can embrace all kinds of elements and spheres of human existence.

Third, even the first-person perspective and the self-relation prove to be vulnerable.

Fourth, during the awareness-building process of one's own vulnerability and of one's own first-person perspective, humans put themselves in a relationship with the self and with all other humans, recognizing their own vulnerability and the vulnerability of all other humans. They become equal in terms of vulnerability; they make themselves equal. Humans share this vulnerability—both the fundamental and the selective and variable kinds. Vulnerability is a dominant force in human existence, and we realize, according to Debra Bergoffen, "that our humanness lies in the fact that we are neither autonomous nor homogenous—that justice concerns the heteronomy of our mutual vulnerability" (Bergoffen 2003:133). This leads to the conclusion that "when we recognize the depth and the breadth of our vulnerability, we realize how much we need the help of others to protect us from our weaknesses and our infirmities" (Hoffmaster 2006:44).

Fifth, during the awareness-building process of their own vulnerability and of their own first-person perspective, humans understand that they share not only a vulnerability but also the individual first-person perspective on individual vulnerability and on the vulnerability of all humans, and the individual self-relation that every human is the subject of his/her life. They recognize the equality of all humans in their vulnerability, the first-person perspective, and self-relation. They realize that the first-person perspective and self-relation are prerequisites for human life.

Sixth, on the basis that humans perceive the vulnerability of their own first-person perspective and their own self-relation, they understand the same vulnerability for the first-person perspective and the self-relation of others. Based on this entire multilayer awareness-building process leading to recognition of the vulnerability of the first-person perspective and the self-relation shared with all humans, a human is prepared to entitle all humans and him/herself to human rights in order "to reduce vulnerability and human defenselessness and fragility in the process of developing their existential project" (Kottow 2004:284) and to actively balance and compensate in the case of a transformation from vulnerability to violations.

The motivation of humans to guarantee each other protection of the essential elements and spheres of human existence by means of human rights is reinforced by the open invitation to exploitation by other humans which their vulnerability constitutes—exploitation in the sense of pursuing one's own interest to benefit from the vulnerability and from the violations of other humans (see Wood 1995:136–158). From a sociological perspective, it can be observed that humans build social institutions and grant each other human rights because of the principle of vulnerability (see Turner 2006:26). Elena Pulcini proposes "the possibility to think—or rather to rethink—responsibility not as arising from an abstract ethical imperative or an altruistic sentiment, but from the subject's (emotionally founded) perception of his own vulnerability and recognition of his dependence (or interdependence)" (Pulcini 2009, 2010:456).

Following on from the six points discussed above, the seventh is the *principle of vulnerability*, which corresponds to vulnerability, with the first-person perspective and with the self-relation, which possesses moral quality, and which is of normative nature, unlike vulnerability itself. Based on the principle of vulnerability, humans entitle each other to human rights.

Therefore, humans are not right-holders because they are vulnerable, but because humans deliberate their own vulnerability and its relevance. They become aware of the first-person perspective and of the self-relation of themselves and all humans, and they get to know the former as a prerequisite for human life. They recognize the vulnerability of the first-person perspective and the self-relation shared with all humans—because of the principle of vulnerability—and correspondingly, they assign each other human rights. Humans differentiate vulnerability based on experiences of suffering, violation, and injustice, and due to the principle of vulnerability establish a protection of essential elements and spheres of human existence with specific human rights. The principle of vulnerability is therefore a starting point for justifying human rights per se and specific human rights.

Eighth, the principle of vulnerability can be the basis for confronting new experiences of suffering, violation, and injustice. This correlates with a dynamic understanding of human rights: if such new threats make the protection of essential elements and spheres of human existence by human rights necessary, a further development of human rights is possible in order to ensure that human rights meet these new challenges. The principle of vulnerability can be understood as having an "exploratory function," provoking new updates and differentiations of the protection system of human rights.

The eight points above can be summarized as the first step in filtering the justification model based on the principle of vulnerability. Not all elements and spheres of human existence are protected by human rights, but only those where protection is required by the principle of vulnerability. On a meta level, one can state at this point that this justification model has justified the following affirmations:

- All humans have the *same* human rights.
- If someone is human, then he/she possesses human rights.
- All humans are holders of human rights.

Second Step of Filtering

The second step of filtering builds on the considerations above and goes into more detail regarding the elements and spheres of protection to which all humans are entitled as holders of human rights. Naturally, the consensus about protection against the possible consequences of vulnerability does not include all elements and spheres of human existence. Which elements and spheres of human existence should be placed under the protection of human rights? What criteria should inform the selection of these elements and spheres of human existence?

As a starting point, historical experiences of injustice under which humans are suffering or could suffer because of the principle of vulnerability must be considered. These experiences of injustice and the principle of vulnerability make humans take action against those injustices and do something to prevent or eliminate such violations.

On a meta level, one can state at this point that this justification model seeks to combine the steps of justifying human rights in a complementary way, and to build a hermeneutic circle contributing reciprocally to the understanding of the other step. Furthermore, the response to the question regarding the justification of specific human rights builds on the response to the question regarding the justification of human rights per se.

Should all historical experiences of injustice under which humans are suffering or could suffer because of the principle of vulnerability be protected by human rights? For example, the violation of a particular interest of person A in a business transaction, or the individual vulnerability of not being able to buy a Ferrari indicate that not every historical experience of a violation must be avoided as a human right, and that there is also a need for a selection of historical experiences of injustice that warrant protection through human rights.

The call for selection leads to the question of which criteria should be used. Because the selection pursues the identification of specific human rights, it is necessary to take a closer look at the understanding of human rights per se in order to understand which characteristics of human rights must be expected in a historical experience of injustice in order to be considered for human rights protection.

The response to this question corresponds with the definition of human rights to which all humans are entitled, and is also based on a moral decision. In order to adequately face up to the vulnerability of all humans, and in order to avoid or stop experiences of injustice, human rights protect elements and spheres of human existence in order to enable humans *to survive* and to enable humans *to live as humans*. The principle of vulnerability therefore means that it is necessary to protect those elements and spheres of human existence that are needed for survival (which humans share with other creatures) and necessary for life as a human (which are specifically human).

Based on the points listed above, the following six characteristics of human rights can be identified:

1. Universality (see Kirchschlaeger 2011:301–312) (all humans have human rights—always, everywhere, and in every case);
2. Categorical nature (all humans have human rights without any conditions; e.g., they do not have to pay taxes or respect the law in order to enjoy human rights);
3. Egalitarian nature (all humans have human rights; this means all humans in the same way, to the same extent, and with the same access);
4. Individual validity (every human has human rights as an individual, not as part of a collective);
5. Enforceability (human rights must be legally enforceable);

6. Fundamentality (human rights protect a minimum standard of essential elements and spheres of human existence that a human needs in order to survive and in order to live a life as a human, preserving his/her humanity and dignity).

These six characteristics inform the selection of specific human rights as criteria to decide whether a historical experience of injustice should be placed under the protection of human rights with a specific guarantee.

On a meta level, it can be observed that this justification model within the process of differentiation considers not only the question as to why *all* humans are holders of human rights but also the question of why humans are holders of *these specific* human rights.

The second step in filtering the justification model based on the principle of vulnerability involves an imminent openness to new dangers, risks, and experiences of injustice that may arise in the future and that are not yet in the conscience or the imagination, and to experiences of injustices that occur in different traditions, cultures, civilizations, religions, value systems, and worldviews.

At the same time, the second step of filtering leads to the challenges of applying these six criteria to the historical experiences of injustice—for example, the challenges of historical contingency and of the universalization of particular experiences of injustice.

Third Step of Filtering

The third step of filtering involves application of the six criteria mentioned above in order to identify the elements and spheres of human existence that need to be protected by human rights.

Concerning the criterion of universality, also addressing the above-mentioned challenges of historical contingence and the universalization of particular experiences of injustice based on the principle of vulnerability, including the first-person perspective, fulfillment of this criterion must be shown by stating "good reasons" that enable the transition from a *subjective* experience of injustice to a *universalizable* experience of injustice.

Concerning the criterion of categorical status, fulfillment is achieved by proving that there are no requirements expected from a human for sharing this vulnerability or violation, or for holding the corresponding right offering protection from this vulnerability or violation.

Concerning the criterion of egalitarian nature, fulfillment lies in the possibility that every human could enjoy a corresponding right in the same way without any distinction.

Concerning the criterion of individual validity, fulfillment implies the possibility of enjoying a corresponding right as an individual, independent of any collective.

Concerning the criterion of enforceability, fulfillment depends on the possibility of implementing the right in a legal system.

Concerning the criterion of fundamentality, fulfillment depends on the result of an examination into whether the historical experience of injustice touches an element or a sphere of human existence necessary for survival or for a life as a human.

At this point, the question arises as to whether the justification model of human rights based on the principle of vulnerability fulfills all the above-mentioned requirements of a justification model for human rights which have not yet been addressed explicitly in the process of this approach.

This model of justification aims to respect the requirements of a rational and critical moral framework in the process of both steps of justification. The steps in the justification model are exclusively developed with "good reasons." This means that they are based on arguments that are plausible and acceptable for all humans in the sense of a model of thought and not a real referendum. It seems that this model of justification is successful in respecting the requirements of a rational and critical moral framework.

In the following, this justification approach based on the principle of vulnerability will be applied to the right to human rights education in order to examine whether the right to human rights education can be justified.

Following the justification model based on the principle of vulnerability, the first step involves analyzing whether there are historical experiences of injustice in the sphere of human rights education. If one considers numerous humans worldwide who do not have access to or do not enjoy human rights education, it seems obvious that experiences of violation of the right to human rights education lead to an awareness that demands that these violations be put to an end and prevented.

Next, the question needs to be clarified as to whether this right embraces elements and spheres of human existence that are necessary for survival and for life as a human, and therefore require the protection of human rights. Six criteria can be used to identify the elements and spheres of human existence requiring the protection of human rights as highlighted above: universality, categorical status, egalitarian nature, individual validity, enforceability, and fundamentality.

In order to prove the universality of the right to human rights education, the possibility must be excluded that these experiences of injustice in the sphere of protection of the right to human rights education are only particular experiences of injustice which cannot be universalized. A positive outcome of this examination would mean the transition from a subjective experience of injustice to an experience of injustice that can be universalized. The universality of the right to human rights education is justified because there cannot be good reasons (meaning that it must possess a basis of plausible and acceptable reasons, and that it must be imaginable that every human—within a model of thought and not within a real worldwide referendum—would agree upon the reasons) that would legitimate the exclusion of an individual human or a group of humans from this right.

In order to show the categorical status of the right to human rights education, it is plausible that the right to human rights education does not rely on any requirements expected from a human for sharing historical experiences of injustice in the sphere of human rights education or for holding the corresponding right which protects every human from a vulnerability or a violation of the sphere protected by the right to human rights education.

The egalitarian nature of the right to human rights education is based on the possibility that every human can enjoy the protection of the sphere of human rights education in an identical manner.

The right to human rights education is an individual right that protects the individual right-holder's access to human rights education, and does not depend on their being part of a collective, which proves its individual validity.

The right to human rights education is enforceable because a violation of this right can be identified, it can be a reason to take legal action, a verdict can be delivered, the perpetrator of the violation can be convicted (e.g., required to make amends to the victim of the violation), a sentence can be served, and this can be controlled and enforced. The right to human rights education can therefore be implemented in a legal system.

The fundamentality of the right to human rights education—belonging to the essential elements and spheres of human existence—is justified because, first, human rights education entails that the holders and the duty-bearers of human rights know their rights and corresponding duties, that they possess the competence to claim their rights for themselves and in solidarity with others; and further, they are convinced, interested, willing, and able to take action for the cause of human rights. Human rights education plays a constituting role for human rights per se and all specific human rights.

Second, human rights education has therefore a procedural significance for the implementation and enforcement of human rights because it enables and encourages the holders of human rights and the duty-bearers to contribute to the realization of human rights.

Third, without human rights education, human rights declarations and treaties run the risk of remaining wonderful pieces of paper without any impact on the reality of the lives of humans who are actually human rights holders and duty-bearers (see Kirchschlaeger 2014). Thus, it can be argued with good reason that the right to human rights education is universal, categorical, egalitarian, individual, enforceable, and fundamental.

Conclusion

The explicative and so-called "negative" approach based on the principle of vulnerability justifying the right to human rights education benefits from its inherent differentiation and combination of the justification of human rights per se and of the justification of the right to human rights education. Both steps of justification are necessary to address the question of how human rights education can be justified because of its fundamental character for the human right to human rights education—whether as a specific human right, or as human rights representing the aim, focus, and essence of human rights education. This inherent differentiation and combination acknowledges the fundamental nature of the human right to human rights education—namely human rights per se—and addresses adequately the aspects that need to be addressed in a moral justification, and respects the necessary criteria. At the same time, the necessary specificity and precision are attributed to the justification of the specific human right to human rights education, never losing sight of its being embedding in the interdependent and indivisible catalogue of human rights.

Beyond that, it has the advantage that it does not have to explain on which capabilities or characteristics humans merit being entitled to human rights, or which capabilities or characteristics make humans human. Rather, the justification model based on the principle of vulnerability starts with the violations that humans suffer or could suffer and that must be stopped, avoided, and prevented in order to protect humans in the essential elements and spheres of human existence.

Furthermore, the justification model based on the principle of vulnerability remains open to new violations that may arise, and therefore corresponds to the dynamic nature of human rights. In addition, it can be applied to experiences of injustice that occur in various traditions, cultures, civilizations, religions, value systems, and worldviews, because the principle of vulnerability possesses diverse and multilayered links. Its openness can be distinguished from an examination of the moral of respect, thereby guaranteeing the universal and egalitarian validity of the justification model.

Finally, it can be connected with religious and secular conceptions of human rights because it remains consciously minimalistic without excluding a religious or theological "adaptation" of human rights (see Kirchschlaeger 2013b:162–184). Justifying human rights education also emphasizes the raison d'être of human rights education which could be perceived by human rights actors and human rights educators. Human rights education is a contribution to the prevention of human rights violations and to the realization of human rights, and must respect the principles of the universality, indivisibility, and interdependence of human rights. So the raison d'être of human rights education includes, on the one hand, these necessary expectations for human rights education. On the other hand, access to human rights education and training requires the implementation of all rights that underlie the comprehensive and interdependent nature of human rights. This is a clear message to nation-states that have a poor human rights performance to not hope that they can compensate for their weak human rights performance with some human rights education activities.

Notes

1. The author has contributed as a consultative expert to the development of the UN Declaration on Human Rights Education and Training during the entire preparation process of the declaration.

2. Rollo May states: "No human being can stand the perpetually numbing experience of his own powerlessness" (May 1969:14).

3. Martha C. Nussbaum elaborates that "the peculiar beauty of human excellence just is its vulnerability" (Nussbaum 1986). Roberto Andorno observes: "Incongruously, modern medical science is focused in an almost obsessive way in reducing human vulnerability and disease as if they were the absolute evil to be eradicated. Instead of viewing human vulnerability as an intrinsic element of existence, it tends sometimes to treat it as a merely technical fact that could be overcome simply through more technological progress. This approach is utopian because the possibilities of science are limited, and will always be limited, in spite of all scientific advances that can be done, at least by the fact that we are mortal beings" (Andorno 2011:136).

References

Alexy, Robert. 1998. "Die Institutionalisierung der Menschenrechte im demokratischen Verfassungsstaat." In Stefan Gosepath and Georg Lohmann, eds., *Philosophie der Menschenrechte* (pp. 244–264). Frankfurt am Main: Suhrkamp.

Alfredsson, Gudmundur. 2001. "The Right to Human Rights Education." In Asbjorn Eide, Catarina Krause, and Allan Rosas, eds., *Economic, Social and Cultural Rights: A Textbook* (pp. 273–288). Dordrecht: Martinus Nijhoff Publishers.

Andorno, Roberto. 2011. "Four Paradoxes of Human Dignity." In Jan C. Joerden, Eric Hilgendorf, Natalia Petrillo, and Felix Thiele, eds., *Menschenwürde und moderne Medizintechnik* (pp. 131–139). Baden-Baden: Nomos.

Bergoffen, Debra. 2003. "Toward a Politics of the Vulnerable Body." *Hypatia* 18(1):116–134.

Butler, Judith. 1977. *Excitable Speech: A Politics of the Performative.* New York: Routledge.

Davis, Wayne A. 1987. "The Varieties of Fear." *Philosophical Studies* 51:287–310.

Forst, Rainer. 1999. "Das grundlegende Recht auf Rechtfertigung: Zu einer konstruktivistischen Konzeption von Menschenrechten." In Hauke Brunkhorst, Wolfgang Köhler, and Matthias Lutz-Bachmann, eds., *Recht auf Menschenrechte* (pp. 66–105). Frankfurt am Main: Suhrkamp.

Fultner, Barbara. 1998. "The Politics of Vulnerability: On the Role of Idealization in Butler and Habermas." *Philosophy Today* 42:94–103.

Gut, Walter. 2008. "Eine Sternstunde der Menschheit: Die Allgemeine Erklärung der Menschenrechte von 1948." *Schweizerische Kirchenzeitung* 49(176):816–819.

Hoeffe, Otfried. 1991. "Transzendentale Interessen: Zur Anthropologie der Menschenrechte." In Walter Kerber, ed., *Menschenrechte und kulturelle Identität* (pp. 15–36). Munich: Kindt.

Hoffmaster, Barry. 2006. "What Does Vulnerability Mean?" *Hastings Center Report* 36(2):38–45.

Honnefelder, Ludger. 2012. "Theologische und metaphysische Menschenrechtsbegründungen, in Menschenrechte." In Arnd Pollmann and Georg Lohmann, eds., *Ein interdisziplinäres Handbuch* (pp. 171–178). Stuttgart: J. B. Metzler.

Huntington, Samuel. 1997. *The Clash of Civilizations and the Remaking of World Order*. New York: Simon & Schuster.

Kant, Immanuel. 1977a. "Grundlegung zur Metaphysik der Sitten." In Wilhelm Weischedel, ed., *7 Werkausgabe* (p. 79). Frankfurt am Main: Suhrkamp.

Kant, Immanuel. 1977b. "Metaphysik der Sitten Rechtslehre." In Wilhelm Weischedel, ed., *8 Werkausgabe* (pp. 434–535). Frankfurt am Main: Suhrkamp.

Kirchschlaeger, Peter G. 2007. "Brauchen die Menschenrechte eine (moralische) Begründung?" in Peter G. Kirchschlaeger, Thomas Kirchschlaeger, Andrea Belliger, and David J. Krieger, eds., *Menschenrechte und Kinder, Internationales Menschenrechtsforum Luzern (IHRF) IV* (pp. 55–63). Bern: Stämpfli.

Kirchschlaeger, Peter G. 2011. "Das ethische Charakteristikum der Universalisierung im Zusammenhang des Universalitätsanspruchs der Menschenrechte." *ARSP-Beihefte, Gleichheit und Universalität* 128:301–312.

Kirchschlaeger, Peter G. 2013a. "Die Multidimensionalität der Menschenrechte—Chance oder Gefahr für den universellen Menschenrechtsschutz?" *Menschen-RechtsMagazin* 18(2):77–95.

Kirchschlaeger, Peter G. 2013b. "Wie können Menschenrechte begründet werden? Ein für religiöse und säkulare Menschenrechtskonzeptionen anschlussfähiger Ansatz." *ReligionsRecht im Dialog* 15.

Kirchschlaeger, Peter G. 2014. "Human Rights and Corresponding Duties and Duty Bearers." *Journal of Human Rights and Constitutional Studies* 2(4):309–321.

Kirchschlaeger, Peter G. 2015a. "Adaptation—A Model for Bringing Human Rights and Religions Together." *Acta Academica* 47:163–191.

Kirchschlaeger, Peter G. 2015b. "Das Verhältnis von Religion und Grund- und Menschenrechten." *Salzburger Theologische Zeitschrift* 19:98–116.

Kirchschlaeger, Peter G. 2016. "Building Bridges to Religions by Justifying Human Rights." In Joseph Zajda and Sev Ozdowski, eds., *Globalisation, Human Rights Education and Reforms* (pp. 169–185). Dordrecht: Springer Netherlands.

Koller, Peter. 1990. "Die Begründung von Rechten." In Peter Koller, Csaba Varga, and Ota Weinberger, eds., *Theoretische Grundlagen der Rechtspolitik: Ungarisch-Österreichisches Symposium der internationalen Vereinigung für Rechts- und Sozialphilosophie, ARSP 54* (pp. 74–84). Stuttgart: Franz Steiner Verlag.

Kottow, Miguel H. 2004. "Vulnerability: What Kind of Principle Is It?" *Medicine, Health Care and Philosophy* 7:281–287.

Lovell, Alan. 2002. "Moral Agency as Victim of the Vulnerability of Autonomy." *Business Ethics: A European Review* 11:62–76.

May, Rollo. 1969. *Love and Will*. New York: Norton.

Nussbaum, Martha C. 1986. *The Fragility of Goodness: Luck and Ethics in Greek Tragedy and Philosophy*. New York: Cambridge University Press.

Nussbaum, Martha C. 1993. "Menschliches Tun und soziale Gerechtigkeit: Zur Verteidigung des aristotelischen Essentialismus." In Micha Brumlik and Horst Brunkhorst, eds., *Gemeinschaft und Gerechtigkeit* (pp. 324–363). Frankfurt am Main: Fischer.

Nussbaum, Martha C. 1995. "Human Capabilities, Female Human Beings." In Martha C. Nussbaum and Jonathan Glover, eds., *Women, Culture, and Development: A Study of Human Capabilities* (pp. 61–104). Oxford: Clarendon Press.

Pulcini, Elena. 2009. *La cura del mondo: Paura e responsabilità nell'età globale.* Torino: Bollati Boringhieri.

Pulcini, Elena. 2010. "The Responsible Subject in the Global Age." *Science and Engineering Ethics* 16:447–461.

Rabossi, Eduardo. 1990. "La teoria de los derechos umanos naturalizada." *Revista del Centro de Estudio Constitucionales* 5:159–175.

Rorty, Richard. 1996. "Menschenrechte, Rationalität und Gefühl." In Stephen Shute and Susan Hurley, eds., *Die Idee der Menschenrechte* (pp. 144–170). Frankfurt am Main: Fischer.

Runggaldier, Edmund. 2003. "Deutung menschlicher Grunderfahrungen im Hinblick auf unser Selbst." In Günter Rager, Josef Quitterer, and Edmund Runggaldier, eds., *Unser Selbst—Identität im Wandel neuronaler Prozesse,* 2nd ed. (pp. 143–221). Paderborn: Schöningh.

Salmon, Wesley C. 1983. *Logik.* Stuttgart: Reclam Verlag.

Schroeder, Doris, and Eugenijus Gefenas. 2009. "Vulnerability: Too Vague and Too Broad?" *Cambridge Quarterly of Healthcare Ethics* 18(2):113–121.

Turner, Bryan S. 2006. *Vulnerability and Human Rights.* University Park: Pennsylvania State University Press.

United Nations. 1999. *Right to Human Rights Education: A Compilation of Provisions of International and Regional Instruments Dealing with Human Rights Education.* New York: United Nations.

United Nations. 2014. *Right to Human Rights Education: The Right to Human Rights Education—A Compilation of Provisions of International and Regional Instruments Dealing with Human Rights Education.* http://www.ohchr.org/EN/Issues/Education/Training/Compilation/Pages/Listofcontents.aspx.

United Nations Human Rights. 2002. "E/C.12/1/Add.76." http://tbinternet.ohchr.org/_layouts/treatybodyexternal/Download.aspx?symbolno=E/C.12/1/Add.76&Lang=En.

United Nations Human Rights. 2003a. "CCPR/CO/79/PHL." http://tbinternet.ohchr.org/_layouts/treatybodyexternal/Download.aspx?symbolno=CCPR%2FCO%2F79%2FPHL&Lang=en.

United Nations Human Rights. 2003b. "CERD/C/62/CO/4." http://tbinternet.ohchr.org/_layouts/treatybodyexternal/Download.aspx?symbolno=CERD/C/62/CO/4&Lang=En.

United Nations Human Rights. 2007. "CEDAW/C/KAZ/2." http://tbinternet.ohchr.org/_layouts/treatybodyexternal/Download.aspx?symbolno=CEDAW%2FC%2FKAZ%2F2&Lang=en.

United Nations Human Rights. 2008. "CEDAW/C/LBN/CO/3." http://tbinternet.ohchr
.org/_layouts/treatybodyexternal/Download.aspx?symbolno=CEDAW/C/LBN
/CO/3&Lang=En.

United Nations Human Rights. 2009. "CCPR/C/79/Add.119." http://tbinternet.ohchr
.org/_layouts/treatybodyexternal/Download.aspx?symbolno=CCPR
%2FC%2F79%2FAdd.119&Lang=en.

United Nations Human Rights. 2010. "CEDAW/C/UKR/7." http://tbinternet.ohchr.org
/_layouts/treatybodyexternal/Download.aspx?symbolno=CEDAW/C/UKR/CO
/7&Lang=En.

Wood, Allen W. 1995. "Exploitation." *Social Philosophy and Policy* 12:136–158.

PART II

Global Research in Human
Rights Education

CHAPTER 5

Challenges and Complexity in Human Rights
Education: Teachers' Understandings of
Democratic Participation and Gender Equity
in Post-Conflict Kurdistan, Iraq

Audrey Osler and Chalank Yahya

Introduction

This paper examines tensions and challenges facing schools in implementing human rights education (HRE) in the autonomous region of Kurdistan, Iraq. Across the globe, both international organizations and governments recognize the potential of education to contribute to the processes of democratization and development. In post-conflict societies, programs of citizenship education and HRE are often introduced with the express aim of developing skills for learning to live together and the peaceful resolution of conflicts.

Following the 2005 Constitution of Iraq, which established Iraqi Kurdistan as a federal entity, the current unified Kurdistan Regional Government (KRG) administration was established. From 2006 on, the KRG has focused on developing Kurdistan's economy and infrastructure, and in 2009 it turned its attention to educational reform. This reform extends the number of years of compulsory education from six to nine; introduces new learning objectives; and places greater emphasis on human rights and democratic citizenship, making a specific commitment to gender equity. In implementing reform, we suggest the KRG is not merely recognizing the potential of education to contribute to immediate and longer-term economic and social development, but is also acknowledging the critical role of education in creating a just and sustainable democracy, in which the rights of traditionally disadvantaged and vulnerable groups and individuals, including women, children, and minorities, are protected.

We understand education policy to be a dynamic process in which teachers, administrators, and students are actors. These various actors can support, subvert, or undermine the original goals of policymakers, both unintentionally and/or deliberately. Our program of research, therefore, not only focuses on policy documents and textbooks, but also extends to an examination of the perspectives of teachers, school administrators, and school inspectors. In this chapter we focus on professionals' perspectives and on their understandings of democracy, development, and human rights, specifically human rights education and gender equity. We argue that these perspectives are critical to a proper understanding of the impact of education reform and its impact on young people, schools, families, and communities. If the KRG is to be effective in realizing democracy, development, and equity through education, professionals' experiences, needs, and understandings need to be taken seriously. Their insights enable us to identify appropriate strategies and plans to strengthen democratic dispositions among the young.

Education Policy Reforms in a Post-Conflict Context

Iraqi Kurdistan experienced considerable conflict and instability in the later twentieth century and the early years of the twenty-first, resulting in a severely damaged infrastructure at home and a notable Kurdish diaspora across the globe. The conflicts which impacted on Kurdistan include a long history of border disputes with Iran; the Iran–Iraq war of 1980–1988; and the Anfal genocidal campaign against the Kurds of 1986–1989, led by the Iraqi military under Saddam Hussein. The year 1991 saw the Gulf War, followed by the Kurdish uprising, resulting in mass displacement and a subsequent humanitarian crisis. The uprising was followed by a brutal crackdown on the Kurdish population, a subsequent withdrawal of the Iraqi administration and military, and an Iraqi internal economic blockade. At the same time, the region suffered the consequences of UN sanctions and international embargo against Iraq from 1990 to 2003 (McDowall 2003; Yildiz 2004).

By 1991, the region had gained ad hoc autonomy (Stansfield 2003), and in 1992 a regional government was established, following a closely contested and inconclusive general election. But the Kurdish leadership was responsible for further difficulties. The rivalry between the Kurdistan Democratic Party (KDP) and the Patriotic Union of Kurdistan (PUK) resulted in a de facto partition of the region (McDowall 2003). By 1994, power-sharing agreements between the parties had broken down, leading to civil war, referred to in Kurdish as "brother killing brother" (*brakuzhi*). Open conflict between the KDP and the PUK was brought to an end under the 1998 Washington Agreement. Nevertheless, the civil war and conflict between the two dominant parties have shaped contemporary Iraqi-Kurdish politics (Stansfield 2003).

Following the 2003 invasion of Iraq and the subsequent political changes, it is the 2005 Constitution of Iraq that defines the internal political, socio-economic, and judicial autonomous governance of Kurdistan. The current unified Kurdistan Regional Government (KRG) operates under a power-sharing agreement, introduced in 2009. The federal region, comprising three governorates—Erbil, Sulaimaniyah, and Duhok—borders Iran to the east, Turkey to the north, Syria to the west, and the rest of Iraq to the south. The region continues to feel the impact of instability in neighboring jurisdictions as well as ongoing tensions with the Baghdad government, fueled by concerns over disputed areas, including Kirkuk. An opposition movement, *Gorran* (Change), challenges the power-sharing arrangements, placing substantive democracy on the political agenda.

It is within this complex post-conflict context that education reforms are being implemented. In the immediate preconflict era, Iraq led the region in school enrollment and completion rates (UNESCO 2011). But Iraqi Kurdistan's infrastructure, including educational infrastructure, was adversely affected by the conflicts. Some fourteen years after the civil war, there remains considerable pressure on the system, with insufficient school buildings and continuing and notable disparities in basic facilities between urban and rural areas. There remain huge challenges in providing appropriate facilities to meet students' needs in a fast-changing socioeconomic and political context.

The challenge for education policymakers is not only to make good the damaged educational infrastructure and ensure that schools are staffed with effectively trained teachers. It is also to ensure appropriate educational measures to support other societal priorities, such as anticorruption measures and guarantees for the rights of women and minorities. Education needs not only to prepare young people for successful economic integration but also to play a full and active part in shaping society in accordance with democratic ideals that embody equity and social justice. In other words, the education system, and schools in particular, has a key role to play in strengthening democratic development and human rights.

The conflict disproportionately impacted women and children, limiting educational opportunities in Iraqi Kurdistan. Before the conflict, girls across Iraq already had lower school enrolment and attendance rates than boys (UNESCO 2003). Following the conflict, the majority of internally displaced persons were women and children, with some 50 percent of the most vulnerable children unable to access schooling, according to UN reports (UN-HABITAT 2001; UNDG/World Bank 2003). In this respect, Iraq, including the autonomous region of Kurdistan, reflects a wider regional and global picture of discrimination and disadvantage faced by women and girls. Security problems may place girls at greater risk of gender-based violence (Harber 2004) (for example, in traveling to and from school), further impacting on school attendance.

In 2000, the world's nations made a promise to free people from extreme poverty and multiple deprivations. This pledge was formulated into eight Millennium Development Goals (MDGs). Two goals aim specifically to address gender equity in education, recognizing that challenges remain at different points throughout the system. MDG 2 is to promote universal primary education, and MDG 3 is to promote gender equality and empower women (UN 2000). Girls from the poorest households face the greatest barriers to education, with subsequent impacts on their ability to access the labor market.

The UN Girls' Education Initiative (UNGEI) is a specific project to operationalize MDGs 2 and 3.[1] Effectively, education is recognized as a prerequisite for sustainable human development (UNGEI 2000; WEF 2000). These initiatives are concerned with enacting international human rights standards on gender equality, including the Convention on the Elimination of All Forms of Discrimination Against Women (CEDAW, Article 10) (UN 1979) and the Convention on the Rights of the Child (CRC, Articles 2 and 28) (UN 1989), which confirm the equal rights of girls and women in education.

The MDGs seek to realize both gender parity in education, through *formal equality* (parity in access and participation rates) and *substantive equality* (equal opportunity *in* and *through* education) (Subrahmanian 2005). In Iraqi Kurdistan, some steps have been taken to guarantee formal equality in access and participation rates. Since 2006, the KRG has put in place arrangements to enable young women who were not enrolled at the standard age, or who had their education disrupted, to continue or restart schooling. The education reform states that:

> schools or classes will be opened for accelerated learning programs. Students should not be younger than 9 for boys starting at grade 1 and not older than 20 whilst the girls should not be younger than 9 starting at grade 1 and not older than 24. (KRG 2009, 13, Article 15)

This provision recognizes the traditional disadvantage that girls experience in Iraqi Kurdistan (Griffiths 2010; UNICEF 2010; UNESCO 2011), and thus creates some flexibility, by extending the age range within which women can complete schooling.

We are interested in exploring the contribution that HRE might play in realizing *substantive equality*, in education and through education, by examining professionals' understandings of human rights and HRE. The right *to* education is insufficient to realize gender equality, since here we are concerned largely with equivalence in enrollment and completion rates between girls and boys. By focusing on rights *in* education (guaranteeing achievement and learning outcomes) and rights *through* education (the ability to utilize knowledge and skills to claim rights within and beyond the school), we can focus on girls' empowerment (Wilson 2003). This means recognizing and overcoming inequalities and instances of discrimination, through an examination of learning content, teaching methods, assessment modes, management of peer relationships, and learning outcomes (Chan and Cheung 2007). The realization of substantive equality requires us to rethink how both girls and boys are educated.

Diversity and Gender in Iraqi Kurdistan

It is widely recognized that schools both produce and reflect broader social norms and inequalities, related, for example, to poverty, structural inequalities, historical disadvantage, institutional discrimination against women and minorities, gender-based violence, and traditional practices that harm or impact unjustly on women and girls (Tomaševski 2005). We present here a brief outline of Iraqi Kurdistan's demographic features, contextualizing the struggle for human rights for both women and minorities. This struggle is taking place within a multicultural setting and within communities characterized by gender inequalities and growing economic disparities.

One significant challenge is the successful accommodation of diversity. Although the majority of the region's population is Kurdish, it is also characterized by long-standing religious, ethnic, and linguistic diversity. The Kurdish majority has for many centuries lived alongside smaller numbers of Assyrians, Chaldeans, Turkmenians, Armenians, and Arabs. According to the KRG, the region has a population of around 5 million, of which more than 50 percent are younger than twenty. There has been no census, so we do not know what proportion of the KRG-administered territory considers themselves to be Kurdish, but estimates suggest Iraqi Kurds may comprise as much as 25 percent of the total Iraqi population (Yildiz 2004). A carefully crafted set of policies is needed to ensure that all groups can claim their rights within the democratic framework.

There is also considerable religious and linguistic diversity in Iraqi Kurdistan. The majority of inhabitants, including Kurds, Iraqi Turkmenians, and Arabs, are from the Sunni Muslim tradition. Within this grouping there is further diversity, with some individuals being observant and others adopting more skeptical or secular positions. The region also has populations of Assyrian Christian, Shiite Muslim, Yezidi, Yarsan, Mandean, and Sahbak faiths (Begikhani, Gill, and Hague 2010). KRG official languages are Kurdish and Arabic. The two most widely spoken Kurdish dialects are Sorani and Kurmanji.[2]

Diversity is a highly politicized issue since territorial disputes between the federal Baghdad and Erbil regional governments, including Kirkuk, require political solutions that guarantee the protection of minority rights and interests. This diversity demands pragmatic solutions in the public sphere, including schools, where learners' rights and societal outcomes may be weighed against each other. For example, choices made to guarantee linguistic rights through separate schooling for specific language communities impact on the ways in which young people of the next generation are prepared (or not) for living together in a multicultural society.

The region's diversity has also increased as a consequence of internal migration, with the protection of migrant rights adding to the complexity of the picture. Many are new populations drawn to Kurdistan because of instability elsewhere in Iraq, while others are former inhabitants who fled past conflicts. They include internally displaced persons (IDPs), drawn from other parts of Iraq; refugees and migrants from neighboring countries; and returnees, including highly educated elites, from the wider diaspora. In 2012, the KRG appealed to the International Organization for Migration (IOM) for more help in dealing with the needs of refugees fleeing war in Syria.[3] While some Syrian refugees are accommodated in a camp near Duhok, others are spread across the region, supported by families and communities (IOM 2012). Child refugees may lack appropriate papers to access schooling. Iraqi Kurdistan's rapid economic development also attracts labor migrants from around the globe, as well as irregular migrants (including victims of trafficking) whose undocumented status leaves them vulnerable (IOM 2010).

In a society characterized both by patriarchy and post-conflict dislocation, one pressing issue is gender equity (al-Ali and Pratt 2011). Three interrelated challenges to realizing gender equity and the human rights of women and girls are violence against women, traditional inheritance laws (Sharia law and traditional inheritance practices across faith communities that favor men), and low female school attendance rates.

Efforts to tackle violence against women, an issue highlighted by both local women's organizations and international nongovernmental organizations (INGOs), has resulted in the establishment of women's shelters to support victims of domestic violence (Begikhani, Gill and Hague 2010). Since 2003, there has been some discussion in local media of a societal failure to support such women, who, although protected by law, remain vulnerable.[4]

Traditionally, married women are expected to receive support from their husbands. For this reason, many families, particularly in rural areas, consider it shameful to allow daughters to inherit property. While courts may rule in their favor, it is still difficult for women to claim their inheritance. Under Islamic (Sharia) law, women are entitled to one-third, while their brothers receive two-thirds. But in practice, even this unbalanced division is unlikely to occur.

Female school attendance is rising, with the Duhok governorate recording one of the highest levels of attendance and lowest differentials between boys and girls, both in Kurdistan and across Iraq (Griffiths 2010, UNICEF 2010). Local women's rights NGO Harikar (2011) reports that rural parents are readier to send their daughters to school when there are women teachers. Harikar quotes an education supervisor as confirming that the number of female teachers now exceeds the number of males in Duhok governorate.

In Kurdistan, where deeply rooted inequalities persist among children, it is critical that the type of human rights education (HRE) offered at school is appropriate to their needs and supports them in claiming their rights. Acknowledging and addressing the roots of inequalities, within and beyond school, is essential, whether these arise from gender-based discrimination or that related to ethnicity, religion, or other differences. Thus, equalities in education require more than merely translating international instruments into national policies or implementing educational reforms. They imply a holistic approach that includes policies and practices inside schools to empower students. Additionally, they imply opportunities to transform knowledge into the application of rights, both in and beyond the school (Stromquist 2006). Such a holistic approach to quality education requires sincere commitment from policymakers and civil society (Wilson 2003).

We have identified some pressing human rights concerns that impact on schooling and to which schools might be expected to respond. It is not difficult to make the case for human rights education (HRE). But in this paper we argue that there is not just a pressing *need* for HRE, there is also a *right* to HRE (see also Chapter 4 in this book). We turn now to this right, focusing specifically on its meanings within a multicultural context.

The Right to Human Rights Education

While the right to education is commonly understood, the concept of a right to HRE (Osler and Starkey 1996) tends to be less familiar, even among education professionals and policymakers. The right to HRE is set out in the 1948 Universal Declaration of Human Rights (UDHR), which underlines "the dignity and worth of the human person" and "the equal rights of men and women." Article 26 of the UDHR specifies the aims of education, which include "the strengthening of respect for human rights and fundamental freedoms"; the promotion of "understanding, tolerance and friendship among nations, racial or religious groups"; and "the maintenance of peace." This is the first international official articulation of the right to HRE. It is confirmed and explicated in subsequent human rights instruments, including the 1989 Convention on the Rights of the Child (CRC; Article 29) (Osler 2012). The right to HRE was reiterated and further strengthened by the UN Declaration on Human Rights Education and Training, adopted in December 2011.

CRC Article 29 confirms the right to an education that promotes human rights, intercultural understanding, and learning to live together; an education that promotes gender equity; and conditions that guarantee certain cultural and linguistic rights of parents and children. It stresses the obligation of the nation-state, as the ratifying authority,[5] to promote education for peaceful coexistence in their communities, the nation, and the wider world:

> States Parties agree that the education of the child shall be directed to . . . [t]he development of respect for human rights and fundamental freedoms . . . [and] preparation of the child for responsible life in a free society, in the spirit of understanding, peace, tolerance, equality of sexes, and friendship among all peoples, ethnic, national and religious groups and persons of indigenous origin. (UN 1989)

This implies that children have some level of engagement with learners from different backgrounds than their own and educational structures that enable a degree of integration between children from different ethnic, religious, and linguistic backgrounds. It recognizes, albeit indirectly, that all children have the right to an intercultural education that recognizes differences at the level of the community and the nation (Osler 2010). Yet education cannot focus exclusively on children's immediate communities or home nations since it also needs to address global identifications and our common humanity. This type of learning, where young people are enabled to learn to live together with differences at different scales is what has been termed "education for cosmopolitan citizenship" (Osler and Vincent 2002; Osler and Starkey 2003, 2005).

As Article 29 also notes, each child also has the right to an education that promotes:

> respect for . . . his or her own cultural identity, language and values, for the national values of the country in which the child is living, the country from which he or she may originate, and for civilizations different from his or her own. (UN 1989, Article 29)

Thus, all children in Iraqi Kurdistan have not only the right to be educated for tolerance and diversity, but also the right to an education that supports their own cultural heritage and that of their families, as well as Kurdish cultural heritage and values. This education must be consistent with human rights principles. This is not a cultural-relativist position where anything goes, but a critical examination of cultural norms within a broad human rights framework. So, for example, harmful cultural practices that impact on girls and women would be challenged as failing to conform to human rights standards, as would cultural norms that give another cultural group enemy or inferior status.

Education for tolerance and social justice, in line with the provisions for the CRC, cannot be fostered where there is complete educational segregation: "educating for peace will require states to mandate some kind of educational integration of schoolchildren from diverse ethnic, religious, cultural and language groups" (Grover 2007:60). Currently, the child's right to education is frequently interpreted, legislatively and judicially, as a parental liberty right (to have a child educated according to parental wishes). Grover (2007:61) argues that this tends to work against children's rights and that "the notion of minority education is frequently erroneously translated into *completely segregated school systems*" (our emphasis). She suggests (2007:61) that "the minority and non-minority child's legal right to free association (each with the other) in the educational context is frequently disregarded both by the legislature and the courts" in nation-states across the globe. The international community has agreed on a definition of HRE in the UN Declaration on Human Rights Education and Training. This suggests that:

> Human rights education and training comprises all educational, training, information, awareness-raising and learning activities aimed at promoting universal respect for and observance of all human rights and fundamental freedoms and thus contributing, inter alia, to the prevention of human rights violations and abuses by providing persons with knowledge, skills and understanding and developing their attitudes and behaviours, to empower them to contribute to the building and promotion of a universal culture of human rights. (Article 2.2)

The declaration specifies that this should include education *about* rights, education *through* rights, and education *for* rights. Education about rights includes knowledge and understanding of human rights norms and principles, implying that this education is both founded on and makes reference to international standards. Education through human rights includes learning and teaching in a way that respects the rights of both educators and learners and within schools, operating within education policy frameworks that guarantee rights. It addresses educational structures (as discussed above) and young people's experiences of schooling. It has methodological implications related to teaching and learning processes in which young people's participation rights are respected. Finally, education for human rights includes empowering learners to enjoy and exercise their rights and to respect and uphold the rights of others. This implies a transformative education, in which learners' own contexts and struggles for justice are considered and addressed, and in which learners are empowered (Osler and Zhu 2011).

Clearly, realizing social justice in education, including gender equity and the rights of minorities, means more than simply translating international instruments into national policies or implementing educational reforms. It means designing a curriculum in which learners are provided with knowledge about their rights and equipped with the skills to claim them.

Our Methods and Fieldwork

In assessing the potential of HRE to contribute to social justice, democracy, and development in the multicultural context of post-conflict Iraqi Kurdistan, we draw principally on fieldwork visits to two Iraqi Kurdistan governorates—Erbil and Duhok—between 2010 and 2012. In Duhok we engaged in classroom observations in two schools and later conducted interviews with teachers whose classes we observed.[6] In Erbil we interviewed a range of education professionals, including teachers, a school principal, and education inspectors. We also participated in a focus group discussion (Yahya 2012).[7]

In total, fifteen professionals agreed to act as research respondents, with interviews taking place in July 2011 and January and February 2012.[8] Of the fifteen respondents (seven female and eight male), five elected to answer the questions in writing rather than through a face-to-face interview. Although we stressed that we wanted professionals' own opinions, and guaranteed anonymity and confidentiality, feedback from three of these five suggests they were, to a greater or lesser extent, ill at ease with an interview format, preferring to give considered answers. Interviews were conducted in either Arabic or Kurdish, transcribed, and then translated into English.

The Duhok teachers were working in two schools as part of a two-year study, and contact was established though a mix of official channels and

personal contacts (Ahmad et al. 2012). The Erbil respondents were a conve-
nience sample, identified through personal contacts and snowballing methods, with interviewees suggesting colleagues or friends to interview. This
method proved appropriate since it was difficult to make personal contact
until we were in Kurdistan.[9] We do not claim the small sample represents all
teachers or all school inspectors, but our analysis identifies some common
emergent themes from a range of individuals and across two different geographical locations. This, we suggest, gives authenticity to the perspectives
presented here.

All interviews were conducted by a researcher familiar with local cultural norms and practices. In Duhok, our respondents were approached by
colleagues from the University of Duhok, with whom they had been working
for some months and whom we characterize as having insider positions. In
the Erbil district, subjects were interviewed by one of us (Chalank), who is
familiar with local cultural norms, having grown up in the city, but whose
secondary and higher education has been in Europe.[10]

Our fieldwork is informed by our study of documentary sources, notably
the reform of the basic and secondary schools (KRG, 2009) and the human
rights text books (Rauof 2007), for which we have had professional (nonof-
ficial) translations made.

Professionals' Perspectives

Here we report on respondents' understandings of HRE and specifically
their observations on diversity and gender equality. Since teaching for gender equality and diversity are taking place within a context of education reform, we also invited our respondents to reflect on this, with some focusing
on broader social issues and some on the relationship between active student-
centered teaching methods and education for human rights, citizenship,
and democracy. Table 5.1 lists the professionals interviewed. All names are
pseudonyms to protect respondents' anonymity.

Understandings of Human Rights Education

A number of individuals link the need for HRE to the Kurdish struggle for
human rights and political recognition. They focus on the need for children

Table 5.1. Research Respondents: Professional Roles and Characteristics

No.	Participant	Professional Role	Gender	Religious Tradition/ Ethnic Background
1	Kamaran	General school inspector	M	Muslim/Kurd
2	Kawthar	School inspector, student counseling	F	Muslim/Turkmenian
3	Foad	Principal, urban model school, and school inspector	M	Christian
4	Asem	Teacher: Arabic, grades 7–12	M	Muslim/Kurd
5	Hassan	Principal, rural school*	M	Muslim/Kurd
6	Sarkawt	Acting principal, rural school	M	Muslim/Kurd
7	Payman	School inspector, social studies, and HRE, grades 1–6	F	Muslim/Kurd
8	Fawzi	Teacher, social studies and HRE, grades 7–10	M	Muslim/Kurd
9	Sawsan	Teacher, social studies and HRE	F	Christian
10	Azad	School inspector, social studies and HRE	M	Muslim/Kurd
11	Sherko	Teacher, social studies and HRE, grade 5	M	Muslim/Kurd
12	Ahlam	Teacher, social studies and HRE, grades 7–9	F	Muslim/Kurd
13	Halat	Teacher, social studies and HRE, grades 7–9	F	Muslim/Kurd
14	Tara	Teacher, English, up to grade 6	F	Muslim/Kurd
15	Loreen	Teacher, civic education and HRE, grade 5	F	Muslim/Kurd

* This is the only school in which our teacher respondents worked where boys and girls were taught separately, attending different shifts.

to know Kurdish history and to understand the fragility of society when the rights of minorities are overlooked:

> Of course, human rights and HRE are very important to know about and be aware of. Especially in our society and due to past experiences of conflicts and violations, we need to be educated about

our rights. . . . Each of us needs rights and also to understand our rights and how to claim them. However, HRE as a subject in our education system does not have as much emphasis as it should. We lack expertise in this discipline and we do not have specialized teachers. . . . For the time being, social studies teachers are required to teach this subject.

(Payman)

Thus, despite the new emphasis on HRE in the 2009 curriculum reform, the subject lacks trained teachers. Respondents confirmed our impression that the textbooks (particularly for older students) are dry and uninteresting, containing long extracts from international instruments, such as the Universal Declaration of Human Rights, but with little or no guidance as to what they mean or how they might be made accessible to teachers and relevant to students. Respondents suggest the emphasis is on knowledge, not on developing human rights dispositions or values:

The content is very dry and very limited. It would have been better if HRE was not simply regarded as just another curriculum subject, examined to test students' knowledge.

(Ahlam)

This subject should be designed and taught in all grades, according to students' age and needs. For example, as a child in grades 1–6, you have specific rights/needs that need to be provided by school and society. If they don't learn about human rights and entitlements at a specific age, then they will not understand or be aware they have these rights. . . . It's important for them to be . . . able to demand them.

(Kawthar)

Generally speaking, respondents place considerable emphasis on the place of human rights in creating a just and sustainable society. They recognize the importance of human rights but express concerns both about a general understanding of human rights in contemporary Kurdish society and about teachers' lack of training in human rights education.

When it comes to the subjects of human rights education and democracy, I do not have very close knowledge of them. Only that my daughter has taken these subjects, and from my perspective, it's important to teach these subjects to school students.

(Kamaran)

In general, not only in Kurdistan, but across the Middle East, we're not aware of our rights. We don't really understand what is meant by human rights. So a good awareness campaign is needed.

(Kawthar)

I don't think the subject [HRE] is given the attention and development it deserves. . . . It should be included in all grades . . . as it's very important for our teachers and students to behave according to human rights standards. . . . Most importantly, it's insufficient to learn about human rights as a paper exercise, there should be genuine opportunities to practice them.

(Asem)

Although Kamaran is a general school inspector, responsible for nine schools, he admits he knows relatively little about HRE and citizenship as taught in those schools, even though he acknowledges their importance. This viewpoint is echoed by others who criticize the minimal coverage of human rights in the curriculum and stress limited societal knowledge of human rights.

A number of respondents suggest that for HRE to seem relevant, both children and adults in Kurdistan need to be in a position to *claim* their rights. Among several respondents, there is an implied criticism of the Kurdish administration for not fully securing the rights of citizens and enabling them to practice these rights. There is a general impression that human rights are important but that both human rights and HRE are ill-understood.

Children learn about authority, but the obligations of authority figures (parents, teachers, government officials) to uphold children's rights are not addressed. Kawthar observes:

It is not enough just to teach our children about rights in books, as individuals we also need to be able to practice these rights outside schools. However, in reality, there are many rights that we know of and yet cannot claim. It would be better that these subjects are taken up to the political level and enacted through laws.

In some institutions HRE was so low in status that schools might adopt corrupt practices to hide the fact they were neglecting the subject.

> Some HRE teachers . . . make the lesson available for other subjects, such as English or mathematics. . . . In such cases, HRE topics will be limited to a few classes before the exams and all students will be graded as if they have mastered their rights very well!
>
> (Fawzi)

Practicing HRE

In order to bring the subject alive, a number of respondents suggested more active learning methods, including group work, the use of stories, and the involvement of NGOs to bring the subject alive to the students:[11]

> [With active methods] . . . the student will understand the topic and s/he will never forget it because s/he takes part in explaining, present-ing and discussing.
>
> (Tara)

> When I use role play, the student takes over the role of the teacher and explains the topic. This makes them feel responsible and will improve performance.
>
> (Loreen)

Foad, who works as a school principal and school inspector, observed that some teachers feel HRE should not be examined, because a student should not fail in something as fundamental as human rights. He strongly opposed this argument, pointing out the importance of the subject matter in learning about responsibilities and rights.

Teaching Rights Where Rights Are Denied

One specific challenge raised by a number of respondents was that of teach-ing rights in contexts in which rights are denied, both in society and in school. Efforts to reform the education system have occurred rapidly, and in many places, school building programs and the provision of basic facilities have not kept pace with demand.

> Right now, the [education reform] process is being implemented with many shortages, which has caused chaos and confusion amongst professionals, students and their families. . . . You hear now of the current student demonstrations that are going on in various towns/ regions in Kurdistan. This is because [of] lack of understanding and [failings in] the system. . . . As a consequence we have been witnessing school children demonstrating on the streets for some years.
>
> (Payman)

One school principal spoke of being instructed by his superiors to drop an investigation into a teacher's professional behavior, and to turn a blind eye to equality and justice:

> Human rights norms should apply to staff as well as students. Very often, you are forced to drop taking it to the next level, because, someone on a higher level instructs you to do so. This contradicts genuine implementation of human rights rules and equality.
>
> (Sarkawt)

Equally, professionals felt it important that HRE not be restricted to children but be extended into communities. One suggested that HRE has been introduced merely to conform to international standards, rather than with commitment and clearly articulated educational and social justice aims:

> I don't think HRE fits with our reality. Our society is still based on a tribal/agricultural system, which is not ready to digest the message behind human rights norms . . . including in the curriculum. I think it has more of a political benefit than a genuine social one. It's more to show to the West that we adhere to human rights norms and have included that in our schooling, without first focusing and addressing real societal problems and injustices.
>
> (Sawsan)

In order to make HRE content more meaningful, we need to add more practical activities. For instance, bring pupils to universities,

visit different NGOs, and show documentary films ... and stories
about human rights. ... It's important to make a link between HRE
and the existence of [human rights] organizations so students are
aware of the need to address human rights issues in our region.

(Fawzi)

HRE teachers need to be continuously trained. ... It would be good
to have HRE professionals from local universities and even abroad to
provide teacher training.

(Azad)

While the examples discussed above relate largely to broader societal de-
nials of rights, another challenge is responding to children who have personal experience of human rights abuses. The example below illustrates how
making HRE relevant to children's everyday lives may empower teachers to
address sensitive questions of child abuse. It also illustrates how giving the
child the right of expression in class (participation rights) may serve to guarantee children's rights to protection:

Sometimes, students give examples of human rights violations they
themselves are ... experiencing at home, such as parents beating
them or verbally undermining their personality. ... I give my students freedom to participate, including time to reflect upon the topic
and discuss examples. ... Sometimes, a student will come to say they
have understood the content, but this is not practiced at home. In
such situations, we inform the principal and school board, investigating the home situation and inviting parents to school to talk. ...
HRE can contribute in building up the student's personality. Many
young learners are not taken seriously at home. Their rights may be
neglected, denied or even violated. Some may grow up in fear, not
daring to speak up.

(Sherko)

HRE, Gender, and Diversity

Among our respondents we observe a preference for talking about gender issues, rather than ethnic or religious diversity, when considering the potential

of HRE to contribute to social justice and learning to live together. Although a number of respondents made direct reference to past conflict, few elaborated on it. One teacher adopted what we have termed a "paradise narrative" (Ahmad et al. 2012), in which she denied past conflict within Kurdistan:

> In our society co-existence stretches from time immemorial. There's no discrimination between nations, races and religions and history testifies to this. . . . We have always been brothers who love and tolerate each other, in class, in the neighbourhood, in the village and in the city.
>
> (Tara)

Such claims form part of a wider political discourse in Iraqi Kurdistan in which the recent conflict among Kurds is denied. We would argue that this discourse, while undoubtedly part of the rhetoric of Kurdish nationalism and shared political destiny, remains deeply problematic within the context of schooling since it denies realities to which children will be exposed, namely past conflict and ongoing inequalities.

By contrast, other teachers responded pragmatically to diversity. Halat proposed asking children questions to find out what they knew about their multicultural, multifaith society and about different religions and cultures "because the more information a person has the stronger their personality and ability to express themself."

Kamaran spoke at length about his understandings of schooling and gender equity and teachers' responsibilities within this area:

> There is no doubt that our society is a *closed* society, strongly based on customs and traditions, where religion also plays a vital role. The only way, in my view, to bring these two sexes closer to each other and enhance gender equality is via school. Our society is a male-dominated society. Men have the power and women are looked down on to a certain degree. . . . Schools play an important role in enhancing general knowledge about gender equality and its advantages in society. . . . I try to encourage a sense of responsibility in every teacher and stress each individual's role in changing cultural norms to incorporate gender equality awareness.

Nevertheless, like a number of other professionals, he did not underestimate the scale of the challenge or the conservative forces undermining equality initiatives, recognizing that schooling needs to be complemented by a comprehensive awareness raising strategy and legal reform:

> We need to acknowledge the fact that tribalism plays a big role in our Kurdish society, in combination with traditions and religion, which all work against the idea of gender equality. Women are viewed as second-class citizens and sometimes used as a commodity to be exchanged in marriage.

Most respondents felt that schools had a key part to play in fostering gender equity, although few were able to articulate the precise contribution of HRE. However, many were aware of how the move toward mixed-sex schools had led to a loss of community confidence, and some had their own reservations about girls and boys being educated together:

> School has a major role in establishing positive gender relationships, because, if from very early stage children get used to studying and playing together . . . it will become normal for girls and boys to interact, communicate and study together.
>
> (Kawthar)

Sherko suggested:

> Gender equality has to start at home. Parents need to treat their boys and girls equally without any differences. . . . But parents interfere in school business. . . . Very often we hear parents complain about the fact that their daughter is placed next to a boy in class.

> Our culture isn't ready yet to mixing the two sexes at this sensitive age [teenage]. I can bring you to a mixed-sex school and just look at the classroom walls! They're filled up with love messages between boys and girls. . . . They do not understand yet how to treat each other respectfully as a sister-brother or as friends. Consequently, the number of mixed-sex schools is decreasing day-by-day. Teachers are sometimes unable to control the situation and many parents are against the idea of sending their daughters to a mixed school, even if it's close to home.
>
> (Azad)

Mixed-sex schooling should begin in pre-school. In the secondary school or college, it is already too late. . . . Ours, the only mixed-sex school in this district, will close next year and boys and girls will be separated. . . . There are no big differences in gender relationships between rural and urban areas. On the contrary, in some rural areas, girls and boys are freer to interact. For example, in the Spring, it's normal for a group of girls and boys to have a picnic together. Agricultural work has made interaction a regular habit. Although we find more educated people in urban areas, gender relations there are not as free as one might imagine.

(Hassan)

Hassan was not alone in noting anomalies in gender relations, whereby in certain contexts boys and girls are free to mix:

We still have many families that are against the idea of sending their children to a mixed-sex school. . . . [T]his is a matter of getting used to the idea. In our Kurdish culture, it is not acceptable for a girl to look at a boy . . . yet it's normal at a wedding to dance hand-in-hand with a strange boy. The latter practice is common and culturally acceptable.

(Fawzi)

Yet it appears that adult professionals were in some cases perpetuating problems by their own reluctance to engage on the basis of equality with their opposite-sex colleagues, preferring the familiarity of same-sex social relationships:

There are many schools, where the female and male teaching staff have two separate teachers' rooms. If this is still the dominant mode of thinking amongst teachers, how can they address gender equality with their students or support interaction between the sexes?

(Payman)

Religion, Values, and Gender

Fawzi told a shocking story of a student who committed suicide after her brother prevented her from joining her classmates on a school visit. He suggested that the case raised fundamental questions about societal recognition of girls' capabilities, as well as questions about home–school communications:

> Yesterday, a young female student, aged between 16–17 years, committed suicide by burning 65 percent of her body. She did it because her brother didn't allow her to join her class in an out-of-school visit.... This is ... a classic example of lack of communication and cooperation between schools and families in grasping curricular activities.... Gender equality is tied to cultural understandings of girls' and boys' roles, and this is not based either on religion or science.... It's an example of false perceptions of girls' potential and behaviour.

Fawzi also expressed concerns both about the power of tribalism and the influence of mullahs in preventing the realization of gender equity:

> The biggest limitation is the tribal mind-set controlling society. Society isn't open to the modernisation we so strongly need.... Another important concern is the lack of well-educated religious personalities.... We have many mullahs that play an important role in society, but very few that are sufficiently well-educated to understand the real meaning of the Qur'an. Our religion allows equal rights for women and men, but this isn't properly understood. To be honest, we need a mind-set ready for religious reformation, according to societal needs. This is allowed in Islam. I'm not talking about reducing prayer from five times a day to three, but we need to understand that time when our Prophet was living is very different from today's age.

Swasan, herself a Christian, agreed:

> [We need to] link gender equality to our religious ideals, which stress equal treatment. Even Islam highlights the need for gender equality. I was just now teaching history and our topic is the history of Islam, where the Prophet Mohammad highlights gender equality.

Finally, we observe that few, if any, of our respondents appeared familiar with the CRC and that child rights were absent from the textbooks reviewed. Although it appears that respondents were more comfortable discussing gender than ethnic diversity, a number insisted that any class discussion that might be construed as political, religious, or gender-related remained problematic:

> Misunderstandings happen very easily in our community . . . if we talk about political, religious or gender-related issues. Class discussion may be counterproductive. For example, if we talked about Valentine's day in class, it may lead to misunderstanding . . . even their families might interfere. . . . So you consciously avoid opening any gender-related topic in the classroom.
>
> (Ahlam)

Ways Forward: Principles and Strategies

We have sought to illuminate the practices of HRE in Iraqi Kurdistan by drawing on the perspectives of teachers and school inspectors responsible for enabling and monitoring quality education. Claiming rights implies knowledge about rights, yet, as we have noted, teachers appear to be ill-equipped to address this subject matter, lacking specific training and operating in a prevailing social climate where considerable inequalities remain between women and men and in which fast-changing economic development is widening the gap between rich and poor.

Teachers' professional education needs to incorporate child rights as an essential feature of the curriculum. The focus within the current school curriculum is on knowledge *about* rights, yet there is a gap between the ideals expressed in international instruments, and reiterated in the political rhetoric of KRG leaders, and the everyday realities of both teachers and children. Teaching about human rights in school (including efforts to teach students about gender equity) takes place in contexts where children's rights (and particularly those of girls) are denied, and in family and societal contexts where powerful conservative and patriarchal values prevail. Urgent attention needs to be given to textbook development and to the assessment of human rights learning, so that books, pedagogy, and assessment procedures support, rather than undermine, stated policy goals relating to human rights and gender equity.

The limitations of current HRE approaches is not a reason to abandon HRE, but rather to ensure that teachers have appropriate support, including training in active methods, and opportunities to discuss how to support children in claiming their rights and the tensions between rights and cultural norms. There also needs to be awareness raising and opportunities for learning for parents and other members of the local community, focusing particularly on child rights and basic human rights standards relating to children's daily lives.

Students are likely to feel disempowered if, despite the human rights they learn about, societal conditions undermine these rights. HRE is a right and a part of quality education. Students not only need knowledge about rights but also education *in* human rights. Such education, as characterized by the UN Declaration on Human Rights Education and Training (Article 2.2)—"Education through human rights, which includes learning and teaching in a way that respects the rights of both educators and learners"—implies consideration of educational structures and young people's experiences of schooling (Osler 2010), as well as the more student-centered methodological approaches that a number of our respondents noted. In other words, learners need to be given opportunities to experience rights within the community of the school. These issues have not yet been addressed within the HRE framework for Kurdistan.

Finally, HRE within a post-conflict society such as Iraqi Kurdistan needs particular focus on "Education *for* human rights, which includes empowering persons to enjoy and exercise their rights and to respect and uphold the rights of others" (UN Declaration on Human Rights Education and Training, Article 2.2). This implies skills training and creating a sense of solidarity between the genders and across ethnic and religious groups, so that learners are encouraged to show responsibility toward and defend the rights of others, particularly those who are different from themselves or with whom they may disagree. This is what Osler and Starkey (2005) have characterized as "education for cosmopolitan citizenship." Learners will only realize their rights if they are equipped and ready to struggle for them.

Powerful conservative forces, including religious leaders and tribal authorities, combine to undermine efforts to promote gender equity. While gender is a sensitive area for discussion, religious and ethnic diversity is often off-limits. Thus, HRE requires much more than merely translating international instruments into national policies or implementing educational reforms. It implies an approach that includes school policies and practices that empower students and provide them with a language to discuss sensitive issues.

It is the responsibility of government to uphold human rights, but this can best be done in cooperation with civil society. Programs of teacher education and training are best implemented in cooperation with local and international NGOs and specialist trainers. This should support Kurdistan's development and enable the best use of human resources, especially the contributions women and girls can make to strengthening democracy and development.

One critique of current approaches made by professionals is that HRE in school is taking place in a vacuum, without sufficient attention to measures beyond the school to raise awareness of the rights of girls and minorities. Such a multidimensional approach might make fuller use of television and other media to influence families and invite them to work in partnership with schools. It might also indirectly counter conservative religious forces who suggest that women's human rights are counter to religious teaching.

We conclude, from the complex and occasionally divergent perspectives of educational professionals in Kurdistan who took part in our study, that education *about*, *in*, and *for* human rights has the potential to strengthen educational quality and gender equity, challenging patriarchal values and tribalism from the grass roots. It is only one tool, and will not be effective, as a number of education professionals have noted, without effective political leadership and legal provisions across a range of policy areas. In a society that is multifaith but that also includes secular perspectives, and particularly in a post-conflict context, recognition of the universal nature of rights and the obligations which this places, not only on governments but also on all actors within civil society, has the potential to promote solidarity and cohesion across cultural and religious boundaries. It is this solidarity that is critical for a just and peaceful future.

Notes

This chapter first appeared in *Education Inquiry*, and we thank the journal for allowing its reprinting in this volume. The full citation for the original article is as follows: Osler, Audrey, and Chalank Yahya. 2013. "Challenges and Complexity in Human Rights Education: Teachers' Understandings of Democratic Participation and Gender Equity in Post-Conflict Kurdistan-Iraq." *Education Inquiry* 4(1):189–210.

1. Launched in Dakar in 2000, UNGEI aims to support the realization of girls' fundamental human right to education, emphasizing its role in realizing other human rights, such as labor market access, health care, and freedom from gender-based violence.

2. Kurmanji is spoken in Duhok, while Sorani is used in Erbil.

3. While some Syrian refugees are accommodated in a camp near Duhok, others are spread across the region, supported by families and communities (IOM 2012).

4. Women may lack access to shelters, which in any case may close for lack of support. Some claim that shelters have allowed women at risk to be returned to their families.

5. In the case of Iraqi Kurdistan, responsibility for guaranteeing children's rights to education lies with the KRG, since education is a devolved responsibility within the autonomous region.

6. The data was collected as part of a small-scale research and development initiative funded by the British Council's DelPHE program (British Council 2010). A paper from this project, INTERDEMOCRATE (intercultural and democratic learning in teacher education), is published as Ahmad et al. (2012). The project builds on a long-standing partnership between Buskerud University College, Norway, and Duhok University, Iraq. We are grateful for the support of the principal investigator, Dr. Lena Lybaek, and project members Niroj Ahmad, Adnam Ismail, and Nadia Zako for data collection.

7. Chalank Yayha would like to thank the Falstad Centre, Norway, for the award of a scholarship that enabled her to complete a second round of data collection for her M.Sc. thesis in February 2012.

8. In Duhok, all three teacher respondents gave us written answers. In Erbil governorate, two of our twelve respondents, both education inspectors, chose to respond in writing.

9. Most schools lack modern communication tools such as websites and public email.

10. This gave Chalank both insider and outsider status, with research participants frequently making reference to shared cultural reference points, but also accorded her, as a young woman educated abroad, particular respect and courtesies which cut across commonly observed standards between the generations, where such courtesies are generally shown to those older than oneself.

11. This was the case for the Duhok teachers, who had each been experimenting with introducing student-centered methods in their own classrooms, as a central feature of the INTERDEMOCRATE project.

References

Ahmad, N., L. Lybaek, I. Mohammed, and A. Osler. 2012. "Democracy and Diversity: Teaching for Human Rights and Citizenship in Post-Conflict Iraqi Kurdistan." *Race Equality Teaching* 30(3):28–33.

al-Ali, N., and N. Pratt. 2011. "Between Nationalism and Women's Rights: The Kurdish Women's Movement in Iraq." *Middle East Journal of Culture and Communication* 4:337–353.

Begikhani, N., A. Gill, and G. Hague. 2010. "Honour-Based Violence (HBV) and Honour-Based Killings in Iraqi Kurdistan and in the Kurdish Diaspora in the UK." Centre for Gender and Violence, Bristol University, UK, and Roehampton University, UK, in partnership with Kurdish Women's Rights Watch. http://www .bristol.ac.uk/sps/research/projects/reports/2010/rw9038reportenglish.pdf.

British Council. 2010. *DelPHE-Iraq.* http://www.britishcouncil.org/delphe-iraq.htm.

Chan, A. W. H., and H. Y. Cheung. 2007. "How Culture Affects Female Inequality Across Countries: An Empirical Study." *Journal of Studies in International Education* 11(2):157–179.

Griffiths, M. 2010. "Girls Education in Iraq." http://irak.alterinter.org/IMG/pdf /UNICEF_Girls_Education_in_Iraq_2010.pdf.

Grover, S. 2007. "Children's Right to Be Educated for Tolerance: Minority Rights and the Law." *Education and Law* 19(1):51–70. doi: 10.1080/09539960701231272.

Harber, C. 2004. *Schooling as Violence.* New York: Routledge.

Harikar. 2011. "Enhance Women Rights Education: Heritage and Life in Dohuk and Nineveh Governorates." http://www.harikar.org/index.php?page=view&id=68.

International Organization for Migration (IOM). 2010. Mission Iraq. *IOM Iraq Newsletter* 2 (January–March). http://www.iom.int/jahia/webdav/shared/shared /mainsite/activities/countries/docs/iom_iraq_vol210_newsletter.pdf.

International Organization for Migration (IOM). 2012. "Northern Iraq Seeks More Aid for Syrian Refugees." Press release June 12, 2012. http://www.iom.int/jahia /Jahia/media/press-briefing-notes/pbnAF/cache/offonce/lang/en?entryId=31884.

Kurdistan Regional Government (KRG). 2009. As cited in Osler, A., and C. Yahya. 2013. "Challenges and Complexity in Human Rights Education: Teachers' Understandings of Democratic Participation and Gender Equity in Post-Conflict Kurdistan-Iraq." *Education Inquiry* 4(1):189–210.

McDowall, D. 2003. *A Modern History of the Kurds.* London: I. B. Tauris.

Osler, A. 2010. *Students' Perspectives on Schooling.* Maidenhead: Open University Press.

Osler, A. 2012. "Universal Declaration of Human Rights." In J. A. Banks, ed., *Encyclopedia of Diversity in Education,* vol. 4 (pp. 2256–2260). Los Angles: Sage Publications.

Osler, A., and H. Starkey. 1996. *Teacher Education and Human Rights.* London: David Fulton.

Osler, A., and H. Starkey. 2003. "Learning for Cosmopolitan Citizenship: Theoretical Debates and Young People's Experiences." *Educational Review* 55(3):243–254.

Osler, A., and H. Starkey. 2005. *Changing Citizenship: Democracy and Inclusion in Education.* Maidenhead: Open University Press.

Osler, A., and H. Starkey. 2010. *Teachers and Human Rights Education.* Stoke-on-Trent: Trentham.

Osler, A., and K. Vincent. 2002. *Citizenship and the Challenge of Global Education.* Stoke-on Trent: Trentham.

Osler, A., and J. Zhu, J. 2011. "Narratives in Teaching and Research for Justice and Human Rights." *Education, Citizenship and Social Justice* 6(3):223–235.

Rauof, A. 2007. *Manual of Instruction for Human Rights Education*. Erbil: Ministry of Human Rights.

Stansfield, G. R. V. 2003. *Iraqi Kurdistan: Political Development and Emergent Democracy*. London: Routledge Curzon.

Stromquist, N. P. 2006. "Gender, Education and the Possibility of Transformative Knowledge." *Compare* 36(2):145–161.

Subrahmanian, R. 2005. "Gender Equality in Education: Definitions and Measurements." *International Journal of Educational Development* 25(4):395–407.

Tomaševski, K. 2005. "Girls' Education Through a Human Rights Lens: What Can Be Done Differently, What Can Be Made Better." *Human Rights and Poverty Reduction* 1–8. http://www.odi.org.uk/events/docs/529.pdf.

United Nations. 1979. "Convention on the Elimination of All Forms of Discrimination Against Women." Geneva: United Nations. http://www.un.org/womenwatch/daw/cedaw/.

United Nations. 1989. "Convention on the Rights of the Child." Geneva: United Nations. http://www2.ohchr.org/english/law/pdf/crc.pdf.

United Nations. 2000. "Millennium Development Goals." www.un.org.

United Nations Development Group (UNDG)/World Bank. 2003. *Republic of Iraq: Housing and Urban Management Sector Report*. September 10, 2003.

UNESCO. 2003. "Situation Analysis of Education in Iraq 2003." Paris: UNESCO. http://unesdoc.unesco.org/images/0013/001308/130838e.pdf.

UNESCO. 2011. "World Data on Education: Iraq," 7th ed. Geneva: UNESCO/IBE. http://unesdoc.unesco.org/images/0021/002114/211439e.pdf.

UN-HABITAT. 2001. "IDP Site and Family Survey." http://www.unhabitat.org/list.asp?typeid=3&catid=203.

UNICEF. 2010. "Girls' Education in Iraq. A Situational Analysis." http://www.ungei.org/resources/files/full_report_iraq_2010.pdf.

United Nations Girls' Education Initiative (UNGEI). 2000. "United Nations Girls' Education Initiative." New York: United Nations. http://www.ungei.org/whatisungei/index_211.html.

Wilson, D. 2003. "Human Rights: Promoting Gender Equality in and Through Education." Background paper for EFA GMR 2003/4.

World Education Forum (WEF). 2000. *The Dakar Framework for Action*. Education for All: Meeting Our Collective Commitments. Text adopted by the World Education Forum Dakar, Senegal, April 26–28. http://www.unesco.org/education/wef/en-conf/dakframeng.shtm.

Yahya, C. 2012. "Human Rights Education in Kurdistan-Iraq: A Means Towards Gender Equality?" Unpublished M.Sc. thesis, Buskerud University College, Drammen, Norway.

Yildiz, K. 2004. *The Kurds in Iraq: The Past, Present and Future*. London: Pluto Press.

CHAPTER 6

Human Rights Education
in Postcolonial India

Monisha Bajaj and Rachel Wahl

Human Rights Education is acquiring greater
importance in the changing national and global scenario
in the wake of globalization. . . . Human rights are in
themselves ends as well as means. They are ends in terms
of standards to be attained and are means as they
enable and empower the people to use the rights to
enjoy the rights. It is both an area of academic enquiry
and also a part of every day life experience of humans as
members of a society.
                —University Grants Commission, India, 2007

It is said that the awareness of human rights is largely
limited to the educated sections of society, while ideally
it is necessary to create awareness about human rights
at all levels. There has been a growing realization that
human rights cannot be taught only from formal
documents. Indigenisation of human rights education
thus, can be one of the crucial components of human
rights education in India.
          —Justice S. Anand, former Chair of India's National
                      Human Rights Commission, 2005

Human rights education has evolved significantly over the past three decades in policy discussions and at the level of practice in India, with rights language figuring prominently in textbook reforms, policy frameworks, and the work of diverse nongovernmental organizations (NGOs) across the country. In this chapter, we chart the increasing convergence of Indian educational policy and human rights language and discourse from the 1990s onward. We then discuss the diverse government-run educational institutions and NGOs that have sought to operate in the space opened up by the "policy talk" on human rights education (Tyack and Cuban 1997). Monisha Bajaj discusses her research on postprimary human rights education in India, examining how NGOs localize internationally circulating discourses on rights vis-à-vis Indian realities to offer transformative visions of HRE to marginalized youth (Bajaj 2012b). Rachel Wahl offers insights from her research on postsecondary human rights education in India, examining how professional training programs and higher education courses address human rights. The chapter offers a complex case study of how, in one nation-state, diverse actors give multiple meanings to and differentially constitute a particular education project: human rights education. We draw on anthropologist Sally Engle Merry's (2006) concept of human rights vernaculars to explore how local actors make meaning of human rights concepts; in this case, however, we argue that in a single country, there are a variety of vernaculars in formation—beyond mere translation of agreed-upon concepts—around human rights education that suggest differing motivations, ideologies, and outcomes driving the HRE project in India.[1]

Education in India

India offers a complex case study of vernacularization due in part to its diversity. The country's tremendous diversity in religions, cultures, and languages (1.2 billion residents in twenty-nine states) and uneven socioeconomic development across regions, social groups, and gender complicate the ways that educational efforts figure into larger goals of economic and political development. Despite India's record economic growth in recent years, estimated to be around 7 percent per annum (World Bank 2010), income inequality has *increased* in the last two decades (OECD 2010). An estimated 42 percent of Indians (nearly 500 million people) survive on less than $1.25

per day, and 75.6 percent of all Indians live on less than $2.00 per day (UNDP 2009).

Educational enrollments have increased significantly since India's independence in 1947. At that time, a mere 16 percent of Indians could read and write, reflecting colonial policies of limited educational access for a select few, who were trained for service in the British colonial administration. The structure of education still reflects colonial legacies, though efforts toward mass expansion have resulted in an average literacy rate of almost 75 percent as of the last census (GOI 2011). Article 26 of the UN Universal Declaration of Human Rights (UDHR) cites access to education as its first component and, as its second, an education that leads to the "full development of the human personality and to the strengthening of respect for human rights and fundamental freedoms." In similar order of priority, the Indian government has focused primarily on access, with only relatively recent attention to the *type* of education that might foster respect for rights.

Human Rights Talk in Education Policy

Since the 1980s, discussions of human rights education have permeated virtually all Indian national entities concerned with education or with human rights, such as the University Grants Commission (UGC), the National Council for Teacher Education (NCTE), the National Council of Educational Research and Training (NCERT), and the National Human Rights Commission (NHRC). The role of these institutions varies and includes a mix of regulatory powers, policy setting, accreditation, and resource provision. Each government institution responds to different pressures for HRE-related reforms, but all are largely energized by UN and international mandates that prioritize human rights education (Bajaj 2012b). The increasing influence of human rights discourses in Indian policymaking has been linked to the country's increased global integration after liberalizing its economy in the early 1990s (Bajaj 2012b). While rights discourses have become more prevalent in Indian policy arenas since the 1990s, Bajaj (2014) has also argued that discussions of the right to education (particularly those that led up to the passage of the 2009 Right to Education Act) have used rights language as an organizing framework for educational ideas and movements that predate this turn to rights language, and which have existed in India since the 1960s. Whether human rights education encompasses a new educational project or the repackaging of older, local ideas into new "fashionable" discourses (Ramirez, Suárez, and Meyer 2007), it is important to situate the rise and influence of human rights education in policy discussions in India within its recent history.

In the 1990s, in line with the UN Decade for Human Rights Education (1995–2004) and subsequent international efforts, the government of India began to develop a plan of action to integrate HRE into schools nationwide, with the support of high-level officials such as the then-president, K. R. Narayan, and, in more recent years, several national-level entities and authorities. India enacted a Right to Education (RTE) Act in 2009, offering a new dimension of human rights discourse in framing how social services are conceived. The RTE Act, which came into force in 2010 after being passed a year earlier, shifted education from a nonbinding "directive principle" to an enforceable "fundamental right" in Indian constitutional law. As a result, students and families can sue the government if schools are not available within a specified distance (1 kilometer for primary schools) and if they don't meet the designated quality standards related to available learning materials and pupil–teacher ratios. Ensuring access is not necessarily a linear process, however; once enrolled, many factors, such as discriminatory practices, inadequate facilities, and poor instructional quality, push children out of school (UNICEF 2010).

The increasing framing of education as a human right has also influenced discussions of curriculum and teaching. Previous curricular frameworks, which provide a national vision for states that then determine curriculum, textbooks, and the content of teacher training, highlighted concepts such as "Gandhian values of education such as non-violence, truthfulness, self-discipline, self-reliance, dignity of labor" (Panda 1978). Recent iterations have focused squarely on human rights. For example, the 2009 National Curriculum Framework for Teacher Education states the following:

> [With regard to teacher education], we need to reconceptualise citizenship training in terms of human rights and approaches of critical pedagogy; emphasize environment and its protection, living in harmony with oneself and with natural and social environment; promote peace, democratic way of life, constitutional values of equality, justice, liberty, fraternity, secularism, caring values . . . and zeal for social reconstruction. (cited in Bajaj 2012b:44)

Similarly, recent efforts have incorporated human rights terms, concepts, and examples into model textbooks prepared at the national level, often adopted in large part or wholesale by states. Policy discussions around human rights education do not necessarily signal meaningful change or impact, as has been discussed in Chapter 1 of this book. They do, however, offer a space in democratic societies for organizations, initiatives, and educational projects to take these circulating ideas and make meaning of them in their own ways. There are numerous and diverse examples of this in India, and the following section highlights some of these efforts.

Differing Scope and Intensity of HRE

In order to situate the different types of human rights education in India across policy and community/school contexts, it is important to understand that not all human rights education looks the same. As discussed in Chapter 1 of this book, HRE as an educational project can and does incorporate diverse goals and multiple actors that are differentially situated; this is true across the globe, and certainly in India.

Figure 6.1 charts different initiatives in India in terms of their scope and intensity (Bajaj 2012b). Analysis was limited to programs and initiatives that specifically use the term "human rights education," excluding similar efforts that did not self-identify in this way. Scope refers to the reach of the intervention, from the school and community to regional and national levels. Intensity is defined by the form that the intervention takes: low intensity is characterized by nonmandatory, self-directed instruction and continues toward high intensity, where trained educators offer sustained instruction over at least one year in human rights concepts (Bajaj 2012b). While these programs may be self-selecting on some level (either by the individual in the case of higher secondary or university courses, or by the school that has chosen to introduce HRE), once enrolled, human rights instruction is a core component of study and is an integral part of the regular life of the school, college, or university.

Figure 6.1 also groups initiatives into different levels. Scope and intensity are often inversely related: the more people affected by an intervention, the more likely that intensity declines. However, more intense contact, instruction, and engagement are seen primarily in initiatives of limited scope.

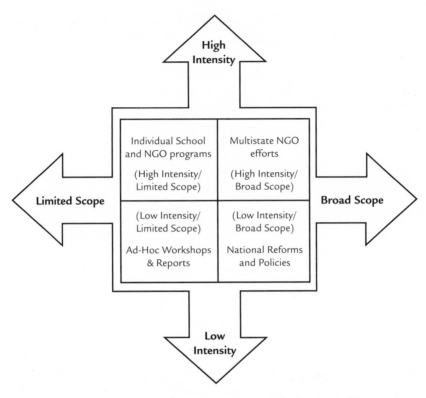

Figure 6.1. Scope and intensity of HRE initiatives in India (Bajaj 2012b).

National-level initiatives such as human rights education modules for teachers, workshops for university students, and training manuals prepared by
the National Human Rights Commission for suggested use are efforts that
have a broad national scope but are low-intensity since they do not mandate
or evaluate implementation. Nongovernmental organizations that run one-
to three-year courses or degree programs in human rights may have highly
intense and thorough educational programs, but their scope is limited to
those students who enroll.

   Given the policy space created by wide-scope efforts, examples are
provided of the types of human rights education being offered by diverse
organizations at the local level. It is important to note that NGO-run programs can be of high or low intensity, regardless of their scope, and there
exists a wide variety among the examples presented in subsequent sections.

The purpose of illustrating the range of programs that situate themselves under the umbrella of human rights education is precisely to demonstrate how the educational project has come to encompass a wide range of actors and programs making meaning in diverse ways across India. There are many more initiatives that could have been included, but it is beyond the purview of this chapter to offer an exhaustive list of human rights education efforts in India.

Diverse Vernaculars of HRE in Different Domains

The Indian experience with HRE, viewed broadly, has more than one trajectory. While there is no doubt that the current momentum owes to the perceived obligations of the Indian state under the action plan of the UN HRE decade and the Human Rights Protection Act of 1994, this situation was preceded by two voluntary initiatives. First was the need felt by the civil liberties and human rights action groups within civil society in terms of disseminating human rights perspectives within the rank and file of the organisations, which lead to organising numerous human rights literacy sessions. Even though those sessions were not "public" sessions, since the objective was to disseminate the rights literacy to largely people associated with the work of those organisations, it could be viewed as a pre-cursor to the current phase of initiatives. The second pre-cursor was the higher education initiatives in human rights supported by voluntary foundations from the North. (Jain 2005)

As was noted earlier in this chapter, it is impossible to reduce the proliferation of human rights education in India to external influences alone. Human rights education initiatives and programs have emerged in India since the 1980s in a variety of ways and through multiple coalitions, discussions, and linkages. It is the confluence of pressure from below (the work of civil society actors), from above (international organizations), and through the circular nature of how transnational advocacy networks (Keck and Sikkink 1998) link global ideas such as human rights education with local struggles that accounts for the rise and prominence of human rights education in contemporary India. The following sections chart various domains and how governmental, nongovernmental, private, and social movement actors have localized human rights in diverse and multiple ways.

School and Cocurricular Programs

Whole-School Approaches

Human rights education at the upper primary and secondary school levels occurs across different contexts including government-run schools, NGO-run schools, and private schools. Two approaches tend to characterize most approaches to human rights education: (1) whole-school approaches to human rights education that are infused into the school's operations, and (2) integrated school-based programs run by external organizations occurring in schools on a regular basis.

Several elite private schools have adopted content, pedagogy, and extra-curricular approaches to human rights, citizenship, and social awareness in India. Since 2001, the Riverside School in Ahmedabad, Gujarat, has been structuring its educational experience around civic responsibility and leadership development among students. While the school is novel in many ways (e.g., its design focus on the lived environment, international partnerships, artist residencies), Riverside's citizenship curriculum partners its economically and socially privileged students with NGOs in Ahmedabad, where students regularly interact with children from different socioeconomic backgrounds. For example, sixth standard (or grade) students are given a project that simulates the conditions of a child laborer. One secondary school student at Riverside, reflecting on her experience, narrated the following:

> We were all put in a small room and we had to make *agarbattis* [incense sticks] from 9 o'clock to 5 o'clock. We were given the same sort of food that child laborers typically get. The main idea was to really experience being stuffed into that room where we hardly get space to even stand, and we had to make 1000 *agarbattis*. After the experience, we shared it with our parents. Some of the parents had child laborers working in their homes and factories. After that, after us experiencing this and sharing it with our parents, those child laborers are no longer in our homes [and workplaces]. We also told others about what we did and sold the *agarbattis* we made for a higher price, and gave

the money raised to a charity that works with child laborers. (Bajaj 2012a:7)

Riverside is a high-cost private school and works primarily to prepare socially conscious and responsible future leaders. Human rights awareness is meaningful for affluent children who may come to be in positions of power and privilege in the future. Significant experiences in early adolescence, when children's sense of justice and morality are being formed (Gilligan 1982; Kohlberg 1981; Noddings 1984), can contribute to greater social responsibility; moreover, student transformations can have a ripple effect on the actions of, for example, their parents. Nevertheless, questions remain as to what actually happened to child laborers who worked in these children's home and how families make sense of human rights education when it counters societal norms; further research could help elucidate the impact of rights education in such contexts.

Conversely, private schools run by nongovernmental organizations and serving extremely marginalized groups in society are also innovating with human rights instruction. Whereas students at the Riverside School were *simulating* the lives of child laborers for a day, some of the children at the NGO-run Navsarjan schools were *themselves* former child laborers. Navsarjan is a human rights and advocacy organization focused on the rights of Dalits (formerly called "untouchables," a social group with high poverty rates), and one of their primary areas of work is on "Human Rights Value Education." Navsarjan's three self-operated schools and hundreds of after-school clubs, called *bhimshalas*, constitute this program area of the organization's work.

In response to widespread caste discrimination in schools and the resulting high dropout rate for Dalit students, Navsarjan has set up three residential schools for Dalit children, which are free of cost to them. These schools draw on children from the poorest communities and most excluded castes in the state of Gujarat. Children have reported that prior to joining these schools, they were forced to sit separately, beaten, and mistreated in other ways by teachers in government schools. The basic provision of an education that does not discriminate against these children is the first element of human rights education in Navsarjan's schools (Bajaj 2012a).

Navsarjan schools also seek to disrupt conventional educational practice through the curriculum and structure of its schools. For example, Navsarjan's curriculum includes greater participatory activities, such as children performing skits and sitting in a circle in class to facilitate interaction.

Classes and assemblies reiterate messages about caste equality and eradicating the notion that Dalit children are less than their higher-caste peers. In terms of structure, the schools use ecosanitation toilets that all students and teachers are required to learn about and empty once they are full—a significant intervention, given the common and widely documented discriminatory practice of making Dalit children clean toilets while other children are in class (Bajaj 2012a, 2012b; Human Rights Watch 2014; Nambissan and Sedwal 2002). Ecosanitation toilets are latrines that collect fecal matter, sanitize it, and then make it usable as fertilizer for farming.

Children in Navsarjan schools are introduced not only to innovative sanitation practices but also to distinct practices around gender. Both boys and girls take part in cooking school meals, with boys often learning to make *chapattis* (flat bread) for the first time. Boys and girls wear the same uniforms, unlike government and other schools, where girls wear skirts and boys wear trousers. Children's books written by the organization's founder, noted Dalit activist Martin Macwan, focusing on caste and gender equity, are also utilized in the classroom. The impact of the alternative norms related to caste and gender equity in Navsarjan educational programs are extensively discussed elsewhere (Kropac 2007), but several of the deliberate practices and initial responses suggest promising results for this variant of human rights education.

School-Based and Cocurricular Approaches

Various nongovernmental organizations work with schools to offer human rights education programs during the school day to students. For example, Amnesty International works with thirty schools in the city of Bengaluru to create spaces for students, teachers, and parents to discuss human rights issues. Various Indian NGOs also offer programs on children's rights and human rights. The Institute of Human Rights Education (IHRE), the educational wing of the Indian human rights organization People's Watch, based in the southern Indian state of Tamil Nadu, began operating in 1997 when teachers asked activists at the organization how they might incorporate human rights principles in the classroom (Bajaj 2012b). Starting as an experiment with a handful of schools, the organization developed a curriculum, delivered trainings for teachers, and attempted to translate and expand their human rights work (at first primarily on caste discrimination and police abuse) into a broad-based educational program. As connections were made with the UN Decade for Human Rights Education (1995–2004), IHRE was able to gain support by aligning with international efforts to promote human rights and translating these interests into funding for their work. At present, IHRE operates in nearly 4,000 schools in eighteen Indian states. Textbooks have been developed in multiple regional languages, and more than 500,000 Indian students have participated in a three-year course in human rights (Bajaj 2012b). Year one introduces students to human rights; year two focuses on children's rights; and year three deals with discrimination and inequality.

IHRE's model attempts to offer breadth and depth to human rights education in the schools in which it works. By securing permission from the government, IHRE has been able to enter into thousands of schools, mainly those serving Dalits, those considered on the lowest rung of the caste system, and "tribal" or indigenous students—both groups comprising the most marginalized sections of Indian society.[2] IHRE aims to secure two hour-long periods per week in which students in the sixth, seventh, and eighth grades are taught by teachers who are trained by IHRE staff, and who use textbooks developed by affiliated curriculum experts. Textbooks and trainings include concepts related to general human rights, children's rights, and issues of discrimination based on caste, gender, religion, ability, skin color, and ethnicity, among others. IHRE's approach to educational reform vis-à-vis human rights differs greatly from conventional Indian education, with interactive activities, learner-centered pedagogy, and participatory approaches to both teacher training and student learning.

The organization has also expanded cocurricular efforts for human rights through the creation of secondary school–level human rights and children's rights clubs (some of which work in collaboration with the National Commission for the Protection of Child Rights in New Delhi to report violations youth document in their communities). Additionally, the organization has run human rights camps for students in the summer holidays, has worked with teachers to create a CD of human rights songs in local languages, and has developed educational videos to complement their textbooks on human rights. Efforts in upper primary and secondary schools in India offer students who participate in these programs a framework for understanding the conditions that surround them. Moreover, the programs have had significant impacts related to students' and teachers' community actions after learning about human rights (Bajaj 2012b).

HRE in Universities and Colleges

Universities and colleges have adopted a variety of approaches to human rights education. Differences also exist between the types of programs and institutions that offer HRE. These include degree programs in elite universities, which in India tend to be national, public universities supported by the federal government. More widely accessible certificates and courses in human rights are also available, such as through distance-learning programs administered by institutions that cater to a broader student population. Many of these programs are funded by the UGC, though not all accept or have been given government funding.

A significant number of tertiary HRE programs are offered at the postgraduate level, such as through master's degrees or certificate programs in human rights. Many others are available within legal studies. Even within postgraduate and legal education, though, HRE programs vary significantly in scope, method, and content. Below we discuss a few examples that demonstrate the different ways in which colleges and universities have implemented HRE.

Elite Institutions and HRE

The prestigious Jawaharlal Nehru University (JNU) in New Delhi has coordinated human rights teaching and research activities within its School of International Studies since 1981. Currently, the school houses the Centre for Promotion of Human Rights Teaching and Research (HURITER). The center primarily facilitates and promotes human rights research and teaching, rather than offering degree programs. Faculty produce research on human rights and assist graduate students and scholars whose research relates to human rights, host seminars and colloquia, and oversee a human rights documentation and information center. The center also offers elective courses in human rights at the postgraduate level (Jawaharlal Nehru University n.d.).

Jamia Millia Islamia, another national, public university in New Delhi, offers a master's degree in human rights and duties education. Housed within the Political Science Department, the program provides students with knowledge of human rights principles and laws. It also cultivates the capacity to implement human rights laws, such as by preparing students to work with an NGO, or by encouraging them to take a rights-sensitive approach to their work in other professions. In keeping with this goal, the sixteen-course degree includes an internship component and visits to sites such as jails, police stations, slums, and local NGOs. The department also hosts lectures and symposia on human rights topics and houses a human rights library (Jamia Millia Islamia Political Science Department n.d.).

HRE in Law Schools

Many HRE programs are housed in law schools. Indeed, one of the National Human Rights Commission's first efforts to promote HRE at the tertiary level focused on legal education (National Human Rights Commission n.d.b). The National Law School of India University has benefited from an especially close partnership with the NHRC. The commission worked with this university, which is ranked among the best in the country (India Today and Nielson Company 2013), to establish the National Institute of Human Rights (NIHR).[3] Faculty affiliated with the institute collaborate with the NHRC to produce research and publications, such as a handbook on human rights for judicial officers (National Law School of India University n.d.). The institute also trains judicial officers in human rights, and offers a postgraduate diploma in human rights law through a distance-learning program.[4]

Similarly, Banaras Hindu University is a selective national university that offers a human rights program within the Law School. The LL.M. in human rights and duties education is a four-semester degree that prepares students for careers as legal professionals. Accordingly, coursework consists of instruction in international and domestic human rights law.

Focus on Accessibility

Other degree and certificate programs in human rights are more accessible than those housed in the elite institutions. The Indira Gandhi National Open University (IGNOU), for example, offers a certificate course in human rights.

This program reflects the university's unique design. IGNOU was founded with the mission of making education accessible to all, "particularly the disadvantaged segments of society," through affordable distance learning and open admissions.[5] Their three-course certificate caters to professionals such as teachers, police officers, and judges, but is open to all interested students. Similarly, the Indian Institute of Human Rights offers a master's degree in human rights through a distance-learning program. Like IGNOU, this university-affiliated NGO seeks to make HRE accessible to a diverse population of learners.

Diversity in Tertiary HRE

HRE at the tertiary level spans a wide variety of approaches and institutions. While some centers focus on facilitating research, others offer degrees that prepare students for careers in which they protect human rights. And while many elite institutions have benefited from UCG funding and offer human rights programs, HRE is also available through programs that reach a broader spectrum of students.

Moreover, the names of these programs indicate the diversity in conceptual approaches. Some program titles refer to both rights and duties, while others refer exclusively to rights. This reflects a long-standing debate within both academic and government institutions as to whether it is appropriate to expand beyond a narrow focus on "rights" to include concepts such as "values" and "duty" in HRE (Bajaj 2012b:38). Indeed, a faculty member in one university HRE program emphasized in an interview the importance of including "duties" in their program's title. For him, this was a crucial modification of what he saw as the West's overemphasis on rights alone.[6]

The NHRC recognizes the issue as a legitimate and open question. In its 2007 report, for example, the commission emphasized the importance of ensuring that HRE is made relevant within Indian contexts. In exploring how to do this effectively, the report admits ambivalence regarding the use of terms such as "duty" in curricula and program titles. The report notes that such issues remain unsettled, though it suggests that the exclusive use of rights language in referring to HRE programs may be better aligned with its mission (Bajaj 2012b:51). The range of programs in existence suggests, however, that the promotion of HRE by the national government has allowed for a diversity of ideological and structural approaches in Indian colleges and universities.

HRE for the Professions

HRE also takes the form of professional training offered by the government, professional organizations, and NGOs. Government agencies such as the NHRC have played an especially significant role in the promotion and facilitation of such education. For example, the commission publishes resources such as model curricula and recommendations on HRE for professionals including teachers and police, hosts activities such as human rights debate competitions for the police and military, and provides HRE directly by offering profession-specific trainings.

Law enforcement is a rare example of a profession in which such training is required for entry. Police at all levels are required to complete a course that covers domestic and international human rights law as part of their preservice training. For the lower-ranking State Police Services, such training takes place at the state level and is the responsibility of the state to oversee. For the higher-ranking Indian Police Service, this training occurs at the national police academy. The military and paramilitary agencies also now offer courses in human rights to their officers.[7]

These human rights trainings are hardly uniform in content or delivery. For one, the trainers vary greatly. Police, representatives from the NHRC, human rights professionals employed by domestic NGOs, or academic experts on human rights may conduct the trainings. The different types of trainers likely offer different content and varying perspectives.[8]

Moreover, there is diversity in the format of the trainings. The required preservice police training often consists only of abstract lectures on human rights laws, without instruction in how to implement such laws—a form of education that human rights professionals and police alike report has little effect on or interest for police. At other times, activists from NGOs take the initiative to create innovative, interactive courses that involve pedagogical techniques such as role-play.[9] Subsequent trainings for midcareer or senior officers may take the form of two- to five-day workshops and conferences, and are not required for all officers at these later stages.[10]

Some of these trainings take the form of distance learning. For example, the NHRC and Indira Gandhi National Open University (IGNOU) have

worked in partnership to develop online training modules to sensitize police to human rights laws and principles. These trainings include instruction
in relevant laws and engage police in reflection about how they can better
protect rights in their work. In a departure from the more typical lecture
format, these modules involve time for interaction between the police trainees and faculty of IGNOU's Law School. This interaction occurs first through
the online platform, and then in person at IGNOU for a smaller group of
police who will become trainers within their own districts.[11]

Other professions have also been the focus of human rights educational
efforts, though such trainings are not typically required for admission to the
profession. For example, civil servants can now take courses in human rights
at the national training institute for the prestigious Indian Administrative
Service. These courses are offered to senior members of the civil service, and
take the form of weeklong conferences (National Academy of Administration n.d.).

Judges are also recipients of professional training in human rights. The
NHRC has created a Foundation Course on Human Rights for recently appointed judges, as well as a refresher course for more senior judges. In addition, the National Judicial Academy offers courses in human rights,[12] and
some state judicial academies include human rights courses, though this is
not a uniform practice across the country.[13]

Teachers, too, are targets of state HRE efforts. The National Council for
Teacher Education (NCTE) has facilitated HRE for teachers by highlighting
human rights concepts in its National Curriculum Framework for Teacher
Education, which outlines priorities for the preparation of teachers (Bajaj
2012b:43). The NCTE has also produced HRE modules for teachers and distributed them to the teacher training colleges, along with videos and sporadic workshops (Bajaj, 2012b:45).

The NHRC has moreover played a role in the direct provision of HRE
for teachers. The commission has created a series of HRE teacher-training
modules and published handbooks for teachers, some in conjunction with
the NCTE (Bajaj 2012b:46; NHRC n.d.a). For example, in 2003 the agencies
partnered to create a handbook on *Discrimination Based on Sex, Caste, Disability and Religion* that was geared toward the training of teachers (Bajaj
2012b:46).

Efforts to integrate HRE into professional training have ranged from requiring it for entry into the profession, to more sporadic efforts that encourage voluntary participation. While human rights courses are required for

law enforcement and many security officers, not every teacher, judge, or civil servant must take a human rights course as part of their preparation. For example, only thirteen of India's twenty-nine states require that human rights topics be covered as part of teacher training (Bajaj 2012b:46). However, national agencies such as the NHRC attempt to make such courses available through professional organizations and training institutes, as well as through direct provision of materials and trainings. It is possible that such courses could be made into requirements in the future, though that remains to be seen.

Nonformal Human Rights Education

While universities and professional training programs often seek to "credentialize" human rights knowledge, adult nonformal educational programs have as their primary aim the empowerment of marginalized communities. The approaches in this section differ from NGO-run programs in schools in that their participants are not involved in formal education and may never have attended schools. Nonformal approaches often use popular education, given the illiteracy of many of the participants. Using participatory methods such as street theater, role-plays, or interactive discussions with visual materials, various groups and movements have integrated rights concepts into their activities. For example, the National Federation for Dalit Women has prepared materials for women to engage with instances of rights violations—many of which participants know about firsthand—in a way that promotes a more critical understanding of the guarantees that exist.

Other popular education programs utilize rights concepts to train individuals from marginalized communities about the law and how violations they face can be countered. Kapoor's (2007) work on human rights popular education programs for Dalit women in the state of Orissa on the Prevention of Atrocities Act—a 1989 law that outlaws and provides recourse for various forms of caste discrimination—highlights the need for rights educators to be attentive to local conceptions of education and action. Kapoor notes that "human rights education has encouraged Dalit women's organizations (of which there are 75 in the region) to engage in the community organizing process . . . and to develop and sustain a parallel women's organizational structure that continues to encourage mobilization around materials issues (e.g. land rights and food security)" (Kapoor 2007:284). He

cautions, however, that Dalit women in these human rights training programs seek not to advance a "Euro-American" notion of individual rights,
but rather to work together to advance Dalit rights alongside men—from
whom they may face mistreatment—in their struggle for greater dignity and
collective rights. Such research further contributes to HRE having different
registers and vernaculars when operationalized in distinct settings and with
diverse populations.

Many other groups utilize popular education and community-based trainings to educate on various legal rights to health, land, food security, education,
and justice, among others. It is important to note that, while not always considered part of the human rights education endeavor, nonformal efforts do indeed
comprise important linkages between activists, educators, and marginalized
communities seeking to make the promise of human rights meaningful.

Concluding Thoughts

High-level policies create opportunities for local programs to emerge. In
India, the proliferation of HRE was encouraged by international initiatives
such as the UN World Program for Human Rights Education. Likewise, policies and initiatives at the national level in India have facilitated the kinds of
subnational programs we describe above. Such global and national efforts
also spread a shared language and network that have likely informed how
HRE has developed.

But within some general parameters suggested by global and national
initiatives (as well as the constraints set by their funding priorities), the goals,
structures, and content of these programs differ greatly across the country.
In a process referred to by Sally Merry as vernacularization, local actors
translate human rights concepts into local contexts, resulting in myriad different approaches. Moreover, the way local actors vernacularize is likely to
vary, ranging from the near "replication" of global models to "hybrids"
wherein global models are combined innovatively with local symbols, structures, and values (Merry 2006).

At one extreme of the translation process, local actions may become
decoupled from the discourse used to describe them (see Chapter 1 and
Meyer et al. 1997). Bringing Dalit children into classrooms but forcing
them to sit in the back row or clean toilets is one example of a practice that

has become decoupled from the right to education it is meant to fulfill. At the other end of the spectrum, Indian NGOs have drawn on the right to education in an effort to abolish caste inequality, giving local meaning to a global language.

This use of rights talk to address caste inequality highlights a second point. The Dalit struggle predates the global rise of rights discourse, as do Indian efforts to broaden access to education. These domestic movements have a long history within India. They were not merely a response to the international human rights movement, nor were they created by national government policies. But activists in these movements have made use of both to expand their work. Thus, global and national policies likely shape how longstanding movements for social justice are articulated and pursued, but such policies cannot be credited with creating or driving these movements.

Both of these factors—the vernacularization of human rights by local actors and the use of global agendas in the service of social justice struggles that predate the predominance of human rights talk—help explain why HRE looks so different across the world and, as we have shown, within one country.

The development of so many different HRE initiatives across the country also reveals a third point: HRE has blossomed in India. Although the quality and impact of these programs vary, it is clear that HRE has become part of the policy and practice of many Indian education and rights institutions.

Several questions arise from these conclusions that would benefit from further research. First, what is the impact of vernacularization on human rights protection? Research suggests that appropriation by local actors can have vastly different meanings, depending on factors such as the roles these actors play within a society and what they hope to achieve. Bajaj (2012b) has shown, for example, how an Indian NGO uses a human rights framework to meaningfully engage children and teachers in local struggles for justice, while Wahl has demonstrated that Indian state officials use rights discourse to defend illiberal practices (Wahl 2017). More research on how human rights are interpreted and enacted within the many initiatives that run under the banner of HRE would enrich our understanding of the significance of this diffusion.

A second area of inquiry could focus on how international HRE initiatives have informed local programs in ways that are fruitful, and on the ways in which the global arena has impeded local efforts. A heated debate exists within the field of human rights on the effect of international initiatives, with critics asserting that global efforts undercut local social justice move-ments.[14] Scholars have noted the importance of localizing HRE curricula, and have documented that such localization occurs, such as through networks that encourage open discussion between global actors (e.g., the staff of international organizations), and national actors (e.g., the staff of domestic NGOs) (Suárez 2007). But further research could provide a more robust understanding of whether and when global HRE efforts support or impede local initiatives.

Finally, future research could explore what accounts for the success of HRE among Indian policymakers. Why and how did the political will emerge that made the spread of HRE possible within India? A large body of research examines why governments comply with global norms,[15] as not all norms are successful in spreading either at the national or subnational level. Research could fruitfully uncover the pathways by which HRE proliferated in policy discourse and in practice in India. Such an investigation may illuminate whether and how HRE might be able to take root in other countries with fewer such initiatives, such as the United States.

Notes

1. Sections of this chapter are adapted and excerpted from the original publications (Bajaj 2012a, 2012b).

2. Dalits (literally translated as "broken people") constitute 15 percent of India's population. Human Rights Watch (2007) finds that "Entrenched discrimination violates Dalits' rights to education, health, housing, property, freedom of religion, free choice of employment, and equal treatment before the law. Dalits also suffer routine violations of their right to life and security of person through state-sponsored or -sanctioned acts of violence, including torture" (1).

3. The NIHR was established in 1998. This institute developed out of the Human Rights Centre, housed in the university from 1991 to 1998. https://www.nls.ac.in/index .php?option=com_content&view=article&id=67%3Anational-institute-of-human -rights-nihr&catid=6%3Aacademic-programmes&Itemid=32.

4. NHRC n.d.b.; National Law School of India, http://targetstudy.com/university /1969/national-law-school-of-india-university.

5. IGNOU, http://mhrd.gov.in/ignou_hindi.

6. Mahatma Gandhi Kashi Vidyapeeth faculty member, interview by Rachel Wahl, August 2010.

7. Bureau of Police Research and Training staff, interview by Rachel Wahl, New Delhi, 2012; NHRC n.d.b.

8. National Human Rights Commission and Bureau of Police Research and Development human rights professionals and staff, interview by Rachel Wahl, New Delhi, 2011–2012.

9. Navaz Kotwal, interview by Rachel Wahl, Commonwealth Human Rights Initiative, New Delhi, 2012.

10. Bureau of Police Research and Development staff, interview by Rachel Wahl, New Delhi, 2011–2012.

11. Dr. K. Elumalai, Director of the IGNOU School of Law, interview by Rachel Wahl, New Delhi 2012; NHRC, http://nhrc.nic.in/nhrc_ignou.htm.

12. National Judicial Academy Training Calendar.

13. National Judicial Academy, http://www.nja.nic.in/round-up-on-sjas.html, http://www.ipsnews.net/1999/11/rights-india-judges-law-students-train-in-human -rights-issues/.

14. See, for example, the discussion in OpenGlobalRights in "Funding for Human Rights," https://www.opendemocracy.net/openglobalrights/funding-for-human-rights.

15. This is a vast field of study, but see, for example, Krasner 1983; Keohane 1984; Katsenstein 1996; Wendt 1995; Adler 1991.

References

Acharya, Keya. 1999. "Rights-India: Judges, Law Students Train in Human Rights Issues." International Press Service News Agency. http://www.ipsnews.net/1999/11 /rights-india-judges-law-students-train-in-human-rights-issues/.

Adler, Emanuel. 1991. "Seasons of Peace: Progress in Postwar International Security." In Emanuel Adler and Beverly Crawford, eds., *Progress in Postwar International Relations* (pp. 128–173). New York: Columbia Univrsity Press.

Amnesty International. 2014. "Holistic Human Rights Education Needed to Make Schools Safer." www.amnesty.org/en/for-media/press-releases/holistic-human -rights-education-essential-make-schools-safer-2014-07-25.

Bajaj, Monisha. 2012a. "Human Rights Education in Small Schools in India." *Peace Review* 24(1):6–13.

Bajaj, Monisha. 2012b. *Schooling for Social Change: The Rise and Impact of Human Rights Education in India*. New York: Continuum.

Bajaj, Monisha. 2014. "The Productive Plasticity of Rights: Globalization, Education and Human Rights." In Nelly P. Stromquist and Karen Monkman, eds., *Globalization and Education: Integration and Contestation Across Cultures*, 3rd ed. (pp. 51–66). Lanham, MD: Rowman and Littlefield.

Careers 360. 2014. "Top Law Colleges in India." http://www.law.careers360.com /articles/top-law-colleges-in-india.

Gilligan, Carol. 1982. *In a Different Voice: Psychological Theory and Women's Development*. Cambridge, MA: Harvard University Press.

Government of India (GOI). 2011. "Census of India 2011." Ministry of Home Affairs, Government of India. http://censusindia.gov.in/.

Human Rights Watch. 2007. *Hidden Apartheid: Caste Discrimination Against India's "Untouchables."* New York: Human Rights Watch.

Human Rights Watch. 2014. "'They Say We're Dirty': Denying an Education to India's Marginalized." http://www.hrw.org/news/2014/04/22/india-marginalized-children-denied-education.

India Today and Nielson Company. 2013. "India's Best Colleges." http://indiatoday.intoday.in/bestcolleges/2013/ranks.jsp?ST=Law&LMT=1&Y=2013.

Indira Gandhi Open University. n.d. "Distance Learning." http://mhrd.gov.in/ignou_hindi.

Jain, Devika. 2005. "Making Human Rights Education Inclusive: The Indian Experience OR Locating Human Rights Education in the Broader Human Rights Landscape." http://www.devakijain.com/pdf/jain_makinghuman.pdf

Jamia Millia Islamia Political Science Department. n.d. http://jmi.ac.in/upload/programme/cs_fss_ps_ma_hrde.pdf.

Jawaharlal Nehru University. n.d. "Centre for Promotion of Human Rights Teaching and Research (HURITER)." http://www.jnu.ac.in/sis/huriter/huriterold.htm.

Kapoor, Dip. 2007. "Gendered-Caste Discrimination, Human Rights Education, and the Enforcement of the Prevention of Atrocities Act in India." *Alberta Journal of Educational Research* 53(3):273–286.

Katzenstein, Peter J. 1996. *The Culture of National Security: Norms and Identity in World Politics.* New York: Columbia University Press.

Keck, Margaret, and Kathryn Sikkink. 1998. *Activists Beyond Borders.* Ithaca, NY: Cornell University Press.

Kohlberg, Lawrence. 1981. *The Philosophy of Moral Development: Moral Stages and the Idea of Justice.* New York: Harper & Row.

Krasner, Stephen D. 1983. *International Regimes.* Ithaca, NY: Cornell University Press.

Kropac, Michael. 2007. "Dalit Empowerment and Vocational Education: An Impact Study." *Working Paper Series.* New Delhi: Indian Institute of Dalit Studies.

Merry, Sally. 2006. "Transnational Human Rights and Local Activism: Mapping the Middle." *American Anthropologist* 108:38–51.

Meyer, John, John Boli, George Thomas, and Francisco Ramirez. 1997. "World Society and the Nation-State." *American Journal of Sociology* 103:144–181.

Nambissan, Geetha B., and Mona Sedwal. 2002. "Education for All: The Situation of Dalit Children in India." In R. Govinda, ed., *India Education Report* (pp. 72–86). Oxford: Oxford University Press.

National Academy of Administration. n.d. "The Training Canvas." http://www.lbsnaa.gov.in/splleft/index/aboutus/296.

National Human Rights Commission, Government of India. n.d.a. "IGNOU Program." http://nhrc.nic.in/nhrc_ignou.htm.

National Human Rights Commission, Government of India. n.d.b. PowerPoint presentation on Human Rights Education.

National Judicial Academy. n.d. "Links to State Judicial Academies." http://www.nja.nic.in/round-up-on-sjas.html.

National Law School of India University. n.d. https://www.nls.ac.in/index.php?option=com_content&view=article&id=67%253Anational-institute-of-human-rights-nihr&catid=6%253Aacademic-programmes&Itemid=32.

Noddings, Nel. 1984. *Caring: A Feminine Approach to Ethics and Moral Education.* Berkeley: University of California Press.

OECD. 2010. "Tackling Inequalities in Brazil, China, India and South Africa." Paris: Organisation of Economic Co-operation and Development.

Panda, Pranati. 2010. "Responsiveness of Teacher Education Curriculum Towards Human Rights Education in India." http://www.hurights.or.jp/archives/human_rights_education_in_asian_schools/section2/2005/03/responsiveness-of-teacher-education-curriculum-towards-human-rights-education-in-india.html.

Ramirez, Francisco, David Suárez, and John Meyer. 2007. "The Worldwide Rise of Human Rights Education." In Aaron Benavot, Cecilia Braslavsky, and Nhung Truong, eds., *School Knowledge in Comparative and Historical Perspective* (pp. 35–52). Hong Kong: Springer.

Robert, Keohane. 1984. *After Hegemony: Cooperation and Discord in the World Political Economy.* Princeton, NJ: Princeton University, 20.

Suarez, David. 2007. "Education Professionals and the Construction of Human Rights Education." *Comparative Education Review* 52:48–70.

Tyack, David, and Larry Cuban. 1997. *Tinkering Toward Utopia: A Century of Public School Reform.* Cambridge, MA: Harvard University Press.

UNDP. 2009. "India Situation Analysis: Are the MDGs Attainable?" New Delhi: United Nations Development Programme.

UNICEF. 2010. "India: Education." http://www.unicef.org/india/education.html.

Wahl, R. 2014. "Justice, Context, and Violence: How Police Explain Torture." *Law and Society Review* 48(4):807–836.

Wahl, R. 2017. *Just Violence: Torture and Human Rights in the Eyes of the Police.* Stanford, CA: Stanford University Press.

Wendt, Alexander. 1995. "Constructing International Politics." *International Security* 20(1): 71–81.

World Bank. 2010. "India Economic Update." Washington, DC: World Bank.

CHAPTER 7

Politics, Power, and Protest: Rights-Based Education Policy and the Limits of Human Rights Education

Sam Mejias

Introduction

Just after 8:00 A.M. on a cold winter morning, outside the gates of Bucking-ham High School in south London, over four hundred students assembled on the street, intending to strike during school hours to protest a perceived in-justice. They aimed their ire at the school's Senior Leadership Team, chal-lenging what they believed was the unfair firing of a popular teacher. Some students walked around the interior and exterior of the school, while others sat down together in the parking lot, obstructing incoming car traffic. Students filmed events outside the school using mobile phones and cameras, focusing on the gathering police presence and describing events on the ground, later uploading their videos to YouTube. A small group of Year 11 students de-manded to see the head teacher to request the reinstatement of the beloved teacher. In just under an hour the number of protestors had increased, as students entered the school and marched through the halls encouraging their fellow students to leave their classes and join in the protest. They chanted the aggrieved teacher's name over and over: "Kohli! Kohli! Kohli!"

The protesting students were organized and media savvy, calling the BBC, a local newspaper, the *Guardian* national newspaper, and even the

UK's national education inspection agency Ofsted (Office for Standards in Education) during the protest to alert them to their actions. Prior to the day's events, the students had organized themselves through Facebook. These students were beneficiaries of significant changes in school policies over the previous several years that had instilled in them a conviction that they had a legitimate voice, and were entitled to have a say in how their school was run. Their actions were based on a simple thought: if we protest, then we can change what has happened to one teacher and correct an injustice.

Their goals were laudable, except for the inconvenient fact that the students had been misinformed and misled into supporting a teacher guilty of gross misconduct toward a student.

Meanwhile, the school's Senior Leadership Team, faced with hundreds of students peacefully protesting, closed the school for health and safety reasons. Only eighteen months earlier, Buckingham had entered into partnership with Amnesty International, with the utopian goal of instilling a human rights ethos across the school, and now faced a revolution of teachers and students fighting for social justice that would eventually tear the school apart. Two months after the protest, a key senior leader was forced to resign in disgrace, the accused teacher was reinstated despite being found guilty by an independent commission, and the school had abandoned its partnership with Amnesty International and the rights-based ethos it had championed. The outcomes of the two-year Amnesty partnership appeared to have had the opposite of the intended effect of making the school more harmonious and human rights–friendly.

In 2009, Buckingham signed an agreement with Amnesty International to participate in a two-year pilot of the Human Rights Friendly Schools (HRFS) project, the organization's ambitious attempt to create a global model for rights-based education policy. Amnesty began the pilot in fourteen secondary schools in fourteen countries, and in 2011 expanded the project to seventy countries. This chapter presents data from a study of the piloting of HRFS at Buckingham, in an attempt to make sense of how the project simultaneously influenced and became affected by dramatic events within the school. The study this chapter is based on explored how Amnesty and Buckingham envisioned and enacted whole-school human rights education (HRE), examining the influence of rights-based approaches to school development in a neoliberal age, and elucidating how the micropolitical relationships between teachers, administrators, and students at Buckingham not only influenced the implementation of HRFS, but also were themselves influenced by the human rights discourse of the project in a negatively dialectical relationship.

The Whole-School Approach to Human Rights Education

Over the past decade, HRE projects promoting holistic rights–based school policies have increased in popularity, and emerging research and practice in the field has demonstrated the potential of such approaches for improving schools and for promoting human rights (Amnesty International 2012; Covell, Howe, and McNeil 2010; Hantzopoulos 2012; Mejias 2013; UNICEF UK 2008). These approaches have been championed in particular by non-governmental organizations (NGOs). Since 2000, six major NGOs[1] have developed whole-school citizenship education and HRE projects to extend rights-based pedagogy beyond the classroom and into school-wide policies and practices. The approach is rooted in the notion that human rights must be simultaneously learned and practiced throughout the school in order to be successful, and that a rights-based school ethos can lead to improved outcomes. This view has support not only in theoretical and empirical literature on HRE approaches (Bajaj 2011; Covell et al. 2010; Hantzopoulos 2012; Osler and Starkey 2010; Sebba and Robinson 2010), but also in official policies and initiatives of international and regional government organizations, notably the United Nations (UNESCO 2006) and the Council of Europe (Backman and Trafford 2007; Council of Europe 1985). The approach is consistent with international discourses on HRE since the mid-1980s that have advocated holistic approaches to teaching human rights (Council of Europe 1985; Cunningham 1991; Osler and Starkey 2005).

Amnesty International and Human Rights
Friendly Schools

Amnesty International (Amnesty) is perhaps the best-known human rights organization in the world, with global name recognition and a history of pioneering human rights advocacy and development efforts worldwide. Amnesty began in 1961 in England as an international network of campaigns to free "prisoners of conscience," and transformed itself into a global human rights watchdog with an established currency of moral authority (Hopgood 2006). Throughout its existence, Amnesty has cultivated a strong reputation for protecting and defending human rights, advocating on behalf of human rights victims and causes, and raising awareness of the importance of human rights in all societies. In the twenty-first century, the organization continues to use education as a key tool for promoting their mission. Amnesty's first coordinated global education project for secondary schools, HRFS sets an ambitious agenda for participating schools to incorporate ten core principles, developed from key international human rights instruments, into four areas of school life: governance, curriculum, extracurricular activities and school environment, and community relations (Amnesty International 2009).

Amnesty International defines a human rights friendly school as:

> a school that embraces the potential of human rights as core operating and organizing principles, [and] that fosters an environment and a community in which human rights are learned, taught, practiced, respected, defended and promoted. It is a place in which all are included and encouraged to take part, regardless of status or role, where cultural diversity is celebrated. In short, a human rights friendly school ensures that equality, dignity, respect, non-discrimination and participation are at the heart of the learning experience and present in all major areas of school life. (Amnesty International 2009:12)

This definition constructs human rights as a school-wide policy framework, emphasizing the role of human rights in the school environment and community as well as in the classroom. Inclusion and equality are particularly strong features of this definition, delineating a significant set of challenges for schools interested in employing the approach. Amnesty's definition is fundamentally idealistic and utopian; it charts a clear vision of a rights-friendly school without elaborating how schools can operationalize the vision.

Research in schools suggests that fundamental changes in school culture and operations are required in order to successfully embed rights-based policy frameworks (Carter and Osler 2000; Covell 2010). Recent research conducted by UNICEF UK on its own whole-school HRE program, the Rights Respecting Schools Award (RRSA), suggests that rights-based policy frameworks can improve schools by reducing conflicts and bullying, improving relationships among students, and creating an atmosphere more conducive to learning (Sebba and Robinson 2010).

Challenges to Rights-Based Education Policy

Although there is widespread support for various forms of HRE in schools, the political climate in which such projects operate plays a critical role in how such initiatives are received and implemented. Schools face external pressures to meet standardized state targets for attainment, which are predominantly based on a neoliberal script of market-based performance and enhanced choice as the solution for problems. Furthermore, schools are not immune to organizational politics, which can affect the enactment of education policy at the grassroots level.

Neoliberalism in Education

Since the 1980s, the influence of neoliberal perspectives on education in Western nations has increased, as U.S. and European policymakers frame educational goals using performance-related terminology, while promoting policy approaches reflecting the principles of market-based capitalism. School policies become soaked in economistic, managerial language. The decision as to where to send children to school is presented as a choice for parents to make based on performance of the school "product" (Apple 1988). These parental choice initiatives argue that schools should be accountable for improving their performance to state standards or risk losing students, and subsequently government funding (Whitty and Power 2002). Neoliberal political ideologies have produced a marketization of education systems, typified by the quasimarkets of parental choice and school autonomy, coupled with an increased focus on public accountability and government regulation (Apple 1988). The use of league tables in England and the importance of Ofsted inspections for schools demonstrate how competition and results have become the benchmarks for success, and thus for strategy. Critics of the marketization of education assert that "narrow curricula, results-driven pedagogy and the myopic tyranny of externally imposed targets" prevent schools from providing quality education for all (Fielding 2008:56). Politically mainstream, the doctrine of neoliberalism is strongly supported by mainstream political parties, and has become the dominant educational policy innovation of the past decade. Progressive and democratic education advocates have noted the ability of market-based educational discourses and practices to significantly influence how schools operate (Ball 2009).

Neoliberalism and HRE: Disjunctures and Possibilities

Scholars appear to generally view neoliberal educational policies as threatening or appropriating rights-based approaches (Apple 2004; Ball 2003; Bowring 2012; Ravitch 2011). Critics argue that a heightened emphasis on economic performance and standards undermines education by shifting discursive emphasis from curriculum and instruction to markets and choice (Ravitch 2011). Some assert that neoliberal policies produce "differential realities" that favor the privileged classes of society by reproducing traditional power structures in schools (Apple 2004; Ball 2003). Others link the development of global citizenship discourses to emerging economic globalization discourses, arguing that neoliberalism is one of several "ideological currents" in a contested discursive space around global citizenship education, where global citizenship education (and thus HRE) can help make individuals more competitive (Schattle 2008:74).

In England, school discipline and classroom behavior management are key areas of concern in formal education policy and practice (Maguire, Ball, and Braun 2010). Managing behavior has become part of the current neoliberal construction of effective education, as schools emphasize strong behavioral and disciplinary policies to make themselves more attractive to parents who wish for their children to attend "safe" schools (Maguire et al. 2010). Parental concerns about school discipline have in the past decade been justified and amplified by a growing policy literature declaring the ill effects of poor behavior on schools and arguing for improved measures for managing behavior (DCSF 2010; DFES 2003; NUT 2006; Ofsted 2005; Steer 2009). Such policy documents link improved student behavior to increased student achievement, aligning discourses of control with discourses of school improvement (Maguire et al. 2010).

There is less support in the literature for HRE as potentially cohering with neoliberal educational perspectives. However, literature on the links between human rights and public services provides a means of exploring potential intersections. Gavrielides (2008) argues that among British policymakers, implementation of the UK Human Rights Act (HRA) has stirred debate over the role of human rights in influencing the delivery of public services. He notes that human rights and the HRA are "viewed as drivers that could improve the experiences and overall satisfaction of users of health, social, prison, transportation and other public services" (Gavrielides 2008:190). The relationship between human rights and a public services discourse reliant on neoliberal managerialism highlights the intersecting and potentially complementary ways to envision HRE as contributing to neoliberal conceptions of student "customer" satisfaction.

Micropolitics and Education

Alongside neoliberal educational policy directives, *micropolitical* activity can influence policy enactment and school outcomes (Ball 1987; Blase and Anderson 1995). Micropolitics refers to the "daily interactions, negotiations and bargains" taking place within schools, driven by informal networks and communications among individuals and groups (Lindle 1999:171). Anyone affiliated with a school—including students, teachers, leaders, parents, and members of the local community—participates in micropolitical activity. Micropolitics addresses the negotiated realities of everyday life for teachers, students, and leaders, offering a foundation for examining policy enactment and organizational management practices. Micropolitics explores how both informal and formal power is used to influence actions in schools, how conflict creates competition for resources, and how people cooperate to achieve individual and collective goals.

Schools are "riven with actual or potential conflict between members" (Ball 1987:19), and thus efforts to understand how they function as organizations must interrogate the nature of political conflict. Micropolitics attends to stakeholders' use of power (through either authority or influence) to manage conflict, mobilize support, enact agendas, circumscribe behavior, and maintain discipline (Blase 1991; Hoyle 1988). It focuses on strategies of "persuasion, compromise, bargaining, and destabilization . . . the conflictive interests that swirl around schools" (Mawhinney 1999, 168). Micropolitical research aims to illuminate the hidden and unspoken interactions that occur at the social level and to explore their influence on the work and culture of schools. It is thus particularly relevant for examining the impact of a rights-based—and fundamentally political—agenda for schools.

Studies of school micropolitics have drawn direct links between effective leadership and moral influence, citing evidence showing that moral education promotes "cooperative political relationships between the principal and teachers and also among the teachers themselves" (Blase 1991:3). Exploring micropolitics in the implementation of HRFS, the study described in this chapter focused on how micropolitical activity among members of the school's Senior Leadership Team (SLT), teachers, and students directly influenced the teacher and student strikes that destabilized Buckingham School and ousted a key senior leader.

Implementing HRFS at Buckingham School

Buckingham School[2] was in many ways an ideal candidate for piloting HRFS. It had strong support from the school leadership for human rights, student voice, and international education as part of its school-wide work. Prior to partnering with Amnesty, the school had implemented initiatives aimed at fostering understanding of international issues (e.g., an annual international conference that invited students from around the world to participate, and fair trade awareness-raising campaigns in the school's cafeteria), as well as democracy and student voice (e.g., democratically elected student leadership teams and house councils providing peer mediation, and events such as an annual "democracy week"). School leaders directly linked participation in HRFS to an expansion of these existing initiatives as a way to support and integrate the project. The school had also already begun work in 2008 on a separate whole-school HRE program, UNICEF UK's Rights Respecting Schools Award. Finally, the school's demographic profile was distinctly international and culturally diverse, with 98 percent of students from minority backgrounds, and many from immigrant families from Asia, Africa, and the Middle East. The school's Somali, Sri Lankan, and Afghan students, in particular, were from war-afflicted backgrounds and areas where human rights are under threat every day. HRFS was seen as a way to progressively advance the school's agenda as a twenty-first-century cosmopolitan school.

Methodology

This chapter provides a brief overview of a doctoral study spanning two years of data collection that explored HRFS implementation in one case-study setting using qualitative methods. The data collected consisted primarily of participant observation of the school's enactment of HRFS at various points over two years; focus groups with teachers and students (including the school's democratically elected Junior Leadership Team responsible for promoting school-wide democratic policies and practices among fellow students); individual semistructured interviews with school leaders and teachers; school and NGO policy documents; and various media documents (including journalistic sources such as the *Guardian* and the BBC, along with social media sources including YouTube and Facebook). The research explored how the policy framework of HRFS interacted with existing school policies and practices, and how school stakeholders (primarily teachers and students) conceptualized and enacted HRE through a whole-school approach.

The findings describe how HRFS became woven into school life at Buckingham: through the pragmatic lens of school performance (relating primarily to improving school behavior and conforming to a neoliberal script of making the school more attractive and "competitive" vis-à-vis school inspections), and through the micropolitical interactions governing school life before, during, and after the introduction of the HRFS pilot. The findings are not meant to be generalizable or representative; rather, they offer a window into the potential complexities of whole-school HRE implementation, as experienced in a British context that was particularly supportive of school-based HRE.

Utopianism vs. Pragmatism: Conceptualizing Whole-School HRE

Data showed that conceptions of whole-school HRE operated in tension between the utopian, unchallenged ideas about the positive effects of human rights principles and practices for schools, and the pragmatic, policy-driven imperatives that shaped the actual teaching and learning practices at Buckingham.

The study found that HRE was considered a "utopian good" that elicited widespread rhetorical support and little opposition to its practice, particularly due to its close association with student voice initiatives, which have a high profile in British schools.[3] Prior to the launching of HRFS, there was a school-wide language about and understanding of overarching concepts of human rights among most students, teachers, and leaders. Students had been given several high-profile platforms for developing basic knowledge and skills about democratic participation and using their voice to express their views. Teachers interviewed recognized the potential of HRE and HRFS to improve student relationships at the school. Buckingham's existing student voice project, Buckingham Student Voice (BSV), created a favorable environment for partnership with Amnesty because school community members were all familiar with and recognized the value of a democratic, rights-based approach. HRFS was thus implemented in practice as broadly reflective of the school's existing student voice initiatives; essentially, these activities were rebranded under one larger, project-driven umbrella.

Data on the majority of participants' perspectives reflects an overwhelmingly positive framing of the potential of HRFS. However, statements of support for HRE by teachers and leaders were mediated by two forces: the pragmatic realities of "getting by" in the daily life of schools, typified by the sometimes difficult choices staff must make in order to accomplish their tasks; and dominant policy and practice regarding effective performance, accountability, and behavior that influence the talk and work of teachers and leaders in British schools. Such pragmatic realities can act as powerful motivators for justifying innovations in school policy and practice, including so-called "progressive" policies. Staff perspectives on the potential of HRFS often reflected (in some cases, literally word-for-word) official educational policy discourse on improving behavior and performance.

Regarding the influence of neoliberal perspectives on the enactment of HRFS, the emphatic promotion by school leaders of the Amnesty partnership as "value-adding" and "performance-enhancing" demonstrated how HRFS was seen as adding to an already substantial portfolio of activity designed to increase the effectiveness of Buckingham as a center for innovation and competition. School leaders conceptualized partnership with Amnesty as a value-enhancing project that would improve the school's reputation and make the school more competitive relative to other schools, cohering with the current neoliberal educational agenda in British schools. The clearest example is the school's use of Amnesty's brand and reputation as a way to demonstrate the strength of overall performance was seen during the 2010 Ofsted schools inspection. A member of the Amnesty HRFS project team was asked to participate in the inspection and encouraged by school leaders to report on the positive impact of HRFS on school performance, despite the clear lack of project-related activity or evidence of impact.

Buckingham staff also viewed HRFS as one more tool for improving outcomes and solving traditional school problems, particularly poor student behavior. Data showed that, among a number of different meanings ascribed to it, HRE was partially understood as a strategy for behavior control. The data collected offers further empirical support for the existence in England of an interpretation of rights as being explicitly linked to responsibility and ultimately behavior, confirming earlier research findings (Howe and Covell 2010; Sebba and Robinson 2010; Trivers and Starkey 2012). However, there is also evidence that school leaders conceptualized human rights as a strategy for encouraging positive working relationships between students and teachers, and between students. For example, the school's extensive work on restorative justice approaches using student juries to mediate disputes demonstrated a commitment to rights-based (rather than control-based) approaches to managing student behavior. Overall, however, the influence of neoliberal policies and pragmatic concerns (in particular concerning issues of behavior and community cohesion) on Buckingham management and teaching practices acted as a prism through which HRE efforts were interpreted and appropriated.

Implementing Human Rights Friendly Schools: Pragmatic and Piecemeal

Analysis of project implementation gathered voices from students, teachers, and particularly leaders who were the key actors in the implementation stage. From the outset of the launch of HRFS, Amnesty viewed the project operationally as a means to inform and deepen their HRE work, and strategically to provide new avenues for advancing their organizational mission. Amnesty's implementation scheme was primarily front-loaded, consisting of the establishment of structured project materials and agreements on the school's process for planning, assessing, and reporting their participation in HRFS during the first year. During the first two pilot years, their contact with the school was largely supportive (providing materials and trainings to teachers and students) and administrative (conducting and participating in assessment and steering group meetings). Overall, Amnesty used its expertise in developing HRFS to offer a significant set of inputs for Buckingham to begin implementing the project. In line with its pilot strategy to create a project model that would be sustainable without Amnesty support, the organization gave Buckingham wide latitude to implement the project as it saw fit.

Buckingham's attempts during the first two years to implement HRFS were mainly integrative and focused on students. The data showed that Buckingham school leaders and teachers implemented HRFS primarily by rebadging Buckingham Student Voice activities to fulfill HRFS requirements. This form of implementation is logical and pragmatic; Amnesty selected Buckingham to act as a pilot based on its progressive student voice initiatives, and Buckingham saw HRFS as an effective means of supporting and expanding its student voice agenda (supporting democratic structures, but also providing justification for expanding curricular hours for HRE-related subjects, notably citizenship). Perhaps because of the school's intensive work on student voice, there were significant missed opportunities to use the HRFS framework to expand the focus from student to teachers. For teachers, HRFS was seen as an initiative mainly meant for students. With few exceptions, it was not seen as something that could either improve teaching practices or improve teacher relationships with either students or the school's management.

A tension was also apparent in the relatively high visibility of rights-based work in the school and the low levels of awareness of HRFS among most students and teachers. Several key signposts conferred a high level of visibility and status to HRFS in the first pilot year. A speech by the head teacher at the school's annual international conference at the beginning of the first pilot year explicitly set out the goals of HRFS. Similarly, the school developed a "rights charter," which was developed as a result of participation in HRFS and was signed by all students and displayed outside the school's auditorium. Existing visual displays posted in and around the school encouraging students to respect each other, act responsibly toward their environment, and resolve conflict peacefully encouraged values linked with human rights principles, although some displays (e.g., the sign "Show some thought," showing a shoe stepping in gum) could just as easily be interpreted as messages of behavioral control. Finally, ongoing Buckingham Student Voice initiatives and the school-wide International Week and Democracy Day were considered important annual initiatives in the school, yet these school practices were not explicitly linked to HRFS in the school's implementation strategy. This epitomized a wider problem across the school: efforts to promote rights-based practices were disconnected from each other, and crucially, not explicitly named as rights per se or constructed as components of HRFS. Buckingham leaders and Amnesty staff missed opportunities to link the promotion of rights-based approaches to a wider utopian agenda and to unify them under a whole-school framework. Most importantly, there was little evidence that HRE was taught in any meaningful sense to members of the school community, who in interviews and focus groups displayed limited and superficial understandings of specific human rights concepts.

Rights, Micropolitics, and Collapse: The Impact of Competing Discourses

Data collected during the study showed that the micropolitical climate at Buckingham prior to the launch of HRFS played a key role in how rights-based discourses were interpreted and used. The dramatic events described at the beginning of the chapter provide vivid illustration of the power of rights discourses within schools, the critical role that leadership and governance plays in creating an atmosphere conducive to embedding rights, and the potential for HRE to empower students and teachers to take political action. Buckingham was a site of discursive tension between school-wide messages of control (evidenced by authoritarian decisions and practices) and of human rights (evidenced by Buckingham Student Voice and HRFS). The micropolitical activity contributing to and generated by this tension played a significant role in undermining HRFS and in destabilizing Buckingham, and suggests that positive micropolitical relationships among members of the school community are a critical determinant of success for whole-school HRE projects.

It is clear from interview, focus group, and documentary material data that preexisting tensions between teachers and members of the school's administrative Senior Leadership Team (SLT, composed of school leaders) played a decisive role in instigating both teacher and student strikes that seriously destabilized the school. The starting point for the unrest described in this chapter was a visit by the government's education inspectorate Ofsted, the first inspection the school had undergone since receiving a "Good" award in 2007. The outcome of that inspection, an awarding of a lower "Satisfactory" grade as compared to 2007's "Good" rating, marked Buckingham's official decline in performance. The political symbolism of performing poorly on an Ofsted inspection was amplified by the troubling nature of some of the unofficial allegations made by teachers to Ofsted inspectors concerning problems with members of the SLT.

Data from interviews and from the voices of key actors involved in the protests paint a surprisingly uniform portrait of a school in which both teachers and students reported the use of intimidating and heavy-handed tactics by a specific key school leader. Teachers spoke of living under anxious conditions. A local politician attending a teachers' union rally supporting teacher strikes at the school said:

> There is a lot of tension between staff members at the school right now. A lot of them feel as if there is a culture of fear. This is a very big issue. I have listened to the people who have gone on strike and they feel that they are being bullied.

The Ofsted inspection represented a flashpoint, not only for the macro (government) and meso (community) political implications of dropping down a score in rated performance, but for the forum it provided for school community members to speak—ironically, off the record—to Ofsted about their discontent. In an interview, the school's assistant head teacher said:

> The staff had gone behind [the SLT's] back. When we were getting feedback from Ofsted the chief inspector pulled [them] out of the office and said, "I'm not going to say this in front of everybody but I want you to know that I've had feedback from staff, that there is a climate of fear at this school." And that was never officially put down on paper. And we were in this position where we had to say, "Well I think some do feel it."

This frank discussion of the mood and atmosphere at the school by SLT members is revealing because it shows that while some SLT members were aware that teachers were questioning their leadership and authority, others were not.

Further analysis of the nature of the micropolitical relationships between members of the school community revealed that

1. deep fissures within the school around undemocratic leadership practices starkly contrasted with school-wide human rights messages, leading to accusations of hypocrisy (*discourses of control*); and
2. the existence of HRFS and popular student voice initiatives at Buckingham provided a form of symbolic and material support for students and teachers seeking justice within the school through direct collective action (*discourses of rights struggles*).

In both areas the role of HRFS was clear. HRFS provided a counter-narrative of school culture that teachers and students compared to their actual (reportedly undemocratic and authoritarian) experiences in the school. Although the extent to which HRFS directly influenced students to become politically engaged is impossible to determine, HRFS clearly provided a platform and reference point for making rights claims within the school.

The timeline of key events at Buckingham (Table 7.1) provides context for examining the intersections between HRFS and micropolitical activity. Events are in chronological order, although specific dates of each month are omitted to preserve the anonymity of subjects.

Timeline of Events

As the timeline indicates, school strikes were driven mainly by discontent with the school leadership over a series of controversial decisions. The strikes were extremely high-profile and highly political attempts to confront the school's leadership over perceived problems being caused by improper management. In the case of the teacher unions, several high-profile incidents, and what appear to be years of anecdotal evidence of tension between the SLT and teachers, fed an emerging narrative of an authoritarian and undemocratic leadership style that frayed relationships and reputations over time. Data revealed that teachers felt disempowered, mismanaged, and "bullied" (the most commonly used word to describe the SLT's actions), and a sense of resentment fed into teacher action, evidenced by key actors within the school

Table 7.1. Timeline of Events

Date/Event

May (Summer Term, Year 1)—Buckingham receives a "satisfactory" rating from their Ofsted inspection. Several teachers privately voice their dissatisfaction with the school's leadership to Ofsted inspectors, which is shared by inspectors with school leaders on an unofficial basis.

June—Teachers represented by the National Union of Teachers (NUT) forward a letter of complaint to Amnesty's UK section, outlining some of their grievances with the SLT and making the specific point that Buckingham, ostensibly meant to be working toward becoming human rights–friendly, is not a place where their rights are being respected.

July—Teachers send a petition of complaint to the school's board of governors, signed by seventy-six staff members.

Summer—The SLT makes the controversial decision to close one of the school's canteens to save money, resulting in some staff having to work longer mornings and some classes having to be covered by nonspecialists. In a letter to parents justifying these actions, an SLT key senior leader explains: "This change has been one of the best changes we have ever made. Unfortunately, a few staff are against this change. As a result I have to inform you that about 30% of staff voted to take strike action. I have told them that their actions are selfish and irresponsible."

August (Autumn Term, Year 2)—A deputy head reports to a key senior leader in the SLT that two students asked him questions about a recently fired science teacher, claiming that the head of the science department, Mr. Kohli, informed them that the SLT "forced him to resign." Mr. Kohli has taught at Buckingham for twenty-eight years and is also the school's current National Union of Teachers (NUT) representative.

September—A key senior leader launches a disciplinary investigation into the alleged comments made by Mr. Kohli to students, appointing the assistant head to lead the investigation. The assistant head questions the two students, who confirm Mr. Kohli's statements to them, alleging SLT impropriety in the firing of the teacher.

October—The disciplinary investigation into Mr. Kohli's actions is dismissed by the head of governors on a technicality. The assistant head leading the investigation had failed to adhere to updated disciplinary guidelines, which required informing students that they were answering questions as part of an investigation, and also informing the students' parents.

November—In response to complaints from teacher unions, school governors and the SLT issue a joint statement rejecting accusations of bullying and mismanagement.

November—The local NUT and the Association of Teachers and Lecturers (ATL) chapters announce that they will strike over what they allege as "mismanagement and bullying" by the SLT.

November—A key senior leader sends a letter to parents explaining management's views on the proposed strike.

(*continued*)

Table 7.1. Timeline of Events (Continued)

Date/Event

November—The local paper publishes a letter expressing opposition to the head, signed by twenty-five former pupils.

December—Unions and staff circulate leaflet explaining their views.

December—The local NUT chapter convenes a public meeting at a local community center to explain the union's decision to strike to parents. A local councilor and a local MP attend.

December—NUT walks out of Advisory, Conciliation and Arbitration Service (ACAS)–mediated negotiations with the SLT at 3:00 p.m., intending to strike the next day. A key senior leader claims that the SLT had already agreed to all of the union's demands.

December—A key senior leader sends a letter to the parents informing them that the school has a "minor and troubling element of rogue teachers preventing a democratic outcome," and reiterates the SLT's position of wanting to negotiate with the unions.

December—Members of NUT and ATL conduct the first-ever teacher strike in Buckingham's history, creating a picket line outside the school. The SLT chooses to partially close Buckingham. Ninety students who are meant to take exams are allowed to attend school. The school's remaining 1,200 students are unable to attend school. Eighty-seven out of a total of 178 staff go on strike. Union members hold a rally afterward at a nearby restaurant. The area ward councilor speaks in support of the striking teachers. A parent reports being barred from attending the meeting despite the ward councilor's invitation at the request of parents.

December—NUT, ATL, and Buckingham's SLT conduct further ACAS-mediated negotiations. It is agreed that they will continue talks later in December.

December—A parent lodges a complaint with the SLT about a staff member who inappropriately dealt with their daughter, a fifteen-year-old female student. The staff member in question is Mr. Kohli. The SLT is now faced with launching a new investigation against the same teacher whose last investigation was dismissed. This allegation is more serious, suggesting that he physically (violently pushed) and verbally abused (shouted at) a student.

January (Winter Term, Year 2)—The local newspaper reports that progress has been made in ACAS-led negotiations. The SLT confirms its support for the agreement reached during the negotiations, and the NUT spokesperson also issues a positive statement announcing victory.

February—Evidence collected by the assistant head as part of a second, separate investigation against Mr. Kohli is brought before a three-member committee of the board of governors. Based on the evidence presented, all three governors agree that Mr. Kohli is guilty. Two governors vote to fire Mr. Kohli with immediate effect. Mr. Kohli is fired.

(continued)

Table 7.1. Timeline of Events

Date/Event

February—Students, encouraged by fellow teachers, stage a sit-in strike and protest at the school. Approximately 70 percent of the students arrive at school on time on the day of the strikes. None of the Year 11 students arrive. At 8:10 A.M., 250 students appear outside the school gate and proceed to enter the school together, chanting "Kohli! Kohli! Kohli!" The protest continues until 3:30 P.M. Police arrive and attempt to contain students in certain areas. A key senior leader intentionally triggers the fire alarm to force students to leave the school, which succeeds in removing 60 percent of students.

February—Year 10 and 11 students amass over 1,000 signatures (including parents) on their petition to reinstate Mr. Kohli. Students gather in a local park to prepare to march on the school in further protest.

February—NUT announces a two-day strike to be held the following week, citing the SLT's failure to abide by the ACAS agreement, specifically highlighting the firing of Mr. Kohli.

February—The local authority intervenes. A spokeswoman announces that the local council has requested a meeting with the SLT and the chair of the governing body.

February—Over 400 parents from the school convene an afternoon meeting to discuss the situation at the school.

February—The proposed NUT two-day strike is called off after a key senior leader enters an "agreed leave of absence."

February—Following the departure of the key senior leader, the chair of governors commissions an independent report into the incidents surrounding Kohli's dismissal.

March—The school's board of governors is replaced with a new set of governors, who overturn the decision to fire Mr. Kohli at an emergency governors meeting appealing the decision. Although the decision to fire Mr. Kohli is overturned, the board of governors conclude that the evidence proved his guilt and that he would receive a letter of written warning.

March—The key senior leader on leave submits his resignation.

---

who used the teacher unions to engage in direct political action against the SLT. This push for teachers' rights in the school may have involved collusive action by teachers to encourage students to strike on their behalf.

Ultimately, conflicting discourses of authoritarian control and rights played a key role in destabilizing Buckingham. The existing school culture was recognized by teachers, students, Ofsted inspectors, and even in the media as being driven by a powerful, unpopular, and authoritarian leader. In a climate described by various school community members in largely negative terms, HRFS was viewed as hypocritical and focused exclusively on students to the detriment of the staff. This demonstrates how student voice and rights-based initiatives can sometimes become a destabilizing force within schools. Nonetheless, HRFS provided political tools for students to draw on that might not have been available otherwise, which may have impacted the choices students made about their political behaviors.

The study found that in Buckingham School, the micropolitical context—namely, the prevailing feeling within the school that the SLT's authority and power was mismanaged and/or contributing to poor teacher and student morale—played a significant role in the way in which rights discourses were interpreted by school community members. Amnesty's presence—and HRFS—played a clear role in the movement for change and justice at Buckingham. Teachers and the National Union of Teachers (NUT) appealed to the moral authority of Amnesty in writing to inform them that this was not a human rights–friendly school. Students drew on Amnesty's organizational presence at and relationship with Buckingham, seeking their advice and support when conducting their strikes.

What is harder to discern is the extent to which strikes were either student-driven or influenced by teachers. It is clear is that teachers shared information about Mr. Kohli's firing with students before it was made public. Questions remain as to why students chose to protest: while it was publicly clear during the strikes that students acted because they supported a teacher who they felt was being treated unfairly, there was also clear indication that students were encouraged by teachers who themselves had strong links to the teachers' unions and a far-left socialist political party.[4] The possible manipulation of student voice by teachers shows the power of micropolitical activity to misdirect rights learning opportunities toward agendas of self-interest.

Discussion: On the Neoliberal and the Micropolitical

At Buckingham, existing relationships among students, teachers, and leaders played a vital role in influencing the manner in which democratic and rights-based discourses were interpreted and implemented. The evidence showed that while whole-school HRE helped to politicize unjust and problematic relationships of power, these very same problematic relationships prevented the establishment of authentic foundations for whole-school HRE and engendered accusations of hypocrisy. Although the vision and direction of Buckingham's leadership enabled establishment of HRFS in the first place, commitment to progressive and rights-based visions were unsuccessful in an educational climate where rights were perceived to be violated, particularly by leaders. In particular, the symbolic construction of control through undemocratic and reactive practices—suspending entire year groups, suspending individual students for simply saying a fired teacher's name, and publicly arresting students in school assemblies, to name a few actual examples of practices that occurred at the school—sharply conflicted with the articulation of school-wide rights messages and critically undermined the potential for rights-based policy approaches to succeed.

A pressing challenge for the promotion of rights-based education in schools concerns the intersections and divergences between HRE discourses, and neoliberal and behavior management discourses in education. The study identified a clear tension between notions of HRE for empowerment (utopianism) versus HRE for school improvement and control (neoliberalism). The findings amplify existing evidence that education in England is strongly influenced by neoliberal government policies, which shape the priorities and language of school leaders (Ball 2012; Camicia and Franklin 2011; Olssen 2004). This agenda places significant strain on teachers and leaders by demanding that schools do more with less, and by asserting the need for schools to *control* students in order to get results. Competition, performance, and accountability have become guiding principles of school policy, and government accountability protocols such as Ofsted inspections, despite their extremely limited and decontextualized examinations of individual school life and performance, are major events by which the school is measured in the public eye. Politicians and policymakers inform parents that they are consumers who should demand a better product, and are encouraged to rely on Ofsted inspections and school ranking systems to inform decisions about where to send their children to school. As a result of widespread rhetorical support for neoliberal views on the importance of parental choice in education, making schools attractive to parents has become a condition for the survival of those schools. As government policies and high-stakes inspections have emphasized the importance of discipline in creating effective schools, behavior management is also a key feature of the increasing marketization of schools (Maguire et al. 2010). Research at Buckingham showed how the current neoliberal educational landscape in England has influenced how rights-based education approaches were interpreted and implemented.

This supports previous empirical assertions about the dominance of neoliberal over democratic discourses in education (Camicia and Franklin 2011).

It is possible that neoliberal discourses of "improved performance" and "added value" can potentially be used to make stronger policy arguments for implementing rights-based frameworks for school development assisted through external organizational collaboration. In exploring the interactions between neoliberal and human rights perspectives in education, I discussed how key actors within school systems use neoliberal frames in everyday practice as a response to state policy mandates that stress market-based approaches to education. I suggest that the idea of "improved performance" can act as a bridge between neoliberal imperatives placed on schools by the state and rights-based solutions for the challenges schools face (such as attainment, addressing cultural diversity, and dealing with violence in schools). Yet this construction of HRE as potentially cohering with the neoliberalization of education is challenged by theoretical and empirical arguments about the reproduction and exacerbation of class, race, and gender inequality caused by such educational policies (Apple 2001). More worryingly, findings from the study suggest that the discursive construction of behavior and control in schools as a way of improving performance and accountability can severely restrict schools' effectiveness in promoting human rights. This then poses a larger, more salient question as to how HRE can either align with or further challenge the neoliberal approach.

Micropolitical analysis of Buckingham demonstrated how authoritarian management practices undermined attempts at promoting human rights. Notwithstanding the unique events surrounding Buckingham, attempts to implement utopian projects for democratizing school management around shared rights values will always be situated in the context of a traditionally hierarchical and authoritarian school structure, and thus subjected to struggle. Attempts by schools to introduce actions aimed at giving students and/or teachers more power, or to introduce greater choice as a function of democratizing the school's work, are set against this context. Unsurprisingly, leadership plays a vital role in facilitating or undermining democratic approaches. Partnership with explicitly political organizations such as Amnesty, on the other hand, may have unintended consequences. At Buckingham, the existence of HRFS and the Amnesty partnership provided a clear outlet for students and teachers seeking justice through direct collective action. Their engagement of Amnesty during political struggles against school leaders reflected an understanding of Amnesty's reputation for protecting and fighting for the rights of others. This shows that students and teachers were able to conceptualize HRE not only in terms of improving schools, but also in terms of the role it plays in struggles for justice.

Micropolitical analysis of school community relations provides an effective means of gauging potential challenges to rights-based approaches and understanding the limits of HRE. Schools' internal dynamics, closed micropolitical relationships, and tendencies toward prioritizing pragmatism can also potentially disadvantage the possibilities of successful implementation of whole-school HRE.

At Buckingham, there was a clear tension between, on the one hand, notions of human rights as a response to micropolitical discontent, and on the other hand, the forms of HRE taught through HRFS. HRE was seen by leaders and teachers as a way to encourage better behavior and even conformity through the linking of rights to responsibilities. HRE was interpreted as bestowing on students certain rights, *provided* they undertook the responsibility of behaving in a manner that would earn those rights. Most of all, HRE was seen as a utopian good mainly intended for students. Human rights, on the other hand, were conceptualized differently by teachers and students in response to micropolitical activity, and put into action through the strikes at the school that clearly violated school rules. In this sense *human rights* were seen as supportive of liberation struggles, incompatible with self-discipline and rights-respecting behavior, and primarily reliant on conflict in order to secure rights claims. *HRE*, on the other hand, was seen as something apolitical for students that encouraged their democratic participation and taught them the value of being responsible toward each other. This binary of HR for struggle (influenced by micropolitics) and HRE for control (influenced by neoliberalism) merits further investigation.

Notes

1. Amnesty, ActionAid, Oxfam, Plan, the British Institute of Human Rights, and UNICEF UK.

2. Pseudonyms have been used for all places and people discussed.

3. Student voice and HRE have all received support in England's education system through the country's mandatory national citizenship curriculum, which teaches students about local, national, and global citizenship. Claims as to how "citizenship" should be taught in the UK are still subject to politicization; for example, after the Tories assumed power in 2010, newly installed education ministers began consultation

on and revision of the citizenship curriculum, which included removing references to human rights as a component of citizenship. Recent changes have shifted curricular focus from human rights to, more broadly, the rule of law.

4. The UK's Socialist Workers Party, based on Marxist political principles.

References

Amnesty International. 2009. *Guidelines for Human Rights Friendly Schools*. London: Amnesty International—International Secretariat.

Amnesty International. 2012. *Becoming a Human Rights Friendly School: A Guide for Schools Around the World*. London: Amnesty International.

Apple, Michael W. 1988. "Economics and Inequality in Schools." *Theory into Practice* 27(4):282–287.

Apple, Michael W. 2001. "Comparing Neo-Liberal Projects and Inequality in Education." *Comparative Education* 37(4):409–423.

Apple, Michael W. 2004. "Creating Difference: Neo-Liberalism, Neo-Conservatism and the Politics of Educational Reform." *Educational Policy* 18(12):12–44.

Backman, Elisabeth, and Bernard Trafford. 2007. *Democratic Governance of Schools*. Strasbourg: Council of Europe.

Bajaj, Monisha. 2011. "Human Rights Education: Ideology, Location, and Approaches." *Human Rights Quarterly* 33:481–508.

Ball, Stephen J. 1987. *The Micro-Politics of the School: Towards a Theory of School Organization*. London: Methuen.

Ball, Stephen J. 2003. *Class Strategies and the Education Market: The Middle Classes and Social Advantage*. London: Routledge Falmer.

Ball, Stephen J. 2009. "Privatising Education, Privatising Education Policy, Privatising Educational Research: Network Governance and the 'Competition State.'" *Journal of Education Policy* 24(1):83–99.

Ball, Stephen J. 2012. "Performativity, Commodification and Commitment: An I-Spy Guide to the Neoliberal University." *British Journal of Educational Studies* 60(1):17–28.

Blase, Joseph, ed. 1991. *The Politics of Life in Schools: Power, Conflict, and Cooperation*. Newbury Park, CA: Sage.

Blase, Joseph, and Gary L. Anderson. 1995. *The Micropolitics of Educational Leadership: From Control to Empowerment*. Teacher Development Series, Andy Hargreaves, ed. London: Cassell.

Bowring, Bill. 2012. "Human Rights and Public Education." *Cambridge Journal of Education* 42(1):53–65.

Camicia, Steven P., and Barry M. Franklin. 2011. "What Type of Global Community and Citizenship? Tangled Discourses of Neoliberalism and Critical Democracy in Curriculum and Its Reform." *Globalisation, Societies and Education* 9(3–4):311–322.

Carter, C., and A. Osler. 2000. "Human Rights, Identities and Conflict Management: A Study of School Culture as Experienced Through Classroom Relationships." *Cambridge Journal of Education* 30(3):335–356.

Council of Europe. 1985. *Recommendation No. R(85)7 of the Committee of Ministers to Members States on Teaching and Learning About Human Rights in Schools*. Strasbourg: Council of Europe.

Covell, Katherine. 2010. "School Engagement and Rights-Respecting Schools." *Cambridge Journal of Education* 40(1):39–51.

Covell, Katherine, R., Brian Howe, and Justin K. McNeil. 2010. "Implementing Children's Human Rights Education in Schools." *Improving Schools* 13(2): 117–132.

Cunningham, Jeremy. 1991. "The Human Rights Secondary School." In H. Starkey, ed., *The Challenge of Human Rights Education* (pp. 90–104). London: Cassell.

DCSF. 2010. "School Discipline and Pupil-Behaviour Policies—Guidance for Schools." London: Department for Children, Schools and Families.

DFES. 2003. "Advice on Whole School Behaviour and Attendance Policy: Key Stage 3 National Strategy." London: Department for Education and Skills.

Fielding, Michael. 2008. "Personalisation, Education and the Market." *Soundings* 38:56–69.

Gavrielides, Theo. 2008. "Human Rights and Customer Satisfaction with Public Services: A Relationship Discovered." *International Journal of Human Rights* 12(2):189–204.

Hantzopoulos, Maria. 2012. "Considering Human Rights Education as U.S. Public School Reform." *Peace Review* 24(1):36–45.

Hopgood, Stephen. 2006. *Keepers of the Flame: Understanding Amnesty International*. Ithaca, NY: Cornell University Press.

Howe, R. Brian, and Katherine Covell. 2010. "Miseducating Children About Their Rights." *Education, Citizenship and Social Justice* 5(2):91–102.

Hoyle, Eric. 1988. "Micropolitics of Educational Organisations." In Adam Westoby, ed., *Culture and Power in Educational Organisations* (pp. 255–269). Milton Keynes, UK: Open University Press.

Lindle, Jane C. 1999. "What Can the Study of Micropolitics Contribute to the Practice of Leadership in Reforming Schools?" *School Leadership and Management* 19(2):171–178.

Maguire, Meg, Stephen Ball, and Annette Braun. 2010. "Behaviour, Classroom Management and Student 'Control': Enacting Policy in the English Secondary School." *International Studies in Sociology of Education* 20(2):153–170.

Mawhinney, Hanne B. 1999. "Reappraisal: The Problems and Prospects of Studying the Micropolitics of Leadership in Reforming Schools." *School Leadership and Management* 19(2):159–170.

Mejias, Samuel A. 2013. "NGOs and Human Rights Education in the Neoliberal Age: A Case Study of an NGO-Secondary School Partnership in London." Institute of Education, University of London.

NUT. 2006. "Learning to Behave: A Charter for Schools." London: National Union of Teachers.

Ofsted. 2005. "Managing Challenging Behaviour." London: Ofsted.

Olssen, Mark. 2004. "Neoliberalism, Globalisation, Democracy: Challenges for Education." *Globalisation, Societies and Education* 2(2):231–275.

Osler, A., and H. Starkey. 2005. *Changing Citizenship: Democracy and Inclusion in Education.* Maidenhead: Open University Press.

Osler, A., and H. Starkey. 2010. *Teachers and Human Rights Education.* Stoke-on-Trent: Trentham.

Ravitch, Diane. 2011. *The Death and Life of the Great American School System: How Testing and Choice Are Undermining Education.* New York: Basic Books.

Schattle, Hans. 2008. "Education for Global Citizenship: Illustrations of Ideological Pluralism and Adaptation." *Journal of Political Ideologies* 13(1):73–94.

Sebba, Judy, and Carol Robinson. 2010. *Evaluation of UNICEF UK's Rights Respecting Schools Award: Final Report, September 2010.* Sussex: Universities of Sussex and Brighton.

Steer, A. 2009. "Learning Behaviour: Lessons Learned. A Review of Behaviour Standards and Practices in Our Schools." Nottingham: Department of Children, Schools and Families.

Trivers, H., and H. Starkey. 2012. "The Politics of Critical Citizenship Education: Human Rights for Conformity or Emancipation?" In Richard C. Mitchell and Shannon A. Moore, eds., *Politics, Participation and Power Relations* (pp. 137–151). Rotterdam: Sense Publishers.

UNESCO. 2006. *Plan of Action: World Programme for Human Rights Education, First Phase.* Paris: UNESCO.

UNICEF UK. 2008. "UNICEF UK Rights Respecting Schools in England." London: UNICEF UK.

Whitty, Geoff, and Sally Power. 2002. "The School, the State and the Market: The Research Evidence Updated." *Curriculo sem Fronterias* 2(1):i–xxiii.

CHAPTER 8

Contentious Human Rights Education: The Case of Professional Development Programs on Sexual Orientation and Gender Identity– Based Refugee Protection

Oren Pizmony-Levy and Megan Jensen

Introduction

Over the past decade, the cause of individuals who seek international protection from persecution based on their sexual orientation and gender identity (SOGI) has been advanced by national and transnational organizations. International documents such as the 1951 Geneva Convention Relating to the Status of Refugees and the 1967 New York Protocol Relating to the Status of Refugees define a refugee as any person who

> as a result of events . . . and owing to well-founded fear of being persecuted for reasons of race, religion, nationality, *membership of a particular social group* or political opinion, is outside the country of his nationality and is unable or, owing to such fear, is unwilling to avail himself of the protection of that country. (Article I, 1951 Geneva Convention; emphasis added)

Notably, this definition does not explicitly designate SOGI as a legitimate claim for asylum.

Starting in the 1990s, contemporary interpretations of these documents began to expand the definition of a refugee and treat SOGI as a case of "membership of a particular social group" (Fullerton, 1993). By 2008, this cause had gained enough momentum that the UN High Commissioner for Refugees (UNHCR) published its *Guidance Note on Refugee Claims Relating to Sexual Orientation and Gender Identity*.[1] In 2010, the UNHCR began hosting international meetings to further develop legal and operational guidance on the issue of persecution based on SOGI.

To date, scholarship on asylum claims related to SOGI has focused on socio-legal analysis of cases and the ways in which governments and legal systems (courts) worldwide have engaged with the issue (e.g., Berg and Millbank 2009; Dauvergne and Millbank 2003; Morgan 2006; Ponce 2012; Swink 2006). David Frank (2012) examined developments in the global institutional context that led to the emergence of an international discourse on SOGI-based refugee protection. He argues that three interrelated developments—the globalization of society; the individualization of society that legitimized lesbian, gay, bisexual, transgender, intersex and/or queer (LGBTIQ) individuals; and the rise of the global human rights regime—enabled this international discourse to emerge.

Importantly, Frank (2012) argues that the emergence of the international discourse on SOGI-based refugee protection exists because societies vary intensely in their approaches toward nonconforming SOGI and LGBTIQ individuals. Indeed, as we write this chapter, more than eighty countries maintain laws deeming same-sex consensual relations between adults a criminal offense, and same-sex marriages are fully legalized in just seventeen countries (International Lesbian, Gay, Bisexual, Trans and Intersex Association 2013). Public opinion research also suggests that, although there has been a general shift toward greater acceptance of homosexuality, this trend varies across countries. For example, acceptance of homosexuality is more prevalent in high-income countries, Judeo-Christian cultures, less religious populations, and countries that have enacted gay rights legislation (Pew Research Center 2013; Smith, Son, and Kim 2014).

Scholars have given little attention to the work of local actors—staff in UNHCR offices, nongovernmental organizations (NGOs), and governmental agencies—who engage with this international discourse in their work. Researchers who conducted a global survey of leaders of NGOs servicing refugees and asylum seekers found significant gaps in attitudes toward individuals seeking refuge due to their SOGI status between NGOs located in high-income countries and those located in low-income countries (Pizmony-Levy and McManus 2012; McManus and Pizmony-Levy 2012). A key question thus emerges: How do frontline workers learn about and engage with this contentious international discourse?

In this chapter, we examine one professional development (PD) workshop offered by the Organization for Refuge, Asylum, and Migration (ORAM), an international NGO, which is intended to professionalize frontline work around protection from SOGI-based persecution. The workshop was implemented in eight countries, most of them considered to be hostile environments for LGBTIQ individuals. This is not an evaluation study, but rather a "window" into human rights education (HRE). Following Tibbitts (2002), we posit that ORAM's workshop is a case of the Accountability Model of HRE, as participants were already "associated with the guarantee of human rights through their professional roles" (165) (see also Chapter 3 in this book).

We make three contributions to the growing field of HRE by exploring trainees' experiences in ORAM's workshop. First, while most HRE research is conducted in the formal education system (at the primary, secondary, and recently tertiary levels), this study focuses on teaching and learning in the nonformal education system (on "on-the-job" training). Second, and related, while the target population in most HRE research includes young participants, the target population in this study consists of adults age twenty-one and over. Third, this study addresses the surprising lacuna in HRE scholarship regarding nonconforming SOGI and LGBTIQ individuals. A review of the literature points to a very small number of publications examining this issue—for example, the Human Rights Education Associates (2003) study guide titled "Sexual Orientation and Human Rights."

In addition, we contribute to the broad scholarship in comparative and international education by looking at the dissemination process of an international discourse or global script to local actors (Wahl 2014). Scholars have long argued that local actors make discourses and scripts into reality (e.g., Anderson-Levitt 2003). This study shed light on one mechanism—short-term PD—that aims to align local actors with an emerging international discourse or global script on SOGI-based refugee protection.

The chapter continues as follows: The next section will situate the case of PD on SOGI-based persecution within the broad literature on HRE, and will outline key challenges in the implementation of HRE. Next, we will present background information about ORAM's workshop, data, and methods. Then we will offer the results from mixed-methods analysis. After discussion of the results and the limitations of this study, we will make suggestions for further research.

Background: Situating Professional Development on SOGI-Based Persecution Within HRE

Over the past two decades, HRE has grown in authority among departments of education, educational nonprofits, human rights groups, educators, and intergovernmental and regional agencies (see Chapter 1 by Russell and Suárez in this book). HRE is viewed as an important means through which students and professionals can move beyond simply valuing and respecting others' rights to actually advocating for the guarantee of those rights (Tibbitts 2002). This becomes particularly important when considering the work of professionals in the refugee field, as they hold a responsibility to assess refugee claims of persecution and advocate for the protection of those rights that have been violated. Scholars argue that developing a greater familiarity with human rights will lead professionals to more openly or strongly "believe in upholding rights" and become "committed to upholding the rights of others" (Kinderman and Butler 2006; Redman et al. 2012). To first build that familiarity with rights, HRE focuses on developing skills within the individual. These skills include recognizing one's own biases, accepting differences, taking responsibility for defending the rights of others, and mediation and conflict resolution (Flowers 2000; Tibbitts 2002).

Scholars have identified various approaches to and models of HRE, with some distinguishing between an "activist approach" and a "psycho-educational approach" (Flowers 2000; Kinderman and Butler 2006; Redman et al. 2012). Tibbitts (2002) expands on these approaches to develop three models of HRE: the Values and Awareness Model, the Accountability Model, and the Transformation Model (discussed at length in Chapter 3). We will use the Accountability Model in this study, as that model takes a political/legal approach to human rights, and is commonly used with professionals who are directly or indirectly "associated with the guarantee of human rights through their professional roles" (Tibbitts 2002:165). Those professional responsibilities involve either "(a) directly monitoring human rights violations and advocating with the necessary authorities; or (b) taking special care to protect the rights of people (especially vulnerable populations) for which they have some responsibility" (165). It is important to note that personal change is not an explicit goal within the Accountability Model, since it assumes that a participant's professional responsibility is "sufficient for him or her to have an interest in applying a human rights framework" to his/her work. Instead, the model endeavors to create structural and legal "norms and practices related to human rights" (Tibbitts 2002:165).

Challenges of HRE Training with Professionals

General Challenges

Several general challenges to incorporating a human rights–based approach to PD are noted in the literature (Celermajer and Grewal 2013; Redman et al. 2012; Teleki 2007). A primary concern with HRE training remains on building local relevancy of the content shared. If participants do not view the content as ultimately transferable to their work, they may not link the human rights concerns presented with their work contexts. An additional concern lies in the use of active and participatory learning strategies such as technology/ multiple modalities, interactive exercises, and engagement of critical thinking skills. While these have a significant impact on adult learning, many HRE trainings "report difficulty in balancing a range of teaching methodologies and resources" (Teleki 2007:13). Finally, programs must utilize trainers who are both familiar with human rights content and able to apply that content to the local context to build relevancy and application of skills learned.

Celermajer and Grewal (2013) note several of these challenges in their study on HRE trainings on the prevention of torture in Nepalese and Sri Lankan security sectors. The authors note that, while there was "an assumption that training can contribute to enhancing adherence by security personnel to human rights principles" (243), the training's standardized approach raised doubts about how content was understood and incorporated into local contexts. The authors also question how the training actually impacts the views and behaviors it seeks to target among participants, noting that "more attention must be paid to the lived realities" of the participants to identify how their views may impact their senses of professional responsibility to apply the content learned at these trainings (243).

Redman et al. (2012) similarly target the need to be aware of and acknowledge participants' existing views in HRE trainings. In their look at HRE training for UK-based medical staff working with patients with learning disabilities, the authors note that staff should not feel "'railroaded' into change"; rather, they should be guided to see how a human rights–based approach can foster "service improvements" in their workplaces (82). To avoid participants' ambivalence toward the training or the overall approach of human rights, the authors recommend allowing participants opportunities to "share their experiences and practice and retain a sense of congruence with their own thoughts and beliefs" throughout the training (82). This recommendation is consistent with Rose and Holmes' (1991) suggestion that creating an environment in which participants can increase their knowledge while openly expressing their own views may enable greater attitudinal change among participants.

LGBTIQ-Specific Challenges

While there is limited literature on the challenges of using HRE training with professionals working with LGBTIQ refugees, established fields such as social work, education, and psychology yield insights into incorporating LGBTIQ-specific content into PD and training programs (e.g., Murphy 1992; Sears 1992; Van Den Bergh and Crisp 2004). This literature often notes how participants' existing beliefs and attitudes toward nonconforming SOGI may present a challenge to the teaching and implementation of human rights–based approaches to working with LGBTIQ individuals.

In studying educators' and school counselors' personal beliefs about homosexuality, Sears (1992) noted how their attitudes were actualized in school settings with adolescent students. While the counselors and teachers often expressed that "they should be more proactive and supportive as professionals committed to the welfare of all of their students," high levels of personal prejudice, ignorance, and fear toward LGBTIQ topics rendered that professional support limited, if not negligible, in their actual work settings (29). Trainings on working with LGBTIQ individuals—regardless of context—must consider how participants' attitudes toward nonconforming SOGI influence their willingness to be open to the content matter, and then to applying the skills learned in their workplaces. As human rights for

LGBTIQ individuals may not be explicitly valued or seen as integral to human rights enterprises in many countries, an HRE model may provide a framework in which participants' views are acknowledged in ways that allow those participants to engage more directly with the notion of LGBTIQ rights.

Murphy (1992) finds a similar challenge in addressing professionals' attitudes while training them to work with LGBTIQ persons. In her study of mental health workers' education on LGBTIQ topics, she urges training programs to directly address "the interaction between the attitudes, feelings, and sexual orientation of the clinician and of the client" (229). Ideally, she envisions trainings that encourage participants to "explore their degree of comfort with their own sexual orientation, and the ways in which their attitudes and beliefs about gay men and lesbian women interact with those of their clients" (240). More recently, Van Den Bergh and Crisp (2004) have applied the notion of culturally competent practice to social work with LGBTIQ clients, also asserting the need for professional training to address participant attitudes when working with sexual minorities.

While this literature indicates a clear need for participants to build self-awareness of their attitudes toward SOGI in order to more mindfully apply the skills learned to their work with LGBTIQ clients, implementing such direct discussion about sexualities—and about participants' own sexualities—may yield the hesitation and reluctance to apply the methods suggested by Redman et al. (2012; see above). As such, there is a need for trainings on LGBTIQ topics to find a balance between allowing participants to share their experiences and attitudes, and then to explore how those attitudes may impact their work with LGBTIQ persons. Failure to find that balance may result in participants feeling "railroaded" into certain positions and thus more likely to avoid accepting and applying the information being presented (Redman et al. 2012).

To help participants contextualize information on LGBTIQ topics in their own work lives, Murphy (1992) suggests incorporating content on those topics in "all aspects of the training and professional practice of mental health professionals" (236). In that way, training—particularly ongoing workshops, in-service education, and continuing education programs—can encourage participants to apply it broadly to their workplaces and tasks. To that same end, Murphy highlights the significance of educating training participants about the "inextricable link between the individual, his/her/their sexuality, and society" to further help participants contextualize a client's "concerns or struggles within their lived realities in order to yield a treatment plan that best responds to those realities" (Murphy 1992:238).

Study Setting

Our data come from a collaborative research project conducted with ORAM, an international NGO with a mission of "advocating for LGBTI refugees fleeing brutalization due to sexual orientation or gender identity" (Hand Foundation 2014). ORAM's PD program was designed to enhance the knowledge, skills, and sensitivity of staff working directly with these refugees. In alignment with the Accountability Model of HRE, the program aims to professionalize organizations and create an infrastructure in which nonconforming forms of SOGI are both accepted and embraced.

Created as a two-day workshop, the PD's curriculum includes five units that engage participants with contemporary understanding of and approaches toward SOGI-based claims in the humanitarian world. The first unit, sensitization and identification, focuses on key terminology and concepts (e.g., sexual orientation, gender identity, gender expression, etc.) and founding international documents (e.g., the 1951 Geneva Convention Relating to the Status of Refugees, the 2006 UNHCR Guidance Note on Refugee Claims Relating to SOGI, and the 2012 UNHCR Guidelines on International Protection: Claims to Refugee Status Based on SOGI).[2] The second unit, protecting SOGI-nonconforming refugees, presents the specific protection needs of these refugees, such as the double marginalization they experience due to their foreign status and SOGI status. While the first two units are more conceptual and theoretical, the final three units are more applied and practical. The third unit, working with SOGI-nonconforming refugees, discusses the importance of and ways to create a welcoming space for those refugees. For example, participants receive a poster with the slogan "You are safe here" in eighteen languages, to be displayed in their offices (see Figure 8.1). The fourth unit, assessing credibility for SOGI-based claims, discusses best practices for conducting interviews and considerations for assessing these claims. The fifth unit, resettling SOGI-nonconforming refugees, discusses considerations relevant to resettlement and ways to address the specific needs of these refugees.

ORAM's PD includes participatory teaching methods such as role-playing, storytelling, and personal contact with openly LGBTIQ trainers.

Figure 8.1. Poster from ORAM workshop (2014). Courtesy of Organization for Refuge, Asylum, and Migration.

Adult education theory emphasizes the role of participatory methods in building the contextual relevance of the content presented, and then driving participant understanding of that content. Understanding and developing adult learning requires "attending to both the curriculum and the pedagogy" of PD—to what adults learn, and how they are taught (Wilson and Burne 1999:176). Desimone (2009) urges that effective professional training must provide opportunities for active learning, as it is likely to increase adults' application of learned content to their workplaces. Particularly in human rights training, these experiential methods are "only as useful as how relevant [their] subject matter is" to participants' particular areas of work or interest in the human rights field (Teleki 2007:13). Relevancy is thus key to developing the "norms and practices related to human rights" that the Accountability Model of HRE endeavors to achieve (Tibbitts 2002:165).

The PD's staff includes facilitators from ORAM as well as local LGBTIQ activists. While the organization's main facilitator taught sections that required a high level of technical and professional knowledge, LGBTIQ activists taught sections that highlighted their local expertise and connected their personal experiences with the content. Scholars have documented that contact with LGBTIQ persons is associated with more positive evaluations of the group and more support for pro-LGBTIQ policies (Barth and Parry 2009; Briceno, Cuesta, and Attanasio 2011; Vonofakou, Hewstone, and Voci 2007). Therefore, ORAM provided opportunities for participants to interact directly with LGBTIQ trainers, including sharing meals and break times, whenever possible.

The incorporation of local LGBTIQ activists as facilitators may also impact the likelihood that participants will apply the knowledge learned to their work practices. In an evaluation of twenty-six human rights training programs for adult professionals, Teleki (2007) found that the most common participant criticism was that the trainings "did not relate closely enough to participants' daily work or local situations" (13). Local facilitators are able to bring contextualized information to these trainings, and thus have the potential to guide participants in making clear connections between the information used and their actual work experiences. That deeper understanding of local LGBTIQ experiences and concerns may result in greater sensitivity and professional responsibility toward SOGI-nonconforming refugees.

With funding from the U.S. Department of State's Bureau of Population, Refugees, and Migration, ORAM offered the PD program free of charge to

Table 8.1. Attitudes Toward Homosexuality in Eight Countries

Country	Homosexuality Should Not Be Accepted by Society (percent)	Homosexuality Is Morally Unacceptable (percent agree)
India		67
Israel	47	43
Jordan	97	95
Kenya	90	88
Malaysia	86	88
Malta	N/A	N/A
Senegal	96	68
Turkey	78	78

Source: Pew Research Center 2013.

partner organizations worldwide. Eight locations were selected for the first wave of training sessions: India (New Delhi), Israel (Tel Aviv), Jordan (Amman), Kenya (Nairobi), Malaysia (Kuala Lumpur), Malta (Valletta), Senegal (Dakar), and Turkey (Istanbul). Recent public opinion research shows that attitudes toward homosexuality are negative in most of these locations (Pew Research Center 2013). In five countries—Jordan, Kenya, Malaysia, Senegal, and Turkey—a large majority of the public endorse the statements "homosexuality should not be accepted by society" and "homosexuality is morally unacceptable" (see Table 8.1). Therefore, one could expect program participants in these countries to be more resistant to ORAM's PD.

Data and Methods

Data for this chapter come from a larger research project that aims to evaluate the impact of ORAM's PD in eight countries. The research design includes a baseline survey collected before the training, an evaluation survey collected during the training, and two follow-up surveys: one collected six weeks after the training and another collected three months after the training. All surveys except for the evaluation survey are conducted online using Qualtrics, a common and secure survey platform. Participation in the research project was voluntary, and training attendees were allowed to opt out from any part of the research. To address the need to link records across data points (surveys) while maintaining respondents' anonymity, a unique identifier code (UIC) was assigned to each respondent. Following work in the field of HIV/AIDS (e.g., World Health Organization 2012), the UIC consisted of the first letter of the first name, the last letter of the last name, the first two letters of the city of birth, the month of birth, and the year of birth.

To examine the experiences of PD participants, we used data from the evaluation survey component. Respondents were asked to complete a total of four surveys, each administered after the completion of a training module. The evaluation survey was developed by the research team in collaboration with ORAM. The questionnaire was based on similar evaluations conducted by the Gay, Lesbian, and Straight Education Network (GLSEN) (Greytak and Kosciw 2010) and scholarship on teacher PD (Haslam 2010). The final questionnaire included items on four themes: (1) attitudes toward LGBTIQ trainers; (2) attitudes toward learning styles and techniques; (3) accomplishment of training goals—empathy, self-efficacy, likelihood of application after training; and (4) general evaluation of training. Eighteen out of twenty items in the questionnaire were closed-ended and Likert-type questions, and the remaining two items were open-ended questions. We included qualitative data to allow participants to voice their opinions and concerns about the training, and to better understand any patterns among their responses. On average, respondents completed the questionnaire within ten minutes. Two-thirds of the sample (66.2 percent) answered the open-ended questions, with an average length of twenty-two words (110 characters).

The final sample includes 1,264 valid questionnaires. Using the unique identifier code, we identified 355 individuals who completed the evaluation survey two, three, or four times (105, 118, and 132, respectively). We were not able to match records across modules for slightly more than one-seventh of the sample (13.6 percent/172 questionnaires).

For the purpose of describing the sample, we examined the characteristics of participants who completed the evaluation survey after the first module of the first day of the training. Slightly more than one-fifth of the participants (21.4 percent) came from the training in Kenya. Two other large groups included participants from Malaysia (15.7 percent) and Turkey (15.2 percent). The rest of the participants came from the training in Jordan (10.8 percent), India (10.0 percent), Israel (10.0 percent), Malta (8.4 percent) and Senegal (8.4 percent). As for organizational affiliation, close to two-fifths of the participants (37.6 percent) were affiliated with the UNHCR, one-fourth (25.1 percent) with local NGOs, and less than one-fourth (17.9 percent) with governmental agencies. The rest of the participants were affiliated with Re-settlement Service Centers (RSCs; 13.6 percent) and other agencies (e.g., the International Organization for Migration and the UN Relief and Works Agency; 5.8 percent). The average age of the participants was 34.2 years, with a standard deviation of 8.4.

Measures

To assess respondents' dispositions toward LGBTIQ trainers and speakers, we used two questions from the evaluation survey. The first question was "How comfortable did you feel in the presence of openly LGBTIQ facilitators/trainers?" with a four-point scale ranging from "very uncomfortable" to "very comfortable." The second question was "People have different preferences for training styles and techniques; which of the following modes do you find most effective and useful?" with the following options: (1) oral presentations, (2) interactive exercises (such as role-play), (3) question and answer sessions, (4) multimedia (such as movies), and (5) meeting LGBTIQ trainers.

To evaluate respondents' attitudes toward ORAM's PD, we used a series of ten statements describing different aspects of the training. Respondents were asked to indicate the extent to which they agreed or disagreed with each statement. The alpha Cronbach coefficient for these statements was high (.86). That is, the internal consistency of the items is high, and the series of statements is reliable. In addition to quantitative measures, respondents were asked two open-ended questions: "What did you like most about the training?" and "What did you like least about the training?"

Finally, to gauge the outcomes of ORAM's PD, we operationalized three concepts: empathy, self-efficacy, and likelihood of implementation. To measure empathy, we used respondents' indication of the extent to which they agreed or disagreed with the following statement: "I have an understanding of what individuals persecuted based on their sexual orientation and gender identity go through in their country of origin." To measure self-efficacy, we used respondents' indication of the extent to which they agreed or disagreed with the following statement: "I am confident in my ability to promote a welcoming environment in my organization so that all individuals, including LGBTIQ people, feel both safe and respected." To measure likelihood to implement, respondents were asked: "Which of the following statements best describes the likelihood that you will apply what you learned in the ORAM training in your organization/work?" with the following options: (1) I have already applied this in my organization/work; (2) I intend to apply this in my organization/work in the future; (3) I would like to apply it, but I don't have the materials I need; (4) I don't know whether the opportunity to apply it will ever arise; and (5) I don't think this will work in my organization/work.

Analytical Strategy

To analyze the evaluation survey data, we employed a mixed-methods design (Creswell 2013). First, we analyzed closed-ended and Likert-type questions using descriptive statistics and bivariate statistics. Second, we analyzed open-ended questions by identifying and coding themes in participants' responses. Together, these methods provide the best understanding of participants' experiences in ORAM's PD training.

Findings

Dispositions Toward LGBTIQ Trainers and Speakers

We begin by describing participants' dispositions toward LGBTIQ trainers and speakers, a crucial element in ORAM's PD. Although the training took part in relatively hostile environments where homosexuality is not acceptable (see Table 8.1), we found that a large majority of the participants felt comfortable in the presence of openly LGBTIQ trainers. This figure increased over the course of the training: after the first module, 76.2 percent of respondents felt comfortable, and after the fourth module, 87.7 percent felt comfortable ($\chi^2 = 27.52$, DF = 9, $p < .01$). As illustrated in Table 8.2, changes in participants' dispositions toward LGBTIQ trainers varied across organizational affiliation. Among participants affiliated with UNHCR, we found a significant increase in the percentage of participants who felt comfortable in the presence of openly LGBTIQ trainers, from 70.2 percent to 88.4 percent.[3]

Feeling comfortable in the presence of openly LGBTIQ trainers is a useful indicator for assessing participants' experiences during the training

Table 8.2. Percent of Respondents Feeling Comfortable in the Presence of Openly LGBTIQ Facilitators/Trainers, by Affiliation and Module ($n = 1,264$)

Affiliation	Module 1	Module 2	Module 3	Module 4	Chi Square	Sig.
UNHCR	70.2	80.2	91.4	88.4	$\chi^2 = 20.62$	$p < .01$
Nongovernmental organization	86.8	90.0	87.7	85.7	$\chi^2 = .69$	$p = .88$
Resettlement service center	73.3	80.3	87.5	87.3	$\chi^2 = 5.61$	$p = .13$
Governmental agency/office	72.9	81.4	90.2	90.9	$\chi^2 = 7.10$	$p = .07$
Other	84.2	95.0	88.9	92.3	$\chi^2 = 1.36$	$p = .71$

(process) and a means of capturing the impact of the training (content). To further explore participants' attitudes toward learning from LGBTIQ trainers, we used responses to the question: "People have different preferences for training styles and techniques. Which of the following modes do you find most effective and useful?" While close to half of the sample (46.3 percent) indicated that "multimedia (such as films and movies)" are effective and useful tools for learning, close to two-fifths of the sample (38.6 percent) indicated "meeting LGBTIQ trainers" as such. This pattern suggests that participants appreciated the opportunity to meet—and have direct contact with—LGBTIQ individuals.

These positive sentiments toward meeting LGBTIQ trainers were also evident in participants' open-ended comments. Overall, participants appreciated firsthand testimonies and personal stories from openly gay and lesbian individuals. Respondents saw contact with LGBTIQ individuals as a way to learn about and better understand the needs of the LGBTIQ community. For example, one participant from Israel mentioned that "hearing about LGBTIQ people's experiences and their difficulties regarding society, 'coming out' to family and friends, and getting to know this community a little better" was useful in her work. Another Israeli participant noted the importance of hearing personal narratives, sharing that "meeting and hearing personal stories gave good context and understanding of (the) state of mind of an LGBTIQ person." Many respondents indicated that contact with LGBTIQ individuals, especially those who might break additional stereotypes, such as "LGBTIQ individuals are not taking part in organized religion," is more effective than other modes of teaching and learning. One participant commented that he "really enjoyed the interaction with an openly gay Muslim! . . . His personal story was more effective in understanding the issue than any other tool in training." A Kenyan participant also noted that he found it important that the facilitator took pride in his identity, commenting: "What I liked most about the session is the fact that the victims [the LGBTIQ] came out bold and said it the way it is. [They were] not ashamed." Interestingly, the participant still used the language of victimhood in his description of the facilitator. While comments like these indicate that participants were open to and appreciative of direct contact with LGBTIQ individuals, they also point to how trainings can build on that openness to further explore participants' views on LGBTIQ individuals' human rights.

Evaluation of Professional Development

Next, we evaluated ORAM's PD using both quantitative and qualitative measures. Table 8.3 presents summary statistics for ten statements describing different facets of the training. In addition to mean score and standard deviation, Table 8.3 includes percent agree (combination of strongly and somewhat agree) and percent disagree (combination of strongly and somewhat disagree). The statements are sorted by the mean score. A large majority of participants (more than 93.0 percent) responded positively to the training. For example, almost all participants agreed with the statements "Facilitators treat all participants with respect" (97.9 percent) and "Facilitators are fair and impartial when dealing with all participants" (97.5 percent). In their open-ended comments, respondents echoed this pattern and offered insights about differences between speakers. One participant from Malaysia commented that "the main speaker was very respectful, professional and humble. It was easy to communicate with him." That same participant also asserted that other facilitators were "trying to shove their perception/info/ opinion down on us. I think there should be mutual understanding of differences." These patterns are especially imperative when considering the facilitation styles used in PD on the sensitive and potentially contested topic of SOGI-based refugee protection.

While analyzing the open-ended comments, we found that most respondents valued the pedagogy of ORAM's PD. Specifically, respondents benefited from experiential learning methods such as role-play and group

Table 8.3. Respondents' Evaluation of ORAM's Training, Percent Agree/
Disagree, Means, and Standard Deviations (n = 1,264)

Statement	Agree (percent)	Disagree (percent)	Mean	SD
The facilitators treat all participants with respect.	97.9	2.1	3.81	.46
The facilitators are fair and impartial when dealing with all participants.	97.5	2.5	3.77	.51
My religious beliefs and values were respected by facilitators.*	96.0	4.0	3.68	.60
My religious beliefs and values were respected by participants.*	96.5	3.5	3.63	.60
This training is relevant for my work at the organization.	96.2	3.8	3.63	.59
The material was presented in an organized, easily understood manner.	96.5	3.5	3.61	.58
This training increased my knowledge in the area of. . . .	95.0	5.0	3.51	.62
I would rate the facilitators as outstanding.	94.9	5.1	3.48	.62
This training increased my skills in the area of. . . .	93.2	6.8	3.40	.65
I would rate the quality of this training as outstanding.	94.5	5.5	3.36	.61

* Sample size is 1,212.

discussion. A Kenyan participant noted that the "role-play section was very informative and closely mirrored realistic situations." The role-play conversations allowed her to "learn new ways to handle people who are reluctant to divulge sensitive information as well as some who are hostile." Another participant from India noted that the role-play allowed him to better understand the people he might be serving. He noted that the role-play "put us in their shoes and [made] us understand a little more about how they feel and what they go through." Beyond the importance of role-play, participants indicated the importance of having an opportunity to ask questions and have discussions on topics that they might not be able to speak about normally. One Turkish respondent noted that this was a rare opportunity to explore issues of sexual orientation and gender identity, explaining that it was helpful to "hear other people ideas and discuss about these during group exercises." These comments suggest how participatory pedagogy may foster an environment in which participants can develop their knowledge while expressing their own views, which may lead to greater participant buy-in and thus more self-directed application of newly learned content and skills in their workplaces (Redman et al. 2012.)

Beyond the pedagogical tools that were used to facilitate a space for discussion and other forms of interaction, respondents indicated the importance of learning about the legal context of protecting LGBTIQ individuals. For some respondents, this was their first discussion on this issue. This was particularly true for participants from Kuala Lumpur. One respondent noted that "the facilitator shared a good deal of information about the law on LGBTIQ, in my country, which I was not aware of. I [found] it very helpful." Another participant in Malaysia noted that "the penal code is hardly used, but more laws [can be] used to target transgender." Similarly, respondents indicated the importance of learning practical and relevant skills for working with LGBTIQ refugees and asylum seekers. Respondents noted that the information was up to date and relevant to the kind of fieldwork they are engaged in.

Overall, Table 8.3 suggests that participants felt their religious beliefs and values were respected by facilitators and other participants (96.2 percent and 96.5 percent, respectively). These items, however, had a relatively high number of missing values (~4 percent). That is, participants were more likely to skip or refuse to answer items about religious beliefs and values and their place in the training. One way to explain this pattern is that most participants were not religious and thus did not experience conflict between their beliefs and values and the topic of the training. Another possible explanation is that religious respondents opted out and did not answer these questions. Social research show a consistent relationship between religiosity and attitudes toward homosexuality and LGBTIQ rights (Pizmony-Levy and Ponce 2013; Powell, Yurk Quadlin, and Pizmony-Levy 2015). Nevertheless, even after accounting for the missing values, the large majority of participants felt their religious beliefs and values were respected.

Further exploration of the relationship between these two items—religious beliefs and values were respected by facilitators and other participants—presents an interesting pattern. The majority of the sample (84.6 percent) answered these questions in a similar fashion (e.g., agree with both statements or disagree with both statements). While approximately 10.4 percent found the facilitators to be more respectful than other participants, only 5.1 percent found other participants to be more respectful than the facilitators.

The issue of respecting differences and having different religious beliefs and values was a central theme in the open-ended comments. While respondents commended the overall quality of the PD, they also resisted cultural acceptance of homosexuality. One Jordanian respondent noted that while he liked the facilitators and the materials used, he "did not like the whole subject. This issue is not accepted in our culture, especially in the refugee community." Another Jordanian argued that this training was a form of imparting Western beliefs, saying that it "impos[ed] a vision of Westernized liberal society in a way that doesn't take into consideration other societies particularities." A Kenyan participant did not go so far as to say that the training was imparting Western values, but mentioned that she "felt that some comments made by the trainers could be disrespectful to certain people's beliefs and morals, and they could have been a bit more sensitive."

The issue of Western values was not the only pushback that participants noted. Some respondents disliked how some facilitators drew on their own religious beliefs in an effort to address the potential conflict between religion and working with LGBTIQ refugees and asylum seekers. One Muslim participant from Kenya explained that being a true Muslim did not allow for tolerance of homosexuality, commenting, "The two who so called themselves as 'Muslims' totally misinterpreted my religion in the name of Islam. SHAME ON THEM AND WOO UNTO THEM" (emphasis in written response). The same participant then noted that "human rights are universal so they shouldn't use a religious point of view or perspective." Another Kenyan claimed that the use of religious texts by the facilitators was wrong. "Some of the trainers used religious quotes that weren't quite true. I understand the point [they're] making. Everyone has a right to live as they please. Just don't bring religion into it." A Turkish participant also asserted that there was no need to bring religion into the discussion: "My work with LGBTIQ is not dependent on my religion . . . my work is LEGAL and HUMANITARIAN, NOT religious" (emphasis in written response).

Finally, participants indicated that the training was not only clear and well organized, but also relevant to their daily work. For example, almost all participants agreed with the following statements: "This training is relevant for my work at the organization" (96.2 percent), "This training increased my

Table 8.4. Percent of Respondents Agreeing with the Statement "I Have an Understanding of What Individuals Persecuted Based on Their SOGI Go Through in Their Country of Origin," by Module ($n = 1,264$)

	Module 1	Module 2	Module 3	Module 4	Total
Strongly disagree	3.0	1.8	.6	2.1	1.9
Somewhat disagree	5.7	1.5	1.9	1.7	2.8
Somewhat agree	40.7	37.4	35.2	28.8	35.8
Strongly agree	50.6	59.3	62.3	67.4	59.6
Total	100.0	100.0	100.0	100.0	100.0

Pearson $\chi^2 = 33.30$, DF $= 9$, $p < .001$.

Table 8.5. Percent of Respondents Agreeing with the Statement "I Am Confident in My Ability to Promote a Welcoming Environment in My Organization So That All Individuals, Including LGBTIQ People, Feel Both Safe and Respected," by Module ($n = 1,264$).

	Module 1	Module 2	Module 3	Module 4	Total
Strongly disagree	1.5	1.8	1.6	1.1	1.5
Somewhat disagree	4.5	2.7	2.6	2.8	3.2
Somewhat agree	37.4	32.0	32.6	23.5	31.6
Strongly agree	56.6	63.5	63.3	72.6	63.7
Total	100.0	100.0	100.0	100.0	100.0

Pearson $\chi^2 = 18.88$, DF $= 9$, $p < .05$.

knowledge in the area of . . ." (95.0 percent), and "This training increased my skills in the area of . . ." (93.2 percent).

Evaluation of Professional Development Outcomes

In this section we explore three self-reported outcomes. The first outcome is empathy toward LGBTIQ refugees and asylum seekers. As illustrated in Table 8.4, a large majority of the sample (95.3 percent) agreed with the statement "I have an understanding of what individuals persecuted based on their sexual orientation or gender identity go through in their country of origin." The second outcome is self-efficacy to promote a welcoming environment.

Similar to the previous outcome, and as illustrated in Table 8.5, a large majority of the sample (95.3 percent) agreed with the statement "I am confident in my ability to promote a welcoming environment in my organization so that all individuals, including LGBTIQ people, feel both safe and respected." Although figures were high after the first module of the training, statistically significant increases were recorded after the fourth module of the training for both outcomes.

With regard to the third outcome, likelihood of implementing change in the organization, we find that slightly more than two-fifths of the respondents (42.8 percent) intend to apply what they learned at the PD in their organizations, and approximately one-fifth (19.6 percent) intend to apply what they learned but don't have the materials they need. Only a small minority of the respondents (13.9 percent) remained skeptical about applying what they learned, whether because they did not see the opportunity to do so or because their organization is not susceptible to change. Importantly, close to one-fourth of participants (23.7 percent) reported already applying what they learned in their organizations.

In the final step of the analysis, we examined whether a sense of respect of religious beliefs and values is associated with the PD's outcomes. Respondents who felt that the facilitators and other participants respected their religious beliefs and values were more likely than others to report empathy toward LGBTIQ refugees and asylum seekers and self-efficacy to promote a welcoming environment for this group (Figure 8.2). Moreover, respondents who felt their religious beliefs and values were respected are more likely than others to implement change in their organizations. All these patterns are statistically significant, and thus we conclude that addressing, incorporating, and respecting participant attitudes and values fosters participant learning and application of PD content in their workplaces (Figure 8.3).

Discussion and Conclusion

In this chapter we examined the experience of frontline professionals in a two-day HRE workshop on SOGI-based refugee protection. Overall, workshop attendees in these eight countries were very satisfied with their experiences, with nine out of ten attendees ranking their experience in the

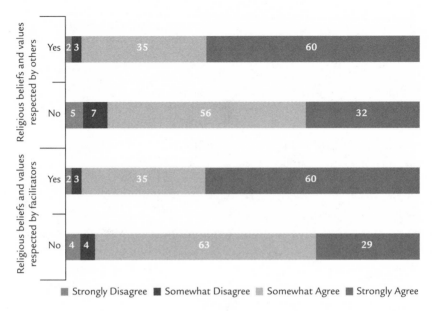

Figure 8.2. Self-efficacy to promote a welcoming environment to LGBTIQ refugees, by sense of respect for religious beliefs and values ($n = 1,212$).

PD positively. Quantitative and qualitative analyses of data from exit surveys point to two factors that contributed to this positive experience. The first factor was the inclusion of openly LGBTIQ individuals—foreigners and domestic—in the teaching staff. By including these individuals, the workshop facilitated what is known in social psychology as a *parallel process*, where the content of the workshop was also reflected in activities and interactions that played out during the workshop. The second factor was the use of learner-centered pedagogy with multiple modalities for teaching and learning. This approach is especially relevant for adult learners in nonformal settings. Workshop attendees indicated that the combination of these factors led to an open and respectful environment where learning could happen. Indeed, we find that respondents who felt that their religious beliefs and values were respected were more likely than others to report high levels of empathy, self-efficacy, and motivation to become agents of change in their organizations. Although the workshop was only two days in length, patterns suggest that attendees experienced meaningful changes during that time.

While these findings are very promising, they were not universal. A small number of respondents, particularly those with orthodox religious

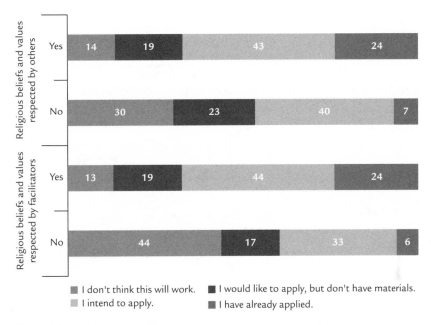

Figure 8.3. Attitudes toward implementation of materials learned at the training, by sense of respect for religious beliefs and values ($n = 1,212$).

beliefs, were not moved in their willingness to help LGBTIQ refugees. In a few cases, the fact that LGBTIQ trainers claimed to share their religious beliefs offended some workshop participants, perhaps closing them off from experiencing higher levels of empathy. While this is concerning, it is encouraging that these reactions were seen in less than a handful of the nearly 500 trainees surveyed.

These patterns suggest that good HRE requires more than the simple transmission of knowledge about universal human rights. Rather, HRE training should include pedagogy that respects various backgrounds and opinions (e.g., religious beliefs and values) and creates a safe space for learning and confronting contentious perspectives. Also, HRE training should address the diversity of learning styles—especially with adults—to maximize engagement with the content and the likelihood of implementing change.

All empirical studies have limitations, and this study is no exception. One weakness of this study is the limited background information available on workshop attendees. Additional background information would allow more in-depth examination of how sociodemographic characteristics (e.g., education and political ideology) and previous contact with LGBTIQ individuals affect engagement with the training. Another weakness is the sample size. Although the data set includes 1,264 questionnaires, it actually represents fewer than 500 individuals. Moreover, the sample size in each location varies significantly: from 88 questionnaires in Senegal to 349 questionnaires in Kenya. This relatively small sample size puts constraints on the sophistication of the analysis using multivariate methods. Nevertheless, these limitations do not jeopardize the findings of this first-ever study.

Nevertheless, this study offers an evaluation model for HRE programs. Evaluation is important not only for program improvement, but also for securing funding and mobilizing support. This is especially true in a policy context that celebrates evidence- and data-based interventions. By drawing on longitudinal survey data (quantitative and qualitative), this study provides insights regarding the pedagogy of ORAM's PD and engagement. Further, by drawing on survey data from different locations, this study confirms that ORAM's PD works in different sociocultural contexts.

Moving forward, research on PD about SOGI-based refugee protection could develop in three ways. One line of inquiry should focus on the impact of training on knowledge, competencies, and attitudes toward SOGI-based protection. Using quantitative methods, scholars could examine not only the overall short-term and long-term impacts, but also the ways in which the impact of training varies across individual characteristics (e.g., gender, education, values/beliefs) and organizational characteristics (e.g., governmental vs. nongovernmental). Another line of inquiry should focus on teaching and learning processes that take place during the training. Here, ethnographic methods (i.e., participant observation and in-depth interviews) could help us to better understand interactions and dynamics between trainers and trainees as they codefine key concepts. In addition to informing the development of "best practices" in training, these directions will shed light on the ways in which actors on the ground engage with and are affected by the promising but still abstract international discourse on protection from persecution based on SOGI.

Notes

1. UNHCR issues Guidance Notes on thematic legal issues in accordance with its mandate and as part of its practice to "clarify applicable law and legal standards" and

to provide "guidance in the particular thematic area concerned" (UNHCR 2008). In 2012, UNHCR replaced this document under the revised name, *Guidelines on International Protection No. 9: Claims to Refugee Status Based on Sexual Orientation and/or Gender Identity*.

2. See note 1.

3. This pattern is significant even when we limit the analysis to individuals who completed at least two surveys (results are available upon request).

References

Anderson-Levitt, K., ed. 2003. *Local Meanings: Global Schooling Anthropology and World Culture Theory*. New York: Palgrave Macmillan.

Barth, J., and J. Parry. 2009. "2 > 1 + 1? The Impact of Contact with Gay and Lesbian Couples on Attitudes About Gays/Lesbians and Gay-Related Policies." *Politics & Policy* 37(1):31–50.

Berg, L., and J. Millbank. 2009. "Constructing the Personal Narratives of Lesbian, Gay and Bisexual Asylum Claimants." *Journal of Refugee Studies* 22(2):195–223.

Briceno, B., L. Cuesta, and O. Attanasio. 2011. "Behind the Scenes: Managing and Conducting Large Scale Impact Evaluations in Colombia." New Delhi: International Initiative for Impact Evaluation. http://www.3ieimpact.org/media/filer/2012/05/23/working_paper_14.pdf.

Celermajer, D., and K. Grewal. 2013. "Preventing Human Rights Violations 'from the Inside': Enhancing the Role of Human Rights Education in Security Sector Reform." *Journal of Human Rights Practice* 5(2):243–266.

Creswell, J. W. 2013. *Research Design: Qualitative, Quantitative, and Mixed Methods Approach*, 4th ed. Los Angeles: Sage Publications.

Dauvergne, C., and J. Millbank. 2003. "Burdened by Proof: How the Australian Refugee Review Tribunal Has Failed Lesbian and Gay Asylum Seekers." *Federal Law Review* 31:299–342.

Desimone, L. M. 2009. "Improving Impact Studies of Teachers' Professional Development: Toward Better Conceptualizations and Measures." *Educational Researcher* 38(3):181–199.

Flowers, N. 2000. *The Human Rights Education Handbook: Effective Practices for Learning, Action, and Change*. Human Rights Education Series, Topic Book. Minneapolis: Human Rights Resource Center.

Frank, D. J. 2012. "Making Sense of LGBT Asylum Claims: Change and Variation in Institutional Contexts." *NYU Journal of International Law and Politics* 44:485–495.

Fullerton, M. 1993. "Comparative Look at Refugee Status Based on Persecution Due to Membership in a Particular Social Group." *Cornell International Law Journal* 26(1):505–564.

Greytak, E. A., and J. G. Kosciw, J. G. 2010. *Year One Evaluation of the New York City Department of Education Respect for All Training Program.* New York: Gay, Lesbian, and Straight Education Network.

The Hand Foundation, 2014. "Oram." http://www.thehandfoundation.org/newsletter -article.php?ORAM-43.

Haslam, M. Bruce. 2010. *Teacher Professional Development Evaluation Guide.* Washington, DC: National Staff Development Council. https://learningforward.org/docs /pdf/evaluationguide.pdf?sfvrsn=0.

Human Rights Education Associates (HREA). 2003. "Study Guide: Sexual Orientation and Human Rights." http://hrlibrary.umn.edu/edumat/studyguides/sexualorientation.html.

International Lesbian, Gay, Bisexual, Trans and Intersex Association (ILGA). 2013. *Annual Report.* Geneva: ILGA. http://old.ilga.org/documents/ILGA_Annual_Report _2013.pdf.

Kinderman, P., and F. Butler. 2006. *Implementing a Human Rights Approach Within Public Services: An Outline Psychological Perspective.* Report for the Department for Constitutional Affairs. http://research-archive.liv.ac.uk/452/2/implementing_a _Human_Rights_Approach_within_Public_Services.pdf.

McManus, P. A., and O. Pizmony-Levy. 2012. "How Do NGOs Engage with Sexual Orientation and Gender Identity-Based Forced Migration?" Paper presented at the Annual Meeting of the American Sociological Association in Denver, CO.

Morgan, D. A. 2006. "Not Gay Enough for the Government: Racial and Sexual Stereotypes in Sexual Orientation Asylum Cases." *Law and Sexuality: A Review of Lesbian, Gay, Bisexual & Transgender Legal Issues* 15:135–161.

Murphy, B. C. 1992. "Educating Mental Health Professionals About Gay and Lesbian Issues." *Journal of Homosexuality* 22(3–4):229–246.

Pew Research Center. 2013. "The Global Divide on Homosexuality." Washington, DC: Pew Research Center. http://www.pewglobal.org/files/2014/05/Pew-Global-Attitudes -Homosexuality-Report-REVISED-MAY-27-2014.pdf.

Pizmony-Levy, O., and P. A. McManus. 2012. "Global Survey of Non-Governmental Organizations Servicing Refugees and Asylum Seekers: Technical Report." Bloomington: Indiana University, Department of Sociology.

Pizmony-Levy, Oren, and Aaron Ponce. 2013. "Framing Strategies and Public Support for the Legalization of Marriage between Two People of the Same Sex." *Sociological Perspectives* 56(2):169–190.

Ponce, A. 2012. "Shoring Up Judicial Awareness: LGBT Refugees and the Recognition of Social Categories." *New England Journal of International and Comparative Law* 18:185.

Powell, Brian, Natasha Yurk Quadlin, and Oren Pizmony-Levy. 2015. "Public Opinion, the Courts, and Same-sex Marriage: Four Lessons Learned." *Social Currents* 2(1):3–12.

Redman, M., E. Taylor, R. Furlong, G. Carney, and B. Greenhill. 2012. "Human Rights Training: Impact on Attitudes and Knowledge." *Tizard Learning Disability Review* 17(2):80–87.

Rose, J., and S. Holmes, S. 1991. "Changing Staff Attitudes to the Sexuality of People with Mental Handicaps: An Evaluative Comparison of One and Three Day Workshops." *Journal of Applied Research in Intellectual Disabilities* 4(1):67–79.

Sears, J. T. 1992. "Educators, Homosexuality, and Homosexual Students: Are Personal Feelings Related to Professional Beliefs?" *Journal of Homosexuality* 22(3–4):29–80.

Smith, T. W, J. Son, and J. Kim. 2014. *Public Attitudes Toward Homosexuality and Gay Rights Across Time and Countries.* Los Angeles: The Williams Institute, 2014.

Swink, A. 2006. "Queer Refuge: A Review of the Role of Country Condition Analysis in Asylum Adjudications for Members of Sexual Minorities." *Hastings International and Comparative Law Review* 29:251–266.

Teleki, K. 2007. "Human Rights Training for Adults: What Twenty-Six Evaluation Studies Say About Design, Implementation, and Follow-Up." Human Rights Education Associates, Inc. http://reliefweb.int/sites/reliefweb.int/files/resources/74BF 01F5CE2682EEC12574C600519C87-HRA-Aug2007.pdf.

Tibbitts, F. 2002. "Understanding What We Do: Emerging Models for Human Rights Education." *International Review of Education* 48(3–4):159–171.

UNHCR. 2008. *UNHCR Guidance Note on Refugee Claims Relating to Sexual Orientation and Gender Identity.* Geneva: UNHCR. https://www.justice.gov/sites/default /files/eoir/legacy/2014/08/15/UNHCR_Guidelines_Sexual_Orientation.pdf.

United Nations. 1951. *Convention Relating to the Status of Refugees.* http://www.unhcr .org/3b66c2aa10.pdf

United Nations. 1967. *Protocol Relating to the Status of Refugees.* http://www.unhcr.org /3b66c2aa10.pdf.

Van Den Bergh, N., and C. Crisp. 2004. "Defining Culturally Competent Practice with Sexual Minorities: Implications for Social Work Education and Practice." *Journal of Social Work Education* 40(2):221–238.

Vonofakou, C., M. Hewstone, and A. Voci. 2007. "Contact with Out-Group Friends as a Predictor of Meta-Attitudinal Strength and Accessibility of Attitudes Toward Gay Men." *Journal of Personality and Social Psychology* 92(5):804–820.

Wahl, R. 2014. "Learning Norms or Changing Them? State Actors, State Violence, and Human Rights Education in India." Unpublished dissertation, New York University.

Wilson, S. M., and J. Burne. 1999. "Teacher Learning and the Acquisition of Professional Knowledge: An Examination on Contemporary Professional Development." *Review of Research in Education* 24:173–209.

World Health Organization. 2012. *WHO, UNODC, UNAIDS Technical Guide for Countries to Set Targets for Universal Access to HIV Prevention, Treatment and Care for Injecting Drug Users–2012 Revision.* http://www.who.int/hiv/pub/idu/targets _universal_access/en/.

PART III

Transformative Human Rights Education Praxis

CHAPTER 9

Historicizing Critical Educational Praxis: A Human Rights Framework for Justice-Oriented Teaching

Melissa L. Gibson and Carl A. Grant

In a middle school social studies classroom in Guadalajara, Mexico, I (Melissa) have been trying to catalyze discussion about social issues in Mexico—issues such as poverty, government corruption, and organized crime. This is, after all, a civics class, and I want my students to interrogate the idea of critically active citizenship: What are the social issues our communities face, and how can we make social change around those issues? But I am faced with resignation. "Miss," they say, "this is just how Mexico is." My students have what Bryan Brayboy (2011) refers to as "genesis amnesia." Borrowing from Pierre Bourdieu and Jean-Claude Passeron (1990), Brayboy argues that genesis amnesia, or the forgetting of history—the forgetting of how oppressive structures have come to be and what existed before them—is a means of normalizing oppression. Imagining that "this is just the way things are" prevents us from imagining how else the world could be. It is much like the parable of the fish, well told by novelist David Foster Wallace (2008): "There are these two young fish swimming along, and they happen to meet an older fish swimming the other way, who nods at them and says, 'Morning, boys, how's the water?' And the two young fish swim on for a bit, and then eventually one of them looks over at the other and goes, 'What the hell is water?'"

One of our primary challenges as social justice and human rights educators is to get our students to see the water in which they swim. But we don't just want them to name injustice; we want them to understand how the particular conditions of our communities have developed over time, and we then want them to imagine into the future how the world could be otherwise and what they can do to help realize that future. It is a tall order in the face of normalized oppression.

Melissa's students are not alone in their genesis amnesia. For example, in the United States, where both authors are justice-oriented teacher educators, our social problems often seem as if they have always been and that there is little we can do to change them. In the face of dysfunctional governments that win reelection, of colonizing public rhetoric that pathologizes people of color, of educational systems designed to fail, and of systems of domination that shape-shift, such as the transformation of discriminatory Jim Crow laws into our current state of mass incarceration,[1] it is hard to remember—or believe—that our world was never not this way. It is hard to remember or believe that it could ever become something different.

In this chapter, we argue that universal human rights provide a concrete language for resisting the genesis amnesia that makes teaching for social change feel so impossible. The power of a human rights framework is for us not merely theoretical; it has affected concrete change in our classes, and it has enabled our students to begin to see the water in which they swim. In Melissa's social studies class in Guadalajara, when students were eventually introduced to the idea of human rights, new questions began to percolate: If the right to shelter is a human right, why are there homeless people? If we have the right to freedom of movement, why is there a migration crisis at the U.S.–Mexico border? If security of person is a basic right, then why are we doing so little in Mexico to resist police, state, and cartel violence? How can people just be disappeared—*what about their rights?* If countries have signed onto the Universal Declaration of Human Rights, why aren't they doing anything to help us? Indeed, in our classes, we have experienced first-hand how the study of human rights has given students a language to interrogate a normalized but oppressive context.

Therefore, we argue here that the study of human rights gives us a language not only to contest oppression and injustice, but also a language in which to root our work as justice-oriented teachers. Universal human rights are, in many ways, the shared language underlying contemporary liberatory pedagogies; rooting our work as educators in a human rights framework is a way of resisting the genesis amnesia that also threatens our own work. Whether in teacher education programs or in K–12 classrooms, critical pedagogies are easily dehistoricized. After all, as justice-oriented educators, we often teach of the moment and in the moment; these days, we frequently understand our work as contesting the neoliberal context in which we find ourselves. Yet while social justice educators are vigilant about anchoring our students in a critical understanding of history and collective struggle, our own work pushing back against the systemic domination of schools has too often become unmoored from the long history of social and political resistance to which it is anchored, leaving social justice to be an ineffable and ill-defined concept. As social justice critic Friedrich Hayek has said, social justice "is allowed to float in the air as if everyone will recognize an instance of it when it appears" (Novak 2008:11).

In this chapter, we offer a multilayered approach to rooting justice-oriented pedagogies in a human rights history. First, we will briefly describe the history of the Universal Declaration of Human Rights, emphasizing how education came to have a prioritized role in human rights work. We will then connect human rights to American movements for racial, economic, and gender justice, often understood as the genesis of social justice education in the United States to the exclusion of human rights antecedents. Finally, we will bring this historicization to bear on justice-oriented teaching, a form of liberatory pedagogy in the U.S. context. By extending our history of social movements and popular resistance to the drafting of the Universal Declaration of Human Rights, a historical genesis often overlooked in the United States, we hope to offer new ways of understanding our work as critical educators. Ultimately, we believe that mooring our social justice work in a human rights framework can help us better resist the narrowed conceptions of education that are pervasive today. As we will show, the language of human rights speaks back to the one-dimensional reduction of education to test scores and job training. In so doing, it helps us connect not only our frustrations but also our hopes to a broader international struggle for justice.

A Brief History of the Universal Declaration of Human Rights

In the first half of the twentieth century and after two world wars, the Great Depression, and the dismantling of colonial empires, the world wrestled with injustice, aggression, and economic collapse on a massive scale. In the wake of this tumult, there was overwhelming global attention on the codification of a universal moral code. This was ultimately realized when, a few weeks after Germany's 1945 surrender in World War II, fifty-one nations signed the UN Charter (Glendon 2001; Ishay 2004; Morsink 1999).

The UN Charter has four goals: (1) to prevent future wars; (2) to establish international justice; (3) to promote social progress and improved standards of living; and, according to the Preamble of the Charter, (4) "to affirm faith in fundamental human rights, in the dignity and worth of the human person, in the equal rights of men and women and of nations large and small." This affirmation of human rights can be seen as a pragmatic approach to prioritizing global justice, a tool outlining minimum standards of human dignity (Appiah 2003; Ignatieff 2003; Koenig 1997; Mower 1979).

The early years of the United Nations were marked by singular focused attention to this human rights agenda. The first human rights treaties, the Convention on the Prevention and Punishment of the Crime of Genocide and the Nuremburg Principles, were written in direct response to what was seen as an ultimate act of social injustice, the Holocaust (Ishay 2004; Morsink 1999). At its first General Assembly meeting in January 1946, the United Nations established a Human Rights Commission, whose primary task would be to author an international bill of rights—what we now know as the Universal Declaration of Human Rights (UDHR) (Glendon 2001).

The United States, under the leadership of Franklin Delano Roosevelt, played an important role in this work. For example, Roosevelt's "Four Freedoms" speech is often given credit for providing the basic framework of the UDHR (Anderson 2003; Glendon 2001; Ishay 2004; Johnson 1987; Mower 1979):

The first is freedom of speech and expression—everywhere in the world. The second is freedom of every person to worship God in his own way—everywhere in the world. The third is freedom from want—which, translated into world terms, means economic understandings which will secure to every nation a healthy peacetime life for its inhabitants—everywhere in the world. The fourth is freedom from fear—which, translated into world terms, means a world-wide reduction of armaments to such a point and in such a thorough fashion that no nation will be in a position to commit an act of physical aggression against any neighbor—anywhere in the world. (Roosevelt 1941:para. 73)

The "four freedoms" importantly hit on two central points in the consideration of human rights: first, that the rights to be protected were both civil/political and economic/social, and second, that international peace was itself a human right (Mower 1979). These four freedoms laid out a vision of an economic and political system more just than the unbridled capitalism advocated in the United States then, as now: economic freedom meant that individuals should be protected from a freedom from want (Ishay 2004). It was ultimately Eleanor Roosevelt, and not Franklin, who, as chair of the UN Human Rights Commission, helped bring this vision to life in the UDHR (Glendon 2001; Johnson 1987).

Codifying Human Rights

[The UN members] believe that men and women, all over the world, have the right to live . . . free from the haunting fear of poverty and insecurity. . . . They believe that science and the arts should combine to serve peace and the well-being, spiritual as well as material, of all men and women without discrimination of any kind. They believe that . . . the power is in their hands to advance . . . this well-being more swiftly than in any previous age. (UNESCO 1949:259)

In the initial work of the Human Rights Commission (HRC), there was a strong push to define human rights in terms of racial antidiscrimination. This stance was given priority in the aftermath of the Holocaust (Morsink 1999). This focus was widely supported by delegates from the Philippines, Egypt, India, the Dominican Republic, Cuba, France, the Soviet Republics, Latin America, and even the United States (Glendon 2001; Hareven 1968). In fact, in its survey of global rights traditions, UNESCO found antidiscrimination and acceptance of difference to be one of the most shared refrains.[2] The United Nations chose to work toward this goal of antidiscrimination through the naming and protection of fundamental human rights (Ishay 2004). Although some of the most powerful governments strongly resisted this agenda, less powerful nations (China, Syria, India, Argentina) ultimately banded together to insist on the preeminence of human rights in the United Nations' mission (Anderson 2003; Johnson 1987; Morsink 1999; Mower 1997).

As understood by the UN delegates, human rights led to justice by challenging unequal hierarchies of power, amplifying the voices of the weak, and working to eliminate the root causes of conflict: poverty, discrimination, and exploitation (Ishay 2004; UNESCO 1949). President Truman described this nexus of concerns at the signing of the UN Charter: "Experience has shown how deeply the seeds of war are planted by economic rivalry and social injustice" (Glendon 2001:238). Over forty years later, the secretary general of the United Nations, Boutros Boutros-Ghali, echoed Truman in his description of one of the United Nations' primary aims as "address[ing] the deepest causes of conflict: economic despair, social injustice and political oppression" (Andreopoulos 1997:11). This attention to economic, political, and social inequality remains the focus of twenty-first-century social justice and human rights work.

What are the specific rights guaranteed by the UDHR that work toward justice? The UDHR includes two broad categories of rights—(1) political/civil and (2) social/economic/cultural—echoing FDR's four freedoms: "freedom of speech and belief and freedom from fear and want [have] been proclaimed as the highest aspiration of the common people" (UN 1948:Preamble). Furthermore, the UDHR declared the equality of all humans, the right to self-determination, and the freedom from tyranny, oppression, and exploitation. *All* persons—regardless of race, nationality, creed, gender, age, religion, or any other identity status—were granted rights to challenge injustice, barbarism, and oppression.[3]

In its thirty articles, the UDHR outlaws slavery, servitude, torture, arbitrary arrest, detention, and interference in private matters. It affirms equal recognition and protection before the law, fair trials, and innocence until proven guilty. It guarantees freedom of movement, residence, speech, religion, thought, and opinion. It also guarantees the right to asylum, to claim a nationality, to marry and have a family, to own property, to change one's religion, to participate in government, to receive social security, to work at the job of one's choosing, to be paid an equal and living wage, to organize and join trade unions, to enjoy rest and leisure, to secure an adequate standard of living (with specific reference to food, clothing, housing, and medical care), to attend free and compulsory elementary schooling, to participate in an education promoting human rights and self-actualization, to engage in the cultural life of the community, and to experience international peace. Governments should be invested in protecting these rights in order to foster a minimum level of social, political, and economic equality.

As is clear from this catalogue of guarantees, the UDHR conceived of human rights far more broadly than traditional Western civil rights, such as those articulated in the U.S. Bill of Rights. In what was seen as a radical departure from the Western rights tradition, which focused only on personal liberties, the UDHR included rights to economic opportunity, protection, and development. In that regard, two distinct rights traditions are codified. The first tradition, Western civil rights, is associated with the British, French, and American revolutionary documents; civil rights protect property, life, and liberty as well as the freedoms of speech, religion, and assembly. In this tradition, the emphasis is on "individual liberty and initiative more than equality or social solidarity" (Glendon 2001:xvii). On the other hand, dignitarian rights emphasize equality, fraternity, and collective responsibility, balancing individual liberties with social and state responsibility. Dignitarian rights include the right to work, to education, and to basic subsistence. This tradition is most closely associated with social democracies, such as in Scandinavia and Latin America. Early drafts of the UDHR took their list of rights largely verbatim from the 1948 Bogotá Conference's Pan-American Declaration of Rights, a document in the dignitarian rights tradition. However, they also reflected the Roosevelts' American conceptions of social justice (Glendon 2001; Johnson 1987; Morsink 1999; Richardson 2000).

This unlikely combination of rights traditions on opposite sides of the burgeoning Cold War—civil/political rights associated with the United States and social/economic rights with the USSR[4]—demonstrates the HRC's deep understanding of the role of inequality in fomenting aggression and unrest. Reiterated throughout the drafting process were assertions that political independence and economic sovereignty go hand in hand, that international security and civil rights are dependent on economic justice, and that genuine justice ensures an individual's personal *and* economic security. The language of human rights was seen as affording a broader vision of social equality than civil or dignitarian rights on their own (Anderson 2003; Glendon 2001; Ishay 2004; Morsink 1999; UNESCO 1949).

The UDHR also goes beyond American civil rights in its insistence on state responsibility. In Western rights theory, the role of the state is limited to ensuring that individual liberties (e.g., to speech, to property) are not compromised. However, according to the UDHR, the state is responsible for actively ensuring and providing for the economic and social welfare of its citizens through guarantees of equal wages, decent housing, and social services. Whereas the civil rights tradition might simply guarantee an individual the right to work if he or she chooses and if jobs are available, the United Nations' articulation of human rights would instead guarantee that any individual who wants to work *will* work, with government initiatives providing employment when private markets do not, and that he or she will be given equal pay for equal work, earning enough to provide an adequate standard of living. In this, the government does more than protect against intrusions on individual liberty; rather, the government guarantees and provides a certain standard of living. Although contested by Americans, this was a widely supported philosophy, one emphasizing individual liberty and collective responsibility equally (Glendon 2001; Ishay 2004; Morsink 1999; UNESCO 1949).

Promoting Human Rights Through Education

Education shall be directed to the full development of the human personality and to the strengthening of respect for human rights and fundamental freedoms. It shall promote understanding, tolerance, and friendship among all nations, racial or religious groups, and shall further the activities of the UN for the maintenance of peace.
—The Universal Declaration of Human Rights (1948),
Article 26.2

The UDHR guarantees to all people the right to education. While early drafts limited this to free and compulsory elementary education, the final document gives education a more prominent role in fostering respect for human rights. The Preamble itself names education as *the* primary vehicle for doing this: "This Universal Declaration of Human Rights, as a common standard of achievement for all peoples and all nations, to the end that every individual and every organ of society, shall strive by teaching and education to promote respect for these rights and freedoms" (UN 1948:Preamble). Strangely enough, this emphasis on education as the primary arbiter of human rights is the result of one of the central conflicts in the drafting of the UDHR: What was the role of the state in promoting human rights (Glendon 2001)? For example, U.S. Secretary of State John Foster Dulles, who served under President Eisenhower and, like Eisenhower, opposed the UDHR, argued that it was the role of education and not governments to foster a human rights culture (Anderson 2003; Hareven 1968). UDHR drafter and French philosopher René Cassin, who believed in state responsibility for protecting human rights, still saw education as having unparalleled power to promote human rights:

Legal force of itself is only a secondary safety valve: it is the education of young people and even of adults that constitutes the primary and real guarantee for minority groups faced with racial hatred that leads so easily to violence and murder. (Osler and Starkey 2000b:94)

This emphasis on education for human rights is reflected in the declaration's wording, which describes the right to education as more than compulsory and free elementary education (although this is seen as the most basic level of educational right). Instead, UDHR drafters answered the challenge of human rights education becoming "education for acquiescence or education for freedom" (UNESCO 1949:223), coming down firmly on the side of education for freedom. This emphasis was eloquently described by Eleanor Roosevelt, who believed that education was the best means for promoting social justice:

Where, after all, do universal human rights begin? In small places, close to home—so close and so small that they cannot be seen on any maps of the world. Yet they are the world of the individual person; the neighborhood he lives in; the school or college he attends; the factory, farm, or office where he works. Such are the places where every man, woman and child seeks equal justice, equal opportunity, equal dignity without discrimination. Unless these rights have meaning there, they have little meaning anywhere. (UN 2014:para. 3)

In the end, even opponents of the UDHR agreed that education played a central role in maintaining rights, freedom, and democracy.

Critiques of the Universal Declaration of Human Rights

The UDHR is frequently critiqued—for its compromises due to Cold War politicking (Anderson 2003; Glendon 2001; Morsink 1999), for its implicit American exceptionalism embedded within it (Jenkins and Cox 2005), for its ignoring of gender rights (MacKinnon 1993). But perhaps the most worrisome critique is of the UDHR as culturally imperialist. Human rights are often critiqued as a Western construction that invalidates others' right to cultural and political self-determination. In particular, the supremacy of individual rights over collective rights reflects these Western priorities. This perception of cultural imperialism was strengthened when the United

Nations later denied colonial territories' demands for independence (Burke 2006; Glendon 2003; Howard 1997–1998; Ishay 2004). Human rights were universal so long as they did not challenge traditional power structures.

While these are important critiques, it is also important to acknowledge the ways in which they are not entirely true. For example, although the United States did play a heavy-handed role in the codifying of human rights, it was actually *other* member nations that became their most outspoken advocates (Mower 1979): China pushed for the explicit inclusion of human rights, justice, and racial equality in the UN Charter when the United States, the UK, and the USSR resisted. These efforts were later joined by other global leaders, such as Mahatma Gandhi (India), Carlos Romulo (Philippines), Charles Malik (Lebanon), Ho Chi Minh (Vietnam), Kwame Nkrumah (Ghana), Leopold Senghor (Senegal), and W. E. B. Du Bois (United States) (Anderson 2003; Ishay 2004).

In addition, although the codification of rights had largely been a Western undertaking (e.g., the Bill of Rights, the Declaration of the Rights of Man), the UNESCO philosophers' survey of 1949 found that, "where basic human values are concerned, cultural diversity had been exaggerated . . . a core of fundamental principles was widely shared in countries that had not yet adopted rights instruments and in cultures that had not embraced the language of rights" (Glendon 2001:222). Indeed, some of the most compelling arguments for universal human rights came from non-Western thinkers. When drafting the UDHR, the Human Rights Commission was deliberate about including these diverse voices and traditions, and the earliest drafts were particularly influenced by the 1948 Pan-American Declaration of Rights and included rights found in the constitutions of Scandinavia and the Soviet Republics as well as in Asian philosophy (UNESCO 1949).

However, African representation, save for South Africa, was strikingly absent; most African nations were still under colonial yoke (Morsink 1999). Yet by 1966, many independent African nations played a prominent role in writing the binding treaties that became the human rights covenants, namely the International Covenant on Civil and Political Rights (ICCPR) and the International Covenant on Economic, Social and Cultural Rights (ICESCR) (Hareven 1968). Moreover, twenty-two postcolonial African constitutions make explicit mention of human rights, which also figure prominently in the charter of the Organization of African Unity (Mower 1979). Thus, despite the prominence of the United States in codifying universal human rights, the language of human rights became central to anticolonial and anti-imperialist struggles. Even at the 1955 Bandung Conference, one of the first gatherings of what would subsequently come to be called the "Third World" nations, human rights were essential for *challenging*—rather than perpetuating—Western imperialism (Burke 2006).

What is clearly missing, however, is any guarantee of minority or group rights (Burke 2006; Howard 1997–1998). For the postcolonial world, cultural and group rights have been intimately linked to the right to self-determination. During the UDHR drafting process, there was significant pressure to guarantee minority rights and to include the statement "Cultural groups shall not be denied the right to free self-development," but it was defeated (Glendon 2001:119). Eleanor Roosevelt, in particular, believed that minority rights did not apply in the Americas because of what she called the "assimilationist ideal" (Glendon 2001). In the end, the Americans won: There is no guarantee of group or cultural rights in the UDHR.

Universal Human Rights as an International Language of Justice

There are two sides to the human rights program. Freedom of expression, freedom of worship, freedom of suffrage. But much closer to the people in the new world is the question of something to eat and a better life.

—Eleanor Roosevelt (Johnson 1989:36)

By looking to this history of the UDHR, we can see that social justice in the era of human rights included both individual liberties and economic security. Human rights were the specific guarantees—for example, to equal pay, to an adequate standard of living, or to the freedom of thought—that could promote this vision of social justice. By codifying an international language for describing oppression, human rights documents provided a new common language for contesting injustice.

Human Rights and the American Civil Rights Movement

Human rights also became a central tool of the civil rights movement in the United States. In the immediate post–World War II context, the NAACP—under the executive direction of Walter White and the philosophical direction of W. E. B. Du Bois—looked to link the struggle for African American equality and justice at home to the global struggle for human rights. White noted in 1944:

> [African Americans took] literally the shibboleths of the Four Freedoms . . . [and] they intend[ed] to secure and enjoy those freedoms and to put an end to the old order in which men, solely because they are colored, can be worked to exhaustion, exploited, despised, spat upon and derided by those whose chief right to sovereignty is whiteness of skin. (Anderson 2003:17)

The rights specified by the UDHR, such as the right to an equal and living wage and the right to move freely and to choose one's residence, were a "lifeline" for those mired in the injustices of Jim Crow (Anderson 2003).

Moreover, the UDHR drafting process revealed the power of human rights language to shame America's discriminatory practices. Throughout the drafting, both the United States and the Soviet Union regularly used the language of human rights to call attention to one another's hypocrisy, with the United States being periodically lumped together with the burgeoning apartheid regime of South Africa as examples of state-sponsored discrimination (Anderson 2003; Dudziak 2000; Glendon 2001; Hareven 1968; Ishay 2004; Johnson 1987).

A human rights framework also supported post–World War II fights for equality. For example, returning black veterans launched the "Double V" campaign—"Victory at home, victory abroad"—in which they linked their fight for justice and democracy in Europe to the fight for African American equality at home. The NAACP also challenged Winston Churchill's "racing" of the Atlantic Charter—he claimed its freedoms were for whites only—by demanding a seat at the negotiating table at the United Nations. The language of human rights lent weight to African American leaders' challenge to President Truman's belief that African Americans wanted "justice, not social equality" by arguing that social and economic equality were necessary correlates for social justice (Anderson 2003:2).

Most significantly, African American organizations three times petitioned the United Nations to intervene on behalf of the United States' human rights violations against African Americans: the National Negro Congress's 1946 petition, "A Petition to the United Nations on Behalf of 13

Million Oppressed Negro Citizens of the United States of America"; the NAACP's 1947 petition, "An Appeal to the World"; and the Civil Rights Congress's (CRC) 1951 petition, "We Charge Genocide." All three petitions were an attempt to lift the struggle for racial justice in the United States to an international arena, both because such an international focus might pressure the United States into taking greater action at home and because it explicitly connected the struggle for African American equality with the struggle for global justice. Although none of these petitions were ultimately successful, they did succeed at publicly shaming the United States' state-sponsored discrimination (Anderson 2003; Dudziak 2000; Glendon 2001).

The language of human rights thus proved a powerful vehicle, both domestically and internationally, to challenge U.S. inequities and injustices. This power was the very reason that Roosevelt and the other U.S. representatives worked so hard to *prevent* African Americans from linking their domestic struggle with human rights. Opponents knew that doing so might open the United States to international critique. Unfortunately, the tangle of Cold War politics eventually led the NAACP and other civil rights leaders to abandon this human rights platform for the limited equality afforded by civil rights alone (Dudziak 2000; Hobbins 1998). Historian Carol Anderson argues that the civil rights movement ultimately failed because it did not maintain this connection to human rights (Anderson 2003).

Human Rights, Protest Movements, and Social Justice Principles

While early civil rights leaders may have abandoned human rights, later social justice leaders and movements explicitly drew on human rights in their vision of social change. For example, both Martin Luther King Jr. and Malcolm X longed to transform the civil rights movement into a human rights movement (Anderson 2003). King wrote his "Letter from a Birmingham Jail" while imprisoned for work on behalf of the Alabama Christian Movement for Human Rights, and he spoke eloquently in other writings about the demands of the "human rights revolution" (King 1963, 1968). Malcolm X argued, "How is a black man going to get 'civil rights' before he first wins his human rights? If the American black man will start thinking about his human rights, and then start thinking of himself as part of one of the world's greatest people, he will see he has a case for the United Nations" (Malcolm X and Haley 1972:207). In this, he echoed what the NAACP and the CRC had argued in their petitions to the United Nations: *human* rights superseded civil rights. Civil rights, after all, could only be granted to citizens, full human members of a community; as long as the United States continued to deny African Americans their human rights, they would remain less than human in law and society, not considered fully human enough to be granted civil rights.

King and Malcolm X were not alone in their orientation to human rights. In the 1960s and 1970s, the National Organization for Women (NOW), the gay rights movement, and the United Farm Workers (UFW), among others, all described their work in terms of human rights. The charter for NOW declared:

> We ... believe that the time has come for a new movement toward true equality for all women in America, and toward a fully equal partnership of the sexes, as part of the *world-wide revolution of human rights* now taking place within and beyond our national borders. ... We realize that women's problems are linked to many broader questions of social justice; their solution will require concerted action by many groups. Therefore, convinced that human rights for all are indivisible, we expect to give active support to the common cause of equal rights for all those who suffer discrimination and deprivation. (Friedan 1966:paras. 1, 13)

As described here, a human rights framework provided a language for contesting inequality; more succinctly, Cesar Chavez described his labor rights movement as "seek[ing] our basic, God-given rights as human beings" (United Farm Workers 2008:para. 4).

One of the particular reasons human rights was embraced by later social movements was its emphasis on cultural pluralism. Because the codification of human rights originated as a means of resisting state-sponsored racism, the framing of human rights embraces cultural pluralism (Ignatieff 2003; Osler and Starkey 2000a, 2000b). Figueroa explains this connection between pluralism and human rights:

> Citizenship (in a plural society) involves commitment to the society in its diversity; openness to, and indeed solidarity with and respect

for, the different other, in particular the "ethnically" different; acceptance of the basic equal worth of all people, of the rights and responsibilities of all; and a rejection of any form of exploitation, inequitable treatment or racism. (Figueroa 2000:57).

However, a social justice commitment to diversity is about far more than tolerance. Rather, it is intended to be antiracist and antioppressive. After all, the persistence of institutional racism (and sexism, ableism, classism, and homophobia) is a direct threat to human rights and to democracy (Ignatieff 2003; Osler and Starkey 2000a). Many protest movements grew in direct response to the persistence of institutionalized discrimination. In doing so, they articulated a vision of the world in which diverse groups were not merely tolerated, but rather were made integral to civil society—the kind of pluralistic society the UDHR implicitly promotes.

A corollary to pluralism is a commitment to amplifying marginalized voices. After all, at the heart of universal human rights is providing "an avenue of power for the disadvantaged" (Richardson 2000:82) by allowing the claims of victims to speak louder than the claims of oppressors (Ignatieff 2003; Spencer 2000). Amplifying the voices of marginalized people is *how* human rights are realized, and this is the heart the work of social justice movements. For example, the American Indian Movement insists on the rights of indigenous peoples to interpret treaties and to address the federal government (Wittstock and Salinas 2008), while the Human Rights Campaign actively works to elect officials who will speak on behalf of LGBTIQ individuals (Human Rights Campaign 2015). Collectivizing the voices of the less powerful is central to the human right to self-determination.

However, the most fundamental way that social justice movements align with a human rights framework is in their demands for the economic and social rights guaranteed in the UDHR: equal pay for equal work, living wages, adequate health care, social support for the impoverished, equitable and meaningful education, and reducing the gap between rich and poor. Political philosopher Amy Gutmann argues, "Starving people are denied their human agency. They are also being denied their dignity, and they are being degraded. They are not being treated as agents with a human life to lead" (Gutmann 2003:xii).

The social justice movements of the late twentieth century recognized this and advocated for the economic and social rights of all citizens. AIM

vows to "reclaim and affirm health, housing, employment, economic development, and education for all Indian people" (Wittstock and Salinas
2008:para 10). NOW "envision[s] a world where social and economic justice
exist, where all people have the food, housing, clothing, health care and education they need" (National Organization for Women 1998). The Gay Liberation Front, after the Stonewall riots, demanded the right of homosexuals
to own their businesses and run their own organizations (Gay Liberation
Front 1969). The UFW struggled not merely for employment security and
rights but also for the protection of the physical health of farm workers by
protesting the use of pesticides (Chavez 1989). Martin Luther King Jr. and
Myles Horton launched a Poor People's Campaign in which a "multiracial
army of the poor" would demand economic justice. The Individuals with
Disabilities in Education Act mandated that individuals with disabilities be
afforded equal educational opportunities. All of these movements are centrally concerned with the litany of social and economic rights guaranteed by
the UDHR.

Finally, these social justice movements understand the complicity of the
state in perpetuating inequality—and thus the state's *responsibility* for elim-
inating inequality. King famously declared when speaking out against the
war in Vietnam:

> True compassion is more than flinging a coin to a beggar; it is not
> haphazard and superficial. It comes to see that an edifice which pro-
> duces beggars needs restructuring. A true revolution of values will
> soon look uneasily on the glaring contrast of poverty and wealth.
> With righteous indignation, it will look across the seas and see
> individual capitalists of the West investing huge sums of money in
> Asia, Africa and South America, only to take the profits out with no
> concern for the social betterment of the countries, and say: "This is
> not just." (King 1967:paras. 46–47)

This is precisely the perspective called for by a former UN Special Rappor-
teur on the Right to Education when arguing that schools (a vehicle of the
state), rather than trying to correct the "socially excluded" individuals themselves, need to recognize and address the "statal" and systemic exclusions
and discriminations that oppress students—to understand that "socially excluded" students are excluded through state actions and inactions—and to

understand that it is a *human rights obligation* to address these systemic inequalities (Alderson 2000).

Connecting Justice-Oriented Pedagogies with a Human Rights Framework

Teaching for social justice might be thought of as a kind of popular education—of, by, and for the people—something that lies at the heart of education in a democracy, education toward a more vital, more muscular democratic society. It can propel us toward action, away from complacency, reminding us of the powerful commitment, persistence, bravery, and triumphs of our justice-seeking forebears— women and men who sought to build a world that worked for us all.

—William Ayers (2008)

Justice-oriented teaching can be understood as the descendant of this human rights framework. Whether looking at critical pedagogy, antiracist teaching, multicultural education, or social justice education, all of these liberatory approaches to teaching embody the human rights commitments to cultural pluralism, amplifying marginalized voices, social and economic rights, and analyzing systems of (in)justice. Thus, justice-oriented pedagogies are fulfilling the vision of global justice and human dignity promoted in the UDHR and expected to be spread through education. To support this claim, we first need to define justice-oriented teaching.

Two theories of justice are often used to frame justice work in education. The first is John Rawls' theory of distributive justice, in which injustice is rooted in macro-level, political and economic structures that cause exploitation and material deprivation and prevent self-actualization (Rawls 1971). The second framework is Nancy Fraser's dualism of redistribution and recognition. In this theory, injustice can stem not just from one's unfair exclusion from the macro-level political and economic order but also from the denial of one's lived experience, identity, and culture. Justice, then, is not simply the redistribution of material resources but also the recognition and acceptance of diverse perspectives and experiences. Justice is about economic rights, political rights, and cultivating authentic pluralism (Fraser 2003).

Theories of justice in education use these frameworks as a jumping-off point. For example, Cochran-Smith describes teaching for social justice as an intellectual approach to the inescapably political work of schooling. The three key components to her theory—equity of learning opportunities, respect for social groups, and teaching through tension—lead to the promotion of students' learning and the enhancement of their life chances. Teaching for social justice must connect "distributive justice, which locates equality and autonomy at the center of democratic societies, with current political struggles for recognition, which challenge the school and knowledge structures that reinforce the disrespect and oppression of social groups" (Cochran-Smith 2009:451). Another formulation is North's: If the ultimate goal of social justice is the restructuring of the political economy—ensuring the economic and political segment of human rights—then social justice education must "challenge the existing hierarchies of power, embracing difference [and] challenging cultural imperialism" (North 2006:510). Grant and Agosto (2008) describe social justice as the aim of education, in that social justice is a regulative system of fairness that ensures the security of citizens, pushes for distributive equality and interrogates why distributive inequalities exist, and aims for the elimination of institutionalized domination. Finally, Westheimer and Kahne's framework of citizenship can also be applied to pedagogy. In their typology, "justice-oriented citizens critically assess social, political, and economic structures and consider collective strategies for change that challenge injustice and, when possible, address root causes of problems" (Westheimer and Kahne 2004:243). Likewise, justice-oriented teachers are similarly attuned to the structures and the root causes of educational inequalities, and they strive to enact pedagogies of change. By embracing cultural differences and promoting pluralism, by challenging cultural imperialism and unequal hierarchies of power, by interrogating material inequalities and advocating for economic justice, by equipping students with the skills necessary to be active and responsible democratic citizens, and by trying to enact equity within the classroom, social justice education works for a world that honors fundamental human rights by offering an education for "the full development of the human personality" (UN 1948 :Article 26.2).

To realize the vision for education established in the UDHR, justice-oriented pedagogies emphasize equipping students with the tools necessary to fulfill their democratic responsibilities (Ayers 2008; Cochran-Smith 2009; Grant and Agosto 2008). One of the central tools of all liberatory pedagogies is critical thinking, which is honed through curricular attention to inequality, injustice, and the violation of human rights (Applebaum 2009; Cochran-Smith 2009; Freire 2008; Gutmann 1999; Sleeter and Grant 1999). For example, students can use basic math skills to analyze injustices and inequalities in their communities—such as access to water, neighborhood displacement, and educational inequity (Denny 2013; Gonzalez-Carillo and Merson 2013; Gutstein 2013). In justice-oriented teaching, mastery of skills raises students' critical consciousness and develops their ability to advocate for justice and rights. This is the precise role of education laid out in the UDHR.

A former director general of UNESCO explained, "Education for human rights and democracy in the last analysis means the empowerment of each and every individual to participate with an active sense of responsibility in all aspects of political and social life" (Spencer 2000:28). This type of education is a means of resisting the systemic perpetuation of inequality and discrimination. By encouraging students to examine their world through sociopolitical critique, justice-oriented educators—like human rights educators—are "working in the small places" to promote a culture of justice and rights. The emphasis on working in the small places stands in stark contrast to contemporary discourses of education reform, which emphasize test scores, narrowed curriculum, market preparation, cultural assimilation, and obedience. Instead, by prioritizing human rights values and rooting our work in this global language of justice, justice-oriented educators bring the support of a global community to their pedagogies of action, critique, pluralism, and critical thinking.

Conclusion: Taking the Long View

In the globalized landscape of the twenty-first century, struggles against oppression transcend national boundaries and group identities. In fact, neoliberalism works by weaving race, class, and hierarchies of privilege together to create entrenched systems of economic, political, and racial oppression. More insidiously, these newly magnified inequalities are designed to convince those on the losing end that they are, truly, to blame. We see this in popular school reform, where teachers and communities of color are simplistically blamed for educational "failings"—never mind the processes of global capital, social privatization, and hegemonic culture that have successfully stripped neighborhoods of their civic and economic resources (Lipman 2013). We see this, too, in discourses of "no excuses" schooling and the "new paternalism" of urban schooling (Thernstrom and Thernstrom 2001; Whitman 2008). We see it as well in the blurring of ideologies—where "liberal" has come to mean conservative, where "social justice" is used even by far-right politicians, and where "postracial" color blindness masks strengthened racial hierarchies and systems of mass oppression (Alexander 2010; Kumashiro 2008; Obama 2009; Office of the Press Secretary 2007).

It is within this context that justice-oriented teachers work. While individual actions in our classrooms matter greatly, they are not enough on their own to challenge the multiheaded hydra of neoliberalism, as the New York Collective of Radical Educators describes our current educational moment. Rooting our work in the language and history of human rights is one way of collectivizing our daily struggles and of acknowledging that our work falls within a broader tradition of antioppressive education. Moreover, a human rights framework challenges us as educators to look beyond the siloed categories of critical pedagogies in an American context. Cultural relevance, social justice, critical pedagogy, antiracist, multicultural—while there are certainly important differences in these approaches, all share a commitment to the same economic, political, social, and civil rights articulated in the UDHR. This is, after all, at the heart of what many justice-oriented educators believe they are working for.

In addition, by locating our work as critical educators in the broader struggle for human rights, we are encouraged to think about our work intersectionally. Oppression and injustice—and likewise, privilege and power—operate in multiple dimensions. Race matters, class matters, gender matters, sexuality matters, migration status matters—taken collectively, each magnifies and complicates the others (Grant and Zweir 2011). A human rights framework invites us to consider the intersection of, for example, political power, economic exploitation, and racial injustice; it invites us to consider how personal liberties intersect with security of person; it invites to consider how state responsibility for injustice affects the individual; and so on. These human rights violations occur across multiple identity dimensions, and thus a human rights framework urges us to consider how forms of oppression intersect with one another. Of course, as with human rights in general, there is the danger of whitewashing: ensuring that "all children" have access to a high-quality education can quickly become color-blind language that reentrenches injustice. The "intersectionality" of human rights can easily obfuscate the unique and powerful ways that individuals experience oppression—raced, classed, politicized, gendered oppressions. However, by marrying our critical pedagogies with a human rights framework, we are hopeful that sharply honed critical analysis can resist these obfuscations.

Finally, rooting our work in a human rights history acknowledges what is at the heart of justice-oriented teaching and liberatory education: a belief in the need for third-order change. Unlike many approaches to social change that tinker with the mechanical details of resources, access, and law, third-order change seeks to change individuals "core normative beliefs about such matters as race, class, intelligence, and educability" (Renee, Welner, and Oakes 2009:156). Within the context of education, third-order change is essential for achieving equity and justice. No amount of tinkering can change the deficit views of marginalized communities; no amount of tinkering can push privileged constituencies to share power. Instead, third-order change acknowledges the long view: Society will change only when hearts and minds change. We must continue in the political arena to demand justice, but we must also look to the next generation and, as Eleanor Roosevelt urged, "work in the small places." As Bryan McKinley Jones Brayboy regularly remarks, justice is a long-term project; as educators, we must take the long view. After all, sixty-five years later, we are *still* working for "the advent of a world in which human beings shall enjoy freedom of speech and belief and freedom from fear and want . . . the highest aspiration of the common people" (UN 1948:Preamble).

Notes

This chapter is a reworking of our earlier collaborations on human rights and the genesis of social justice education. Please see Melissa Gibson and Carl Grant, "'Working in the Small Places': A Human Rights History of Multicultural Democratic Education," in Rumjahn Hoosain and Farideh Salili, eds., *Democracy and Multicultural Education* (Charlotte, NC: Information Age Publishing, 2010), 43–71; Carl Grant and Melissa Gibson, "These Are Revolutionary Times: Human Rights, Social Justice, and Popular Protest," in Thandeka Chapman and Nikkola Hobbel, eds., *The Practice of Freedom: Social Justice Pedagogy Across the Curriculum* (New York: Routledge, 2010), 9–35; and Carl Grant and Melissa Gibson, "'The Path of Social Justice': A Human Rights History of Social Justice Education," *Equity and Excellence in Education* 46(1) (2013):81–99.

1. Jim Crow laws refer to the system of legal segregation in place in the United States after Reconstruction, or after the end of the Civil War and slavery. Jim Crow laws created a system of separate and unequal societies in which black Americans were legally treated as inferior citizens. See Michelle Alexander's book, *The New Jim Crow:*

Mass Incarceration in the Age of Colorblindness (New Press, 2010), for an analysis of how today's state-sponsored racism is a direct descendant of these Jim Crow laws.

2. Concurrent with the Human Rights Commission's work on drafting the UDHR, the UN Educational and Scientific Committee (UNESCO) set about surveying philosophers, politicians, scholars, scientists, and educators the world over in order to determine whether there were such things as *universal* human rights. UNESCO collected its responses and submitted them to the Human Rights Commission as evidence of and guidance for universal human rights as well as a warning about the limits of crafting a universal declaration. While the HRC did not use UNESCO's survey, most of UNESCO's findings correspond to the UDHR (Glendon 2001; UNESCO 1949).

3. While sexual minorities are outspoken advocates for social justice in contemporary society, and while they often figure in a listing of marginalized and oppressed identities, it is important to note that LGBTIQ individuals were not explicitly included in the original concern for human rights or in the United Nations' codification of human rights.

4. Of course, aligning social/economic rights and civil/political rights along Cold War ideologies is a gross oversimplification, particularly its conflation of socialism and communism. As pointed out, dignitarian rights have long been associated with socialist societies—especially the social democracies in Scandinavia, Latin America, and Europe. Socialism is an economic system built on cooperative management of the economy, as opposed to an economy of unregulated free markets. There is a vast range of what this can look like in practice. Communism is a frequently totalitarian political and economic system with an ideal of a classless and stateless society. A socialist economy is compatible with a democratic political system; communism is not.

References

Alderson, Priscilla. 2000. "Practicing Democracy in Two Inner City Schools." In Audrey Osler, ed., *Citizenship and Democracy in Schools: Diversity, Identity, and Equality* (pp. 125–132). Stoke-on-Trent: Trentham.

Alexander, Michelle. 2010. *The New Jim Crow: Mass Incarceration in the Age of Colorblindness.* New York: New Press.

Anderson, Carol. 2003. *Eyes off the Prize: The United Nations and the African American Struggle for Human Rights, 1944–1955.* New York: Cambridge University Press.

Andreopoulos, George. 1997. "Human Rights Education in the Post-Cold War Context." In George Andreopoulos and Richard Pierre Claude, eds., *Human Rights Education for the Twenty-First Century* (pp. 9–20). Philadelphia: University of Pennsylvania Press.

Appiah, Kwame Anthony. 2003. "Grounding Human Rights." In Amy Gutmann, ed., *Michael Ignatieff: Human Rights as Politics and Idolatry* (pp. 101–116). Princeton, NJ: Princeton University Press.

Applebaum, Barbara. 2009. "Is Teaching for Social Justice a 'Liberal Bias'?" *Teachers College Record* 111(2):376–408.

Ayers, William. 2008. "Social Justice and Teaching." http://billayers.wordpress.com /2008/05/07/social-justice-and-teaching/.

Bourdieu, Pierre, and Jean-Claude Passeron. 1990. *Reproduction in Education, Society, and Culture* (Richard Nice, trans.). London: Sage.

Brayboy, Bryan McKinley Jones. 2011. "Genesis Amnesia, Indigenous Knowledge Systems, and Indigenous Peoples." Paper presented at the annual meeting of the American Educational Research Association, New Orleans, LA, April 11, 2011.

Burke, Roland. 2006. "'The Compelling Dialogue of Freedom': Human Rights at the Bandung Conference." *Human Rights Quarterly* 28(4):947–965.

Chavez, Cesar. 1989. "Address at Pacific Lutheran University, Tacoma, Washington." http://www.ufw.org/_page.php?menu=research&inc=history/10.html.

Cochran-Smith, Marilyn. 2009. "Toward a Theory of Teacher Education for Social Justice." In Andy Hargreaves, Ann Lieberman, Michael Fullan, and David Hopkins, eds., *Second International Handbook of Educational Change* (pp. 445–467). New York: Springer International.

Denny, Flannery. 2013. "Beyond Marbles: Percent Change and Social Justice." *Rethinking Schools* 27(3):24–29.

Dudziak, Mary L. 2000. *Cold War Civil Rights: Race and the Image of American Democracy.* Princeton, NJ: Princeton University Press.

Figueroa, Peter. 2000. "Citizenship Education for a Plural Society." In Audrey Osler, ed., *Citizenship and Democracy in Schools: Diversity, Identity, and Equality* (pp. 47–62). Stoke-on-Trent: Trentham.

Fraser, Nancy. 2003. "Social Justice in an Age of Identity Politics: Redistribution, Recognition and Participation." In Nancy Fraser and Alex Honneth, eds., *Redistribution or Recognition: A Political-Philosophical Debate* (pp. 7–109). London, England: Verso Books.

Freire, Paulo. 2008. *Education for Critical Consciousness.* New York: Continuum Books.

Friedan, Betty. 1966. "The National Organization for Women's 1966 Declaration of Purpose." http://www.now.org/history/purpos66.html.

Gay Liberation Front. 1969. "A Radical Manifesto: The Homophile Movement Must Be Radicalized." http://www.fordham.edu/halsall/pwh/1969docs.html.

Gibson, Melissa, and Carl Grant. "'Working in the Small Places': A Human Rights History of Multicultural Democratic Education." In Rumjahn Hoosain and Farideh Salili, eds., *Democracy and Multicultural Education* (pp. 43–71). Charlotte, NC: Information Age.

Glendon, Mary Ann. 2001. *A World Made New: Eleanor Roosevelt and the Universal Declaration of Human Rights.* New York: Random House.

Gonzalez-Carillo, Selene, and Martha Merson. 2013. "Transparency of Water: A Workshop on Math, Water, and Justice." *Rethinking Schools* 27(3):18–23.

Grant, Carl, and Vonzell Agosto. 2008. "Teacher Capacity and Social Justice in Teacher Education." In Marilyn Cochran-Smith, Sharon Feiman-Nemser, D. John McIntyre, and Kelly Demers, eds., *Handbook of Research in Teacher Education: Enduring Questions in Changing Contexts* (pp. 175–200). New York: Taylor & Francis.

Grant, Carl, and Melissa Gibson. 2010. "These Are Revolutionary Times: Human Rights, Social Justice, and Popular Protest." In Thandeka Chapman and Nikkola Hobbel, eds., *The Practice of Freedom: Social Justice Pedagogy Across the Curriculum* (pp. 9–35). New York: Routledge.

Grant, Carl, and Melissa Gibson. 2013. "'The Path of Social Justice': A Human Rights History of Social Justice Education." *Equity and Excellence in Education* 46(1):81–99.

Grant, Carl, and Elisa Zweir. 2011. "Intersectionality and Student Outcomes: Sharpening the Struggle Against Racism, Sexism, Classism, Ableism, Heterosexism, Nationalism, and Linguistic, Religious, and Geographical Discrimination in Teaching and Learning." *Multicultural Perspectives* 13(4):81–88.

Gutmann, Amy. 1999. *Democratic Education*. Princeton, NJ: Princeton University Press.

Gutmann, Amy. 2003. "Introduction." In Amy Gutmann, ed., *Michael Ignatieff: Human Rights as Politics and Idolatry* (pp. vii–xxvii). Princeton, NJ: Princeton University Press.

Gutstein, Eric. 2013. "Whose Community Is This? Mathematics of Neighborhood Displacement." *Rethinking Schools* 27(3):11–17.

Hareven, Tamara. 1968. *Eleanor Roosevelt: An American Conscience*. Chicago: Quadrangle Books.

Hobbins, A. John. 1998. "Eleanor Roosevelt, John Humphrey, and the Canadian Opposition to the Universal Declaration of Human Rights: Looking Back on the 50th Anniversary of UNDHR." *International Journal* 53(2):325–342.

Howard, Rhoda E. 1997–1998. "Human Rights and the Culture Wars: Globalization and the Universality of Human Rights." *International Journal*, 53(1):94–112.

Human Rights Campaign. 2015. "Mission Statement." http://www.hrc.org/about_us/2528.htm.

Ignatieff, Michael. 2003. "Human Rights as Politics and Idolatry." In Amy Gutmann, ed., *Michael Ignatieff: Human Rights as Politics and Idolatry* (pp. 3–98). Princeton, NJ: Princeton University Press.

Ishay, Micheline. 2004. *The History of Human Rights: From Ancient Times to the Globalization Era*. Berkeley: University of California Press.

Jenkins, Alan, and Larry Cox. 2005. "Bringing Human Rights Home." *The Nation*, June 27.

Johnson, M. Glen. 1987. "The Contributions of Eleanor and Franklin Roosevelt to the Development of International Protection for Human Rights." *Human Rights Quarterly* 9:19–48.

King, Martin Luther, Jr. 1963. "Letter from a Birmingham Jail." http://mlk-kpp01
.stanford.edu/index.php/encyclopedia/documentsentry/annotated_letter_from
_birmingham/.

King, Martin Luther, Jr. 1967. "Beyond Vietnam." http://mlk-kpp01.stanford.edu
/index.php/encyclopedia/documentsentry/doc_beyond_vietnam/.

King, Martin Luther, Jr. 1968. "I've Been to the Mountaintop." http://mlk-kpp01
.stanford.edu/index.php/encyclopedia/documentsentry/ive_been_to_the
_mountaintop/.

Koenig, Shulamith. 1997. "Foreword." In George Andreopoulos and Richard Pierre
Claude, eds., *Human Rights Education for the Twenty-First Century* (pp. xiii–xvii).
Philadelphia: University of Pennsylvania Press.

Kumashiro, Kevin. 2008. *The Seduction of Common Sense: How the Right Has Framed
the Debate on America's Schools.* New York: Teachers College Press.

Lipman, Pauline. 2013. *The New Political Economy of Urban Education: Neoliberalism,
Race, and the Right to the City.* New York: Routledge.

MacKinnon, Catherine. 1993. "Crimes of War, Crimes of Peace." In Stephen Shute &
Susan Hurley, eds., *On Human Rights: The Oxford Amnesty Lectures, 1993*
(pp. 83–110). New York: Basic Books.

Malcolm X and Alex Haley. 1972. *The Autobiography of Malcolm X.* New York: Bal-
lantine Books.

Morsink, Johannes. 1999. *The Universal Declaration of Human Rights: Origins, Drafting, and Intent.* Philadelphia: University of Pennsylvania Press.

Mower, A. Glenn. 1979. *The United States, the United Nations, and Human Rights: The
Eleanor Roosevelt and Jimmy Carter Eras.* Westport, CT: Greenwood Press.

National Organization for Women. 1998. "Declaration of Sentiments for the National
Organization for Women." http://www.now.org/organization/conference/1998
/vision98.html.

North, Connie E. 2006. "More Than Words? Delving into the Substantive
Meaning(s) of 'Social Justice' in Education." *Review of Educational Research*
76(4):507–535.

Novak, Michael. 2008. "Defining Social Justice." *First Things* 108:11–13.

Obama, Barack. 2009. "Remarks by the President to the Hispanic Chamber of Com-
merce on a Complete and Competitive American Education." http://www.whitehouse
.gov/the_press_office/Remarks-of-the-President-to-the-United-States-Hispanic
-Chamber-of-Commerce/.

Office of the Press Secretary. 2007. "Fact Sheet: Advancing the Cause of Social Justice
in the Western Hemisphere." http://www.whitehouse.gov/news/releases/2007/03
/20070305-4.html.

Osler, Audrey, and Hugh Starkey. 2000a. "Citizenship, Human Rights, and Cultural
Diversity." In Audrey Osler, ed., *Citizenship and Democracy in Schools* (pp. 13–18).
Stoke-on-Trent: Trentham.

Osler, Audrey, and Hugh Starkey. 2000b. "Human Rights, Responsibilities and School Self-Evaluation." In Audrey Osler, ed., *Citizenship and Democracy in Schools* (pp. 91–109). Stoke-on-Trent: Trentham.

Rawls, John. 1971. *A Theory of Justice.* Cambridge, MA: Belknap Press of Harvard University Press.

Renee, Michelle, Kevin Welner, and Jeannie Oakes. 2009. "Social Movement Organizing and Equity-Focused Educational Change: Shifting the Zone of Mediation." In Michael Fullan and David Hopkins, eds., *The Second International Handbook of Educational Change* (pp. 153–168). New York: Springer International.

Richardson, Robin. 2000. "Human Rights and Racial Justice: Connections and Contrasts." In Audrey Osler, ed., *Citizenship and Democracy in Schools* (pp. 79–90). Stoke-on-Trent: Trentham.

Roosevelt, Franklin Delano. 1941. "Annual Message to Congress on the State of the Union, January 6, 1941." FDR Library at Marist University. http://www.fdrlibrary .marist.edu/pdfs/fftext.pdf.

Sleeter, Christine, and Carl Grant. 1999. *Making Choices for Multicultural Education: Five Approaches to Race, Class, and Gender*, 3rd ed. Upper Saddle River, NJ: Merrill Prentice Hall.

Spencer, Sarah. 2000. "The Implications of the Human Rights Act for Citizenship Education." In Audrey Osler, ed., *Citizenship and Democracy in Schools* (pp. 19–32). Stoke-on-Trent: Trentham.

Thernstrom, Stephan, and Abigail Thernstrom. 2001. *No Excuses: Closing the Racial Gap in Learning.* New York: Simon & Schuster.

United Farm Workers. 2008. "Education of the Heart—Quotes by Cesar Chavez." http://ufw.org/_page.php?menu=research&inc=history/09.html.

United Nations. 1948. "Universal Declaration of Human Rights." http://www.un.org /Overview/rights.html.

United Nations. 2014. "Resources for Speakers on Global Issues." http://www.un.org /en/globalissues/briefingpapers/humanrights/quotes.shtml.

United Nations Educational, Scientific and Cultural Organization (UNESCO). 1949. *Human Rights: Comments and Interpretations.* New York: Columbia University Press.

Wallace, David Foster. 2008. "David Foster Wallace on Life and Work." *Wall Street Journal*, September 19. http://online.wsj.com/articles/SB122178211966454607.

Westheimer, Joel, and Joseph Kahne. 2004. "Educating the 'Good' Citizen: Political Choices and Pedagogical Goals." *Political Science & Politics* 37(2):241–247.

Whitman, David. 2008. *Sweating the Small Stuff: Inner-City Schools and the New Paternalism.* Washington, DC: Thomas B Fordham Institute.

Wittstock, Laura Waterman, and Elaine J. Salinas. 2008. "A Brief History of the American Indian Movement." American Indian Movement. http://www.aimovement .org/ggc/history.html.

CHAPTER 10

Expanding the Aspirational Map: Interactive Learning and Human Rights in Tostan's Community Empowerment Program

Beniamino Cislaghi, Diane Gillespie, and Gerry Mackie

Introduction

In 2010, a new cycle of the nongovernmental organization (NGO) Tostan's three-year Community Empowerment Program (CEP), a human rights–based education program, was beginning in rural Senegal. The CEP had been linked with various community results—for example, better health practices, higher participation of women in public decision making, and effective lobbying of local government (Gillespie and Melching 2010; Diop, Moreau, and Benga 2008; CRDH 2010; Kuenzi 2005). The Tostan staff knew from experience that the human rights education classes in the first six months of the program were critical for communities to achieve those results in a sustainable fashion. However, nobody had really studied the ways in which those classes helped participants, most of whom had never been to public schools, to act for community well-being and the promotion of human rights. Knowing how Tostan's human rights curriculum contributed to these results seemed important both practically and theoretically.

An evidence-based corpus of theory and praxis in nonformal transformative HRE would be beneficial for development practitioners working to empower resource-poor rural communities. The HRE literature does not offer many practical models of effective instructional strategies for the nonformal setting. Yet such models have long been called for and bear promising results. Merry (2006), for instance, has argued that we need examples of "community-based" human rights interventions grounded in the belief that "local arrangements can promote human rights and social justice" (104). Examining local conditions as they interface with human rights would be part of an educational approach that values interactive pedagogy, one that would awaken participants' potential for envisioning more just community practices as they arise out of what is already culturally given.

In contrast to the lack of nonformal models, practical models for integrating HRE into formal education are abundant. As Bajaj (2011) observed, many of the models that have emerged in the last two decades have addressed the integration of human rights within school curricula, as advocated by international organizations working in cooperation with national governments (see, for instance, Starkey 1991a, 1991b; Ray 1994; Spring 2000; Osler and Starkey 1996, 2010; Best 2002; McQuoid-Mason, O'Brien, and Green 1991; Hornberg 2002; Suárez, Ramirez, and Koo 2009). However, the fact that these models are designed to work with people who have access to schooling might limit their efficacy at scale. Cardenas (2005) criticized HRE programs that are inaccessible to vulnerable and marginalized peoples because those programs could unwittingly reinforce existing patterns of abuse and subjugation, as they would benefit only existing social and economic elites. HRE should empower communities as a whole, its main challenge being "to change the expectations of those who hold power (current and future generations) so that HRE does more than simply widen the gap between human rights demands and state practice" (375).

In the last few years, the number of practical guides for implementing HRE activities in the nonformal setting has increased (see, for instance, Amnesty International 2011; Elbers et al. 2008; Brander et al. 2012). These guides are helpful as they provide practitioners with a set of activities that they can use in the field, but most lack an evidence-based understanding, grounded in participants' experiences, of what empowers them to advance human rights locally. To our knowledge, none of them have focused on how expanding aspirations through nonformal interactive HRE methods can empower people in rural African communities for human rights protection and promotion.

This chapter was drawn from a larger research study (Cislaghi, Gillespie, and Mackie 2016), which explored how participants described their experiences with the pedagogy and curriculum during the first module of the CEP. That module includes, among other content, sessions on visioning and human rights and responsibilities. We found that participants in the rural communities came to advance human rights in their larger communities and beyond; they did so in a way that aligned local practices with specific human rights in efforts to actualize their vision of community well-being. Our purpose in this chapter is to look more closely at the relationship between Tostan's visioning and human rights sessions, the type of pedagogy used to teach them, and their effects on participants' realization of their aspirations.

In the next section we present the work of the NGO Tostan, its CEP, and its approach to HRE, including its sessions on visioning and human rights. We also explain the methods used in the larger study and explain the concept of "the capacity to aspire." In the second section, we discuss the themes that emerged from participants' descriptions of their learning during the visioning and human rights sessions. Finally, we discuss how the interactive strategies throughout these sessions prepared many of the program participants to imagine and create, individually and collectively, more just relationships and social conditions.

Study Background

Tostan and the CEP

Since the 1990s, Tostan has worked in remote rural villages in West Africa, primarily Senegal, providing its nonformal education program to those who request it. In an earlier study, Gillespie and Melching (2010) described the ways in which, over time, the curriculum changed and how the sessions on human rights came to be included in what originally was solely a literacy-focused curriculum. This new curriculum proved transformative for participants and their communities. A full description of Tostan's thirty-month CEP and its different components can be found in Cislaghi et al. (2016). The first module, the focus of our study, lasting about twelve months, is called the *Kobi* (a Mandinka word meaning "to prepare the field for planting"); it includes sessions on democracy, human rights, problem solving, and health and hygiene. Two classes of twenty to fifty participants—one for adults and one for adolescents—participate in the sessions. These sessions are two hours long, usually meet three times a week, and are taught by a trained facilitator who lives in the village for the duration of the program. The classes are taught in the participants' first language (as much as possible when dealing with multiethnic groups of participants), and both curriculum and pedagogy draw on participants' cultural background, their daily experiences, and their existing knowledge and abilities. To increase the reach of the program, facilitators require each participant to share the new knowledge acquired in class with one "adopted learner," a nonparticipating member of their family or group of friends. Tostan also equips participants with skills they can use to organize awareness-raising activities in their village and in surrounding villages. The NGO calls this knowledge-sharing strategy "organized diffusion."

The first twenty-four sessions of the CEP include, among others, sessions on visioning (session 3) and human rights (sessions 10–24). The eight sessions we selected and studied among the first twenty-four were: (1) the first introductory session, (2) the visioning exercise, (3) the human right to life, (4) the human right to be protected against all forms of discrimination, (5) the human right to peace and security, (6) a review of all human rights learned up to that point, (7) the human right to health, and (8) the right to vote and be elected. From the larger study, we look here at how the interactive pedagogy used throughout the CEP and the visioning session set the stage for teaching human rights interactively in the adult classes.

Individual and Collective Aspirations

In session 3, on visioning, the facilitator puts a poster in the middle of the class and invites each participant to draw his or her vision for the future of the community ten years from that moment. Participants typically draw such features as health huts, better roads, and peaceful interactions among community members. As the sessions unfold and participants learn about human rights, they revisit and revise that vision. This exercise helps participants share the hopes they hold for the future, both individually and collectively, and discuss ways to achieve them—to bring that positive future into being.

Cultural anthropologist Appadurai (2004) called the capacity to visualize a future that is different from the present and the actions required to navigate toward that future the "capacity to aspire." This capacity is usually more highly developed among the most privileged—those who are exposed to a variety of possibilities that open up their imagination and who possess the resources to explore the steps required to achieve their aspirations. The most disadvantaged lack opportunities to discover alternatives to their present conditions and the ways to attain them. Appadurai, as well as the scholars who furthered his work, believed that the capacity to aspire is critical for human development, as it is a fundamental capacity to direct human energy and resources toward positive change (Ray 2006; Genicot and Ray 2015; Dalton, Ghosal, and Mani 2015; Ibrahim 2011).

Appadurai (2004) has further argued that aspirations are as much collective as individual. To advance their common good, social groups need to develop "a culture of aspirations by collectively envisioning their future, and their capacity to share this future, through influencing other groups, the government, and other factors in their physical and social environment" (25). Given the importance of increasing the capacity to aspire for community development, we studied the human rights curriculum in the Tostan classes, investigating to what extent and through what dynamics it could help participants develop individual and collective aspirations for their future.

The literature on aspirations also alerted us to the potential spillover effects of participants' expanded aspirational capacity to nonparticipating members of the community. Macours and Vakis (2009) argued that spillover can indeed happen. They showed how a cash transfer program in Nicaragua increased the aspirations not only of participating women but also of those in their social networks. Capacity spillover seemed to be a concrete possibility in the CEP, particularly because of its organized diffusion strategy. Tostan participants are encouraged in many ways to share what they learn in the classes. As we reexamined our data from the larger study looking at aspirations and human rights, we wanted to reflect further on how Tostan's instructional strategies contributed to possible spillovers, if at all.

Study Methods

Participants in the larger study (Cislaghi et al. 2016) were men and women who attended the Tostan classes in three different resource-poor communities in central Senegal. It is important to note that most were illiterate and had little if any formal schooling. The data, collected over a period of twenty-six months, included video recordings of Tostan's classes, focus groups, and individual interviews. We selected and trained six local interviewers to conduct focus groups and individual interviews, and two local cameramen. All research assistants spoke the same language as the research participants. Living in Senegal during most of the fieldwork, researcher Cislaghi supervised the data collection.

We videotaped, transcribed, and translated eight of Tostan's human rights sessions in three villages, for a total of twenty-four tapes. After each of these sessions, we conducted ten semistructured interviews with class participants (five men and five women in each village after each class); in total, 240 individual interviews were translated and transcribed by local transcribers. After eighteen months, at the end of the second phase of the program, we revisited the same villages and conducted two focus groups and ten individual interviews in each of the three villages. The data included a total of six focus groups and 270 individual interviews.

To analyze the data we used grounded theory methods (Charmaz 2006; Henwood and Pidgeon 2003). With the aid of the interviewers, we immersed ourselves in the data and independently coded the transcriptions by breaking the text into segments made up of words, phrases, and sentences (a process referred to as open coding). As patterns in the data emerged across videotapes, focus groups, and interviews, we revised our codes by comparing and contrasting the codes from the individual work of each of us. Through axial coding, we arranged the data into major categories and subcategories. Eventually, data saturation was reached when no new categories emerged.

For this chapter, we thought more specifically about the interrelationships between the visioning session, the eight human rights sessions, and Tostan's interactive pedagogy as described by the participants. Appadurai makes the case that aspirations need to be tied to meaningful, manageable tasks if they are to be realized. How did culturally relevant interactive instructional strategies and human rights curricular materials enable that? And how did they expand people's aspirations in ways that helped them work together to improve their social situation?

Participant Descriptions of Their Learning Experiences

Participants were very keen to talk about their experiences in the classes. For instance, they reported that they found them engaging and enjoyable. One man, for instance, spontaneously said, "I was surprised at how everyone in class was sharing laughs, talking and exchanging thoughts, and having fun learning" (10: M, A, 22).[1] They also described what instructional strategies stood out to them as having motivated them to come to class and participate in the discussions. Five themes emerged from participants' responses: (1) the use of culturally meaningful curricular materials, (2) experiential learning, (3) democratic dialogue and deliberation, (4) the skits, and (5) a welcoming facilitator.

Use of Culturally Congruent Strategies and Content

As reported by Easton, Monkman, and Miles (2009), the hallmark of Tostan's nonformal education program is its respect for and use of participants' cultural experiences. We also found that culturally congruent strategies and content also mattered to participants. Facilitators were from the same language group and wore the same traditional clothes as participants, a visible sign of common identity. Participants noted repeatedly the importance of the use of their own language in the Tostan classes. One woman, for instance, said, she considered it important to study in Fula "because it is [a language] sacred to humans" (10: W, A, 3). To encourage discussion and interpretation, facilitators used drawings depicting West African people in situations similar to those experienced by participants in their daily lives.

In class, Tostan facilitators made reference to existing proverbs and local cultural events. Participants mentioned, specifically, their surprise at the way the facilitator used the local proverb, "If ten people dig and ten others fill in, there's lots of dust but no hole." Not only were they surprised by its use, they explained how the proverb opened up a discussion around the local values of working together and how they could improve their collaboration to achieve their vision. One man said, "I will tell family and friends about how important it is to work as a team instead of as individuals" (10: M, C, 1); and another man from another village said, "[At home we need to talk about how we] work together. . . . If everyone gets together and works then we can get so much more done" (10: M, A, 1).

All these elements made the classes familiar and inviting. One man said, "Everything I learned today was memorable. I learned about my culture and how things worked" (10: M, C, 1). The language, the local proverbs, and

the depiction of West African people in familiar situations helped participants understand human rights from their set of cultural understandings
and meanings and in a language that was immediately accessible to all of
them.

Experiential Learning

Not only did facilitators use elements from participants' cultural background; they also deliberately asked participants to contribute with their
own life experiences as members of the community. Participants frequently
mentioned this aspect and recalled other people's experiences. For instance, one man, after session 11 on nondiscrimination, said, "I learned
about discrimination and how it is done all over the world. For example,
Amadou went to a village and only slept in the homes of people with the
last name Diallo" (10: M, C, 13). The videos show that the facilitators actively encouraged participants to reflect upon their local reality and to
contribute to the discussion with examples from it. Take, for instance, the
following excerpt:

> Facilitator: Does mutual aid exist among us [in this village]?
> Man: There are some who take your money by force; they do not
>   respect others.
> Woman: There are people that helped me; for example, when
>   my children were born, they helped me to get birth registra-
>   tion papers.
> Facilitator: There are two categories: those that harm and those that
>   help. What are some examples around here of harming or helping?
>   (10: V, A, 12)

Participants connected the use of their own life experiences and their
capacity and motivation to contribute to the discussion. They were also positively surprised by other people's contributions. One woman, for instance,
said, "I did not think people would open up like this" (10: W, B, 13); one man
said, "I was surprised today that we talked about health and everyone in class
was sharing their thoughts and experiences. I did not think everyone would
share so much about their personal lives" (10: M, B, 17).

While the culturally congruent strategies discussed above helped participants understand human rights and contextualize them in their culture, experiential learning helped them recognize the relevance of those rights in their own individual lived experiences. In class, participants contextualized human rights in meaningful examples drawn from their own lives that would help them, over time, look together critically at existing examples of human rights abuses and discuss how to remedy them.

Skits

Participants often cited the skits as the most innovative, engaging, and amusing technique; it was possibly the most frequently mentioned instructional strategy. The participants engaged in a form of performance very similar to Boal's (1979, 1995) theater of the oppressed; the facilitators asked them to enact scenes from their daily lives (for instance, a misunderstanding between a husband and a wife, or a discussion about sending one's daughter to school or marrying her off) and invited the rest of the class to comment on what they were seeing. These skits were very memorable to participants. One man, for instance, said, "Today I was surprised to see a performance about someone marrying a young girl. The father agreed to the marriage but the mother did not. There was lots of arguing but people got together and they talked about it until they came to understanding. A skit about this was really surprising" (10: M, B, 17). Participants also repeatedly described how the skits helped them learn and talk together: "I was happy because it taught me a lot. I have never seen something like this before and it is very interesting" (10: M, A, 14), said one man. A woman remarked, "I was [at first] surprised at what the skits meant, but we sat down and talked about it and that was very interesting" (10: W, B, 14). The videos show that direct discussions among participants increased dramatically in length and intensity during the plays; interestingly, during these discussions the women, when interrupted by the men, would not stop but would speak louder and persist in making their voices heard.

The skits offered participants the opportunity to look together critically at examples of human rights violations or protections. Some of these events might have happened in their villages before, but possibly they had never deliberated on them collectively, deciding how to act on them. The skits helped participants talk about concrete examples of violations of human rights, and together deliberate on their possible solutions.

Democratic Dialogue and Deliberation

Participants also enjoyed having debates around local issues and remarked upon the novelty of doing so. One man said, "I was surprised to get the chance to talk to some of my neighbors and share ideas with them; I never thought we would sit in the same room and do this" (10: M, B, 1). Another man, from a different village said, "Usually at this time of day everyone is off doing their own thing, but it's great that we are here . . . having great conversations and getting an education" (10: M, B, 3). Participants also believed that similar conversations in class were fun, great, memorable, and good.

They also remarked on the differences between conversations in the village and in class, where norms of democratic collaboration had been established. After the first session, one man said, "Here at school participation is the same, but it is different out in the village" (10: M, A, 1). The difference this man referred to, the data suggest, is mostly in gender participation. Although he observed an equitable participation (possibly because it was indeed already more equitable than in village meetings), analysis of videotapes shows that women's participation increased over time. In community A, for instance, in the first session women spoke for 45 seconds, and men for a total of 517. By the time the course had reached session 13, all participants were speaking more, and the women were speaking longer and more frequently than the men.

Toward the end of the human rights sessions, participants all valued their conversations: "Woman: Taking part in the group is good. . . . When you speak, someone might correct you, and persuade you of the contrary view. . . . Man: It's important to speak, because your ideas could be useful for others" (10: V, A, 22). Not only did participants believe the discussions to be important, they found them fun and helpful. Take, for instance, the woman who said, "I was surprised that everyone in class participated, especially after the skits everyone got excited and was laughing and we learned a lot" (10: W, A, 17).

Experiential learning and the skits helped participants discover individually and collectively the relevance of human rights for their own lives.

Democratic dialogue equipped participants with the individual and collective skills they needed for all to be active parts of the conversation.

Welcoming Facilitators

Participants described Tostan's facilitators as friendly, warm, understanding, and culturally familiar. In particular, they linked their facilitators' clarity and enthusiasm. One woman said, "The facilitator is interested in us learning because that is why he is here. He wants to teach us, and every morning he asks us questions to see if we have not forgotten what we learned" (10: W, B, 11). They also appreciated the facilitators' kindness, which made them feel safe and welcomed: "The teacher helps . . . a lot, he is very polite, he will not embarrass you in class, he won't show you up, he is very patient with us and he takes time to explain things to us until we understand and he allows us to ask as many questions as we want" (11: M, B, FG). The videos show facilitators responding with encouragement to all participants at all times, even when they simply repeated what others had just said. Participants said they were motivated to participate in and return to the classes because the facilitator valued their contributions and invited them to experiment without fear of error.

These instructional strategies were important in engaging participants in the human rights curriculum in transformative ways. The use of culturally congruent instructional strategies helped participants engage critically with human rights from their cultural standpoint. Experiential learning and skits showed them the relevance of those rights for their individual and collective daily lives. A welcoming facilitator helped participants join in the dialogic problematization of their social context from their newly acquired human rights perspective, and in the deliberation as to solutions to the problems they identified.

Effect of the Program on Community
Members' Aspirations

In the larger study (Cislaghi et al. 2016), analysis of participants' descriptions of the community before Tostan's HRE classes revealed that aspirations were limited. Participants described themselves and others as being lost, or asleep, without hope for the future. One man, describing life in his village in the first interview, said, "It's like being in a closed house with no keys" (10: M, B, 1); and one woman, commenting on her life conditions, said, "Someone who doesn't know anything can't get anything and can't get anything done" (10: W, B, 1). We don't mean to represent these villages as either hopeless or excluded from the social change processes occurring in their country; rather, we see them as using HRE to become agents of change in their communities. In 2011, reflecting on the CEP, participants remarked that their communities were transforming, but that the CEP had sped up the process and put them in charge of that change (11: M, A, FG).

In this study, reexamination of the visualization session showed that it unlocked participants' hopes and aspirations for the future. Participants began to reflect on how they could achieve change for themselves and others. After the visualization session, one woman, when asked what stood out to her from the class, answered, "What I picked up today was the question, what is life? Life is working and being able to survive and making a difference" (10: W, B, 3); a man, in answer to the same question, replied, "[I have learned that] we all make a difference" (10: M, B, 3). As the classes unfolded, participants began to report an increased capacity to learn and get things done, which, in turn, expanded their awareness of the possible roles they could take. One woman reflected on how she was now capable of actively participating in the public life of her village: "I have learned roads to go through I did not know, and now I know how to talk to others and present myself" (10: W, A, 11). In 2011, reflecting on how she and others in her community (both men and women) had changed, one woman said, "When I attended meetings in the past, I would sit in the back and never say anything but now when I go to meetings I speak. . . . Now, women like me are able to call for meetings and men will sit and listen to what the women have to say" (11: W, B, I).

In the human rights sessions, participants could link each right and responsibility to what they believed to be good for the future of their community. The small-group discussion and the skits helped participants develop the public speaking skills they needed to participate in these class debates. The visualization session (with the drawing exercise and its following revisions) expanded participants' aspirational map; the constructive dialogue around the community's future increased the number of possible future communities available to participants. These aspirational discussions increased as participants looked critically at their reality through the human rights curriculum: experiential learning guided participants in a critical analysis of their community as it was and as they would like it to be. Facilitators then presented participants with practical problems: How can we reach the ideal community we visualized? Not only were participants developing aspirations for the future, they were problematizing the present. This process responds to Appadurai's call for stretching the map of aspirations and increasing navigational capacities of even the most disadvantaged populations.

Most important, we could see how the aspirations had spillover effects. Participants explained to each other interactively in class, in light of their aspirations, why they needed to change unjust social practices, and they actually changed these practices. They and others saw the changes. This visibility created spillover. They said nonparticipating members of their communities had observed them undertake public actions, such as cleaning up the community and speaking in public. They said, too, that they had become models for those nonparticipating members, and that those examples convinced them that together they could achieve even more changes. The spillover reached neighboring communities. Participants said that visitors commented positively on visible changes they had made and asked them how they had accomplished them. Participants reported having explained to them how they had relied on human rights to establish their goals and awaken their aspirations, and that they wished to share what they had learned with their neighbors. Participants in this study said they shared their aspirations and information, but future research could explore how others take up these aspirations as they learn the information from participants in the *Kobi* sessions.

Conclusions

Increasing aspirations is a dangerous process, since it can lead to either frustration, in the case of unreachable aspirations, or to its opposite, a lack of drive to self-betterment, due to underwhelming aspirations. Ray (2006) argued that aspirations expand by opening a gap, or "window," between present conditions and the possible future. The size of the opening is what determines the successful expansion of the capacity to aspire: if the opening is too small, "there is no drive to self-betterment"; if it is too large, "there is the curse of frustrated aspirations" (4). The CEP encouraged participants to open their own aspirational windows and framed the opening in terms of the participants' sociocultural context, so that they could engage proactively and meaningfully with the conditions in that context.

At the beginning of the program participants had some aspirations, but did not know how to move from their present situation to the future. They lacked the practical skills and social technologies to advance their collective well-being together. Through the CEP, participants developed individual and collective aspirations for their future, identified obstacles to those aspirations, and acquired knowledge and skills necessary to address those obstacles together. Their work in their village inspired others to join in the process of change. In this study, we found that participants' expanded aspirational capacity was critical for them to act for the promotion and protection of human rights in their communities. Further studies could enhance our understanding of how the expansion of aspirations and engaging human rights education practices and curriculum reinforce each other in ways that are transformative for participants. We hope these findings will inspire human rights educators working in similar settings to consider integrating visioning exercises in their transformative human rights education curricula.

Note

1. We adopted the following system to identify quotations: the year in which the interview was conducted, 2010 or 2011 (in this case 10): Gender of the interviewee (Man) or V for video, village (A), and number of the session after which the interview was carried out (in this case 22).

References

Amnesty International. 2011. *Facilitation Manual: A Guide to Using Participatory Methodologies for Human Rights Education*. London: Amnesty International, 2011.

Appadurai, A. 2004, "The Capacity to Aspire: Culture and the Terms of Recognition." In V. Rao and M. Walton, eds., *Culture and Public Action* (pp. 59–84). Palo Alto, CA: Stanford University Press.

Bajaj, Monisha. 2011. "Human Rights Education: Ideology, Location, and Approaches." *Human Rights Quarterly* 33(2):481–508.

Best, Francine. 2002. "Les Droits de l'Homme et l'Education." *International Review of Education* 48(3–4):229–238.

Boal, Augusto. 1979. *Theatre of the Oppressed*. London: Pluto Press.

Boal, Augusto. 1995. *The Rainbow of Desire: The Boal Method of Theater and Therapy*. London: Routledge.

Brander, Patricia, Laure De Witte, Nazila Ghanea, Rui Gomes, Ellie Keen, Anastasia Nikitina, and Justina Pinkeviciute. 2012. *Compass: Manual for Human Rights Education with Young People*. Budapest: COE.

Cardenas, Sonia. 2005. "Constructing Rights? Human Rights Education and the State." *International Political Science Review* 26(4):363–379.

Charmaz, K. 2006. *Constructing Grounded Theory*. London: Sage.

Cislaghi, Beniamino, Diane Gillespie, and Gerry Mackie. 2016. *Values Deliberation and Collective Action: Community Empowerment in Rural Senegal*. New York: Palgrave MacMillan.

CRDH. 2010. *Évaluation de l'Impact du Programme de Renforcement des Capacités des Communautés mis en œuvre par Tostan en milieu rural sénégalais dans les régions de Tambacounda et de Kolda, en 2009*. Dakar: Centre de Recherche pour le Développement Humain.

Dalton, Patricio S., Sayantan Ghosal, and Anandi Mani. 2015. "Poverty and Aspirations Failure." *Economic Journal* 126(590):165–188. doi: 10.1111/ecoj.12210.

Diop, Nafissatou J., Amadou Moreau, and Hélène Benga. 2008. *Evaluation of the Long-Term Impact of the TOSTAN Programme on the Abandonment of FGM/C and Early Marriage: Results from a Qualitative Study in Senegal*. Washington DC: Population Council.

Easton, Peter, Karen Monkman, and Rebecca Miles. 2009. "Breaking Out of the Egg." In Jack Mezirow and Edward W Taylor, eds., *Transformative Learning in Practice: Insights from Community, Workplace, and Higher Education* (pp. 227–239). San Francisco: Jossey-Bass.

Elbers, Frank, Colm Regan, Tony Meade, and Nour Hemici. 2008. *Resources for Human Rights Education in the Euro-Mediterranean Region: A Practical Introduction to Methodologies in Non-Formal Education* Copenhagen: Euro-Mediterranean Human Rights Network.

Genicot, Garance, and Debraj Ray. 2015. "Aspirations and Inequality." NBER Working Paper No. 19976. Cambridge, MA: National Bureau of Economic Research.

Gillespie, Diane, and Molly Melching. 2010. "The Transformative Power of Democracy and Human Rights in Nonformal Education: The Case of Tostan." *Adult Education Quarterly* 60(5):477–498.

Henwood, K. L., and N. F. Pidgeon. 2003. "Grounded Theory in Psychology." In Paul M. Camic, Jean E. Rhodes, and Lucy Yardley, eds., *Qualitative Research in Psychology: Expanding Perspectives in Methodology and Design* (pp. 131–155). Washington, DC: American Psychological Association Press.

Hornberg, Sabine. 2002. "Human Rights Education as an Integral Part of General Education." *International Review of Education* 48(3–4):187–198.

Ibrahim, Solava. 2011. "Poverty, Aspirations and Wellbeing: Afraid to Aspire and Unable to Reach a Better Life: Voices from Egypt." BWPI Working Paper, University of Manchester. http://hummedia.manchester.ac.uk/institutes/gdi/publications/workingpapers/bwpi/bwpi-wp-14111.pdf.

Kuenzi, Michelle. 2005. "The Role of Nonformal Education in Promoting Democratic Attitudes: Findings from Senegal." *Democratization* 12(2):223–243.

Macours, Karen, and Renos Vakis. 2009. *Changing Households' Investment and Aspirations through Social Interactions: Evidence from a Randomized Transfer Program.* Washington, DC: World Bank.

McQuoid-Mason, David, Edward L. O'Brien, and Eleanor Green. 1991. *Human Rights for All: Education Towards a Rights Culture.* Claremont, South Africa: David Philip Publisher.

Merry, Sally. (2006). *Human Rights and Gender Violence: Translating International Law into Local Justice.* Chicago: University of Chicago Press.

Osler, A., and H. Starkey. 2010. *Teachers and Human Rights Education.* Stoke-on-Trent: Trentham.

Osler, Audrey, and H. Starkey. 1996. *Teacher Education and Human Rights.* London: David Fulton.

Ray, Debraj. 2006. "Aspirations, Poverty and Economic Change." In Abhijit Vinayak Banerjee, Roland Bénabou, and Dilip Mookherjee, eds., *Understanding Poverty* (pp. 409–423). Oxford: Oxford University Press.

Ray, Douglas, ed. 1994. *Education for Human Rights: An International Perspective.* Paris: International Bureau of Education.

Spring, Joel. 2000. *The Universal Right to Education: Justification, Definition, and Guidelines.* Mahwah, NJ: Lawrence Erlbaum.

Starkey, Hugh, ed. 1991a. *The Challenge of Human Rights Education.* London: Cassell—Council of Europe.

Starkey, Hugh, ed. 1991b. *Socialisation of School Children and Their Education for Democratic Values and Human Rights: Report of the Colloquy of Directors of Educational Research Institutions.* Strasbourg: Council of Europe.

Suárez, Diego, Francisco Ramirez, and Jeong-Woo Koo. 2009. "UNESCO and the Associated Schools Project: Symbolic Affirmation of World Community, International Understanding, and Human Rights. *Sociology of Education* 82(3):197–216.

CHAPTER 11

Human Rights Education's Role in Peacebuilding: Lessons from the Field

Tracey Holland and J. Paul Martin

Some seventy years ago, the authors of the Universal Declaration of Human Rights—perhaps the most thoughtful and resonant international agreement of modern times—felt that human rights education would be so crucial that they wrote it into that great, foundational text. Article 26 reads: "Education shall be directed to the full development of the human personality and to the strengthening of respect for human rights and fundamental freedoms."

Human rights discourse has become an important concept in both popular and diplomatic language. In principle, governments and international agencies as well as NGOs agree that human rights are a necessary component of just societies. In his recent speech at the 27th Session of the Human Rights Council in Geneva in September 2014, the UN High Commissioner for Human Rights, Ra'ad Al Hussein, noted, "Recognition of the inherent dignity and of the equal and inalienable rights of all members of the human family is the foundation of freedom, justice and peace in the world." He went on to underline one of the major arguments supporting the work of the human rights community around the world: "Societies that uphold human rights are more resilient, more sustainable and thus more secure" (Hussein 2015).

In the same speech before the Human Rights Council, the high commissioner also addressed the need for inclusion as part of bringing peace to war-torn societies: "Underlying patterns of violations and discrimination, including corrupt and discriminatory political systems that disenfranchised large parts of the population, created an inflammable backdrop." Here the high commissioner identifies the problem others have also identified (Tutu and Wald 2014)—that most armed conflicts have taken place in contexts that are characterized by social exclusion. When people are denied a voice in political processes, or when they feel a sense of inequality and marginalization in other ways, they are more likely to resort to crime and violence, and they are more likely to have acts of violence committed against them due to impunity for the perpetrators. Furthermore, when governments fail to protect and promote economic and social rights and to respond to the basic human needs of significant segments of their citizens, they leave themselves open to those citizens' feelings of alienation in the form of violent protests. Speaking from his experience in Liberia, James Yarsiah, director of the Rights and Rice Foundation, emphasized the prevention aspect of HRE in peacebuilding contexts:

> In order for there to be lasting peace in our country we must address the root causes of the Liberian conflict. It should come as no surprise that we have incorporated an in-depth analysis of these reasons into the HRE program. And since no such cause runs deeper than the violations of the rights of the ordinary people that were perpetrated by the former rulers of Liberia, we must ensure that Liberia's people not only are aware of their rights but know how to go about defending and protecting them. Above all we must believe that major advances in conflict prevention and resolution will come about only when the rights of people are respected, under a governance system that upholds the rule of law. (Holland 2014:80)

Peacebuilders around the world understand that civil society must be engaged, and human rights education is recognized as key to strengthening communities and citizen engagement. Moreover, all UN member states have affirmed on many occasions their belief in the centrality of HRE as a long-term strategy for the prevention of human rights violations and conflicts, for the promotion of equality and sustainable development, and for the enhancement of people's participation in decision-making processes (Hussein 2015).

While the meanings and interpretations of human rights are common in theory, as seen in speeches, international documents, and agreements in post-conflict situations, concerted action and the financing needed to teach human rights are seriously absent in practice. Unfortunately, many of the national governments that have adopted international treaties that mandate educating citizens in human rights only pay lip service to this promising practice in the peacebuilding operations they support. Most HRE targeted at marginalized social groups remains in the hands of a few local NGOs and their international supporters. Thus, given the fact that only a few NGOs are able to access and mobilize the resources to promote HRE systematically, the overall social impact is limited.

We believe that if there were more awareness of the role HRE has played in peacebuilding it would be easier to garner more support and funding for HRE programs. Thus the purpose of this chapter is to bring some clarity to the role HRE can play in the task of cultivating peace through the promotion of human rights, drawing on the study of various HRE programs in peacebuilding contexts: Liberia, Colombia, Sierra Leone, the Casamance region of Senegal, and Chiapas in Mexico. This chapter underscores the effectiveness of human rights education that grows organically out of the specific needs and experiences of local communities and among specific groups of people.

Defining Human Rights Education

The job of human rights educators is to lay the groundwork for a rights-respecting culture (Mertus 2004). Among the many current definitions of human rights education, one of the most recent by a senior international body is that of the Committee of Ministers of the Council of Europe (2010). According to the committee, human rights education "means education, training, awareness raising, information, practices and activities which aim, by equipping learners with knowledge, skills and understanding and developing their attitudes and behavior, to empower learners to contribute to the building and defense of a universal culture of human rights in society, with a view to the promotion and protection of human rights and fundamental freedoms." As this definition suggests, it is not enough to present people with information and then leave them to take action on their own. Education has to lead students through the steps to act upon their new knowledge. Human rights education is then enacted through people's experiences and the institutions and organizations they develop.

The human rights education organizations we have studied drew the inspiration for their educational work from international and national human rights laws and policies, as well as from constitutional amendments that their governments have recently ratified. Many of these provisions were formulated as part of the transition away from armed conflict and toward peace in these countries. In the majority of cases, these HRE organizations work with populations that have been excluded from participatory processes and often have little or no knowledge of domestic or international rights. Thus, while the educators believe that it is important that the legal and policy discourse around human rights be disseminated widely, they have had to find meaningful ways of teaching human rights to populations that had been historically denied their human rights.

In the end, what has motivated learners to attend and sustain their involvement in HRE has been the fact that it allows them to come together with other people, discuss their problems, and find solutions. Thus, all of the HRE content grew organically out of the needs, desires, and problems of people in their respective contexts. Given this trend, it is not surprising that the educators in HRE programs recognize the influence that the Brazilian educator Paulo Freire has had in shaping their implementation of HRE. Freire has defined education as based on problem-solving and critical analysis rather than on the mere acquisition of new knowledge. In this model, educators act as facilitators, helping learners to discover what they already know, and guiding them, through dialogue and critical thinking, in the acquisition of new ideas. This approach employs a method of self-discovery in which learners of human rights are presented with songs, images, and role-plays as ways to analyze the problems and other issues they face in their communities. In analyzing the graphically presented problems, the participants are encouraged to discover human rights issues for themselves, and to devise solutions and implementation strategies.

This educational process helps to make human rights relevant to the lives of the learners. If learners fail to see such relevance, they may feel alienated and threatened by HRE, especially if it conflicts with their understanding of their own society and its social values and practices. To some learners, the promotion of international human rights can present a challenge to long-held convictions, goals, or aspirations, or it can feel like an imposition of foreign values that benefit one group over another. However, the problem-solving focus of human rights education can help to address this conflict. Educators in the various HRE programs we studied sought to avoid having learners feel that their self-conceptions were being challenged or that the core values of their cultures were under examination. In nearly all of the projects we stud-

Rights	Responsibilities
We are all born free and equal.	Respect and do not violate the freedoms of others.
We all have a right to be seen and treated as equal.	Accept and see all humans as one, no matter their age, color, sex, nationality, tribe, and origin.
We all have a right to life.	Value, protect, and respect your life and the lives of others.
We all have the right to a decent salary in exchange for willing labor.	Do not enslave others or force labor on others. Work toward the greater welfare and improvement of your community and country.

Figure 11.1. Chart from Rights and Rice Foundation HRE Program.

ied, human rights was translated into local meaning-frameworks in ways that made sense to ordinary people and showed them the true benefits of understanding and adopting human rights ideologies.

We can provide many examples of this translation process. In Liberia, for instance, the interpretation and translation of the Universal Declaration of Human Rights into the language and daily experience of the participants is the core methodology of the Rights and Rice Foundation's (RRF) HRE program. The local RRF educators simplify the language of the UDHR's thirty articles and make concrete clarifications with respect to both content and format in ways that correspond to people's daily experiences. Typically, each of the rights is translated into ideas that community members feel will resonate widely throughout their communities. Given the importance of duties and responsibilities in human rights practice in African nations, the related responsibilities and duties are taught alongside the rights. Educators must transpose the new values and rights into particular roles and responsibilities and make the case for the validity of the change. Therefore, they carefully explain the role that taking personal responsibility plays in the context of peacebuilding. The accompanying chart (Figure 11.1) shows some examples of corresponding responsibilities that are taught alongside the rights.

For the purposes of this chapter, we will go into greater detail on four of the nine projects we studied in Mexico, Peru, Colombia, Sierra Leone, Senegal, and Liberia. The legacies of the conflicts—which in some cases have ended only recently—are still present in each location and need to be addressed in order to bring a sense of stability and peace to people's lives. Thus, the remainder of this chapter will take a closer look at the basic characteristics of the curriculum, educators, and outcomes of HRE programs in peacebuilding contexts.

The HRE Projects

The UN Human Rights Council's Working Group on the Universal Periodic Review of Liberia points to three obstacles to human rights education in Liberia: the lack of any human rights awareness among large segments of the society, delays in the domestic dissemination and enforcement of the major regional and international human rights conventions, and inadequate financial resources to implement HRE projects (Hussein 2015).

This situation exemplifies the context in which HRE programs operate, not just in Liberia but in many parts of the world. As described, this context is defined by an overall lack of awareness of human rights, supporting documentation on these rights, and financial resources to implement HRE. All of the programs we studied, with the exception of the one in Lima, Peru, which operates with graduate students at a university, involved community-based HRE projects that were designed to provide human rights education to socially and politically disaffected groups. The common thread in these programs is that each target audience had and continues to experience social exclusion, and in some cases ongoing violence as well. Before these programs began, their audiences did not have access to rights such as health, education, and legal protections, or to opportunities such as jobs and political participation, as they were victims of discrimination before and after the armed conflict. Their subjugation has allowed others to commit acts of violence against them with impunity. In all of the cases we studied, political openings caused by the cessation of armed conflict finally brought human rights into view. The result was that, in each of these cases, a group of oppressed people learned that they have the right to claim their rights in the public sphere. Thus the fulfillment of human rights came to be seen as being dependent on the empowerment of all people, enabling them to take greater control of their lives and to make more informed decisions. This change was accompanied by a growing sense that governments and duty bearers must be held accountable and must fulfill their obligations to promote rights for all groups. These new attitudes forming in individuals and communities were supported to different degrees by broader political and social movements grounded in human rights and social justice.

In Cartagena, Colombia, we studied an HRE project, run by the League of Displaced Women, within the community of displaced women and children known as City of Women. Since the official ending of the armed conflict, thousands of displaced people in Colombia have filed *acciones de tutela*, legal procedures established by the constitution that allow individuals to petition the Constitutional Court directly for protection of their fundamental human rights. After compiling and reviewing these cases, in January 2004, the court issued Judgment T-025/04, which condemned government inaction and accused government officials of outright discrimination toward displaced persons. The League of Displaced Women is among the organizations working with the court in the spirit of UN Security Council Resolution 1325 on women, peace, and security (the Resolution affirms the integral role of women globally in conflict prevention and transformation as well as in peacebuilding and reconstruction efforts after conflict). Their human rights education agenda has been expressly designed to "confront impunity for the crimes committed against internally displaced women and to discover the truth of what led to their forced displacement and to know who was responsible for it" (Ariza, Gonzalez, and Guerrero 2009:19).

The League's HRE workshops focus on understanding the gender gap, the rights of women, the history of discrimination, and above all the importance of women as key players in rebuilding the social fabric, which continues to be frayed by the violence and crime brought on by forced displacement. It should be noted that taking women's testimonials is a vital part of this human rights education process. Through the process of developing these written testimonials and discussing their experiences with others, the women acquire a deeper understanding of their own experiences. As part of the HRE, the women quickly learn that there is a domestic legal system under which they can bring claims and expect those claims to be honored.

In Liberia, we studied the Rights and Rice Foundation's HRE project, which works in the Foya District of Lofa County in Liberia. The postconflict administration of Ellen Johnson Sirleaf called for human rights education to be incorporated into the curricula of all the nation's primary, secondary, and tertiary schools, but the actual implementation of such an agenda has been slow. This commitment to HRE has been taken up primarily by the nongovernmental sector. The Rights and Rice Foundation is one such NGO. The goal of its HRE project is to nurture the growth of local human rights advocacy committees, called Community Peace Committees (CPCs), which adjudicate local, noncriminal conflicts as they arise. RRF provides the members of these committees with extensive training and mentoring in human rights, conflict mediation, and advocacy. Each committee is composed of nine members chosen to reflect proportionately the overall population, and thus typically includes a range of women, men, elders, and young people.

The Rights and Rice Foundation recognizes that the source of many ongoing conflicts between communities is often the scarcity of resources available to the communities. During our study of the program, human rights educators had to deal with a crisis in a community where the people had no access to water. When these people went to a neighboring community for water, the neighboring community shut down the pump, thereby creating conflict between the two groups. Often these conflicts are exacerbated because they fall along ethnic lines. In this case, there had been an especially inflammatory conflict between the Mandingo and Loma tribes in the Foya District and other parts of Lofa County during and after the civil war. Generally speaking, government authority is weak in these places, so the RRF's goal through their HRE project has been to provide ongoing training and mentoring to community members, including training in how to mediate conflicts such as these and spreading awareness of human rights principles and practices as delineated in international and domestic law.

In Chiapas, we studied Project Melel, an organization devoted to promoting and defending the rights of children in San Cristóbal de las Casas. Thousands of children live in precarious situations in the state of Chiapas in Mexico, a community recovering from the violent conflict that took place beginning with the Zapatista uprising of 1994, and that lasted for nearly ten years, between local indigenous communities, the Zapatistas, the military, and the police under the command of the national government. The children with whom Project Melel works have not experienced the armed conflict directly; they are members of the generation born after the Zapatista uprising, whose families fled from the rural to the urban areas of Chiapas during the conflict. This younger generation growing up in San Cristóbal de la Casas suffers from the same social exclusion and lack of security that ignited the Zapatista uprising so long ago. Thus, the struggle for rights is ongoing as the children of indigenous communities continue to be discriminated against by the mainstream Mexican society.

Project Melel directs much of its advocacy and educational programming to child workers and their families. In San Cristóbal, many families rely on their children, both boys and girls, to work on the streets, making money in whatever way possible. Thus, many of these children do not attend school. Project Melel uses learning circles or weekly discussion groups, held either on the streets or at its headquarters, to engage the children in reflective exercises that help them determine what they wish to change about their lives. Through these discussions children learn about their human rights as articulated in the UN Convention on the Rights of the Child (CRC). Specific rights topics contained in the CRC that are identified by the children as being especially relevant to their daily lives include rights against physical abuse and their right to attend school apart from their needing to work. The children learn broader human rights concepts, such as gender equality and governmental responsibility to ensure the protection of citizens' rights. Because the majority of the children in Project Melel are of Totzil ethnic background, the project contextualizes children's rights by relating them back to the Totzil concept of *lekil kuxlejal*, a good life.

In Senegal we studied the implementation of the *D'action Citoyenne* curriculum at the Malick Fall School. This junior high school is located in the Casamance, a region of Senegal, south of The Gambia and thus largely separate from the more developed northern region, which includes Dakar. The Casamance has been rocked by a persistent conflict between the Senegalese army and the Movement of Democratic Forces of Casamance (MDFC). Over the last two decades a host of local human rights organizations have been established in the region, all of them seeking to strengthen the ability of the residents to respect and defend their rights. These organizations see the region's surviving schools as its critical social institutions. By providing the Senegalese with a social space in which they can apprehend the new political structures based on justice and human equality, the schools can slowly change the people's existing mentality of insecurity and fear into one of trust and mutual respect.

Six years ago the Malick Fall School adopted a curriculum entitled *D'action Citoyenne* to teach citizenship and human rights to junior high school students. It is intended to make the fourth- and fifth-grade students in this school more aware of the problems of economic and political development in Senegal and to encourage them to think about how they can contribute to their community. The students in the program study the issues that affect them most closely and those they have expressed a desire to learn about: freedom of expression and worship, the right to have a family, the right to obtain an education, the right to gender equality, the right to experience social solidarity within one's community, and the right to live in a healthy environment. Their capstone HRE experience is working in groups to identify a specific public policy problem in their community. After the students have identified what they deem the most important problems in their communities, the educators help them acquire the knowledge, skills, and techniques they need to conduct accurate surveys and otherwise assemble data about their chosen topics. With the teachers' help, students brainstorm possible solutions, pick the best one, and shape it as a recommendation for public policy. The students then create an action plan designed to convince local or state authorities to adopt their proposed policy.

Common Characteristics of Peacebuilding HRE

Each HRE program that we have studied is unique because it is dependent on the organizational capacity of those who run it, their institutional and funding constraints and mandates, and the unique characteristics of the national and immediate context in which the project operates. Indeed, one of the major characteristics of all HRE programming everywhere is that it conforms to the social reality of the place in which it is being taught. Therefore it must be flexible and adaptable as the local opportunities and obstacles become visible. Despite the large resulting variations, we found major curricular commonalities, which, taken together, help to define the practice of HRE in peacebuilding. In this section we examine three HRE curricular objectives. All of the projects we studied have sought to meet felt needs, improve communication skills, and lead learners to a greater awareness of the various social, cultural, and historical barriers that impede a human rights–respecting culture. All three of these main curricular objectives support the accomplishment of broader peacebuilding goals.

Improving Human Security and Meeting Human Needs

The designers of all of the HRE programs we studied recognize that unmet needs are a potential source of conflict. Thus, the content of these programs always begins and ends with the expressed needs of the learners. The long-term, hoped-for outcome of human rights education is to install a mechanism in communities that addresses the needs felt by the community and the unfair structural inequalities that privilege the needs of some over others, thereby reducing both existing conflict and the potential for future conflict.

The methods of both assessing and addressing needs associated with each group targeted by human rights education varied from place to place. In Chiapas, Melel educators use storytelling and drawing to help the children define their needs. While the Melel children expressed many needs, the three principal needs were: to do well in school, to be protected from violence, and to earn an income. In Chiapas, the fact remains that many children still struggle to stay in school, and many of their needs remain unaddressed. It is clear that the range of their choices is constrained by overwhelming obstacles linked to poverty, discrimination, social marginalization, and violence.

Melel works on the assumption that the children's needs can only be met to a sustainable degree when the children and their families know their rights to basic public services that the government is legally obligated to provide. Melel educators provide HRE to the children's parents and teachers, in part through acting in accordance with these taught rights. For example, all children who participate in Melel's programming must also attend public school. However, while all children have the right to attend school, many still do not. Melel's human rights approach teaches parents that children have a right to attend school, that children's education must come before their work, and therefore that the parents must send their children to school.

When parents fail to send their children to school, Melel educators step in as the children's advocates, especially when children are too fearful to approach a parent or a teacher who may not support a child's right to education. Melel also believes that in order for children's needs to be met, access to decision making in national policy and law is crucial. This access must be based on broader involvement by the civil society organizations that seek to protect the rights of child workers. For example, Melel argues that laws that prohibit children from working are unjust; it mobilizes its participants to advocate for laws and policies that are respectful of children's right to work despite the age restrictions placed by national governments and international organizations.

In another project we studied, we find the same emphasis on need fulfillment as part of human rights education. The League of Displaced Women sees unmet needs as a source of instability in the lives of the displaced women with whom it works. In the wake of their displacement, living in shantytowns on the outskirts of the city of Cartagena, these women faced serious and immediate needs: identification papers, homes, employment, and education for their children. In many cases their living conditions were abysmal, with no running water, no bathrooms, and very few working toilets connected to sewers. The women had no permanent place to live, and faced violence and insecurity. In 2003, the League undertook the creation of the City of Women. While meeting women's needs within the city has reduced the level of stress on these women's lives it has not decreased the conflict in the community outside of the city or their fear of being victims of violence. However, the city has supported the League's notion that basic needs such as shelter and income must be met before women can address their other human rights and participate in struggles for the fulfillment of those rights.

The public school *D'action Cityonne* program in Senegal also recognizes that a chief role of human rights education is to meet unmet needs. Life is difficult for everyone in the Casamance, and this means that the teachers, not just their students and the students' parents, experience on a daily basis the physical insecurity caused by armed conflict, food scarcity, and the continuing, substantial movement of people from rural areas to urban centers. The teachers from the program at Malick Fall School, when interviewed for our study, continually underscored their belief in human rights education, as it allows them to base their teaching on the actual problems that surround them, as they seek to change old, deeply ingrained patterns of thinking, and thereby eventually bring peace to the region. Within the school, teachers learned that it was vital for them to be more in touch with their students' personal needs and experiences. Their students come to school hungry, tired, and sick, and these needs must be addressed in order for children to learn.

Through the program, the students themselves came to the realization that the street children who did not attend school had the same right to education as they did, and they wondered why these children's needs were not being met. The students called on the government to do something to improve the situation of children on the streets. The program led students to be more supportive of rights for others. As the teachers noted, through the curriculum the children became aware that children's rights are often violated in serious ways.

In Liberia, when asked about their most urgent needs, many people cited the need for clean water, medical attention, shelter, schools, and a fair and honest judicial system. While everyone is affected, the basic survival needs of women and their children generally go unfulfilled, particularly because women are often without money to feed their families or provide shelter. The Community Peace Committees struggled to integrate the abstract ideals of human rights and human rights laws into the lives of poor community members, whose most basic human needs went unfulfilled. They did this by providing a mechanism whereby community members could resolve their conflicts and that in turn would free up or enable the financial and human resources to complete their community development projects or address the legal issues and conflicts between neighbors over scarce land, crops, livestock, and water resources.

Fostering Participation and Voice in Public Life

A second common objective among the HRE projects we studied was a commitment to equipping human rights learners with the skills necessary for active participation, which include among others the capacity to describe, articulate, and convey one's needs; to seek and acquire services; and to manage conflicts and resolve disputes. This component of human rights education helps to address a common problem in peacebuilding contexts: failure to recognize the need for civic participation on the part of vulnerable groups, which results in the visible scarcity of resources provided to those communities that do not have a voice.

In Liberia, the Rights and Rice Foundation's human rights educators have recognized the importance of helping people to find a voice as part of an inclusive and secure society. They focused their work on women and youth, two groups they believe need to brought more centrally into decision making. RRF educators have taught basic concepts and speaking skills, which have aided women and youth to name their experiences and describe them to others. Moreover, Community Peace Committee members have been carefully chosen to represent all walks of life. Women and youth in particular were given an opportunity to serve as leaders and to become advocates in their communities. The CPCs serve as a forum where women and young people can practice their public speaking skills as they debate among themselves and air their grievances. In addition to working with women and youth, RRF educators teach local authorities, tribal chiefs, and male leaders about the rights of women and children. In discussion groups attended by these authorities and local women, the educators work skillfully to promote listening skills and to encourage learners' empathy and receptivity to the needs of others. These discussions embody inclusion at a local level through the exchange of ideas and perspectives and the attempt to find a human rights–based solution to human need.

Fostering participation in civic life is also important in the City of Women in Cartagena, where the League of Women's human rights educators see the struggle to include displaced women in political processes, and to make their needs visible, as part of the larger task of holding accountable those who were responsible for the women's displacement. The League's work of recording displaced women's testimonials is the initial step in learning about one's rights. It is also part of the work of having these voices heard in local and national politics, and holding accountable those responsible. Through the process of developing these written testimonials and discussing their experiences with others, the women acquired a deeper knowledge about their own experiences. Through these discussions, women who once were victimized obtain information that enables them to recognize that they have human rights and that these rights have been violated. They learn to rename their experiences in terms of those rights and to use their raised awareness to speak out against those who have violated their rights. Educators firmly believe that it is necessary to help these women to advocate for themselves by giving them the language and skills they can use to redress the wrongs and injustices that they see as keeping them from fulfilling their aspirations.

At Project Melel in Chiapas, in order to promote the inclusion of children in decision making in their homes, schools, and at Melel, the educators work to ensure that the children and their families, as well as their own workers, reflect on and change their roles and responsibilities. Melel also recognizes that the ideas, attitudes, values, and skills that underpin inclusion must be instilled early in life in order to influence the political system and the responsiveness, style, accountability, and trustworthiness of government institutions and officials. Melel's strategy is to improve inclusion at three levels: (1) individual or personal; (2) proxy, those persons with whom the children interact on a daily basis, notably parents and teachers; and (3) collective, that is, those individuals and institutions that define the social environment in which the children live. Action at all of these levels is seen as necessary to ensure the protection and inclusion of children in the governmental and family decision-making processes that affect them.

At the first level, children are taught by Melel educators to advocate for their own needs, which generally involves allowing students to first voice their opinions about their needs in small-group discussions with Melel educators, and then to collectively present their opinions to parents, teachers, and Melel staff. This learning about advocacy often results in the children feeling increased confidence in coming to adults with the problems and needs they face. For example, the Melel director felt it was a major success when one of her students came to her to speak of the abuse she suffered at home. There are limitations, of course, to having children advocate for their own needs. The most obvious in this case is that children speak out against abusers at home but have to return to that abuse because there is no other place for them to go. Even so, the simple inclusion of children within discussion groups constitutes a huge achievement, since, historically in these Mexican communities, children have had no voice in decision making at any level and no opportunity to participate in public life.

The same can be said for the promotion of the voices of their parents, especially their mothers, a group that has also been excluded from participation, which has left them not only without any representation but without any sense of what they or their children are entitled to. After one parent learned why it was important for her children to have their births registered and how this process worked, she was able to demand registration for her children. Thus, parents can serve as proxies for their children and their rights if the parents themselves feel they have a right to public voice and participation. Melel therefore emphasizes the fact that parents need education about their rights in order to safeguard the rights of their children.

At the Malick Fall School in the Casamance, the HRE program's goal is to increase the participation of schoolchildren in the school itself as well as in their community and home life. Teachers at the school have been trained to develop new types of questioning and to give students opportunities to express their views. This exercise is not only about self-expression; it is also meant to encourage the teachers to give much more weight to the students' views. Children are thus acknowledged in the school as active participants, as evidenced by their increased ability to have their views heard by others. Below, one teacher, Ms. Badji, describes how teachers, even those in the school who have not received the HRE training, have become more patient, encouraging the children to voice their opinions, especially when they are working with students who, for whatever reason, do not easily express themselves.

Before, I was a little too hard with the kids. For example, when a child was crying in class I did not even try to understand why, just putting him by the door for the rest of the class. But after this program I have started to manage the children's reactions, talking with them and understanding their problems. I now understand that a child may behave in a way that is not of his or her own volition. Overall this program has brought me closer to the children, and now we have good relations. Indeed, if someone among them has a problem, he or she comes to me and explains the problem, and I help him or her to solve it.

At the end of each academic year, at a public hearing before a panel of civic-minded community members, program participants present in groups on the work they have done. The typical portfolio, a poster made up of four panels, is a summation of the students' acquired knowledge, conveyed in their own voices and with only minimal input from adults, thus teaching its own vital lesson about participation rights. The portfolio project reflects a commitment to young people's participation rights and recognition of children as a source of strength and opportunity for local communities. The students' new consciousness results in their desire to remedy the violations they have identified in their school and their community, among them the *talibes*[1] and child workers who inhabit the streets and marketplaces of their city.

Addressing Inequalities and Subjugation in Historical and Cultural Practices and Patterns

With the intention of contributing to the transformation of men and women who aspire to become members of the National Police, the course in human rights has identified the following as values to develop in students: tolerance, justice, equality, democracy, solidarity, and respect of human dignity. It is important that to reach this end and to transform war into peace, human rights education must always resist the temptation to be ahistorical. On the contrary it is necessary to review the past, demystify it, and utilize it as input that can modify the present. Far from forgetting the past, it is vital that we seriously broach those problems that originated the structural defects in El Salvador's society. Future police agents must be well aware of the historical background of the public security institutions in our country, with our objective being never to repeat the practices that contributed to the weakening of the state of law and social order.[2]

In all the human rights projects we studied, educators realized that they were taking on not just the consequences of the conflict but also deep preexisting cultural patterns and practices that for centuries had supported serious patterns of inequality and discrimination. For example, in many cases the armed conflict was over, but patterns of gender discrimination and child abuse remained. Such traditions and the associated practices in traditional societies might have been largely invisible, or seen as insignificant and natural, but often they enabled the armed part of the conflict. As the above quotation from the El Salvadoran National Police Academy's proposal argues, HRE must include the confrontation and comprehension of historical conditions and patterns that have led to the current state of conflict or post-conflict.

In Liberia, RRF educators addressed these deeply embedded inequalities by involving key male authority figures in discussions of women's rights. The educators sought to engage them in a critique of the social and historical factors that implicitly condone the perpetuation of violence against women and girls. For example, an increased understanding of women's rights in Liberia has led to the enforcement of new local inheritance laws, which in many communities previously prohibited women from inheriting property that was under their husband's name.

In Colombia, there is a long-standing culture of impunity with respect to violence against women. Noting that the problem was not attributable to a single authority but rather a systemic structural deficiency, the Constitutional Court in Colombia concluded:

Given the conditions of extreme vulnerability of the displaced population, as well as the repeated omission by the different authorities in charge of their assistance to grant timely and effective protection, the rights of the plaintiffs in the present proceedings—and of the displaced population in general—to a dignified life, personal integrity, equality, petition, work, health, social security, education, minimum subsistence income and special protection for elderly persons, women providers and children, have all been violated [and this has] been taking place in a massive, protracted, and reiterative manner (Colombian Constitutional Court 2004:10).

In response to continued violence, the League of Women has called for government accountability and decried the ongoing impunity. The League understands that human rights education cannot address impunity directly, but believes that it provides a context in which people can analyze the situation and decide how to assert their rights.

In Chiapas, indigenous children and their families still must endure the discrimination and stereotyping imposed upon them by the prevailing society. Girls in particular are especially victimized. Neither government authorities nor the general public support the rights of indigenous children or the integration of their families into Mexico's economic and political mainstream. Public opinion blames parents for their supposed failure to keep their kids off the streets, and laws that prohibit child labor also criminalize children. As a result, children who work are seen as violating the almost sacred norms of childhood. The prevalence of such a social view enables the government to avoid providing the specific protections the children need. Thus a major challenge faced by Melel and other children's aid organizations in Chiapas is to encourage the Mexican government and Mexico's citizenry as a whole to see indigenous children as rights-holders. Their first and continuing challenge, however, is to convince the children themselves that they have rights.

In all of the studies, educators were quick to point out that the human rights programs especially benefited children and young people in the community. There was a sense that HRE had led to significant shifts in attitudes toward children. The most notable change across studies was that parents who have become aware of their children's rights are beginning to encourage their children to prioritize their schooling. Such trends have led to an increase in primary school enrollment and attendance in those communities where the CPCs are operative. HRE efforts are making children and youth increasingly aware of their rights, including their right to an education. Thus, at home, adults and children are engaging in dialogue about education as a right, and working together to ensure that children receive an education. A trend is emerging: the greater the community members' awareness of human rights, the more cautious they are about doing anything that might be seen as a violation of these rights. This new and still fragile ethos is one that especially benefits women and children, given the historical patterns of disenfranchisement of these groups.

HRE's Impact on Individuals, Multipliers, and Institutions

We found that the impact of HRE was visible on three levels: individuals, multipliers, and organizations or institutions. In the case of individuals, HRE led to changes in personal behavior and improvements in people's own lives. We understand improvements in terms of the reduction or prevention of physical violence, greater inclusion in public life, and new understandings about laws and social relationships. In Chiapas, Melel found that one welcome result was that mothers who were informed about their children's rights obtained birth certificates for their children and reduced the number of hours their girls worked at home, so that they could spend more time on their schoolwork. In one school in Sierra Leone, as a result of children's education about their rights, students used their new awareness of their rights to hold abusive teachers accountable for their actions. Girls then reported feeling less afraid at school. In the Casamance in Senegal, when students took photographs illustrating the school's collapsing walls and ceiling, and presented them to the local authorities, the local government was obliged to repair the school. In Liberia, women now willingly go to CPCs to have their complaints heard. The labor and resources previously expended in settling minor conflicts are now being devoted to community initiatives and to upgrading families' livelihoods.

A second impact area we studied was HRE's impact on multipliers, in the sense that the benefits of HRE were felt not just on those who participated in the HRE programs, but also indirectly on the lives of other vulnerable groups. In Colombia, this impact on others is captured by educators who recognize that the experiences of women are important "not only for those who have decided to give their testimony and denounce what happened to them, but also for the women who continue to have their voices silenced, victims of fear and ignorance" (Ariza et al. 2009:21).

Throughout our research, we found that local educators acted under a broad range of titles such as activist, schoolteacher, social promoter, forest ranger, agronomist, and shopkeeper. In many cases, educators took on direct advocacy and defended someone whose rights were violated. In Sierra

Leone, training in human rights enabled educators to instigate changes on their return to their home communities. One educator, who participated in a HRE workshop organized by the African Human Rights Education Project in 2012, spoke to us of the impact the training on maternal mortality had on her ability to work with those most heavily impacted by the issue:

> I am Alice Koroma. I am a Traditional Birth Attendant, and have served in the Kanthata Bana community for four years. I take care of pregnant women and of children younger than five years old, and sometimes I help to deal with general health problems. After I returned from the human rights education training, I knew much more about the causes of maternal mortality. I have held meetings in my community on how to care for and support pregnant women. So, in turn, I am sensitizing the community to consider local mechanisms, like using hammocks to transport pregnant women whose cases are urgent.

Another teacher's story eloquently attests to the impact that human rights education has had on her ability to advocate for a child in her class:

> Mariama was twelve when her father passed away. Two years later her father's younger brother, (also called her "junior father") took her to live with him in his house . . . [where] he slept in the same bed with Mariama. He said this was the only way to prove he cared, and to protect her. As any child would, she thought that through such sentiments he was proving his love for her, as her father had done when he had been alive. One day, however . . . he raped her and threatened that if she told anyone, he would kill her. He continued this game till the poor girl became pregnant. . . . As her teacher, I often noticed her not cooperating in class and consistently sleeping, so I decided to ask what the matter was. She told me she was fine, but as a parent myself, I was suspicious. I insisted that something must be wrong, and that she should open up to me. Finally she did so. . . . What I learned from the HRE workshop that I attended earlier this year is that all such matters must be reported to the police, and the perpetrator must be brought to justice. The fact that he is a girl's junior father does not give him the right to rape her. Such issues have been prevalent in our

communities for far too long, but they have been constantly kept under the table. . . . The HRE workshop has made us aware that such issues are human rights issues and that we have an obligation to identify and report them, and to follow up on them in court.

These anecdotes illustrate how the consciousness that people have rights becomes a motive and a tool to save people from abuse. The multipliers themselves were perceived as having the requisite credentials as authorities on account of their profession or their level of higher education.

The third impact level we examined was HRE's effect on local institutions. It was important to see that HRE led to the creation of new institutional practices and organizations. The latter's sustainability was crucial, as more people saw in them the needed capacity to improve people's lives on a permanent basis. We also believe that organizations and new institutional practices can sustain a commitment to ongoing human rights education in the community and provide a venue for future conflict reduction and social inclusion.

In Liberia, the Community Peace Committees have grown since 2006, in terms of both their status and acceptance in the communities, and in the effectiveness of their work. Part of the acceptance springs from the fact that the committees have upgraded their capacity to deal with conflicts; as a result, their communities see them as fostering greater social stability and more harmonious social relations within the communities. On a more practical level, community residents have begun to see the CPCs, through their timely intervention in land or ownership disputes, as bringing economic benefits to the community, as there is less need for the more costly intervention of government officials from outside of the community. The CPCs have also opened up opportunities for civic participation by women, and now many women participate fully in decision making about local development projects.

In the Casamance, the schools were previously run in an authoritarian and punitive manner, but the minister of education and other authorities have been convinced that less authoritarian, more caring schools based on rights will promote a culture of respect and dignity, and cultivate the skills in civic participation that a well-functioning society needs. Thus schools like Malick Fall School have been transformed into spaces in which students' views and personal problems are taken into consideration. The school encourages a sense of responsibility among students and teachers, and toward the children on the streets outside of the school. The school has become an environment in which children are able to exercise their rights and have their voices heard. While it is difficult for the teachers to achieve success in conflict prevention in areas such as the home, within the school, teachers report fewer discipline problems, more collaboration, and a greater awareness of human rights and the causes of conflict in the Casamance.

In Cartagena, the City of Women exemplifies a fully functional community of practice that builds on its members continually advancing their knowledge of human rights and their role in running a community of independent homes. Irene, one of the women who lives in the city, said, "One simply wants to learn a little bit more, to be more ambitious; one wants to learn more every day about everything." In principle, building a physical community with all the necessary basic utilities, services, and educational activities ensures a greater degree of permanence than the typical human rights education or training program. One of our broad conclusions is that, as learners become more competent human rights practitioners, they become more involved in the main processes of the particular community. Learning is thus not just the acquisition of knowledge by individuals but also a process of social participation and community building around a shared ethic. The key indicator of impact is the increased participation of women, coupled with their more sophisticated understanding of human rights.

Conclusion

Our study revealed that human rights education works best when it responds to people's desire for change. This form of HRE is based on the growing recognition around the world that all people are entitled to have their human rights respected and protected, and that this is a major responsibility and legal obligation on the part of local governments and officials. Human rights education may not stop bombs from dropping or force border authorities to accept refugees, but it does promote a new emergence of rights claims by people who have historically been denied not only their rights but also knowledge about their rights. When rights were seen as part of the social changes that these countries experienced in a time of peacebuilding, people learned to make claims on their government. They wanted to join in something bigger than themselves, to bring about systemic and institutional changes to make their communities better. Most experts and activists know that it takes many years, perhaps even decades, to ensure stable democratic governments. Many, however, do not recognize that education must support this democratic transition, and that human rights must be taught well and continuously. Human rights educators must continue their work to educate populations about their rights long after people have laid down their arms.

While we found substantial evidence that HRE led to significant changes in individual behavior, in identifiable multiplier effects, and in the development of local institutions, the consistent challenge for educators was how best to provide a comprehensive human rights education. Several of the educators in the programs we studied expressed concern that they had failed because their students could not name specific human rights. For example, in Liberia, when asked what they had learned about human rights, many of the interviewees simply referred to the fact that now they are living in greater harmony with their neighbors, with less conflict and more local conflict resolution. Asked to give an example of human rights, a participant would say something like, "Human rights means to live together peacefully." One exception to this pattern was a fairly widespread understanding of children's rights. When asked to name a specific children's right, the interviewee commonly would cite a child's right to attend school. Many of the human rights educators themselves often had difficulty distinguishing between civil rights, endowed by national constitutions, and universal human rights. Presumably this more detailed knowledge of human rights will come over time, as HRE workers receive more training.

Despite this challenge of providing a comprehensive human rights education, our research showed that it is important for each project to be designed to reduce human suffering and increase opportunity, two things that may have conflict-prevention effects in and of themselves. Furthermore, all of the projects recognized that the needs of young people must be addressed. In particular, children must be given opportunities to learn about human rights; grow up in a rights-respecting culture; and be provided with opportunities to engage socially, economically, and politically in their communities. This is just one example of how human rights education can help reduce conflict and foster political inclusion. More studies are needed to flesh out the connections between HRE in peacebuilding, how it is implemented in diverse social conditions, and how it best contributes to conflict management and economic and political inclusion.

Notes

1. *Talibes* are moved from their villages in Senegal and Guinea-Bissau to attend urban residential Quranic schools. They are forced to endure extreme forms of abuse, neglect, and exploitation, and are forced to beg.

2. Proposal written by senior officials at the Salvadoran National Police Academy, 2000.

References

Ariza Altahona, Alexis, Linda Gonzalez Pineros, and Patricia Guerrero Acevedo. 2009. "Desde el corazón de las mujeres: Una estrategia de resistencia juridica de la Liga de Mujeres Desplazadas." Cartagena de Indias: Liga de Mujeres Desplazadas. www.observatoriogenero.org/DDV/desde%20el%20corazon%20de%20las%20 mujeres.pdf.

Colombian Constitutional Court. 2004. "Colombian Constitutional Court, Decision T-025 of 2004." http://www.brookings.edu/~/media/Projects/idp/Colombia_T-025 _2004.pdf?la=en.

Council of Europe. 2010. "Recommendation CM/Rec(2010)7 of the Committee of Ministers to Member States on the Council of Europe Charter on Education for Democratic Citizenship and Human Rights Education." https://wcd.coe.int /ViewDoc.jsp?p=&Ref=CM/Rec(2010)7&Language=lanEnglish&Ver=original &Site=CM&BackColorInternet=C3C3C3&BackColorIntranet=EDB021 &BackColorLogged=F5D383&direct=true.

Holland, T., and J. P. Martin. 2014. *Human Rights Education and Peacebuilding: A Comparative Study.* New York: Routledge.

Hussein, Zeid Ra'ad Al. 2015. "Keynote Speech by Mr. Zeid Ra'ad Al Hussein, United Nations High Commissioner for Human Rights at the Conference on 'Education for Peace,' Palais des Nations, Geneva, 14 January 2015." http://www.ohchr.org/EN /NewsEvents/Pages/DisplayNews.aspx?NewsID=15482&LangID=E.

Mertus, Julie. 2004. "Improving International Peacebuilding Efforts: The Example of Human Rights Culture in Kosovo." *Global Governance* 10(3):333–351. http://www .jstor.org/stable/27800532.

Tutu, Desmond, and Wald, Mary. 2014. "The Voices of Inclusion and Peace: Missing from the Conversation?" *Huffington Post*, December 8. http://www.huffingtonpost .com/desmond-tutu/the-voices-of-inclusion-and-peace_b_5955828.html.

CHAPTER 12

Leveraging Diversity to Become a Global Citizen: Lessons for Human Rights Education

Carol Anne Spreen and Chrissie Monaghan

Embracing Human Rights in Education to Face Global Challenges: A Conceptual Model

Education can be a powerful tool that urges us to reimagine society as a place for celebrating diversity, supporting human dignity, and promoting human rights. An extensive body of literature identifies and explains the ways in which formal education is central to nation-state building in its capacity to create citizens (Carnoy and Levin 1985; Meyer and Ramirez 1992) and assimilate individuals by transmitting narratives of the imagined national community to which they belong and in which they take part (Anderson 2006). Over the last few decades, human rights education (HRE) has been applied as an "essential part of the preparation for participation in a pluralistic society" (Osler and Starkey 2010:165). During the UN Decade for Human Rights Education (1995–2004), HRE was defined as a:

> training, dissemination and information effort aimed at the building of a universal culture of human rights through the imparting of knowledge and skills and the moulding of attitudes and directed to . . . strengthening of respect for human rights . . . full development of the human personality and the sense of its dignity . . . promotion of understanding, tolerance, gender equality and friendship among all nations, indigenous peoples and racial, national, ethnic, religious

and linguistic groups . . . [and] enabling of all persons to participate effectively in a free society. (United Nations 1994:3)

Over the last thirty years there have been differing and at times divergent models and definitions of HRE, which now circulate on a global scale, put forward by world organizations (e.g., UN agencies), professional associations (e.g., Human Rights Education Associates), and international advocacy groups (e.g., Amnesty International) (Keet 2007:53). Today human rights curricula can be found in many national education policies as part of civics, history, or citizenship education (Lohrenscheit 2002; Mihr 2009; Mihr and Schmitz 2007; Ramirez, Suarez, and Meyer 2007). Throughout its evolution, human rights educators have increasingly recognized that HRE also requires the combining of legal perspectives with an affective dimension (see also Chapter 2 in this book). In laying out the early foundations for HRE, the Council of Europe Recommendation stressed that:

> the study of human rights should lead to an understanding of, and sympathy for, the concepts of justice, equality, peace, dignity, rights and democracy. Such understanding should be both cognitive and based on experience and feelings. School should thus provide opportunities for pupils to experience affective involvement in human rights and to express their feelings through art, drama, music, creative writing and audio-visual media. (Council of Europe 1985)

Despite recognizing the importance of affective and applied understandings of HRE, and while there are many conceptual distinctions across models, much of HRE still remains highly formalized and tends to focus on legal and international frameworks, emphasizing the moral and ethical aspects of human rights. Keet (2007) describes this limitation as "declarationism," where the emphasis is on the presentation of legal texts, facts, and figures, underscoring the importance of incorporating a legal perspective to provide a basic knowledge and culture of human rights law and its relevance to participants' lives. According to Keet, HRE is a concept that is subject to a conceptual eclecticism that "hampers its pedagogical potential as a counter-measure to human rights violations and human suffering" (Keet 2007). He suggests that the dominant conceptual structure of HRE has largely been a "declarationist, conservative, positivistic, uncritical, compliance-driven framework that is in the main informed by a political literacy approach" (2007:1).

We share Keet's critique, and in this chapter we hope to show how "declarationist" or "political literacy" approaches to HRE miss a key opportunity to address human rights violations, and most importantly to begin to tackle human suffering through action. By posing human rights through legalistic frameworks, as something "out there" to be obtained, HRE fails to engage students in deep learning about social injustice or develop in them a concrete understanding about how to enact or advocate for rights, leaving students ill-equipped to make sense of the many global border crossings they will make in their own lives. For many students, particularly those who are most vulnerable and living in highly unequal societies, whose rights are being and continue to be violated, *education about human rights* appears out of synch with their realities of living in an unequal and inequitable global world (Vally and Spreen 2012).

In the United States, school communities are growing increasingly diverse, and students from numerous countries with varying knowledge and experiences are reshaping the educational landscape. By failing to engage these youth in positive or purposeful ways (e.g., that embrace their culture, language, history, experience—or their human dignity), most schools miss an important opportunity to practice human rights in education. Much like its predecessors (multicultural or civics education), HRE must be pushed beyond broad notions of democracy or symbolism of diversity and equality, and beyond the rhetoric of laws and rights, and instead be informed by the lived experiences of those whose rights have been and continue to be violated in an unequal and asymmetrical world. Human rights is most powerful as a learning tool when it centers on action and social transformation as its end goal.

Given its salience and current resonance, educators are beginning to grapple with new ways to incorporate human rights in education. In a recent study of HRE approaches, Bajaj (2011) distinguishes three different outcomes-based models of HRE that differ in content, approach, and action. HRE for Global Citizenship emphasizes "individual rights as part of an international community [that] may or may not be perceived as a direct challenge to the state" (492), while HRE for Coexistence, most often implemented in post-conflict settings, emphasizes "minority rights and pluralism as part of a larger human rights framework" (492). HRE for Transformative Action seeks to alter unequal power relations among individuals, groups, society, and/or the state by making learners aware of injustices that they and others experience. In this chapter we build on these models by demonstrating that in today's diverse school communities, thinking about human rights in education through *global citizenship* and *transformative action* can provide a springboard for exploring problem-based solutions to global problems while investigating and understanding human rights and responsibilities. Specifically, we start from Bajaj's HRE for Transformative Action, illustrating how HRE should be taught in a way that critically considers the continued social, economic, and political inequalities that persist (both locally and globally) in communities. We then go beyond this definition to illustrate how it can also provide a platform for not only becoming aware of injustices, but for learning about what one can do and what role one can play in order to bring about positive social change.

Children today face a new set of challenges in a world that is more globally connected yet ever more unequal, divided, and asymmetrical. And due to the narrowing of the curriculum and the overemphasis on rote learning for standardized testing, too many schools are failing to engage young people in meaningful learning. As Sattin-Bajaj and Suárez-Orozco (2012) explain, "youth the world over need more cultural sophistication, better communication and collaboration skills, and higher-order cognitive skills for thinking, as well as metacognitive skills to reflect on their own learning" (2). In this world of increasing complexity and diversity— the lack of fit between traditional teaching and learning of abstract concepts and lofty declarations versus what education needs to be in order to help students address global complexities head on—is the departure point for our investigation.

We acknowledge from the outset that there have been many responses to and critiques of both HRE and global citizenship education (GCE) (see, for instance, Davies 2006; Keet 2007; Bajaj 2011). Elsewhere we engage in this debate and describe the evolution, critiques, and strengths of HRE in relation to GCE (Monaghan and Spreen 2016). In that article we argued that HRE and GCE share similarly stated goals as well as approaches and strategies; additionally, many of the same institutions and actors that once were at the fore in advocating for HRE have now shifted their attention to GCE. However, we suggest this shift is not without consequences, particularly with regard to developing and implementing educational programming. Importantly, today, for reasons both political and instrumental, GCE has gained global resonance with governments, policymakers, and the international community, and its latest iteration comes from UNESCO's Education First initiative, which explains that "Global citizenship education aims to empower learners to engage and assume active roles both locally and globally to face and resolve global challenges and ultimately to become proactive contributors to a more just, peaceful, tolerant, inclusive, secure, and sustainable world" (UNESCO 2013a).

For our purposes in this chapter, we define GCE as education that is socially engaged and that uses transformative approaches to teach about citizenship, democracy, identity, and rights, while also reflecting on how it can be an important and potentially more radical model of human rights education. Elsewhere, we have presented a theoretical model for "mindful global citizenship education," suggesting that it offers a conceptual framework for supporting human rights education in addressing complex notions of globalization, citizenship, and identity (Hammell et al. 2014). Much of the current scholarship on global citizenship and human rights education is either overly celebratory or overly skeptical of their transformative potential. Additionally, the unit level (i.e., individual, institutional, systemic) on which transformation is supposed to occur with the implementation of GCE or HRE programming is under-theorized and under-researched. This is particularly true of GCE, the advocates of which proclaim, on the one hand, that it "equips students to successfully compete in the global economy," and, on the other, that it seeks to "familiarize students with an intercultural perspective to allow for increasing cooperation in a globalized world" (UNESCO 2014). While the later vaguely aligns with notions of global citizenship that we promote in our work, the former reifies notions of economic competition between citizens of different nation-states. As such, we propose an alternative model of global citizenship education that takes a humanities-oriented, human rights–based approach. We underscore that critically engaging and redefining traditional human rights teaching and placing it more firmly as part an overall socially just, transformative, and rights-based approach to teaching and curriculum can ensure that learning about rights will play a more significant role in an overall project of addressing violations of human rights and human suffering.

We are particularly interested in examining the interaction between human rights education and critical praxis, and the ways in which both facilitate transformative human rights–based educational programming. In this chapter we attempt to capture and explain our curricular and pedagogic processes, students' perceptions of global citizenship and themselves as global citizens, and the students' sense of engagement with their community, and how they used this knowledge to act.

In this chapter we also demonstrate how this approach to global citizenship practice prepares students to explore human rights and then learn to act as responsible citizens in an increasingly complex world (Chickering 2003; Tilak 2008). Our model builds on concepts of social justice, considering civic learning as responsible activism that recognizes the individual's connections to social issues in their own community and throughout the world (Davies 2006; Rhoads and Szelényi 2011; Schattle 2009). Finally, our work illustrates how this approach embraces antioppressive pedagogies such as antiracist pedagogy, social justice pedagogy, critical pedagogy, and multicultural education; we further lay out how this strand of emancipatory global citizenship education aligns closely with the broader goals and ideals of human rights–based education. The following section describes a teaching and research initiative, Becoming a Global Citizen, that was designed to facilitate this form of critical inquiry into notions of global citizenship and human rights through a community-based action research and teaching approach.

Teaching and Learning Global Citizenship Through Relationships and Rights at the High School and Tertiary Levels

While one cannot argue with Education First's lofty goals of "empowering students to engage and assume active roles both globally and locally" (UNESCO 2013b), we are cautious about what schools can and cannot do, given the current political climate around high-stakes testing and accountability. More concretely and perhaps in view of Keet's critique of HRE, in this project we employed global citizenship instead of human rights education to frame our project. Initially, this was done for political reasons: we wanted to enroll a diverse group of learners from across the high school where the program was carried out; however, the teachers and administrators felt that "human rights" would alienate lower-tracked students and English language learners because HRE was viewed as "too difficult and legalistic." It was also seen by some students as "owned" by honors and advanced-tracked students who were part of an Amnesty International club at the school, and who, by and large, ignored the migrant and refugee kids at the school. Interestingly, as the project evolved over the last few years, we also began to recognize the ways that human rights in and of themselves were not a sufficient entry point for engaging the school or as a vehicle for tackling some of the issues of global injustice and inequality students experienced. Instead, *global citizenship for transformative action* took on a different and expanded meaning in our work.

Importantly, this project evolved over a five-year period, beginning with a focus on *human rights in education*, and specifically the *right to education*. In the fall of 2010 we created an interdisciplinary, field research course on comparative perspectives on human rights and education for graduate students, law students, and undergraduates that focused on understanding and examining human rights and education, both locally and internationally. Cotaught with faculty from the law school and the Legal Aid Justice Center, the course was designed to prepare students to work together collaboratively by participating in site visits to local community service organizations, schools, and homes; to conduct interviews with staff/community members, families, and children; and to organize community members who could serve as cultural and linguistic translators and identify needs and interests for improving educational services. Lectures and readings on education and human rights were supplemented by practical skills of academic community engagement, and several sessions were devoted to preparing students on the ethics and practices of conducting community-based research in culturally diverse settings.

As part of the course, we held a two-day international Human Rights in Education Symposium, with legal scholars and education advocates working on human rights and education in various countries throughout the world including India, Pakistan, Suriname, Guatemala, South Africa, Colombia, and the United States. In this symposium, we invited faculty, students, high school teachers, students, administrators, and public service organizations working with migrant communities in the area to examine both the broad underpinnings of international human rights and the specific components of education rights; we then considered these as they related to the experiences of marginalized and underserved youth in various parts of the world (i.e., children in emergency or post-conflict situations, girls with restricted access to schools, educational issues in indigenous communities, disabled and language minority groups, access to and discrimination in schools against migrants and refugees).

Action-oriented research was a critical dimension of the course, because it involved individuals, community organizations, social service providers, and numerous local advocates throughout the research design, data collection, and presentation and dissemination of findings. Importantly, students helped develop a manual on *Rights in Education* for workshop participants, presented their preliminary findings (from course case studies), and created action items to carry out over the coming years.

Building on the course and symposium, during the following year we organized a second workshop on the Right to Education for Refugees. The workshop brought together more than seventy students, parents, immigrant/refugee/migrant advocates, social service providers, lawyers, and educators to discuss the successes and challenges of ensuring the right to education in the local community. Workshop sessions included stories and documentary films developed by local migrant students and their families, and presentations by teachers, social service agencies, legal advocates, and community-based immigrant and refugee organizations. The focus was on understanding and advocating for rights in education in the United States, particularly in the local schools. It included a discussion of local opportunities to create culturally responsive curriculum and address more equitable learning opportunities for all students. During the symposium, we shared research findings from the previous course, developed and distributed a manual that came out of the course Rights in Education in Virginia, and then created action items for participants to carry out over the coming years. We broke into working groups and used adapted versions of Action Aid's "Rights Respecting Schools" guidelines and self-evaluation tool ("How does your school environment promote children's rights?") to discuss issues that were most pressing in the community. The current Becoming a Global Citizen course and related ongoing research were among the main action items identified by the participants in the workshop.

In the fall of 2013, we launched a collaborative teaching and research initiative between the university and the local high school, the core activity of which has been the development and implementation of two interrelated courses: Global Citizenship and Human Rights in Education (which was offered to graduate and undergraduate students one day a week at the university) and Becoming a Global Citizen (which was taught at the high school four days a week as a full-year elective). A key element of this approach was combining a diverse group of students in learning together about global citizenship and human rights from more than a dozen different countries, multiple religions and language groups, and university and high school students, including honors/advanced placement and English language learners (ELL)/migrant/refugee students. Historically, there has been a significant division at the high school level between ELL/migrant students, who comprise approximately 10 percent of the student body, and the student body at large.

Many of the former are political refugees and undocumented migrants who have experienced numerous violations of their rights and often struggle with issues of identity, belonging, and legal/social status. Some are former child soldiers or ethnic minorities, or they have faced various forms of discrimination and/or rights violations. Conversely, many of the American high school and university students enrolled in the course were interested in human rights and involved in a variety of humanitarian and community service–related projects and after-school programs, but their efforts have been mainly directed at working with groups abroad. While the "global subject" was just down the hall, for many of these students it seemed a world away. This initiative set out to remedy that.

Over the course of the year, students learned about core themes of human rights, citizenship, and social justice through readings, films, and experiential lessons. In the first part of the semester they studied various organizations, declarations, and efforts to promote human rights, and they were introduced to the tenets of the Universal Declaration of Human Rights (UDHR) and several treaties that mobilize persons and resources to action when rights are violated. Through media, documentaries, interviews, and guest lectures, students began to explore the relationship between human rights and education through engaging with a range of issues, including but not limited to stereotyping and discrimination, immigration, climate change, and freedom of expression. As they developed a language and vocabulary to understand rights, personal stories and narratives shared by students in the class expanded their understanding and enabled them to connect abstract concepts of human rights, democracy, and citizenship to personal experience and toward practical applications. Through oral historical approaches, students started to evaluate how global citizenship is constructed through "real-life" explorations, which are then converted into stories that contain shared and vital experiences that transcend national boundaries. Throughout the year, students were challenged to consider the ways in which they come to know and understand themselves, each other, the world around them, and their own ability to act as responsible global citizens and agents of change.

Leveraging Diverse Learning Contexts

Becoming a Global Citizen was a rare opportunity for graduate, undergraduate, and high school students to work together to foster a reciprocal learning environment. With approximately 10 percent of the high school population identified as language minority/ELL students and more than fifty languages spoken at the school, teachers lacked the capacity or support to address the social needs and cultural considerations in working with such a varied group of students. In our particular community, there was an International Rescue Committee relocation center, so the languages, relocation, and settlement needs and experiences of international students were very wide-ranging. The most commonly spoken foreign languages in the high school (in descending order) are: Spanish, Mai-Mai (a Somali language), Swahili, Arabic, Krahn (a Liberian language), Farsi, Mandarin, and Burmese. Research on migrant students suggests that schools frequently do not know much about—or more importantly, do not know how to address—the past experiences that refugees and immigrants faced in their country of origin (e.g., issues of trauma, protracted violence, cultural dislocation, loss of social and financial status, etc.) and how these might impact students' lives and learning outcomes.

While many local organizations offered an array of services to migrant and refugee families, these were, by and large, not coordinated or part of a larger advocacy strategy to support students or their learning experiences. And the schools they land in are often ill-equipped to incorporate the experiences and cultural resources that migrant and refugee families bring to the school community. Moreover, many migrant children and their families have never heard of the many international human rights treaties that set forth their rights to, in, and through education, specifically the ways in which human rights should be protected in education, or as a means to define how education should be organized so as to facilitate the full enjoyment of their human rights (Tomasevski 2003). Similar to the refugee and immigrant children whom they teach, many educators are unaware of international human rights treaties that set forth the universal right to education, specifically the normative and practical ways in which education acts as a multiplier for other rights, or how human rights should be protected in education. In many countries, noncitizens do not have a legally recognized right to education, despite provisions of international human rights treaties, such as the Convention on the Rights of the Child. Absence of citizenship may constitute the most widespread legal obstacle to the enjoyment of the right to education.

The underlying premise of the course was to advance the argument that, once children are enrolled in school, their right to education is barely realized if schools and teachers, and the supporting education system, cannot or do not enable epistemological access. The right to education can only be realized when all children have equal access to opportunities for learning, under conditions that respect their dignity and bring their knowledge and experience to light. Becoming a Global Citizen was designed as one of the very few nontracked courses at the school, and was open to all students. Our first year we enrolled a diverse group of eighteen students from their sophomore to senior years, representing the full range of cultural, linguistic, and socioeconomic backgrounds. Describing their status provides but one window into how citizenship and human rights issues enter the classroom: seven of the students were English language learners whose families were placed in the area by the International Rescue Committee as refugees; five of the seven were from war/conflict-affected areas and had spent part of their schooling in refugee camps. Two additional students were ELL students who had immigrated to the United States for economic and political reasons. There was also an exchange student from northern Europe who was taking a "gap year." Among the American students, four were from the advanced placement/honors tracks and one had a documented learning disability. The course was cotaught by the university teaching team and a high school teacher with a background in special education. In contrast, the university had a group of mostly white but socioeconomically diverse students: three were international students, and one had been a political refugee.

An ELL teacher who collaborated with us from the outset on the design and implementation of the course explained its importance:

> About 10% of [our] students are born in another country. Teaching about global citizenship provides a wonderful opportunity for refugee and immigrant students to draw upon their own experiences, cultures, and languages as a powerful resource, to teach their American-born peers about global issues from a personal perspective. At the same time, it provides an environment for English Language Learners and native English speakers to engage in meaningful dialogue with university students on issues that are important to all of them.

These benefits would extend far beyond our classroom, into the high school and the broader community, potentially advancing democratic citizenship.

Teaching Human Rights Through Social Justice Pedagogy and a Rights-Based Approach

In bringing together a group of students with different racial, ethnic, class, and linguistic backgrounds, as well as different legal and social statuses, this course aimed to both reveal and break down many of these existing socially constructed categories (e.g., refugee/migrant, legal/undocumented, exchange/ELL, general/special education, black/white), allowing students to recognize and ultimately challenge these categories and their social and economic salience.

In the first weeks of the course, we discussed our expectation that the classroom was a space for democratic colearning, and we asked all students to try to let go of the "expert–learner" model of education and strive to build meaningful relationships with everyone in the room. Challenging the concept of the "banking model of education" (Freire 2000), we subverted declarationist and political literacy approaches to human rights. Throughout the year, we had to work with students to embrace this approach. It did not come naturally, because outside our classroom the students were still experiencing the multiple discontinuities between learning in and out of school. Typically, learning in school is organized to increasing levels of abstraction, and the focus is primarily on content delivery, while learning outside of school is context-dependent, hands-on, and designed to solve concrete problems. In our classroom we were aware of this, and we explicitly asked that students be open to some experimentation and be willing to try new approaches (e.g., based on what was and was not working in the classroom). Initially, they were uncomfortable with the lack of structure or hierarchy in the classroom; they struggled with ambiguity, and not having one right answer was very disconcerting for many of them. Some didn't like working in groups with students who they perceived to be low performers and not strong students. Others were pleasantly surprised at how much our classroom was "just like a university class," where they were "finally taken seriously" as individuals with opinions and experiences.

By looking at global issues through the broad lens of rights-based approaches, students were able to think differently about the role of culture and tradition, and create new values and attitudes about learning in a diverse classroom and a global society. Through discussions of the intersections of race, class, gender, power, and status, we considered ways that school communities could differently tap into the knowledge, resources, and experiences in the rich diversity of histories to address inequality and promote nondiscrimination. Through action research projects carried out over the second part of the year, students began to think anew about the power and purpose of education and its potential to impact some of the most pressing issues and concerns facing the world today: global migration, poverty and the economy, social and environmental instability, violence, and war.

As previously explained, most human rights programs rely on either delivering human rights content or designing a field-based internship; very few link the two. The combination of developing understanding through content and reflection, without field experience, does not foster purposeful engagement with new concepts, whereas field internship experiences and reflection without rigorous engagement in the content and meaning is also lacking, possibly leaving room to promote stereotypes because core beliefs and assumptions may be left unexamined. Taken together, our emphasis on understanding, reflection, and action was essential, and these three aspects mutually reinforce global citizenship for transformative outcomes.

During the first semester, the major impetus was having the students learn about human rights, citizenship, identity, and inequality and then co-construct activities and lessons they carry out in class, and that they post on the classes' weblog. As part of the organizational framework for the course, we drew on the resources of organizations like the Right to Education (RTE) Project (www.right-to-education.org). Through this framework, we sought to understand and examine the intersections of education rights and educational inequality as they impact refugee, immigrant, and undocumented children in and out of schools. In determining the content for the course, we developed a curriculum that integrates elements of critical pedagogy, recognizing the importance of uncertainty, context, attentiveness, open-mindedness, and emphasizing multiple perspectives. We also incorporated off-the-shelf units, lesson plans, and activities (and even visits) from staff at three nationally recognized human rights–oriented education programs: Amnesty International, Facing History, and Voice of Witness/Valencia 826.

Specifically, students learned about organizations, declarations, and efforts to promote human rights and were introduced to the tenets of the Universal Declaration of Human Rights (UDHR) and several treaties that mobilize persons and resources to action when rights are violated. Students then went beyond this content-based understanding of HRE to explore the relationship between human rights and social justice by engaging with a range of issues, including but not limited to stereotyping and discrimination,

Table 12.1. Becoming a Global Citizen Course

Knowledge and Understanding	Skills	Values and Attitudes
☐ Human Rights laws and declarations ☐ Diversity ☐ Globalization and interdependence ☐ Sustainable development ☐ Peace and conflict	☐ Critical thinking ☐ Ability to analyze arguments ☐ Persuasive writing ☐ Ability to challenge injustice and inequalities ☐ Respect for people and things ☐ Cooperation and conflict resolution	☐ Sense of identity and self-esteem ☐ Empathy ☐ Commitment to social justice and equity ☐ Value and respect for diversity ☐ Concern for the environment and commitment to sustainable development ☐ Belief that people can make a difference

anti-immigration policies and sentiments, concerns about environmental sustainability and climate change, and notions around surveillance and freedom of expression. As Table 12.1 illustrates, a key element of this approach was combining university students, honors and AP (advanced placement) students, and ELL students in learning together about global issues by developing knowledge, skills, and attitudes that form global citizenship. Through stories and narratives shared by students across all these levels (both verbal and written), students were able to connect these abstract concepts of human rights and social inequality and apply them to their own personal experiences. A selection of some of the weekly content and themes is depicted in Table 12.2 to provide an overview of some of the significant units and events that were addressed.

During the second part of the year, the university students were responsible for mentoring the high school students and assisting them with participatory action research projects. The class was divided up into five groups, each focused on a student-generated topic identified by applying their knowledge of global issues and translating those larger issues into local concerns that they could address or raise awareness about in their own community. The groups identified and focused on: segregation and racial inequality, homelessness, poverty, sustainability, and immigration. Each group had at least one university-based mentor to help as they developed research questions, gathered and analyzed data, and put together a final video documentary or public awareness campaign.

Table 12.2. Content, Themes, and Sample Units from High School Course

Content and Themes	*Selection of Special Units and Events*
☐ Identity ☐ Participatory research ☐ Citizenship ☐ Social justice ☐ Equity, inequality, and discrimination ☐ Diversity ☐ Human rights and education rights ☐ Globalization and interdependence ☐ Sustainability ☐ Development ☐ Policymaking ☐ Peace, violence, and conflict	☐ Media and technology: viewed the documentary *9500 Liberty*, helped high school students write policy briefs to prepare for a Skype conversation on immigration policy with U.S. Senator and former Governor Mark Warner. ☐ Conducting oral histories: seminar with representatives from Voice of Witness (a nonprofit with a mission to illuminate human rights abuses through oral histories) and facilitated high school students taking each other's oral histories to make a video for diversity week. ☐ Workshops: participated in workshops with Amnesty International and other training professionals on team building, youth participatory action research, youth activism and visionary practice, and social movements. ☐ Field visits: hosted research days and field trips to the university and community to interview faculty, student leaders, and community members, and to attend public guest lectures on topics.

The final section of this paper explains in more detail what we feel are the essential components of transformative human rights education: First, it is important to create a culture of belonging and trust by helping students move from national to global citizenship, building on the ideas, experiences, understandings, and cultural backgrounds of students. Most importantly, the preservation of identity and the recognition of multiple identities students may hold is a key right in education. Second, it is important to help students develop an understanding of connections—between the global and the local, and to one another—by building relationships. In our class this was done by emphasizing that learning is a dialogue and recognizing that everyone who participates in the dialogue has insights and contributions that can inform our understanding of human rights. Third, we stressed "doing citizenship," emphasizing Freirean ideas about education as a liberating experience and requiring that students participate actively on equal footing in ways in which they could contribute meaningfully. Like Freire, we recognized that participation is not inevitable; it is a process that has to be constructed. So by first building trust, then building relationships, we set the foundation for equal participation and meaningful action. Below we describe in more detail how each of these components was incorporated into our teaching and learning.

Citizenship and Identity: Constructing a Classroom Culture of Belonging

In the United States, where one in every five students lives in a family from another country, issues of identity and citizenship are increasingly central to both the legal status and sense of belonging of many young adults. Immigration reform has become a hot-button issue. For many students in the class, the issue has reached a peak over the last few years, with debates over "undocumented" students, the DREAM Act, and accompanying concerns about access to and financial means for education for those youth who lack legal status and support. Despite our increasing diversification and global human rights movements, our ideas about citizenship and civic engagement are often simplistic and fail to address the complex notions of globalization, migration, and rights in meaningful and purposeful ways. For refugee and migrant students in the class, their curricula have not been sufficient to help them understand and address the accompanying legal and personal challenges that surround migration and status.

We began the semester by deconstructing notions of identity and citizenship, and we identified two main tenets to guide this work. First, we tried to focus on language and classroom culture that are meaningful and empowering by discussing issues of power, designing rules of engagement, and exploring issues of empathy and solidarity. A lot of our activities were about self-identification and occupying multiple identities, and then learning to listen. We also specifically addressed the needs of English language learners in the classroom, who might have needed more time to articulate or share thoughts. We also used arts and performance-based activities, allowing students to express themselves in their language of choice with peer translators, and we assigned group tasks with multiple and diverse activities.

This approach to constructing a culture of belonging underscores what Starkey and Osler have termed "Freedom," "Identity," and "Dignity and Security," referring to the Preamble and several articles in the Convention on the Rights of the Child. In our approach, freedom, identity, dignity, and security were ensured through pedagogy that permitted maximum freedom of expression of thought, conscience, and belief, while underscoring that the responsible exercise of these rights also requires skills, trust, and reflection that are incorporated into the learning activities. Students were able to express opinions and exercise choice in many options in the class activities and projects.

No two classes were alike, though on any given day one would always find university and high school students talking and working together. Most often, the students worked in small groups, discussing themes ranging from poverty to structural racism to the challenges they were having in their own lives. Though we were working through difficult subject material, there was levity and light-heartedness infused in the students' and instructors' interactions. Posters and projects from different activities quickly covered the walls—one wall showcasing students' self-portraits and identity mapping, another depicting students' storyboarding for their documentary film projects, and another featuring the guiding principles for the class they had developed together at the beginning of the year.

We also focused throughout the course on building deepening levels of trust, respect, and security, and helping students process their anxieties and fears, particularly with regard to sharing their backgrounds. Several students in the class had personal experiences with many of the themes and phenomena they were studying (e.g., forced migration, war, racial discrimination). We discussed with the students how to create an environment conducive to sharing (e.g., listening intently and asking open-ended questions) and the importance of bearing witness to and receiving stories from each other even if they are hard to hear.

At the conclusion of the first semester, the class was tasked with preparing a presentation for the annual school-wide "diversity assembly" that synthesized what they had learned up to that point in the course and that included every member of the class. They decided to make a short video that would highlight several tenets of the UDHR that paired with their own lived experiences. They conducted and wrote down brief oral histories with one another; when it came time to do the filming, the students decided that they would read one or two sentences from each other's stories, rather than their own. They appear on camera, against a brick wall, and as a quickening instrumental melody played in the background, they each read one of the UDHR statements and a personal example from their classmates of how issues like racial profiling, immigration, poverty, and war and conflict affected them. The Afghan student read from a description of U.S. racial profiling, stating, "Most people know about racial profiling happening in Arizona and Texas, but did you know it is happening right here? Article 2 of the UDHR states that everyone is equal, despite differences in skin color, sex, religion, or language." After reading a couple of brief sentences about their country of origin and what brought them to the United States, they concluded by explaining that "these stories reveal why many students and their families come to America. Articles 14 and 15 of the UDHR make it possible for students to come and start a new life here." For many of the students, it was the first time they had shared their story at the school with anyone from outside the class.

Understanding Connections and Building Relationships

The relationships built among the high school students who previously had very little interaction with one another, and between the university and high school students were substantive, lasting, and one of the most important outcomes of the course. The flexibility and critical space we created with our approach to acting as global citizens to promote human rights helped students grapple with the challenges of building relationships with people who were seemingly quite different, and gave students an opportunity to confront their points of discomfort about their experience. On more than one occasion, we overheard one student saying to another, "I never knew that about you. . . . I've been in school with you for years and I never had any idea." We focused throughout the course on students' own histories and lived experiences, and we designed activities that allowed students to share in formal and informal ways different aspects of their personalities, interests, and backgrounds. This often took place in small-group discussions, where students were given a prompt (e.g., "Discuss a time in your life where someone saw you differently than you saw yourself"). However, many of the most profound stories about making connections and building relationships were shared spontaneously. Below we highlight two examples and the students who shared them:

> In late October, Lexis mentioned in passing that she and her friends had been stopped by a local police officer at a city park on a recent

Saturday afternoon. Single mother of a two-year-old son, Lexis was frequently absent from school though rarely missed Global Citizenship class (several times bringing her son to class with her). Lexis is African American and explained it was not the first time she had been stopped by the local police for simply being in a public space; this time, however, when she and her friends provided identification (e.g., driver's licenses or school I.D. cards) as requested, the officer demanded they furnish passports. Lexis recounts that as the scene was unfolding and she and her friends (who were Latina) were becoming increasingly anxious as the officer badgered them for more and different forms of identification, she thought back to the stop-and-frisk activity we had in class the previous week and reflected "I knew he didn't have the right to do this and that I had rights." In the hopes of defusing an escalating situation, she also presented her passport, but even then the officer questioned why "somebody like her would even have a passport?" and whether her friends were "legal." Lexis explained that, "he kept saying I shouldn't even need this passport. Then I got mad." At that point, Lexis told the officer that he could not detain her or her friends, then asked for his name and badge number, and let him know she was going to report him for harassment. She did exactly that and several weeks later, after the police had launched an investigation into the matter following the complaint, the officer was suspended from active duty and Lexis was issued a formal apology. Reflecting on the event later in the classroom, Lexis explained, "it was because of this class . . . because we had talked about it and what to do if something like this happened, that I knew how to take a stand and what my rights are."

This sharing of personal stories in the moment and observing how students can "actually do something" was empowering for students on many levels.

Several days after Lexis first described her experience with the police officer, we were reading an excerpt from the Voice of Witness book series, where the narrator, who had immigrated to the United States from the Middle East just after 9/11, describes strangers approaching her in public and demanding she take off her head scarf, telling her "You're in America now." During the in-class discussion that followed, one American student stated she didn't think things like that happened anymore. "It's been over ten years. I see people wearing head scarves at the high school." Then Fatima (a student who had resettled to the United States from Somalia after residing in a refugee camp in Kenya for over two years) turned from her seat in the front row and faced the class. "When I was in seventh grade, I was walking to the pencil sharpener when a boy in the class reached out and grabbed my head scarf, pulling it off. It was in front of everyone and the teacher saw it happen and didn't say or do anything, just kept going like nothing had happened. Since then, I haven't worn a head scarf to class or anywhere in town." The rest of the class was silent until one student spoke up. "That's not right . . . I can't believe that happened to you." Another chimed in: "I have a friend here who says the same thing, that she's been made fun of for wearing her head scarf to school so she stopped doing it." A few days later, Fatima came to class wearing a bright yellow head scarf. When one of the instructors complimented her on it, Fatima said, "After our discussion, I just thought that I can't let people make me feel like my culture is wrong. I know I can at least wear it here and no one will judge me. And if anything happens, someone would stand up for me now."

We expected that the experience of learning about social justice and power relations in conjunction with human rights principles would create a truly emancipatory pedagogy, as learning through dialogue forced students to confront their assumptions and biases and analyze their own preconditioned values and beliefs. The reality is that it was only during these moments of dissonance in the real world that students were able to realize the importance of multiple perspectives or the enormity of how easy it is to fall into mindless patterns of thinking. Recognizing that something as "harmless" as expecting everyone to know a nursery rhyme could possibly alienate students from diverse backgrounds was powerful learning.

Throughout the year, students described their own positionality and how connections and relationships helped them see their own blind spots. Early on they expressed their frustration with a seemingly open-ended, democratic, and less-hierarchical classroom, and explained their preference for a more traditional, top-down learning structure. Yet, instead of adding more structure, we gave the students the opportunity to explore their own discomfort directly with a writing assignment posing the concern as a question. Over time, students began to recognize how the democratic classroom had the potential to take them outside of their traditional, didactic comfort zone and to see that, through the use of reflection, they could begin to analyze the cause of their feelings and the inherent cultural relativism present in applying their experience to others. One student noted:

> There was one point during class when the activity became very disorganized and it seemed like everyone was talking at the same time. I began to compare this classroom to my own high school classroom and briefly thought that my high school classroom [was better] because of how organized it was. Then, I thought of . . . how problematic my comparison was . . . it was just a very different way of managing a classroom than my teachers managed us. Furthermore, my classroom was about one-twentieth as diverse as this CHS classroom, which lends itself to a lot of differences in classroom environment that I cannot understand as a product of an entirely homogenous high school classroom environment.

Nussbaum (2006) has described different aspects of democratic citizenship education: the first is a critical examination of prevailing traditions, habits, and ways of life, and being prepared to questions beliefs and assertions. The second is the adoption of a perspective and ability to see oneself not as simply a citizen of the local region or group, but also and above all, as a human being bound to all other human beings by ties of recognition and concern. And the third is a "narrative imagination," namely the ability to think what it might be like to be in the shoes of a person different than oneself (390). These capacities are described by students in this way:

> We've also taken the time to come together with localized news topics from countries around the world. This combination of academic material and current/present events effectively connect what can seem like distant, abstract concepts with living, breathing people. I think the same has been done with our experiences in the class. In both classes we've had conversations about diversity, identity, democracy, human rights, and developed innovative ways to engage with these ideas.

Another described how the topics both engaged and empowered the students to think beyond the classroom to their possible impact on the world:

> In our class discussions and readings . . . we've touched on large scale ideas and social issues. We have the opportunity to share with high school students these broad based ideas, and they share with us their own unique perspectives and stories. We've had conversations about poverty, child labor, genocide, and a number of other social injustices. The workshop that we attended that integrated Amnesty International presented the students, and myself, with the tangible hope of being able to do something about everything that we've been exposed to this semester. In our class . . . I think the overarching theme has been a push for systematic change and the improvement in the livelihood of our fellow citizens of the world.

So, as "schools are often places where the dignity of students, teachers, and staff are undermined by rules, standards, and testing regimes, disciplinary procedures or their failure to value diversity and difference" (Osler and Starkey 2010:129), in our classroom we embarked on a process of transforming relationships and meanings around the purposes of schooling that were profoundly political. While the project is still in an early phase, we recognize that to continue building a rights-based or rights-friendly school will generate conflict, resistance, and even reaction. We acknowledge that this approach does not avoid conflict, and in fact requires further action.

Doing Citizenship: Social Action Projects

The culminating action-research projects allowed students to apply their conceptual knowledge from the first semester to an immediate problem in their local community. Students were stretched and challenged by every aspect of the project, from developing a research question, to gathering data and information, and, most significantly, utilizing that information to spur action. All groups decided to make a short (5–7 minute) documentary film that would raise awareness at the high school about topics they had learned about, and how these challenges related to their community. We arranged for several community members who were working on similar issues to come to the high school as guest speakers. We also brought the high school students to the university to conduct research by meeting with professors, other student volunteer organizations, and accessing resources and information in the library. In spite of living in a "college town," for many it was their first time visiting the campus.

Each project team met with a variety of university professors who, similar to the community members, had expertise related to the students' projects. During these informal meeting/interview sessions, the students critically engaged with the professors in active, reciprocal discussions, sharing their interests and knowledge they had acquired about their topic throughout the academic year. "It was a really great experience being able to share our ideas with an actual professor and have him listen to us," one student said. The same professor later described how impressed he was by the students' ability to thoughtfully and critically discuss big conceptual ideas and challenges.

This circular flow, combined with the flexibility of the curriculum, added new ideas brought in with guest speakers and current news events. These enabled us to be responsive to the needs of the class, and we found ourselves delving more deeply into concepts that students struggled and/or resonated with. Looking for points of engagement that built on or challenged the experiences of students fostered the most interactions for students, and constantly called on them to apply topics previously covered in the course. The two groups working on action-research projects related to homelessness interviewed several homeless men and women who often spend time on the avenue of shops and restaurants across the street from the university. Many of the students expressed reluctance and anxiety as they prepared to conduct the interviews, wanting to make sure they were asking appropriate questions and still being respectful. Hours later, while having lunch at the university dining hall, the students spoke passionately about their interviews. "I was unsure at first that I should even be asking questions. But then I did and he wasn't offended and spoke about his life and everything that led to him being here. And now I can't stop thinking that every person I see holding a sign and asking for help on all these street corners in this town has a story like this man's."

When the students screened the final films, we expressed how proud and impressed we were at what they had achieved. Importantly, they reflected on how challenging but rewarding the process had been and how raising awareness and making change requires a more sustained commitment than they had previously imagined. One student said, "I didn't really think it was going to be that hard to make a video, but the more we got into it, the more I wanted to know and I cared about making sure that we got it right. People need to know about this and it seems like telling their stories is one of the only ways to really make an impact."

Conclusion

Through this case study of a combined high school and university classroom, we showed how global citizenship education can provide a more complex way of looking at and understanding human rights and responsibilities in a global world by helping students to understand and investigate identity, belonging, and citizenship, as well as through critical historical inquiry, experiential learning, and civic action lessons. Finally, human rights education must be done by looking back and understanding history, and looking forward through teaching and practicing democracy and rights. Through global citizenship education, schools and communities can go beyond rights rhetoric and acontextual learning about democracy to eschew the dominant technical rationality that is currently parading as a solution to our education crisis. This is essential to fostering intercultural learning, critical thinking, and attentive civic engagement.

By employing global citizenship education through the broad lens of a rights-based approach, we can begin to think differently about the role of culture and tradition in education, teaching to create new values and attitudes about living in a diverse and global society. We can consider ways that school communities might use the knowledge, resources, experiences, and rich diversity that exists within those communities to address inequality and promote human rights. The legacy of human rights education and practices of civic or citizenship education can build on the praxis of public participation through social action to provide an important platform to rethink and reform teaching and learning, beyond test scores and developing human capital skills for the labor market. There is a moral imperative for all people, irrespective of citizenship or national legislation, to enjoy universal human rights, among them education. Internationally, the right to education is specifically guaranteed by numerous treaties and conventions promoting principles that give credence to rights within and rights through education. Transformative global citizenship and human rights education can and should allow us to reimagine society as a place for celebrating diversity, supporting human dignity, and promoting human rights.

References

Anderson, Benedict. 2006. *Imagined Communities: Reflections on the Origin and Spread of Nationalism*, rev. ed. New York: Verso.

Bajaj, Monisha. 2011. "Human Rights Education: Ideology, Location, and Approaches." *Human Rights Quarterly* 33(2):481–508.

Carnoy, Martin, and Henry M. Levin. 1985. *Schooling and Work in the Democratic State*. Stanford, CA: Stanford University Press.

Chickering, Arthur W. 2003. "Reclaiming Our Soul: Democracy and Higher Education." *Change: The Magazine of Higher Learning* 35(1):38–44.

Council of Europe. 1985. "Recommendation No. R (85) 7 of the Committee of Ministers to Member States on Teaching and Learning About Human Rights in Schools." https://rm.coe.int/CoERMPublicCommonSearchServices/DisplayDCTMContent?documentId=09000016804c2d48.

Davies, Lynn. 2006. "Global Citizenship: Abstraction or Framework for Action?" *Educational Review* 58(1):5–25.

Freire, Paulo. 2000. *Pedagogy of the Oppressed*. New York: Bloomsbury.

Hammell, Sahtiya Hosoda, Rose Cole, Lauren Stark, Chrissie Monaghan, and Carol Ann Spreen. 2015. "On Becoming a Global Citizen: Critical Pedagogy and Crossing Borders in and out of the University Classroom." In D. Williams and A. Lee, eds., *Internationalizing Higher Education: Critical Collaborations Across the Curriculum* (pp. 213–229). Rotterdam: Sense Publishers.

Keet, André. 2007. "Human Rights Education or Human Rights in Education: A Conceptual Analysis." Ph.D. dissertation, University of Pretoria.

Lohrenscheit, Claudia. 2002. "International Approaches in Human Rights Education." *International Review of Education* 48(3–4):173–185.

Meyer, John W., Francisco O. Ramirez, and Yasemin Nuhoglu Soysal. 1992. "World Expansion of Mass Education, 1870–1980." *Sociology of Education* 65(2):128–149.

Mihr, Anja. 2009. "Global Human Rights Awareness, Education and Democratization." *Journal of Human Rights* 8(2):177–189.

Mihr, Anja, and Hans Peter Schmitz. 2007. "Human Rights Education (HRE) and Transnational Activism." *Human Rights Quarterly* 29(4):973–993.

Monaghan, Chrissie, and Carol Anne Spreen. 2016. "From Human Rights to Global Citizenship Education: Peace, Conflict and the Post-Cold War Era." *International Journal of Educational Sciences* 13(1):42–55.

Nussbaum, Martha C. 2006. "Education and Democratic Citizenship: Capabilities and Quality Education." *Journal of Human Development* 7(3):385–395.

Osler, Audrey, and Hugh Starkey. 2010. *Teachers and Human Rights Education*. Stoke-on-Trent: Trentham Books.

Ramirez, Francisco O., David Suárez, and John W. Meyer. 2007. "The Worldwide Rise of Human Rights Education." In Aaron Benavot and Cecilia Braslavsky, eds., *School Knowledge in Comparative and Historical Perspective* (pp. 35–52). Dordrecht: Springer.

Rhoads, Robert A., and Katalin Szelényi. 2011. *Global Citizenship and the University: Advancing Social Life and Relations in an Interdependent World*. Stanford, CA: Stanford University Press.

Sattin-Bajaj, Carolyn, and Marcelo Suárez-Orozco. 2012. "English Language Learner Students and Charter Schools in New York State: Challenges and Opportunities." New York Governor's Leadership Team for High Quality Charter Public Schools. http://centerforschoolchange.org/wp-content/uploads/2012/09/ELL-Report-.pdf.

Schattle, Hans. 2009. "Global Citizenship in Theory and Practice." In R. Lewin, ed., *The Handbook of Practice and Research in Study Abroad: Higher Education and the Quest for Global Citizenship* (pp. 3–20). New York: Routledge.

Tilak, Jandhyala B. G. 2008. "Higher Education: A Public Good or a Commodity for Trade?" *Prospects* 38(4):449–466.

Tomasevski, Katarina. 2003. *Education Denied: Costs and Remedies*. New York: Zed Books.

UNESCO. 2013a. "Global Citizenship Education: An Emerging Perspective." Outcome Document of the Technical Consultation on Global Citizenship Education. http://unesdoc.unesco.org/images/0022/002241/224115E.pdf.

UNESCO. 2013b. "Teachers for 21st Century Global Citizenship." http://www.unesco.org/new/en/education/resources/online-materials/single-view/news/teachers_for_21st_century_global_citizenship.

UNESCO. 2014. *Global Citizenship Education: Preparing Learners for the 21st Century*. Paris: UNESCO.

United Nations. 1993. *Vienna Declaration and Programme of Action*. http://www.ohchr.org/EN/ProfessionalInterest/Pages/Vienna.aspx.

United Nations General Assembly. 1994. "United Nations Decade for Human Rights Education." A/RES/49/184, 94th Plenary Meeting, 23 December 1994. http://www.un.org/documents/ga/res/49/a49r184.htm.

Vally, Salim, and Carol Anne Spreen. 2012. "Human Rights in the World Bank 2020 Education Strategy." In Steven J. Klees, Joel Samoff, and Nelly P. Stromquist, eds., *The World Bank and Education* (pp. 173–187). Rotterdam: Sense Publishers.

Wendt, Alexander. 2003. "Why a World State Is Inevitable." *European Journal of International Relations* 9(4):491–542.

Afterword

Nancy Flowers

Whence: The Evolution of Human Rights Education

A book entitled *Human Rights Education: Theory, Research, Praxis* would have made no sense thirty years ago when I first encountered human rights education (HRE). There was no theory then, only aspiration; no research, only supposition. And although magnificent praxis was taking place—the People Power Revolution in the Philippines, popular education to oppose military dictatorships in Latin America—educators in other parts of the world learned about and from these heroic efforts only after the fact. Indeed, this book in itself demonstrates the phenomenal growth of HRE since then, with scholars and educators from around the world contributing to a textbook to serve the needs of students in the field. Originally there were no students and no "field" as such.

Early human rights educators were almost all self-taught, except for the lawyers among us, who were grounded in the legal foundations but seldom in an interactive pedagogy of human rights. Because of this dichotomy among practitioners, human rights education projects tended to emphasize legal content, the "learning about" human rights, or what André Keet (2007) has criticized as "declarationism." Typical of these were efforts undertaken in the early 1990s in Eastern Europe. Although HRE had not been a factor in the dissolution of the Eastern Bloc, it offered countries newly independent of Soviet influence a framework for reforming national constitutions and institutions and moving toward political and cultural participation with the rest of Europe. Additional factors influencing a legal bias came from projects undertaken in countries like Ethiopia and Thailand to educate citizens about new constitutions that contained provisions based on international rights language.

However, this legalistic approach and its emphasis on civil and political rights were soon balanced by the dynamic experiences of educators in the Global South. Benito Fernández Fernández (2009) describes this transition in Latin America:

> Education played a key role in resisting dictatorships. Every human rights organization counted on popular education programmes that emphatically condemned the violation of human rights, in particular civil and political rights, calling for a restoration of democracy and the recognition of popular and political organizations. However, as the cycle of political persecution came to an end with the return of democracy, the fight for human rights has shifted to become a struggle for economic, social, cultural, and environmental rights.

This shift to include the full spectrum of human rights was especially carried out through popular education, one of the most creative and flexible strategies of the human rights struggle in Latin America.

The United Nations' Role in Human Rights Education

As Melissa Gibson and Carl Grant have analyzed in their chapter, "Historicizing Critical Educational Praxis: A Human Rights Framework for Justice-Oriented Teaching" (Chapter 9), the earliest UN rights documents recognized HRE as essential to maintaining rights, freedom, and democracy. However, the United Nations did not actively promote HRE until the establishment of the UN Decade for Human Rights Education (1995–2004). Largely a response to pressures from nongovernmental organizations (NGOs) at the 1993 World Conference on Human Rights in Vienna, the Decade called upon "all States and institutions to include human rights, humanitarian law, democracy and rule of law as subjects in the curricula of all learning institutions in formal and non-formal settings."[1]

However, with a few stellar exceptions (e.g., the Philippines, Costa Rica), most governments responded half-heartedly, with many, including the United States, simply ignoring the mandate.[2] However, the Decade did provide a much-needed international forum for practitioners to engage with each other, which, along with the advent of the Internet, made for a rich cross-fertilization among human rights educators in different parts of the world.

It was in this period that both intergovernmental organizations (e.g., UNESCO, UNICEF, the Council of Europe) and established NGOs (e.g., Amnesty International) developed important HRE programs. Also new NGOs dedicated to HRE were founded (e.g., the People's Decade for HRE, Human Rights Education Associates [HREA]). Subsequently, national and regional HRE networks have evolved (e.g., the Asia-Pacific Human Rights Information Center [HURIGHTS OSAKA], the Democracy and Human Rights Education Network in Europe [DARE], Red Interamericana de Intercambio de Experiencias Educativas para Promover la Educación en Derechos Humanos, and Human Rights Educators USA [HRE USA]), as have international coalitions, notably the Right to Education Project, a collaborative initiative, supported by ActionAid International, Amnesty International, Global Campaign for Education, Save the Children, and Human Rights Watch.[3]

Since the UN Decade for HRE, the Office of the High Commissioner for Human Rights (OHCHR) has played a significant role in encouraging HRE around the world. In 2005, it established the ongoing World Programme for Human Rights Education, which has set forth guidelines for effective HRE initiatives and activities. Structured in consecutive phases, the Programme has focused thus far on primary and secondary school systems, higher education and professional training programs, and training for media professionals and journalists.[4]

In 2011, the UN General Assembly adopted the Declaration on Human Rights Education and Training, the first instrument in which international standards for human rights education were officially proclaimed by the United Nations. Although the document stops short of referring to a "human right to human rights education"—language that was lost in the negotiating process between states at the Human Rights Council—the declaration does for the first time recognize governments' specific commitments to promote HRE. It also provides an important tool for civil society to advocate for HRE. For example, HRE 2020, a coalition of fourteen organizations from five continents, was founded in 2013 to ensure a systematic monitoring of states' implementation of HRE in human rights instruments, including the Declaration on Human Rights Education and Training.

The OHCHR continues to promote HRE, providing financial and technical assistance for the development of educational and training materials and the continuing development of resources (e.g., the Database on Human Rights Education and Training).[5] Most recently, the OHCHR has issued a web resource, The Right to HRE, a compilation of provisions of international and regional instruments dealing with human rights education, a valuable tool for advocating for HRE as essential to a basic education.[6]

Human Rights Education Today

More than a decade ago I argued that the definition of HRE depended on whom one asked, whether governments, NGOs, or educationalists (Flowers 2004). Time has only multiplied the players and practices that now define HRE, a diversity amply reflected in the essays in the present volume. The rich complexity of approaches and perspectives examined by its contributors illustrates the state of the field today, as well as exposing some inherent weaknesses and predicting challenges yet to be faced.

In discussing the global diffusion of human rights discourse in "Symbol and Substance: Human Rights Education as an Emergent Global Institution" (Chapter 1), Susan Garnett Russell and David Suárez chart the institutionalization of human rights education as a distinctive field as reflected in the proliferation of educational curricula, textbooks, and implementation in schools. However, they emphasize the great disparity in the manner, commitment, and continuity with which different countries embrace HRE. For some practitioners accustomed to working in more traditional settings of formal education, the rapidly expanding practice of HRE threatens to undermine its hard-won legitimization by becoming too political, too confrontational, and too controversial. For others, this diversity of goals, applications, and methodologies confirms the ultimate effectiveness of HRE.

Nearly fifty years after the publication of *The Pedagogy of the Oppressed*, the voice of Paulo Freire echoes through many of the articles in this book and continues to inform the practice of human rights educators around the world, especially his vision of education as based on problem solving and critical analysis rather than merely the acquisition of new knowledge. The Freirean educational goal of *conscientization*, the process of developing a critical awareness of one's social reality and thus becoming subjects capable of bringing about change, is essentially political, involving both individual and collective identities. Attempts to make HRE "nonpolitical" necessarily stop short of "education *for* human rights," the use of human rights knowledge to further the realization of human rights.

Vernacularization

Directly related to the Freirean emphasis on critical thinking is the growing recognition that local context and individual experience are essential to effective HRE, a "vernacularization" that encompasses both content and methodology.

Repeatedly, the authors of these chapters emphasize that HRE training should encourage local actors to translate human rights concepts into their own contexts and include pedagogy that respects diverse backgrounds and opinions, such as religious beliefs and values. For example, in "Human Rights Education in Postcolonial India" (Chapter 6), Monisha Bajaj and Rachel Wahl affirm that if HRE is to fulfill its transformative vision, NGOs must adapt internationally circulating rights discourses to local realities. This is also the case in "Expanding the Aspirational Map: Interactive Learning and Human Rights in Tostan's Community Empowerment Program" (Chapter 10), wherein Beniamino Cislaghi, Diane Gillespie, and Gerry Mackie describe the NGO Tostan's culturally congruent nonformal human rights education strategies in villages in West Africa. In "Leveraging Diversity to Become a Global Citizen: Lessons for Human Rights Education" (Chapter 12), Carol Anne Spreen and Chrissie Monaghan illustrate this point with their work in U.S. high school classrooms that intentionally included a wide spectrum of students: native-born, refugee, migrant, gifted, and remedial. Through shared personal narratives, students were able to connect abstract concepts of human rights and social inequality and apply them to their own varied experiences.

New Learners

Increasingly, the human rights community has embraced the understanding that the concept of equal rights necessarily implies recognition of the "right to be different." Whereas difference has always been a reason for discrimination and exclusion, the increasing individualization of society has legitimized and intensified HRE regarding the right of vulnerable populations: of often-oppressed minorities like Roma and Dalits; of indigenous peoples; of migrant workers; of women taking a stand against violence in the family and social and political marginalization, of persons with disabilities; of gays, lesbians, transsexuals, and intersex individuals taking collective action to question cultural practices and rules that discriminate against them. An excellent example of HRE for such marginalized groups is the intensive work of the International Disability Alliance to prepare persons with disabilities to advocate for themselves during the drafting process of the Convention on the Rights of Persons with Disabilities, both formally before the drafting committee and informally in the UN corridors. After the adoption of the convention, they continued this work with *Human Rights. Yes! Action and Advocacy on the Rights of Persons with Disabilities* (Lord et al. 2012), the first HRE manual written to educate people with disabilities and their allies about these newly codified rights.

As Oren Pizmony-Levy and Megan Jensen argue in their chapter "Contentious Human Rights Education: The Case of Professional Development Programs on Sexual Orientation and Gender Identity–Based Refuge Protection" (Chapter 8), if marginalized groups are to fully realize their human rights, HRE must also be available to those who work with them, such as teachers, social and humanitarian workers, and government officials. These individuals need to understand how their personal views and values may impact their professional responsibility to respect the human rights of those whom they serve.

New Skills

Educators in all the projects described in this book have recognized that human rights law and theory are ultimately only meaningful if it can be put to direct use, another aspect of vernacularization that directly affects the goals and methodology of HRE: as local actors translate human rights concepts into local contexts, myriad approaches, motivations, ideologies, and outcomes emerge. In "Human Rights Education's Role in Peacebuilding: Lessons from the Field" (Chapter 11), Tracey Holland and J. Paul Martin call for a needs-based approach to learning about human rights that involves identification and articulation of issues directly concerning participants, advocacy, and problem solving. They stress that knowing your rights and teaching others that they have rights is not enough; it is also necessary to develop strategies to secure these rights and the skills to implement such strategies. These prerequisites include speaking skills to describe and convey one's needs, to rename experiences in rights terms, and to use raised awareness to speak out against those who have violated one's rights. Participants also need "street smarts" to seek and acquire services, as well as "people smarts" to attract community support and manage inevitable conflicts and resolve disputes. By acquiring the language and skills to redress the injustices that they see as keeping them from fulfilling their aspirations, participants become advocates for themselves and their communities.

Among the "people skills" needed are internalized abilities to recognize one's own biases, accept differences, and take responsibility for defending the rights of others, mediation, and conflict resolution. Perhaps the more abstract and challenging of these is what Fernández (2009) has called the pedagogy of tenderness, a form of restorative justice that seeks to address social change without hurt or abuse, honoring each individual's rights, including those of oppressors. During periods of oppressive regimes and widespread human rights abuses, social justice movements have typically prioritized adversarial actions such as protests, recrimination, and retribution. The changes in personal attitude required to shift to respect for the rights of all are not so much taught as learned over time, a challenge to HRE programs that seek a "quick fix" to abuses.

New Communications

Before the Internet was widely available, most exchanges among human rights educators were limited to "snail mail" and the rare opportunity to meet at conferences. Until the mid-1980s, for example, Amnesty International's only official HRE activity had been a dedicated group of volunteers in Germany known as the HRE Clearing House. Operating from a member's kitchen table in Bremen, they somehow managed for many years to publish the world's most comprehensive HRE bibliography and to distribute it by mail.

By contrast, today even the smallest of human rights NGOs has some access to the Internet, and the rich collaboration and exchange of materials, ideas, and practices that it has made possible. Curriculum materials, IGO and UN reports, manuals, documents, research findings, and other HRE publications are now accessible online, with many organizations making free electronic publication a matter of policy to ensure their widest use.

Furthermore, services like blogs, dedicated chats, webinars, and Skype make real-time communications between individual educators and even group consultations relatively easy, further enhancing international collaboration.

Of particular importance has been the rise of online courses in human rights, for which Human Rights Education Associates (HREA) has set the international standard. First offered in January 2002, HREA's instructor-led courses now number fifty per year. Its online courses have continually adapted to meet participants' needs, becoming ever more practical in application and shorter and more intense in order to accommodate learners' busy schedules. HREA now offers a variety of formats: not only instructor-led courses, but also self-directed online courses and hybrid courses that include both online and face-to-face components. Between 2002 and 2015, HREA's Distance Learning Program has trained 10,500 human rights defenders, educators, and humanitarian workers; its virtual Human Rights Campus currently has more than 16,500 registered users from 170 countries.

Digital campaigns represent a new space for human rights action, capable of rapidly engaging many people on an issue. Such initiatives clearly increase human rights awareness; however, it remains unclear to what extent long-distance digital involvement instills the values and skills that define HRE. Rebecca Joy Norlander recently evaluated RespectMyRights.com, an interactive educational website developed as part of an Amnesty International HRE project, Education for Human Dignity. She found that dissemination of human rights content via "one-to-many" broadcast channels fails to incorporate the participatory pedagogical approach of HRE. Although Norlander commends RespectMyRights.com for its integration of awareness raising, an interactive educational culture, and the tools for action, she concludes: "More clarity is needed concerning what exactly constitutes the development of human rights values, attitudes, and behaviors in a digital space, or more broadly, what effect the use of digital ICT has on cultivating the ethical capacity of learners" (Norlander 2013).

All-School Approaches to HRE

In 1953, UNESCO started its Associated Schools Project Network (ASPnet), commonly referred to as UNESCO Associated Schools, which now number some nine thousand affiliated institutions in 170 countries. Although

HRE is not the sole focus of these schools, which include intercultural learning, education for sustainable development, and UN priorities, UNESCO Associated Schools were among the first international educational efforts to introduce human rights concepts into schools, and they continue to thrive.

More recently, educators have sought to create all-school approaches to HRE that include faculty and staff, parents, and the wider community, as well as students, in both learning and realizing human rights. For example, in 2009 Amnesty International launched its Human Rights Friendly Schools project, which seeks to put human rights at the heart of the learning experience and to make human rights an integral part of everyday school life.[7] The project has since grown to include twenty-one countries. However, in "Politics, Power, and Protest: Rights-Based Education Policy and the Limits of Human Rights Education" (Chapter 7), Sam Mejias describes how "Schools' internal dynamics, closed micropolitical relationships, and tendencies toward prioritizing pragmatism can also potentially disadvantage the possibilities of successful implementation of whole-school HRE." Educators in many parts of the world continue to struggle with how to make a truly integrated human rights school community.

Whither: Challenges for the Future of HRE

Institutional Integration of HRE

The problems Mejias analyzes in a particular British school point to one of the major challenges facing HRE as a whole: the integration of HRE into existing educational and political systems.

At one extreme, human rights information, values, and skills may be regarded as potentially disruptive or even adversarial. Holland and Martin (in a draft of Chapter 11), for example, elsewhere observe:

> One reason why host governments might not be fully committed to systematic HRE is the fear that it will fuel people's desires for rights and make rights claims on their governments that governments perceive as unwanted and disruptive. HRE can thus be seen as a negative force in peacebuilding contexts.[8]

At another extreme, governments may co-opt HRE for their own ideological ends, denying the interdependence of rights by cherry-picking those
rights they wish to endorse and omitting or ignoring others that may challenge their policies and priorities. Some states have even established "Po-
temkin" showcase HRE projects to evade international criticism. As Osler
and Yahya report, in some institutions HRE was so low in status that some
schools adopt corrupt practices to hide their neglect of the subject, using designated HRE lessons to teach other subjects and grading students as though
they had mastered human rights (Chapter 5).

As Mejias illustrates, even where the motivation for HRE is genuine and
the initiative has the support of the relevant authorities, the institutionalization of HRE in schools is still a work in progress. He critiques the essential
problem with Amnesty's Human Rights Friendly Schools project as "a clear
vision of a rights-friendly school without elaborating how schools can operationalize the vision" (Chapter 7). It is for this reason that some of the most
creative and effective HRE programs, including those reported in these
pages, are being run by civil society, adjacent to and often collaborating with
but not fully integrated into state structures.

Osler and Yahya critique current approaches to school integration of
HRE as taking place in a vacuum (Chapter 5). They emphasize that opportunities for human rights learning for parents and community members are
essential if teachers are to feel safe addressing controversial topics and local
issues, especially those that might be construed as political, religious, or
gender-related. Cases can be cited from around the world of educators being
disciplined or even fired for teaching human rights values that conflict with
local realities. Perhaps the most high-profile case was the 2006 firing of
Mirosław Sielatycki, director of the Polish In-Service Teachers Training Centre, for distributing *Compass,* a Council of Europe HRE curriculum that
includes lessons on discrimination on the basis of sexual orientation. Although Poland is a State Party to the European Convention on Human
Rights and the Convention on the Rights of the Child, the Polish minister of
education justified this dismissal on grounds that Mr. Sielatycki had disseminated materials that could be regarded as promoting homosexuality and
that were contrary to "patriotic education" in Polish schools. The secretary
general of the Council of Europe protested, saying, "I do not understand how
teaching tolerance can be grounds for dismissal." This case underscores how
teachers of HRE can be vulnerable to censure, even with the support of a

powerful IGO like the Council of Europe. HRE that includes the whole community can help to further acceptance of HRE, but it is difficult to implement and is no guarantee of protection.[9]

Besides educational institutions, HRE needs to be incorporated into all relevant state-sponsored systems, especially supports for poor community members whose most basic needs are not being met. As Holland and Martin emphasize in a draft of Chapter 11 and have noted elsewhere, "[H]uman rights education is not a stand-alone activity but rather needs to be linked with, and integrated into, the entire gamut of human needs and social services." However, such integration into state structures clearly constitutes a huge challenge for future HRE.

Insufficient Teacher Training in HRE

Even where HRE is mandated by legislation and supported by the formal education systems, ongoing commitment to train a whole generation of teachers is still required. As a respondent observed in Audrey Osler and Chalank Yahya's study of post-conflict HRE in Iraqi Kurdistan, "Challenges and Complexity in Human Rights Education" (Chapter 5):

> HRE as a subject in our education system does not have as much emphasis as it should. We lack expertise in this discipline and we do not have specialized teachers. . . . For the time being, social studies teachers are required to teach this subject.

In a post-conflict situation like Iraqi Kurdistan, it is not surprising that Osler and Yahya found teachers unprepared for HRE or dull textbooks without guidance as to how human rights might be made accessible to teachers or relevant to students. But in fact, teachers poorly prepared for HRE are not the exception but the rule, even in parts of the world where HRE is well established. A recent national survey of HRE in Denmark revealed that nearly half of all teachers interviewed continued to feel insecure in their knowledge of human rights.[10] A report from Scotland reached similar conclusions: although Scottish teachers were supportive of and interested in HRE, they strongly indicated a lack of training in the area.[11] This lack of skilled human rights educators and a well-established culture of human rights in school communities is a challenge everywhere in the world that only time and persistence can address.

"We're Already Doing That!"

A related challenge is the conclusion reached by preschool teachers and professors of education alike: "We're already doing that." Viewed superficially, HRE can be conflated with a variety of initiatives in education (e.g., antibullying, citizenship, multicultural, global, moral, development) or established school value systems (e.g., social justice, gender equity, diversity). Such confusion arises when HRE is not clearly defined or understood, a common problem where educators themselves have never received HRE. Although HRE may share similar goals with other forms of education, it differs by being grounded in international legal instruments. In practice, this means addressing any social issue like racism or bullying from a human rights perspective. For example, a human rights approach to racism would address it as a violation of the human right to freedom from discrimination, a fundamental human right that comes with the responsibility to protect that right for others. Human rights educators need to continually clarify how HRE differs from other forms of education and to emphasize its concrete advantages.

Unmet Needs

Most educators agree that HRE is everywhere most successful when the content of human rights is directly related to community needs. Identifying and articulating specific local issues are part of the general movement toward vernacularization. Unfortunately, however, human rights educators are ultimately much less successful in fulfilling those needs.

One obstacle to the practical application of HRE is the nature of rights learning itself. Educators know well how to convey a body of information, but imparting a framework of values presents an immense challenge. Research shows that essential values and attitudes are laid down in early childhood and are difficult to alter. Minds are difficult to change and hearts even more so, especially when that change is undertaken with respect for learners' culture and identity and stresses individual critical thinking. As Felisa Tibbitts observes in "Evolution of Human Rights Education Models" (Chapter 3), the Values and Awareness/Socialization Models continue to be problematic within HRE practices. We know well how to indoctrinate, but we are still evolving effective methodologies to convey human rights values *in* human rights.

Another obstacle is the ineluctable fact that HRE takes time. As Michalinos Zembylas observes in "Emotions, Critical Pedagogy, and Human Rights Education" (Chapter 2), a "pedagogy of discomfort" demands time, as does establishing trust in the classroom, strong relationships, and compassionate understandings among people. Indeed, the development of what he calls "strategic empathy" is "an admittedly long and difficult task" that needs the full continuum of the school years:

> But mere understanding is clearly not enough; students will become more susceptible to affective transformation when they enact compassionate action early on in their lives, starting with simple things such as learning to be more patient and tolerant with peers who do not grasp a difficult concept in language or mathematics. As they grow up, children are offered opportunities to enact more complex manifestations of compassion, including action to alleviate the suffering of people who experience difficult times, no matter which community they come from.

Clearly, to be successful, HRE requires a commitment to years of continuous effort on the part of sponsoring institutions, an investment of resources few are willing or able to make. Few school systems have the vision or the means to create and sustain HRE from preschool through high school. In the informal sector, HRE programs typically have a planned trajectory of months or a few years, especially when they are begun in response to crises or post-conflict situations. Although such programs often express the optimistic intention of becoming self-sustaining, that hope seldom materializes. To succeed, they require long-term support and expert training, often from outside the community.

Sufficient time is also required to build advocacy skills, such as articulating issues, gathering community support, and negotiating with authorities. Furthermore, these skills must be honed by direct experience and are highly dependent on personalities and circumstances. While application of education *for* human rights can inspire and energize, it can also raise unrealistic expectations of change. Failure to achieve immediate goals can quickly turn to frustration, disillusionment, and even lead to the abandonment of human rights principles in favor of immediate, violent action.

As important as time is the need for patience in HRE. All involved—funders, administrators, educators, and learners alike—need to be convinced that HRE is effective and they must be willing to wait for results over the long term. This wait often strains patience because the field continues to lack reliable means of evaluation or clear benchmarks for progress. And, as the lessons of the Arab Spring exemplify, the strategies of steady persistence are often overwhelmed by the dramatic appeal of immediate, direct action, with or without a clear strategy.

The Nature of Human Rights

Along with the need for time and patience, HRE is also challenged by the abstract nature of human rights norms themselves. Human wrongs are concrete, whereas human rights are neither "absolute truth" nor divinely ordained, but the evolving consensus of human beings. In "The Right to Human Rights Education: Conceptual Perspectives" (Chapter 4), Peter Kirschlaeger argues that human rights need to be justified to every human being, not only as an individual rights-holder, but also as a protector and respecter of the rights of others. To grasp that justice concerns the recognition of one's own vulnerability and the common vulnerability of all other human beings requires fairly sophisticated conceptual thinking. However, Michalinos Zembylas turns mutual vulnerability into a practical pedagogic principle that can enhance the emancipatory interests of education, especially in contexts of human rights violations (Chapter 2). In his view, mutual vulnerability can provide a "new grammar" for critical pedagogy in HRE, disrupting normative frames of community and promoting a sense of community based on the "shared burden of troubled knowledge carried more or less by all participants in a given society."

Not all learners want or need to enter into the philosophic foundations of human rights, but when challenged by other value systems with claims to absolute authority, educators need to be able to make a clear and credible justification for the universality, indivisibility, and interdependence of rights. Such justifications of HRE are often challenged, however, as reflecting Western European and Christian values, promulgated with an evangelical fervor and unrealistic idealism. In his recent book *The Endtimes of Human Rights*, Stephen Hopgood (2013) faults the human rights movement for a secular religiosity among the middle classes of North America and Europe that in many cases has substituted belief in human rights for a lost religious faith. Ultimately, Hopgood sees the elitist vision of uniting the world under secular human rights law as ultimately futile against the compelling power of ordinary people's traditional cultures and religious beliefs, especially in a world where power is shifting "away from a unipolar American-led system toward a more multi-polar world" (Hopgood 2013:3). Hopgood may be correct in attributing the roots of human rights to nineteenth-century liberal humanism; certainly, like all liberal institutions, human rights is vulnerable to absolutism of all kinds. Principles of equality and respect for human differences may be the most difficult lesson that HRE has to teach, and the most important.

Lack of Scalability

The chapters of this book relate examples of HRE undertaken in many places, with many different goals and learners. As inspiring as they may be, they also illustrate another challenge to HRE: scalability. HRE does not lend itself to spreading as a one-size-fits-all model: what succeeds in Ahmedabad will not necessarily work in Chiapas or Charlottesville, or even in parts of the same city. Although goals and methodologies are transferable, each HRE initiative must be custom designed for a particular setting and group of learners. This means that even as part of an international program like Amnesty's Human Rights Friendly Schools, the success of any individual school will depend in part on how well it adapts the guidelines of the project to local idiosyncrasies and personalities. Quality control of the kind exercised by corporations over their franchises is impossible, as is rapid proliferation of projects conforming to a template imposed from above.

On the other hand, the very fact that no two HRE programs are alike may be an inherent strength. Although "experts" may be imported for training and support, every HRE program is thus sui generis, drawing on the creativity and experience of local people. It is they who genuinely define and have ownership of HRE in their own communities.

Conclusion

For at least two decades, a fellow human rights educator and I have had a lively disagreement about what is and is not HRE. She finds my working definition far too permissive, and I regard hers as too exclusive, to the point that she now entirely eschews the word "education" in favor of "learning." Over the years, however, our debate has challenged us both to shift our ground to include the multiplicity of forms this new field is taking, both in theory and in practice. As the essays in this book richly demonstrate, human rights education is dynamic beyond what either of us could have foreseen thirty years ago.

I am certain that the insight, commitment, and range of experience reflected in these pages will inspire still other scholars and activists to make human rights education their own pursuit and define it in new and personal ways.

Notes

1. Vienna Declaration and Programme of Action, II.D.79. See http://www.ohchr.org/EN/ProfessionalInterest/Pages/Vienna.aspx.

2. Summary of national initiatives undertaken within the Decade for Human Rights Education (1995–2004). See http://www.ohchr.org/EN/Issues/Education/Training/Pages/Initiatives.aspx.

3. See more at http://www.right-to-education.org/page/about-us#sthash.YKaS1orT.dpuf.

4. For more on the UN World Programme for Human Rights Education see http://www.ohchr.org/EN/Issues/Education/Training/Pages/Programme.aspx.

5. http://hre.ohchr.org/hret/intro.aspx.

6. http://www.ohchr.org/EN/Issues/Education/Training/Compilation/Pages/Listof contents.aspx.

7. See http://www.amnesty.org/en/human-rights-education/projects-initiatives/rfsp.

8. Holland and Martin, Chapter 11 of this book.

9. Mr. Sielatycki appealed to the District Court in Warsaw on grounds of unfair dismissal and discriminatory treatment in employment because of his political opinions. The court found in Mr. Sielatycki's favor and awarded him approximately 20,000 PLN (€5,700) in damages, the maximum sum claimed. Subsequently, Mr. Sielatycki was appointed deputy director of the Office of Education of the City of Warsaw and later secretary of state in the Ministry of Education.

10. Danish Institute for Human Rights, *Mapping of Human Rights Education in Danish Schools*. For English summary, see http://www.humanrights.dk/files/media /dokumenter/udgivelser/mapping_of_hre_in_danish_schools.pdf. For full report in Danish, see http://www.menneskeret.dk/udgivelser/udredning/.

11. BEMIS, *A Review of Human Rights Education in Schools in Scotland* (2013), 58. http://bemis.org.uk/documents/BEMIS%20HRE%20in%20Schools%20Report.pdf.

References

Fernández, Benito Fernández. 2009. "Popular Education in the Struggle for Human Rights in Latin America." *Adult Education in Development* 72. Bonn: DVV International. https://www.dvv-international.de/en/adult-education-and-development /editions/aed-722009/contributions/popular-education-in-the-struggle-for -human-rights-in-latin-america/.

Flowers, N. 2004. "How to Define Human Rights Education? A Complex Answer to a Simple Question." In V. B. Georgi and M. Seberich, eds., *International Perspectives in Human Rights Education* (pp. 105–127). Gütersloh, Germany: Bertelsman Foundation.

Hopgood, Stephen. 2013. *The Endtimes of Human Rights*. Ithaca, NY. Cornell University Press.

Keet, André. 2007. "Human Rights Education or Human Rights in Education: A Conceptual Analysis." Ph.D. dissertation, University of Pretoria.

Lord, Janet F., Katherine N. Guernsey, Joelle M. Balfe, Valerie L. Karr, and Allison S. deFranco, eds. 2012. *Human Rights. Yes! Action and Advocacy on the Rights of Persons with Disabilities*, 2nd ed. Human Rights Education Series No. 6. Minneapolis: University of Minnesota Human Rights Center.

Norlander, Rebecca Joy. 2013. *The Contributions of Digital Communications Technology to Human Rights Education: A Case Study of Amnesty International*. Ph.D. dissertation, Saybrooke University, San Francisco, CA. http://gradworks.umi.com /36/11/3611482.html.

Sample Discussion Questions
for Use with This Book

1. How should the diversity of approaches to HRE within a particular country or setting be judged from the perspective of the human rights movement? Should educators encourage a variety of approaches to HRE, or should the movement attempt to create a more universal framework? Why or why not?
2. What lessons from one HRE experience might apply to others? Should cross-learning be encouraged, or should HRE develop purely in its own context?
3. What drawbacks might accompany government support and funding for HRE? How might potential drawbacks be mitigated?
4. What can human rights educators hope to accomplish, and what may be beyond the scope of the educational endeavor? How might human rights educators partner with other types of activists as well as with policymakers to pursue outcomes that are less likely to be obtained through education alone?
5. What are the strengths and challenges of different approaches to HRE (professional vs. school-based, formal vs. nonformal, whole school vs. NGO-led, etc.)?
6. How does the structure of formal schooling limit or facilitate human rights education?
7. How do other forms of education (e.g., social justice, peacebuilding, multicultural) resonate with, compare with, or differ from human rights education?
8. What should human rights education look like at different levels (primary, secondary, tertiary) and in different domains (professional, nonformal, adult education, etc.)?
9. How can the outcomes and impact of human rights education be measured and assessed?
10. What role do families and communities play in human rights education?

APPENDIX B

Further Reading in Human Rights Education

Al-Daraweesh, F., and Dale Snauwaert. 2015. *Human Rights Education Beyond Universalism and Relativism: A Relational Hermeneutic for Global Justice*. New York: Palgrave Macmillan.

Andreopoulos, George J., and Richard Pierre Claude. 1997. *Human Rights Education for the Twenty-First Century*. Philadelphia: University of Pennsylvania Press.

Bajaj, Monisha. 2012. *Schooling for Social Change: The Rise and Impact of Human Rights Education in India*. New York: Bloomsbury.

Bajaj, Monisha, Beniamino Cislaghi, and Gerry Mackie. 2016. "Advancing Transformative Human Rights Education" (Appendix D to the Global Citizenship Commission Report). New York: New York University. https://www.openbookpublishers.com/shopimages/The-UDHR-21st-C-AppendixD.pdf

Cislaghi, Beniamino, Diane Gillespie, and Gerry Mackie. 2017. *Values Deliberations and Collective Action: Community Empowerment in Rural Senegal*. New York: Palgrave Macmillan.

Gerber, Paula. 2013. *Understanding Human Rights: Educational Challenges for the Future*. Cheltenham, UK: Edward Elgar Publishing Ltd.

Hantzopoulos, Maria. 2016. *Restoring Dignity in Public Schools: Human Rights Education in Action*. New York: Teachers College Press.

Holland, Tracey, and John Paul Martin. 2014. *Human Rights Education and Peacebuilding*. New York: Routledge.

Katz, Susan, and Andrea Spero. 2015. *Bringing Human Rights Education to US Classrooms: Exemplary Models from Elementary Grades to University*. New York: Palgrave Macmillan.

Osler, Audrey. 2016. *Human Rights and Schooling: An Ethical Framework for Teaching for Social Justice*. New York: Teachers College Press.

Osler, Audrey, and Hugh Starkey. 2010. *Teachers and Human Rights Education*. London: Trentham Books.

CONTRIBUTORS

Monisha Bajaj is Associate Professor of International and Multicultural Education at the University of San Francisco, where she directs the MA program in human rights education. She is also Visiting Professor and Research Fellow at the Institute for Reconciliation and Social Justice, University of the Free State, South Africa. Bajaj is the editor of the *Encyclopedia of Peace Education* (Information Age, 2008) and *Peace Education: International Perspectives* (Bloomsbury, 2016) and author of the award-winning book *Schooling for Social Change: The Rise and Impact of Human Rights Education in India* (Bloomsbury, 2012), as well as numerous articles. She is the recipient of a National Academy of Education/Spencer Foundation postdoctoral fellowship (2009), the Teachers College Columbia University Distinguished Alumni Early Career Award (2015), and the Ella Baker/Septima Clark Human Rights Award (2015) from Division B of the American Educational Research Association (AERA).

Beniamino Cislaghi is Lecturer in Social Norms at the London School of Hygiene and Tropical Medicine and Adjunct Lecturer in Public Health and Community Medicine at Tufts University. He worked as a human rights volunteer educator and trainer for more than ten years at the national and international level. Before starting his Ph.D. in HRE, he also worked for various NGOs and international organizations, including UNICEF, WHO, and ILO. His past research focused on how HRE can offer participants a space to renegotiate existing cultural meanings and collaborate to increase their own and others' well-being. After finishing his Ph.D., he worked for three years as the Director of Research, Monitoring, and Evaluation of the NGO Tostan, and as a researcher with Stanford and Columbia universities. He is interested in how HRE can empower people for community-based responses to development challenges, a topic he has written on with Diane Gillespie and Gerry

Mackie in *Values Deliberation and Collective Action: Community Empowerment in Rural Senegal* (Palgrave Macmillan, 2017).

Nancy Flowers is a writer and consultant for human rights education. She has worked to develop Amnesty International's education program and is a founding member of Human Rights Educators USA, a national human rights education network. As a consultant to governments, nongovernmental organizations, and UN agencies, she has helped establish national and international networks of educators; develop materials; and train activists, professionals, and military and police personnel in Africa, Asia, the Middle East, Eastern Europe, and the Balkans. She is the author and editor of articles and books on human rights education including *Acting for Indigenous Rights: Theatre to Change the World* (University of Minnesota, 2013), *Local Action/Global Change: A Handbook on Women's Human Rights* (Paradigm Press, 2008), *Human Rights. Yes! Action and Advocacy for the Rights of Persons with Disabilities* (University of Minnesota, 2012), and *Compasito: A Manual on Human Rights Education for Children* (Council of Europe, 2007).

Melissa L. Gibson is Assistant Professor in the College of Education at Marquette University. Her research explores the theoretical and political grounding of social justice in education, justice-oriented pedagogies and teacher preparation, and community work for educational justice. Her writing has appeared in *Equity and Excellence in Education, Multicultural Perspectives,* and *Intercultural Education,* as well as in the forthcoming volume *Rethinking Bilingual Education.* In addition to her work as a teacher educator, Dr. Gibson taught middle and high school for ten years—most recently, middle school social studies in Guadalajara, Mexico.

Diane Gillespie is Emeritus Professor of Interdisciplinary Arts and Sciences at the University of Washington–Bothell. Interested in cultural and psychological issues in education, she has written extensively on interactive learning and the challenges of diversity in higher education. In 2007 she turned her research interest to human rights education, coauthoring with Molly Melching "The Transformative Power of Human Rights Education: The Case of Tostan" (*Adult Education Quarterly,* 2010). She continued this line of research with Ben Cislaghi and Gerry Mackie in *Values Deliberation and Collective Action: Community Empowerment in Rural Senegal* (Palgrave Macmillan, 2017). She has won numerous awards for her teaching, including the 2010 University of Washington Bothell Distinguished Teaching Award. Since retiring in 2012, she has been a volunteer with Tostan, assisting with research and the development of its training center.

Carl A. Grant is Hoefs-Bascom Professor in the Department of Curriculum and Instruction at the University of Wisconsin–Madison. He has authored or edited more than fifty books and has written more than one hundred journal publications. Professor Grant's recent book publications include *The Moment: Barack Obama, Jeremiah Wright and the Firestorm at Trinity United Church of Christ* (with Shelby Grant) (Rowman & Littlefield, 2013); *Intersectionality and Urban Education: Identities, Policies, Spaces and Power* (with Elisa Zwier, eds.) (Information Press, 2014); and *The Selected Works of Carl A. Grant* (Routledge, 2015).

Tracey Holland teaches in the Education Department at Vassar College in Poughkeepsie, New York, and serves as the Faculty Director of Vassar College's Urban Education Outreach Initiative to underserved students in the Hudson Valley. For the past fifteen years Tracey has researched, created, and evaluated HRE in peacebuilding contexts. She is coauthor with J. Paul Martin of *Human Rights Education and Peacebuilding: A Comparative Study* (Routledge, 2014).

Megan Jensen directs a USDOE-funded professional development program for the Literacy Design Collaborative. Her work supports up to eighty schools in the Los Angeles Unified School District in creating aligned, responsive curricula to develop student literacy skills in all content areas, with dissemination to regional and state-level education entities around the United States. Megan has worked as a reading specialist for students with learning differences in grades K–12. While on a Fulbright grant, she worked with a South African high school to develop its on-campus library and literacy programming. She earned her MA in International and Comparative Education from Teachers College, Columbia University, with research interests in the international application of New Literacy Studies and inclusive education practices.

Peter G. Kirchschlaeger is Visiting Fellow in Ethics at Yale University, Senior Research Fellow at the Faculty of Theology of the University of Lucerne, and Guest Lecturer at the Leuphana University, Lueneburg. He is a private lecturer in theological ethics at the Faculty of Theology of the University of

Fribourg, a fellow at the Raoul Wallenberg Institute of Human Rights and Humanitarian Law, and a research fellow at the University of the Free State, Bloemfontein. In 2013, he was a visiting scholar at the University of Technology, Sydney, and 2013–2014 Guest Professor at the Katholieke Universiteit Leuven. From 2011 to 2015 he was Chair ad Interim and from 2013 to 2015 Dean of Research at the Chur University of Theology. He is a consultative expert for international organizations (e.g., UN, UNESCO, OSCE, Council of Europe, European Union), governments, NGOs, and the private sector.

Gerry Mackie is Associate Professor of Political Science, and Co-Director of the Center on Global Justice at the University of California–San Diego. He is a political theorist interested in contemporary democratic theory and in problems of collective action. One main area of interest is democracy, particularly conceptual and normative problems of democratic voting; his first book on voting, *Democracy Defended*, received the Gladys Kamerer Prize from the American Political Science Association. Since 1998, he has worked with the NGO Tostan in West Africa, and since 2004 with UNICEF on collective action to end harmful social practices, including the practice of female genital cutting (FGC). This was declared the "common approach" to the practice by eleven United Nations agencies in 2009. He has worked on harmful social practices since 1995, and has conducted training in the conceptualization and measurement of social norms and their change since 2007. Recently, he conducted a qualitative study on Tostan's HRE practices with Ben Cislaghi and Diane Gillespie: *Values Deliberation and Collective Action: Community Empowerment in Rural Senegal* (Palgrave Macmillan, 2017).

J. Paul Martin is currently Adjunct Professor and Director of Human Rights Studies at Barnard College, Columbia University. Previously, he was founding executive director of Columbia's Center (now Institute) for the Study of Human Rights. His writing focuses on human rights education and on postsecularism.

Sam Mejias is currently a researcher at the London School of Economics and Political Science and a freelance development consultant. His research focuses on citizenship, young people, politics, and media. His past work in the field of human rights education includes the development of Amnesty International's *Human Rights Friendly Schools* project and a doctoral study exploring its implementation.

Chrissie Monaghan is a Research Officer at Watchlist on Children and Armed Conflict and an Instructor at New York University's Steinhardt School of Culture, Education, and Human Development. Her research focuses on three main areas: the contemporary historical development and implementation of human rights education programming; globalization and refugee education; and the impact on children of attacks on schools and hospitals in situations of armed conflict. She has carried out multiple research projects in countries throughout sub-Saharan Africa, including an evaluation of UNICEF's Peacebuilding, Education, and Advocacy (PBEA) program in Ethiopia and Kenya's Dadaab refugee camp. Chrissie holds a doctorate in Social Foundations of Education with a focus on Education in Emergencies from the University of Virginia.

Audrey Osler is Professor of Education at University College of Southeast Norway and Professor Emerita at the University of Leeds, United Kingdom, where she founded the Centre for Citizenship and Human Rights Education. Her research addresses education policy, children's rights, and diversity in a global context, and she has published eighteen books, over a hundred articles in peer-reviewed journals, and contributions to numerous edited collections. International work includes acting as an expert for the Council of Europe, UNESCO, and other international organizations; teaching at the UN University for Peace in Costa Rica; acting as consultant to governments in Europe and the Middle East; and various research and development projects in post-conflict contexts including Aceh, Indonesia; Ethiopia; and Iraqi Kurdistan. She is currently writing a book on human rights and schooling for Teachers College Press in the Multicultural Education Series edited by James A. Banks.

Oren Pizmony-Levy is an Assistant Professor of International and Comparative Education at Teachers College, Columbia University. He holds a Ph.D. in sociology and comparative and international education from Indiana University–Bloomington (2013). His research and teaching focus on the intersection between education and social movements, such as accountability, environmentalism, and human rights. His work has been published in *Comparative Education Review*, *Sociological Perspectives*, the *Journal of LGBT Youth*, and others.

Susan Garnett Russell is an Assistant Professor of International and Comparative Education at Teachers College, Columbia University, as well as

Director of the George Clement Bond Center for African Education. She earned her doctorate in international and comparative education from Stanford University. Her research focuses on education and conflict, human rights, citizenship, and gender, particularly in sub-Saharan Africa. Recent publications appear in *International Studies Quarterly*, *Prospects*, *Compare*, and *International Sociology*.

Carol Anne Spreen is an Associate Professor of International Education in the Department of Humanities and Social Sciences at New York University. Her scholarship focuses on issues of human rights in education, school reform, and educational equity. Her current research focuses on teachers' lives and work, both globally and locally, and using participatory action research to study the impacts of poverty and inequality on educational opportunities. Dr. Spreen received her Ph.D. in comparative education in 2001 from Teachers College, Columbia University. She also holds an M.Ed. in instructional leadership from the University of Illinois, and a B.Ed. in international educational development from the American University.

David F. Suárez is an Associate Professor at the Evans School of Public Affairs. He teaches courses on public management, organizational theory, and leadership in the nonprofit sector. His current work focuses primarily on (1) the emergence and development of human rights education; (2) the relationship between managerialism and organizational outcomes; and (3) the consequences of professionalization for the nonprofit sector. He is particularly interested in collaboration, advocacy, and civic engagement—issues that link nonprofits to public agencies and the policy process. His work has been published in *Comparative Education Review*, *Sociology of Education*, and other outlets.

Felisa L. Tibbitts is a lecturer at Teachers College, Columbia University, and the founder and Senior Advisor of Human Rights Education Associates (HREA), which she directed from 1999 to 2010. She is also Visiting Professor and Research Fellow at the Institute for Reconciliation and Social Justice at the University of the Free State, South Africa. She has worked with numerous government and international agencies in developing curriculum, learning resources, and policies that support the integration of human rights and democratic values into teaching and training, including the Office of the UN High Commissioner for Human Rights, UNICEF, UNESCO, UNDP,

OSCE, the Council of Europe, the Organization of American States, and numerous nongovernmental organizations such as Amnesty International. Tibbitts has written widely on HRE, and her articles have appeared in the *Journal of Peace Education, Intercultural Education, International Review of Education, Prospects,* the *European Journal of Education,* and the *Journal of International Social Studies.*

Rachel Wahl is an Assistant Professor in the Social Foundations Program, Department of Leadership, Foundations, and Policy, in the Curry School of Education at the University of Virginia. Her research has been published in journals such as *Law and Society Review, Comparative Education Review,* and the *Oxford Journal of Human Rights Practice.* Her book *In the Eye of the Torturer: Human Rights from the Other Side* is forthcoming from Stanford University Press as part of their Stanford Studies in Human Rights series.

Chalank Yahya holds an M.Sc. in human rights and multiculturalism from University College of Southeast Norway. She received a scholarship from Norway's Falstad Centre to do research for her master's thesis in Iraqi Kurdistan. The research study focused on the impact of the HRE in enhancing gender equity and diversity rights in a post-conflict setting. Her publications include a study of cases of Kurdish women's self-immolation and women's human rights (KRG Ministry of Human Rights, 2009). Chalank is currently working as Quality Coordinator at the International Organization for Migration (IOM) in Norway.

Michalinos Zembylas is Associate Professor of Educational Theory and Curriculum Studies at the Open University of Cyprus. He is also Visiting Professor and Research Fellow at the Institute for Reconciliation and Social Justice, University of the Free State, South Africa. He has written extensively on emotion and affect in relation to social justice pedagogies, intercultural and peace education, and citizenship education. His recent books include *Emotion and Traumatic Conflict: Re-claiming Healing in Education* (Oxford, 2015), *Methodological Advances in Research on Emotion and Education* (with P. Schutz; Springer, 2016), and *Peace Education in a Conflict-Troubled Society* (with C. Charalambous and P. Charalambous; Cambridge, 2016).

INDEX

ACKNOWLEDGMENTS

This book is the product of countless conversations about human rights education (HRE) over the past two decades that have converged around the need for a contemporary collection of perspectives on the field.

I was introduced to the transformative potential of HRE by scholars and advocates such as the late Richard Pierre Claude, Paul Martin, Betty Reardon, Nancy Flowers, Henri Tiphagne, and Abraham Magendzo, and have seen first-hand how committed activists on the ground across the globe use formal and nonformal education to advance respect for rights and dignity. I express appreciation to the authors who contributed to this book, as well as to the grass-roots movements, activists, and educators whose efforts are documented here.

I would like to offer my gratitude to colleagues at the University of San Francisco (USF), a pioneering institution in advancing human rights education with its first-of-its-kind master's program in human rights education. Special thanks to Emma Fuentes, Shabnam Koirala-Azad, and Susan Katz in the Department of International and Multicultural Education for creating and advocating for the human rights education program at USF. The collegial and collaborative environment of the School of Education at USF has also been particularly useful in developing this book project, and I express my gratitude to Kevin Kumashiro and faculty colleagues Ursula Aldana, Rick Ayers, Sarah Capitelli, Dave Donahue, Rosa Jimenez, Lance McCready, Genevieve Negron-Gonzales, Sedique Popal, Betty Taylor, Brad Washington, Christine Yeh, and Desiree Zerquera. Support from USF's Faculty Development Funds greatly facilitated this project as well, particularly through support for Jazzmin Gota and Noah Romero's excellent assistance with the book. A special thank you to Jennifer Wofford for creating the beautiful image that appears on the cover of this book.

Finally, I express my thanks to my family: my partner Bikku Kuruvila, our son Kabir, and our parents, Asha Bajaj, Dinesh Bajaj, and Sosanna Kuruvila, for their love, support, and encouragement.